THE ABOLITION
OF AGING

*The forthcoming radical extension
of healthy human longevity*

By
David W. Wood
Chair of London Futurists

Delta Wisdom

In times past, visionaries marvelled at birds soaring high above them into the sky, and wondered how humans might, one day, escape gravity in the same way. Other visionaries pondered tales of creatures that never grew old, and wondered how, one day, these tales could become a reality.

This book sets out the framework for how humanity might, at last, within a few short decades, become enabled to escape the vicious downward pull of aging.

Accordingly, this book is dedicated:

To the researchers, engineers, entrepreneuers, and humanitarians who are wrestling with humanity's oldest challenge
— may they receive ample support and inspiration
to speed them, wisely and sure-footedly, on their audacious quest.

Paperback ISBN 978-0-9954942-0-6

Published by Delta Wisdom

"There is nothing in biology yet found that indicates the inevitability of death. This suggests to me that it is not at all inevitable, and it is only a matter of time before the biologists discover what it is that is causing us the trouble, and that terrible universal disease or temporariness of the human's body will be cured"

– Richard Feynman, in his 1964 lecture
"The role of scientific culture in modern society"

A quick note on spelling: This book generally uses British English, except that I have used the simpler spelling "aging" throughout, instead of the longer version "ageing".

Advance praise for
THE ABOLITION OF AGING

"A real tour de force"
– Aubrey de Grey, Chief Science Officer of SENS Research Foundation

"An epic read with stunning references and observations"
– David Doherty, CoFounder & Director at 3G Doctor

"David Wood has provided the ultimate handbook of arguments on behalf of the arresting, reversal and even termination of aging. Wood fights 'mortalists' as Aquinas fought infidels. Although the book is science-led, its most striking feature is Wood's faith in the capacity of liberal democracies to rise to the challenge of conquering mortality. A must-read for believers and sceptics alike."
– Prof Steve Fuller,
Auguste Comte Chair in Social Epistemology, University of Warwick

"*The Abolition of Aging* is a truly revolutionary book, which considers the radical extension of human longevity and sheds light on the possibility of indefinite lifespans. This modern masterpiece will help us all to rethink what it means to live and die."
– José Cordeiro, Founding Faculty at Singularity University

"David Wood has written a very important book. The idea that people in their fifties and sixties today might live to see a time when science enables them to stop aging – and indeed reverse the aging process – is astounding. Wood is a serious-minded person with solid scientific and organisational credentials, and he has studied this subject for many years. This book deserves to reach a wide audience, and we should heed his call for more research into this fascinating area."
– Calum Chace, Author of *Pandora's Brain* and *Surviving AI*

"Science and technology have made remarkable strides against infectious diseases in the last few decades. The next 2-3 decades could see similar progress against the diseases of aging: heart disease, cancer, dementia, and so on. Aging itself can be slowed, reversed, and even abolished. That's the claim made by former smartphone industry executive David Wood in his impressive new book *The Abolition of Aging*. Wood's message is clear: whether or not these outcomes happen depends on positive action from large number of people around the world. His book serves as a clarion call for concerted involvement by everyone concerned about a better future for humanity."

– Zoltan Istvan, US Presidential candidate

"With his new book, David Wood shows once again his knack for clear-headed, pragmatic, open but rigorous 'classical' thinking (he is a Brit, after all), applied to visionary speculations on the near- and long-term future of humanity."

– Giulio Prisco, Board Member, IEET

"This book is a thorough analysis of the background and context of probably the two of the most important questions of our time: When will we be able to control the aging process? And what would be the implications of such a development? In essence, the answer is highly likely to be sometime this century, and the implications would be far reaching. If we are to avoid highly damaging and chaotic outcomes, it is important that we all become much better informed about the issues. And, if we want to see how this development can lead to a better future for us all, there is probably no better place to start than by reading the insights of David Wood's detailed study of the subject."

– Dr Bruce Lloyd, Emeritus Professor of Strategic Management, London South Bank University

"A perfectly-timed, well written book – could be a best seller."

– Peter Morgan, Technical Director, Data Science Partnership

"*The Abolition of Aging* presents interesting new views on the topic of the prevention of aging, summarizing the entire field in a fascinating read. I hope that the book will encourage readers to participate in collective efforts, such as scientific studies, in support of life extension — something that's very important to do at a time when fighting aging can become mainstream."

– Alexey Turchin, Co-founder, Longevity Party (Russia)

Table of contents

Foreword 1

Two objections 1

Two paradigms 2

Two abolitions 3

Motivation 4

The discussion ahead 7

Author's note 9

Enhancing the conversation 9

1. A shocking possibility 11

Beyond future shock 12

Sweetness and lies 14

Complications and perspectives 18

Acceptance and change 19

Raging and calm 23

Optimism and failure 26

Conflicting forces 28

2. Rejuveneering 101 31

Probabilities 31

Beyond "business-as-usual lifespan extension" 32

The plasticity of aging 35

Curing diseases 38

The biology underlying aging 39

Fixing the failures 42

The elixir of life? 43

Entropy and other constraints 44

Immortality 46

Religious concerns 47

Social concerns 51

Conflicting motivations 60

Timescales 66

3. From flight to rejuvenation   69

Criticism from all sides 70

Rapid breakthrough 74

More moonshine 76

Desiring more life 80

4. Rejuveneering starting points   83

Rejuvenation in nature 83

Repairs and replacements 85

Negligible senescence 88

Out-smarting evolution 91

Examples of successful engineering 97

Examples of hybrid engineering 103

Examples of nano-engineering 105

Examples of better genetics 107

More than marginal improvements 110

The legacy of a pioneer of flight 111

5. Scaling up   115

Exponential progress 116

Growing numbers of rejuvenation engineers 119

Surmounting Brooks' Law 121

Slow progress before fast progress 125

Frameworks for collaboration 129

6. Collaborative rejuveneering   133

Accelerating genetic analysis 133

Eroom's Law 136

Learning from failures 139

Changing regulations 142

New methods of testing new medicines..146

From in-vitro and in-vivo to in-silico 149

Understanding "exceptional responders" 152

IBM's medical discovery initiative 156

The unreasonable effectiveness of big data 159

The further growth of deep learning...163

Factoring complexity..167

The CRISPR game-changer..170

7. Runners and riders   **173**

Living long enough to live indefinitely 173

Lifestyle changes..175

Extra supplements..178

Dealing with damage..181

Progress towards SENS...183

Telomere theory of aging 188

Questions about telomeres 192

The shortest fuse?..196

Genomic stability...199

Investigating genetic variation...204

Disruption from deep learning...207

Evolution and rejuveneering 211

The next phase of the race..216

8. Changing minds   **219**

Scientific hostility to continental drift..220

Changing minds on moving continents.......................................223

Washing hands 225

Medical paradigm shifts, resisted 227

Bloodletting 232

9. Money matters   **235**

Hoping that people will die quickly..237

The cost of aging 240

Paradigm clash 243

The Longevity Dividend 245

Quantifying the longevity dividend 248

Financial benefits from longer lives 251

The costs of developing rejuvenation therapies 254

Sources of additional funding 256

The final decision 258

10. Adverse psychology   **263**

Varieties of objection 264

Managing terror 267

Beyond the denial of death 269

Terror Management Theory 272

The paradox of opposition to extended healthspan 275

Engaging the elephant 277

11. Towards Humanity+   **281**

Beyond the freedom card 281

Embracing radical transformation 283

From precautionary to proactionary 285

A better future for humanity 287

The future of faith 292

The Humanity+ vision 295

A manifesto for Humanity+ 297

The future of death 299

12. Radical alternatives   **301**

An ambulance to the future 301

Not freezing 306

The forthcoming surge in cryonics 310

Head transplants 311

Full body prosthetics 316

A roadmap of avatars 320

Brain duplication 322

Chemopreservation vs. cryopreservation 326

Killed by bad philosophy? 330

Mindfiles 333

Copying the dead to the future? 337

Assessment 341

13. Future uncertain   345

Exceptional engineering complications? 345

Social turmoil ahead? 349

Naïve politics? 351

Market failures? 356

Destructive inequality? 361

A broken dialogue? 367

Poor ways of doing good? 369

Public apathy? 375

A lack of conviction? 380

Noise swamping the signal? 382

Making a real difference? 385

Acknowledgements   387

Endnotes   389

Index   405

About the author   415

About Delta Wisdom 416

Foreword

Within our collective grasp dwells the remarkable possibility of the abolition of biological aging.

It's a big "if", but *if* we decide as a species to make this project a priority, there's around a 50% chance that practical rejuvenation therapies resulting in the comprehensive reversal of aging will be widely available as early as 2040.

People everywhere, on the application of these treatments, will, if they wish, stop becoming biologically older. Instead, again if they wish, they'll start to become biologically younger, in both body and mind, as rejuvenation therapies take hold. In short, everyone will have the option to become ageless.

Two objections

The viewpoint I've just described is a position I've reached following extensive research, carried out over more than ten years. My research has led me to become a strong supporter of what can be called "the rejuveneering project": a multi-decade cross-disciplinary endeavour to engineer human rejuvenation and thereby enable the choice to abolish aging.

But when I mention this viewpoint to people that I meet – as part of my activity as a futurist, or when I catch up with my former colleagues from the smartphone industry – I frequently encounter one of two adverse reactions.

First, people tell me that it's *not possible* that such treatments are going to exist in any meaningful timescale any time soon. In other words, they insist that human rejuvenation *can't* be done. It's wishful thinking to suppose otherwise, they say. It's bad science. It's naively over-optimistic. It's ignorant of the long history of failures in this field. The technical challenges remain overwhelmingly difficult.

Second, people tell me that any such treatments would be *socially destructive* and *morally indefensible*. In other words, they insist that human rejuvenation *shouldn't* be done. It's essentially a selfish idea, they say – an idea with all kinds of undesirable consequences for societal harmony or

1

planetary well-being. It's an arrogant idea, from immature minds. It's an idea that deserves to be strangled.

Can't be done; shouldn't be done – in this book, I will argue that both these objections are profoundly wrong. I'll argue instead that rejuvenation is a noble, highly desirable, eminently practical destiny for our species – a "Humanity+" destiny that could be achieved within just one human generation from now. As I see it, the abolition of aging is set to take its place on the upward arc of human social progress, echoing developments such as the abolition of slavery, the abolition of racism, and the abolition of poverty.

It turns out that the can't/shouldn't objections are interlinked. They reinforce each other. It's often *because* someone thinks an effort is technically impossible that they object to any time or finance being applied to it. It would be much better, they say, to apply these resources to other philanthropic causes where real progress *is* possible. That, allegedly, would be the moral, mature thing to do. Conversely, when someone's moral stance predisposes them to accept personal bodily decline and death, they become eager to find technical reasons that back up their decision. After all, it's human nature to tend to cherry pick evidence that supports what we want to believe.

Two paradigms

A set of mutually reinforcing interlinked beliefs is sometimes called a "paradigm". Our paradigms guide us, both consciously and unconsciously, in how we see the world, and in the kinds of projects we deem to be worthwhile. Our paradigms filter our perceptions and constrain our imaginations.

Changing paradigms is hard work. Just ask anyone who has tried to alter the opinion of others on contentious matters such as climate change, gun control, regulating the free market, or progressive taxation. Mere reason alone cannot unseat opinions on such topics. What to some observers is clear and compelling evidence for one position is hardly even noticed by someone entrenched in a competing paradigm. The inconvenient evidence is swatted away with little conscious thought.

The paradigm that accepts human bodily decline and aging as somehow desirable has even deeper roots than the vexatious political topics mentioned in the previous paragraph. It's not going to be easy to dislodge that *accepting-aging* paradigm. However, in the chapters ahead, I will marshal a wide range of considerations in favour of a different paradigm – the paradigm that heartily anticipates and endorses rejuvenation. I'll try to encourage readers to see things from that *anticipating-rejuvenation* paradigm.

Two abolitions

Accepting aging can be compared to accepting slavery.

For millennia, people from all social classes took slavery for granted. Thoughtful participants may have seen drawbacks with the system, but they assumed that there was no alternative to the basic fact of slavery. They could not conceive how society would function properly without slaves. Even the Bible takes slavery as a given. There is no Mosaic commandment which says "Thou shalt not keep slaves". Nor is there anything in the New Testament that tells slave owners to set their slaves free.

But in recent times, thank goodness, the public mind changed. The *accepting-slavery* paradigm wilted in the face of a crescendo of opposing arguments. As with slavery, so also with aging: the time will come for its abolition. The public will cease to take aging for granted. They'll stop believing in spurious justifications for its inevitability. They'll demand better. They'll see how rejuvenation is ready to be embraced.

One reason why slavery is so objectionable is the extent of its curtailment of human opportunity – the denial of free choice to the people enslaved. Another reason is that life expectancy of slaves frequently fell far short of the life expectancy of people not enslaved. As such, slavery can be counted as a major killer: it accelerated death.

From the anticipating-rejuvenation perspective, aging should be seen as the biggest killer of all. Compared to "standard" killers of the present day, such as drunken driving, terrorism, lead fumes, or other carcinogens – killers which rouse us to action to constrain them – aging destroys many more people. Globally, aging is the cause of at least two thirds of human deaths. Aging is the awful elephant in the room, which we have collectively learned to ignore, but which we must learn to recognise and challenge anew.

Every single week the rejuveneering project is delayed, hundreds of thousands more people suffer and die worldwide due to aging-related diseases. Advocates of rejuveneering see this ongoing situation as a needless slaughter. It's an intolerable offence against human potential. We ought, therefore, to be powerfully motivated to raise the probability of 50% which I offered at the start of this foreword. A 50% chance of success with the rejuveneering project means, equally, a 50% chance of that project failing. That's a 50% chance of the human slaughter continuing.

Motivation

In the same way as we have become fervently motivated in recent decades to deal with the other killers mentioned above – vigorously campaigning against, for example, drunk drivers and emitters of noxious chemical pollutants – we ought to be even more motivated to deal with aging. The anger that society has directed against tobacco companies, for long obscuring the links between smoking and lung cancer, ought to find a resonance in a new social passion to uncover and address links between biological aging and numerous diseases. If it's right to seek to change behaviours and metabolism to cut down bad cholesterol (a precursor of heart disease) and concentrated glucose (a precursor of diabetes), it should be equally right to change behaviours and metabolism to cut down something that's a precursor of even more diseases, namely, biological aging.

This is a discussion with enormous consequences. Changes in the public mood regarding the desirability of rejuveneering could trigger large reallocations of both public and private research expenditure. In turn, these reallocations are likely to have major implications in many areas of public well-being. Clearly, these decisions need to be taken wisely – with decisions being guided by a better understanding of the rich landscape of rejuveneering possibilities.

An ongoing surge of motivation, wisely coordinated, is one of the factors which can assist the rejuveneering project to overcome the weighty challenges it faces – challenges in science, technology, engineering, and human collaboration. Stubborn "unknown unknowns" surely lie ahead too. Due to these complexities and unknowns, no one can be sure of the outcome of this project. Despite what some rejuvenation enthusiasts may suggest, there's nothing inevitable about the pace of future medical progress. That's why I give the probability of success as only around 50%.

Although the end outcome remains unclear, the sense of discovery is increasing. The underlying scientific context is changing rapidly. Every day brings its own fresh firehose of news of potential breakthrough medical approaches. In the midst of so much innovation, it behoves us to seek clarity on the bigger picture.

To the extent that my book can provide that bigger picture, it will have met at least some of its goals. Armed with that bigger picture, readers of this book will, hopefully, be better placed to find the aspect of the overall rejuveneering project where they can make their best contributions. Together, we can tilt that 50% success probability upwards. The sooner, the better.

The discussion ahead

Chapter by chapter, here's how this book will unfold.

Chapter 1, "A shocking possibility", provides a fuller introduction to the subject of abolishing aging. To set the scene, it draws upon contributions of great men of letters: the wartime poet Wilfred Owen, the mid-century poet Dylan Thomas, and the Scottish novelist Iain Banks. All three of these writers suffered premature deaths. Their examples help make the case that *all* deaths are premature.

Chapter 2, "Rejuveneering 101", poses and pre-emptively answers 25 questions that frequently interrupt any longer discussion of the possibility of human rejuvenation. This discussion is a necessary prerequisite to clear the way for the material in later chapters.

Chapter 3, "From flight to rejuvenation", looks at some aspects of human existence which were for centuries accepted as "natural"– much the same as aging is often regarded nowadays. For example, it was long held that powered flight through the air was *unnatural and impossible*, and any attempt at it would be bound to fail. These opinions were eventually overturned, faster than almost anyone expected. These reversals of opinion provide important learnings for the debate over human rejuvenation.

Chapter 4, "Rejuveneering starting points", advances arguments against any claim that rejuvenation is inherently impossible. Nature is the best mentor here: nature is full of rejuvenation mechanisms, which human intervention has the potential to magnify and extend.

Chapter 5, "Scaling up", takes that analysis one stage further. Suppose it turns out to be one million times harder to solve the engineering problems of human rejuvenation than it was to solve the engineering problems of powered flight. Would that mean it will take one million times as long to complete the first project, compared to the second? The nature of exponential progress suggests otherwise. Provided suitable forms of collaboration can be arranged, the task can be completed in decades, rather than millennia.

Chapter 6, "Collaborative rejuveneering", reviews how that kind of productive cooperation is possible, via changes in systems, tools, and processes, as well as changes in technology. In other words, larger numbers of contributors can fuel the arena of rejuvenation with exponential growth, rather than a cacophony of disorganised low-quality noise.

Chapter 7, "Runners and riders", looks at different approaches favoured by different rejuveneers, and highlights what seem to be the most promising lines of research.

Chapter 8, "Changing minds", explores the topic of clashing paradigms. Medical orthodoxy at different times has fiercely resisted change, for social and cultural reasons, as much as for intellectual ones. Examples include opposition to improved hospital cleanliness, and a continuing fondness for bloodletting. In these cases, it took painstaking efforts, often by comparative outsiders, to persuade mainstream medical practitioners to adopt a new paradigm.

Chapter 9, "Money matters", continues the theme of paradigm change, by providing a different kind of argument in favour of accelerating the rejuvenation project. This is an economic argument, featuring the concept of the longevity dividend.

Chapter 10, "Adverse psychology", digs further into the factors behind objections to human rejuvenation. Once these factors are made clear, there's greater hope for everyone to take a more measured, reflective decision on whether the project deserves our collective support.

Chapter 11, "Towards Humanity+" describes in more detail how a world without human aging could operate. It's a world with many differences from our present one. The advent of that world will cause us to revise many aspects of our lifestyle. It will challenge some of our treasured thoughts and values. But it's a world where we can be profoundly happy to make our new homes. The positive changes will far outweigh the negative ones. As such, it's a world well worth fighting to bring into being, as soon as possible.

Chapter 12, "Radical alternatives", looks at some alternatives that may be considered by people who face the prospect of significant aging and death before comprehensive therapies for human rejuvenation become widely available.

Chapter 13, "Future uncertain", takes stock: it lists key unknowns that still remain unanswered. It also proposes a course of action to resolve these unknowns in the most effective manner.

Author's note

When rejuveneering is tabled for discussion, many emotions come to the surface. Feelings that have long been suppressed may swell up, with surprising force. Nevertheless, I'll do what I can to maintain an even keel in the chapters that follow.

The pages ahead mix detail with context. The context includes analogies and comparisons. Alongside the details of specific medical topics, I discuss various non-medical engineering problems which were, at one time, viewed as equally intractable and unsolvable as aging. The fact that these other problems have been – or are being – solved, adds extra weight to the idea that rejuvenation likewise lies within our grasp.

Analogical reasoning has, of course, its own limitations. History is more likely to *rhyme* than to *repeat*. But analogies can also be the catalyst for important new insight. I'll leave it to readers to determine whether the analogies in this book live up to that potential.

Enhancing the conversation

One of the themes that run throughout this book is the importance of better systems to enable more sophisticated collaborations between diverse supporters of rejuveneering. We need systems that allow the best ideas and the best techniques to become widely appreciated, regardless of their origin.

As part of a commitment to a better conversation among writers who have important things to say on the subject of rejuveneering – and who say it well – I frequently quote sentences and paragraphs from different writers in the pages that follow.

> These paragraphs are recognisable by being formatted with distinctive background shading and inset margins (like this one).

In all such cases, I have provided links to the original articles, in text that precedes the quotation, so that interested readers can look in more detail at the work of these writers and their publications.

Any writers who I have quoted, but who think I have misrepresented or misunderstood their ideas, are welcome to get in touch with me[1], so I can make amends, and the conversation can improve.

The website https://theabolitionofaging.com/ contains additional pointers to the fast-evolving online discussion of topics raised in these conversations. After all, I could only include in this book a small fraction of the material that I originally thought should be covered. And if I am right that the whole field of rejuveneering is undergoing an exponential increase, the online discussion is poised to grow and grow. Please let me know, via that website, your own thoughts about which areas deserve greater attention.

1. A shocking possibility

We live in an era of sweeping change. Every day brings a fresh wave of Internet news reports about apparent breakthroughs by scientists and engineers. These reports highlight accelerating progress in numerous areas of technology. Human skills are jumping forward in fields such as atomic level manufacturing (nanotechnology), genetic analysis and synthesis (biotechnology), mass data processing (information technology), and brain enhancement (cognitive technology). Reflecting on these trends, we are led to anticipate the imminent creation of new types of machines, new types of lifeforms, new types of algorithms, and new types of minds.

Further extrapolation of these trends suggests some striking conclusions. The robots and software that we humans are creating may take over more and more of the tasks from which we used to earn our living. Technological unemployment might soon be upon us, at an unprecedented scale. In that case, we must develop systems that provide our essential needs even in the absence of us earning an income. We must also learn to find our purpose in roles other than paid employment.

Indeed, new forms of artificial intelligence may quickly become far cleverer than native humans, potentially relegating us to the status of the *second* most intelligent species on the planet, languishing behind new superintelligences. On the other hand, if we humans can absorb technology inside our bodies and brains, in the right way – if, that is, we can successfully *merge* with technology – then the threat of displacement may recede. Instead of being subordinated to artificial superintelligences, we humans might become superhumans, retaining control of our own destiny.

These modifications of our bodies and brains may extend further than just making us stronger and smarter: they might alter our fundamental character. In other words, we may soon have increased power, not only to alter nature, but to alter *human nature*. Rather than continuing to be driven by our present, biologically grounded desires and hopes, we'll have the opportunity to *deeply rewire our brains* so we are driven by new sets of desires and hopes. We'll have to face the question, not just "What do we want?" but "What do we want to want?"

Perhaps most shocking of all, we may gain the ability which is the main subject of this book – the ability to reverse and even abolish aging. If we want to, we could live indefinitely youthfully.

Beyond future shock

As a futurist, when I talk to audiences about the implications of accelerating technology, I'm used to witnessing some powerful reactions. Some of these reactions are intensely positive: "*Wow*, that would be awesome; I love it". Others are intensely negative: "*Yuk*, that would be awful; I hate it". Both sets of reaction – the excitement and the distress – are varieties of future shock.

As a futurist, one of my tasks is to ease people beyond future shock. Our assessment of radical possible future scenarios should be guided, I say, not just by our initial emotional reaction, but by the kind of careful thought that is possible only once these strong emotions are, at least temporarily, set aside.

Our untutored gut reactions to hearing about an unexpected future scenario are liable to lead us astray – *badly* astray. The evaluative principles which served us well in the past may lose their applicability in the very different circumstances that could exist in the future. So as a futurist, I ask audiences: let's avoid rushing to judgement. Let's be ready to free ourselves from the assumptions of the past. Let's be vigilant, against wishful thinking, and also against any overdose of cynicism. Let's be ready to conceive the full potential of new scenarios, so we can see more clearly both the upsides and the downsides they bring.

Therefore, let's try to calmly assess this possibility: practical therapies for the comprehensive reversal of biological aging may be just around the corner.

It's my own carefully considered view that, within 25 years – that is, by around the year 2040 – science may have placed into our hands the means to radically extend human longevity. I'll describe in the pages ahead how a suite of rejuvenation treatments, administered regularly, could periodically undo the accumulated damage of aging in both body and brain. As a result, life expectancy will shoot upwards. Not long afterward, more and more people will start sailing past the current world record for the longest verified human lifespan – a record held, as best as researchers can determine[2], by

Frenchwoman Jeanne Louise Calment, who lived for 122 years and 164 days (1875 to 1997).

To be clear, these new heights of longevity would be achieved, not by extending the period of enfeeblement and decrepitude at the end of someone's life, but by keeping people healthy and invigorated for as long as each person chooses. This would be the extension, not just of lifespan, but of healthspan.

Consider, moreover, that as years pass, quality of life would progressively improve. At the chronological age of sixty, someone might be more resilient, more capable, and more energised than when they were fifty. By the time they reach seventy, they might be every bit as healthy as when they were thirty. (And, moreover, a lot wiser.)

This is the vision of biological rejuvenation. The programme to achieve it can be called "rejuveneering"[3] – the engineering of rejuvenation.

It's a controversial programme. Of all the topics I discuss with people in my role as a futurist, this is the one that tends to generate the most commotion. Eyebrows rise. Chests heave. Nervous chuckles escape. Heads look away, silently imploring the conversation to move to something different – something less close to the bone.

Whilst some people try to duck any exchange of views on this topic, others plunge in, fists flying. "It's simply not possible to reverse aging", they may declare. "The very idea is unnatural." "It's wishful thinking." "Not in a hundred years. Probably not in a thousand years." "Those who say otherwise are quacks." "It's a money-making racket." "It's an egocentric, narcissistic fantasy." "It would be an epic misuse of research funding." "Even *if it could* be accomplished, it would surely have dreadful side-effects." "The bad consequences would outweigh any good that might be accomplished." *You get the flavour.*

After all, if the rejuveneering programme succeeds, we can anticipate a society full of people who are perpetually youthful. *That's going to turn all manner of things upside down.*

Accordingly, as this book examines the prospects for the success of rejuveneering, it also examines how society might cope if, indeed, all manner of things *are* turned upside down.

There are many obstacles standing in the way of a serious discussion on these topics. The very idea of rejuveneering stirs not only objections but also emotional hostility. Expect a lot of rancour in the pages ahead, as I dig into these objections and seek to defuse the hostility, so that calmer minds can prevail. Expect, too, lots of honest intellectual disagreement. Drawing on my decades-long experience as a facilitator of forthright discussion, I'll do my best to referee, and to provide the light of illumination alongside the heat of passion.

Sweetness and lies

Let's start with an uncomfortable question. *Do you want to die?*

In other words: *Do you look forward to the disintegration of yourself – to the permanent cessation of your thoughts, your memories, and your feelings – and to the termination of any possibility for future thoughts, actions, and experiences?*

I'll make a concession. Sometimes, the answer might be "Yes". Sometimes, death can be sweet.

Death can provide a welcome relief, of a sort, from an extended period of drawn-out suffering, from the heartache of personal deterioration, from the awfulness of senility, from spiralling healthcare costs, from humiliating feelings of bodily incompetence, and from the chilling sense of being a burden to caregivers.

What's more, death can enable a fresh start, as relatives and friends of the deceased draw a line under a protracted spell of weary uncertainty, and pick up the pieces in a new phase of their lives.

But go back to a period before the onset of the drawn-out suffering, personal deterioration, embarrassing incontinence, senile dementia, and spiralling healthcare costs. Go back to a period of relative good health. Were the first downward movements of the plunge towards ill health and death welcomed, if they were noticed at that time? Was each subsequent step along the way – each ratcheting of the body's state of collapse – a cause for celebration? *Not likely.*

The only reason that death is, sometimes, comparatively sweet, is because of all the bitter steps that happened earlier, during that person's sorry descent from good health to death's door.

The goal of rejuveneering is to prevent (or subsequently reverse) these earlier, bitter steps, and thereby to entirely avoid any final pressure to accept death in the face of prolonged suffering.

Rejuveneers ask us to imagine that aging was optional. Given a choice between mental senility and enhanced cerebral vigour, who would choose senility? Given a choice between bodily decline and a new flurry of energy, who would choose decline? Given a choice between spiralling physical disintegration and personal rejuvenation, who would choose disintegration? *Not the young. Not the middle-aged. Not even the elderly* – if they really had a free choice, without the weight of powerful social and psychological expectations to the contrary.

We all bemoan the circumstances when someone is, as we say, "cut down in their prime" – when they "die before their time". We are particularly distressed at the deaths of youngsters, who are deprived of the chance to experience all that a fuller life would have given them. They miss the opportunity to fall in love, perchance to marry, to see their children grow, and to get to know their grandchildren. They miss the opportunity to progress through their careers, to master their chosen fields of endeavour, and to travel widely throughout the world. No wonder that we exclaim, of these deceased youngsters, "What a waste", "What a shame". In such circumstances, few critics would be so bold as to ask "What's so bad about death?"

But imagine again. The death of a child is a tragedy, but so is the death of a grandparent. The death of a grandparent is just as much a foreclosing of new opportunity as the death of a youngster. To think otherwise is to be guilty of *ageism* – a prejudice against someone just on account of how old they happen to be. To think otherwise is to imagine that older people must inevitably lose their powers of innovation, and forfeit the rights to re-invention which they possessed while younger.

The only reason that claim may strike us as strange is because we have grown accustomed to the idea that life has a "natural length", lasting around three generations. But why shouldn't grandparents also have the opportunity for renewal, to pursue absorbing new pastimes, to enter and master new fields of endeavour, and to travel even more widely, including journeys in both outer and inner space? Why should all the wisdom in their heads – their capacity to help and inspire – be snuffed out by decline and death? What more could these grandparents still accomplish, enabled by rejuvenation of both body and mind? What new subjects could they learn? What new skills could they acquire? What new experiences could they cherish? What new gifts could they bestow? What new contributions could they make, to the roll out of humanity's tapestry?

As I mentioned, there's a widespread ingrained view that human lifespans are subject to a kind of natural length. This view says that death in just a few decades time is, in a sense, the appropriate destination for all of us. Indeed, it says that death can even be sweet.

This idea is ancient, and comes in many forms. The Roman poet Horace, writing in Latin in the first century BC, penned the famous phrase "Dulce et decorum est pro patria mori": "It is sweet and honourable to die for your country". The same fighting words are inscribed over the entrance of the Arlington National Cemetery Memorial Theatre in Virginia, USA. They can also be found in the chapel of the Royal Military Academy at Sandhurst, UK, and in many other locations worldwide. The sentiment evidently has wide appeal. It can help onlookers find *a sort* of meaning in the tragic, untimely death of soldiers. But another poet, Wilfred Owen, took exception to the idea. Writing in the midst of World War One battle carnage, Owen condemned Horace's phrase as "The old Lie" – with an emphatic capital 'L'.

Owen was no coward. He was awarded the Military Cross in recognition of his bravery in an attack he led at the village of Joncourt, France in October 1918, in which he captured a German unit's machine gun and used it against enemy combatants. Alas, his was a posthumous award. Owen was killed in action just a few days later, the 4th of November, whilst he was leading another attack. Owen's family received that heart-rending news one week later – on the day which, poignantly, also marked as Armistice Day. It is said[4] that his family opened the telegram informing them of Owen's death at the same time as church bells were pealing in celebration of the peace. Armistice came too late for Wilfred Owen. He was just twenty five.

Owen's poem – which appropriates the same phrase "Dulce et decorum est" for its own title – gives a wrenching description of someone dying from a gas attack. Here's how it ends[5]:

> Gas! Gas! Quick, boys!---An ecstasy of fumbling,
> Fitting the clumsy helmets just in time;
> But someone still was yelling out and stumbling,
> And flound'ring like a man in fire or lime.

Dim, through the misty panes and thick green light,
As under a green sea, I saw him drowning.

In all my dreams, before my helpless sight,
He plunges at me, guttering, choking, drowning.

If in some smothering dreams you too could pace
Behind the wagon that we flung him in,
And watch the white eyes writhing in his face,
His hanging face, like a devil's sick of sin;
If you could hear, at every jolt, the blood
Come gargling from the froth-corrupted lungs,
Obscene as cancer, bitter as the cud
Of vile, incurable sores on innocent tongues,---
My friend, you would not tell with such high zest
To children ardent for some desperate glory,
The old Lie: Dulce et decorum est
Pro patria mori.

Imagine, with Owen, if military deaths were no longer lauded as being
"sweet and honourable", despite centuries of tub-thumping pro-nationalist
sentiment. But more than that: imagine if, one hundred years after Owen's
untimely demise, *all* human deaths became a thing to deeply regret, and to
prevent. This rejuveneering viewpoint sees all deaths as being untimely:
each death irrevocably extinguishes vital potential and truncates
opportunity. To borrow adjectives from Owen's poem, each death is *obscene*
and *bitter*. In this alternative imagining, death would no longer be sweet
under any circumstances.

In their hearts, people have frequently intuited that awful truth. But
they have, almost equally frequently, refrained from thinking it. It would
have been a frustrating, demoralising, terrifying truth to contemplate – since
no realistic prospect of rejuvenation was at hand at that time. As a result,
huge swathes of culture were created, as cushions against the thought of the
forthcoming annihilation of each and every one of us (and all whom we
hold dear). Buttressed by art, story-telling, fantasy, and religion – and, yes,
by poetry – we have developed patterns of thought that told us, in various
ways: *death ain't too bad*; death is natural; death can be sweet. We have
reassured each other that we can, and should, make our accommodation
with physical decay and death; we should even welcome death as a
necessary part of the human existence.

But what if science really is on the point of delivering biological rejuvenation? In that case, we ought to collectively rise up, and protest: *It is an old Lie that death is natural, necessary, or in any way sweet or honourable.* Humanity can do better.

Complications and perspectives

Of course, there are many complications en route to reaching such a transformational conclusion. These complications swarm all over the pages ahead. These pages take time to look into questions of biology, engineering, ethics, religion, politics, and economics. It's my task to guide readers through the associated complications. Along the way, I aim to distinguish questions which still remain open – matters where thoughtful experts can legitimately disagree – from others where a firm conclusion ought to be drawn.

One area where a firm conclusion can already be drawn is this: *The time to have this discussion is now.* It's no longer acceptable to laugh at the rejuveneers, or to ignore them, or to dismiss the whole field as the playground of crackpots, dreamers, and charlatans. More and more news reports are carrying tantalising hints about progress towards rejuvenation. There is real science – new science – behind many of these reports. Responding to these hints, online movements are forming, growing, fracturing, coalescing again with greater vigour, and starting to impact the public zeitgeist. These movements channel powerful energy. Accordingly, major corporations are starting to make sizeable investments into the technology of human longevity.

Although some rejuveneering enthusiasts occasionally let their excitement cloud their judgement, and their hopes sometimes run far ahead of prudence, there is considerable merit in what they have to say. In this book, I give voice to these pioneers – as well as to their critics – and I give my reasons for expecting the field to flourish. I also make it clear that the end outcome of the programme is far from settled.

Accordingly, the pages ahead provide a bird's eye report from the frontiers of the emerging field of rejuvenation biology:

- The goals and motivations of key players in this field
- The rapid progress that has been achieved in the last few years
- The challenges that threaten to thwart further development

- The critical questions that still need to be faced.

The book contains material drawn from my discussions with more than a dozen researchers, engineers, entrepreneurs, and humanitarians, who are making it their life's quest to enable human rejuvenation. I sincerely thank everyone for the time they took to talk to me.

What I bring to the book is a combination of five perspectives:

1. My background in doctoral research in history and philosophy of science at the University of Cambridge, when I wrestled with the thorny question of how to distinguish good science from bad science (pseudoscience) – that is, how to distinguish enlightened mavericks from deluded incompetents. That question has remained high in my mind throughout the intervening decades.

2. My twenty five year professional career within the smartphone industry, where I saw many aspirations regarding the breakthroughs that fast-moving technology could enable; these aspirations were that tech could make us all smarter, rather than rejuvenate us, but there are many similarities. Many of the aspirations of the smartphone industry had their own stern critics ahead of time, before eventually becoming widely acknowledged as a kind of common sense.

3. My experience as a writer, presenter, and blogger, in which I have learned (so people tell me) to explain complicated subjects in a relatively straightforward but engaging manner.

4. The eight years in which I have had the privilege, as chair of London Futurists, to organise meetups in London dedicated to futurist and technoprogressive topics – meetings which have featured a wide variety of different attitudes and outlooks, and which have on occasion needed considerable refereeing.

5. My aspiration as a humanitarian to probe for both the human upsides and the human downsides of changing technology – in order to set possible engineering breakthroughs (such as rejuvenation biotech) in a broader social context.

Acceptance and change

At first glance, rejuveneers seem to stand opposed to a profound piece of humanitarian wisdom – wisdom expressed by, among others, Gautama

Buddha, 2nd century Stoic advocate Marcus Aurelius, and 20th century American Protestant theologian Reinhold Niebuhr.

That wisdom urges serenity and acceptance in the face of life's deep challenges. There's no merit in becoming unnecessarily agitated about an issue – such as the onset of aging – if there's nothing that can be done about that issue. Why discuss a painful problem if you can't change the outcome? What's the point of complaining if there's no solution available?

It's as stated in the opening lines of Niebuhr's famous "serenity prayer"[6] (a prayer that everyone can appreciate, without any need to believe in a supernatural deity):

> God grant me
> *The serenity to accept the things I cannot change…*

A similar thought lies at the heart of Buddhism. The "Four Noble Truths"[7] state that suffering arises from attachment to desires, and that suffering ceases only when attachment to desire ceases. To transcend the omnipresence of suffering, we have to learn to accept life as it is, and to set aside desire – such as the desire for better material possessions, pleasure, security, or long life.

The Stoic philosophy of life, developed in ancient Greece and Rome, likewise emphasises an attitude of acceptance. As Epictetus (55-135 AD) stated[8],

> Freedom is secured not by the fulfilling of men's desires, but by the removal of desire.

Stoic advocate Marcus Aurelius (121-180 AD), who was emperor of Rome for the last 19 years of his life, posed the following questions in his "Meditations"[9]:

> Why do you hunger for length of days? The point of life is to follow reason and the divine spirit and to accept whatever nature sends you. To live in this way is not to fear death, but to hold it in contempt. Death is only a thing of terror for those unable to live in the present. Pass on your way, then, with a smiling face, under the smile of him who bids you go.

Admiration of "Stoic calm" persists to the present day. Former American president Bill Clinton has been quoted[10] as saying that "Meditations of Marcus Aurelius" was his favourite book. Stoicism is highlighted by self-education advocate Paul Jun as providing "9 Principles to Help You Keep Calm in Chaos"[11]:

Not only does philosophy teach us how to live well and become better humans, but it can also aid in overcoming life's trials and tribulations. Some schools of thought are for more abstract thinking and debate, whereas others are tools that are immediately practical to our current endeavours.

The principles within Stoicism are, perhaps, the most relevant and practical sets of rules for entrepreneurs, writers, and artists of all kinds. The Stoics focus on two things:

1. How can we lead a fulfilling, happy life?

2. How can we become better human beings?

The goal of Stoicism is to attain inner peace by overcoming adversity, practicing self-control, being conscious of our impulses, realizing our ephemeral nature and the short time allotted—these were all meditative practices that helped them live with their nature and not against it.

It is in contrast to these philosophies of mature acceptance – philosophies that emphasise uncomplaining acknowledgement of our finitude and our limits – that rejuveneers can be portrayed as arrogant, grasping, and juvenile. Rejuveneers dare to complain about the perceived insult of deteriorative aging. Rejuveneers have the audacity to imagine that an outcome unavailable to the greats of the past – including giants such as Marcus Aurelius, Reinhold Niebuhr, and Gautama Buddha – namely, the option of indefinite youthfulness – might shortly be available to present-day folk. Rejuveneers, according to this line of thought, lack the self-awareness to realise how unreasonable their ambition is. Indeed, the hubris of the rejuveneers can seem absurd.

But the quotes given above tell only a part of the story. For example, there's more to Buddhism than acceptance. Buddhist mindfulness coach Sunada Takagi comments as follows[12]:

Acceptance is the first step toward change

I recently had a couple people raise doubts to me about the Buddhist idea of "accepting what is." Isn't it too passive? What if we're in a situation that's really unacceptable?

I've come across a few things recently that speak to this. Each makes a slightly different point, but they all basically say the same thing. "Accepting what is" does not mean passive acquiescence. Far from it, it's the first step in making real and lasting change…

> So "accepting what is" is not about passivity at all. It's about clear seeing... Paradoxically, it's when we take responsibility for our own failings and difficulties, or those of the world around us, that the real process of change can begin to take place. I see it as an essential starting point for anything we take on in life.

Paul Jun, the writer I quoted above on the Stoic philosophy, also adopts a strong action-orientation. For him, being stoical is far from being passive. It can, as he says[13], be the prelude to urgency:

Remind yourself that time is our most precious resource

What I particularly love and find challenging about Stoicism is that death is at the forefront of their thoughts. They realized the ephemeral nature of humans and how this is repeated in many facets of life.

It provides a sense of urgency, to realize that you've lived a certain number of hours and the hours ahead of you are not guaranteed as the ones you have lived. When I think of this I realize that everyday truly is an opportunity to improve, not in a cliché kind of way, but to learn to honestly appreciate what we are capable of achieving and how we are very responsible for the quality of our lives.

This makes our self-respect, work ethic, generosity, self-awareness, attention, and growth ever more important. The last thing any of us wants to do is die with regret, hence why following principles of Stoicism puts your life into perspective. It humbles you and should also deeply motivate you.

That brings us back to the serenity prayer of Reinhold Niebuhr. Above, I quoted the first clause of that prayer – the so-called "acceptance clause". But there are two more clauses: an action clause and a wisdom clause. Here's the entirety:

> God grant me
> The serenity to accept the things I cannot change
> *The courage to change the things that I can*
> *And the wisdom to know the difference.*

Just as people can, rightly, be criticised for foolhardily attempting to change something that cannot be altered, so also can they, again rightly, be criticised for passively accepting some massive flaw or shortcoming which, it turns out, lay within their capacity to fix.

The most important clause in this prayer, arguably, is the "wisdom clause": if we can find out, objectively, whether something lies within our collective ability, it makes all the difference as to whether the right thing to do is to seek accommodation or to seek transformation.

For rejuveneering, I have no doubt that the right thing to do is to seek transformation. Doing otherwise would be akin – to borrow another motif from Christian heritage – to walking past on the other side of the road, keeping well away from an unfortunate traveller who has been mugged, stripped of his clothing, and left half dead. When regarding the unfortunate state of everyone around the world that is already "half dead" due to the approach of diseases of old age, who amongst us will prove to be a "good Samaritan" that sees the plight and provides tangible support? And who, in contrast, will be like the priest and the Levite of the biblical parable, rushing past with eyes averted, preoccupied with whatever else fits the accepting-aging paradigm?

Raging and calm

First World War medal-winning lieutenant Wilfred Owen is by no means the only poet to have reacted angrily to the glorification of death. In 1951, the octogenarian father of Welsh poet Dylan Thomas was dying. In his physical decay, Thomas senior, formerly a long-time teacher of English at Swansea Grammar School, was losing his eyesight. He was on the point of becoming blind. This prompted Dylan Thomas to write one of his best known poems, "Do not go gentle into the good night"[14]. It starts as follows:

> Do not go gentle into that good night
> Old age should burn and rave at close of day
> Rage, rage against the dying of the light

This poem offers no comfort. It avoids saying that blindness and death should be embraced. It provides no reassuring platitudes about accepting fate stoically with a stiff upper lip, about "having had a good innings" (a long time at the batting crease), or about respecting the grand cycle of life – platitudes which are common in polite British society, and which have analogues the world over.

Instead, the poem expresses visceral rage about the prospect of death. It makes no difference that the person who is dying has reached a ripe old age – their demise is still something which deserves rage.

Thomas senior died in 1952. Just one year later, his son, Dylan Thomas, was dead too – aged only 39.

The great Welsh poet was the victim of a self-inflicted gruelling lifestyle, but also, sadly, the victim of an incorrect medical diagnosis. He was, notoriously, a hard drinker. He claimed with some pride, just a few days before he died, that he had consumed "18 straight whiskies" in one drinking binge. Complaining of pain shortly afterwards in his New York hotel room, he was given some steroids by a local doctor[15], before being sedated with morphine. Because his problems worsened, he was admitted to a hospital, where clinical staff initially suspected alcohol-induced brain damage.

Dylan Thomas died without regaining consciousness. His autopsy brought a surprise: the primary cause of death was pneumonia. The morphine treatment he had received was probably ill-advised, since it would have exacerbated his breathing problems. His alcoholic tendency was likely a distraction, hindering a proper diagnosis. Greater awareness of the true cause of his ill-health would, perhaps, have saved him from an early grave. *To remain longer in the full-blooded light of life, it's not sufficient to rage; nor is it sufficient to hope.* We need the best insights that medical understanding can provide, as to the causes of impending bodily failure.

Often, however, even a full diagnosis of someone's illness can do little to help them survive. This is the case with another renowned writer, the Scottish novelist and science fiction author Iain Banks. In 2013, aged 59, Banks thought he was at the peak of his writing powers, except that his back was unexpectedly sore. As he told Guardian journalist Stuart Kelly, for an article published under the title "Iain Banks: The final interview"[16]:

> On the morning of 4th March, I thought everything was hunky dory except I had a sore back and my skin looked a bit funny. By the evening of the 4th I'd been told I had only a few months to live.

One month after this stunning news, Banks went public with the information, in an announcement[17] that mixed calmness with black humour:

> I am officially Very Poorly...
>
> I first thought something might be wrong when I developed a sore back in late January, but put this down to the fact I'd started writing at the beginning of the month and so was crouched over a keyboard all day.

When it hadn't gone away by mid-February, I went to my GP, who spotted that I had jaundice. Blood tests, an ultrasound scan and then a CT scan revealed the full extent of the grisly truth by the start of March.

I have cancer. It started in my gall bladder, has infected both lobes of my liver and probably also my pancreas and some lymph nodes, plus one tumour is massed around a group of major blood vessels in the same volume, effectively ruling out any chance of surgery to remove the tumours either in the short or long term.

The bottom line, now, I'm afraid, is that as a late stage gall bladder cancer patient, I'm expected to live for 'several months' and it's extremely unlikely I'll live beyond a year…

I've asked my partner Adele if she will do me the honour of becoming my widow (sorry – but we find ghoulish humour helps).

Banks was full of praise for the medical staff who had worked with him:

I'd like to add that from my GP onwards, the professionalism of the medics involved – and the speed with which the resources of the NHS in Scotland have been deployed – has been exemplary, and the standard of care deeply impressive. We're all just sorry the outcome hasn't been more cheerful.

But as was clear from his remarks in "The final interview", Banks felt aggrieved at his life being cut short. His regrets spanned Scottish politics, local forthcoming developments in and around Edinburgh, and – especially interesting for an author of science fiction – prospects for understanding outer space more fully:

In the unlikely event that I'm around for the referendum on Scottish independence I'm definitely voting 'yes'. I was saying last year that if we don't get it in 2014 we'll get it in my lifetime and now it turns out my lifetime might not extend as far as the first referendum and that just seems wrong…

I'm annoyed I won't get to vote in the referendum. I'm annoyed I won't get to ride an Edinburgh tram and I'm annoyed I won't get to go on the new Fife crossing [just north of Edinburgh].

And… just not seeing so much of the near future. I'd love to see what's going to happen next, what's happening in the oceans of Jupiter's moon, Europa, and what else we'll find out just in our own solar system. And we're not far from being able to analyse the atmospheres of planets around other stars and maybe spotting the signs of life there. There's so much I would have loved to have seen.

On what seems a more positive note, Banks expressed thanks that his own death would avoid the drawn-out "decrepitude" he saw in some of his elderly relatives:

> You know, I go and see my now very old Mum in her old folks' home, and I saw my Uncle Bob after getting my bloods done this morning and he's not in a good way. You look at the decrepitude of the very old and ill, and at least I'll be spared years of that. It'll be over fairly quickly.

As he suspected, Banks did not live to vote in the Scottish referendum. That would have required him to live for another 18 months. Instead, he died just three months after his cancer was discovered. Even as his body was failing, his mind was full of rich ideas for intriguing new writing projects. The Guardian journalist Stuart Kelly expressed a double regret:

> "You know, this might be my last public statement", Iain Banks said to me on the phone when I was setting up this interview, and at the time that simply didn't seem likely: he was too full of ideas and opinions and schemes. He emailed me a fortnight ago, saying that he was hoping to be out walking around the village again by the end of the week. In fact, he died on 9 June...
>
> To be robbed of 30 years he thought he might have had is one thing: to lose the few months he was cautiously anticipating seems especially cruel.

Optimism and failure

How might a rejuveneering programme avoid the "especially cruel" fate that befalls people of all ages, in all walks of life, the world over, when their minds are full of fine ideas, but cancer (to name just one killer disease) strikes their bodies down and terminates them? Many readers are probably thinking: *How on earth can rejuveneering succeed, given that progress towards a cure for cancer has proven to be so elusive?*

Indeed, already more than four decades have passed from US President Richard Nixon's December 1971 declaration of a "war on cancer" – also known as the "commitment for the conquest of cancer"[18]:

> We are here today for the purpose of signing the cancer act of 1971. I hope that in the years ahead that we may look back on this day and this action as being the most significant action taken during this Administration. It could be, because when we consider what cancer does

each year in the United States, we find that more people each year die of cancer in the United States than all the Americans who lost their lives in World War II.

This shows us what is at stake. It tells us why I sent a message to the Congress the first of this year, which provided for a national commitment for the conquest of cancer, to attempt to find a cure.

Now, with the cooperation of the Congress, with the cooperation of many of the people in this room, we have set up a procedure for the purpose of making a total national commitment...

As a result of what has been done, as a result of the action which will come into being as a result of signing this bill, the Congress is totally committed to provide the funds that are necessary, whatever is necessary, for the conquest of cancer.

Nixon had high ambitions for this battle. His words echoed those of another epic declaration[19] by a previous US President, John F. Kennedy, nine years earlier:

We choose to go to the moon in this decade and do the other things, not because they are easy, but because they are hard, because that goal will serve to organize and measure the best of our energies and skills, because that challenge is one that we are willing to accept, one we are unwilling to postpone, and one which we intend to win...

We shall send to the moon, 240,000 miles away from the control station in Houston, a giant rocket more than 300 feet tall, the length of this football field, made of new metal alloys, some of which have t yet been invented, capable of standing heat and stresses several times more than have ever been experienced, fitted together with a precision better than the finest watch, carrying all the equipment needed for propulsion, guidance, control, communications, food and survival, on an untried mission, to an unknown celestial body, and then return it safely to earth, re-entering the atmosphere at speeds of over 25,000 miles per hour, causing heat about half that of the temperature of the sun... and do all this, and do it right, and do it first before this decade is out...

But whereas Kennedy's moonshot declaration is the stuff of legend, Nixon's war on cancer had no Apollo 11 moment. Nixon's 1971 aspirations proved to be wildly over-optimistic. Dr. Benjamin Neel, head of the Ontario Cancer Institute, and a veteran of four decades of research on cancer, commented pithily[20] on what he saw as the naivety of Nixon's programme. The 1971 declaration of war on cancer was, he said,

...like Kennedy trying to put a man on the moon in the 1600s. We had no fundamental understanding of the disease.

This sentiment suggests we might be 300 years of research and development away from being able to comprehensively cure cancer – the length of time separating the 1600s from the 1900s.

Yet rejuveneering appears an order of magnitude harder even than curing cancer. The rejuveneering programme needs to cure, not only cancer, but also a host of other seemingly intractable diseases, including senile dementia, motor neuron disease, respiratory diseases, heart diseases, and stroke. It's also possible that other diseases will grow in significance, as current killers are gradually tamed.

With all these challenges to be faced, how is a rejuveneering programme even vaguely credible?

Conflicting forces

As later chapters in this book explain, the answer to this question has five parts:

1. A Copernican revolution, switching the roles of disease and aging, in which addressing aging becomes the key to solutions to numerous diseases
2. Exponentially accelerating progress, on account of ever greater numbers of people having ever better tools with which to conduct their research and development
3. Increasing ability to re-engineer biological entities with atomic precision, that is, at the nanoscale
4. The transformational power of improved software (of numerous sorts)
5. The transformational power of profoundly increased public interest in the field.

Each of these changes is a revolution of its own kind. Together, suitably integrated, they can add up to the biggest transformation of human history.

But the factors which could profoundly assist the rejuveneering programme co-exist with other factors which could profoundly destabilise it:

1. The ever greater noise and chaos which the ever-larger number of participants in the field could produce, via poor quality research
2. The potential of unmanaged adverse side-effects from new technologies, with treatments having detrimental outcomes rather than the positive ones expected
3. Over-optimism, simplistic explanations, false diagnoses, and deflated expectations, which could result in a social backlash against the whole initiative, and the onset of a "rejuveneering winter", akin to the periods of "AI winter" in which funding for artificial intelligence research was sharply restricted
4. Badly handled public communications about the possible impacts of rejuvenation biotech, alienating potential supporters rather than inspiring them and harnessing their good will
5. Social fragmentation and hostility, fuelled by rising inequality and economic turbulence, and perhaps by tech-induced environmental damage, resulting in the slowing down and eventual destruction of the engines of innovation upon which rejuveneering depends.

If these destabilising factors gain the upper hand, the bold aspiration of poets and other visionaries for human mastery over health and longevity will remain just that – aspiration, unfulfilled, devoid of practical wisdom – an opportunity that slipped out of our collective grasp.

Can we move beyond poetry to practical wisdom? Can we make the abolition of aging a fact, rather than just a slogan? Can we harness the positive forces for the acceleration of rejuveneering, whilst taming the negative forces that would destroy the project? I believe we can, though the outcome is far from being set. It's going to require a great deal of inspired hard work – perhaps from people who are reading this book and whose will might be strengthened in the process.

2. Rejuveneering 101

It's time to raise, and answer, questions that might otherwise prevent some readers from taking the subject of rejuveneering seriously. In the process, this chapter will cover what can be called "Rejuveneering 101" – the introductory material that establishes a common starting point, before subsequent chapters dive more deeply into controversy.

Probabilities

Q1: What's the basis for calculating a 50% probability for the success of rejuveneering by 2040?

The estimate I have given for the success of rejuveneering is a ballpark figure. I don't claim to assess it as 50.0%, accurate to one decimal place. The actual figure could be anywhere between, say, 25% to 75%. But I picked 50% in order to emphasise that the matter is reasonably balanced:

- There are many forces which, if harnessed properly, could swiftly accelerate progress
- There are many forces which, on the other hand, if they become dominant, could completely derail the project.

At the close of the previous chapter, I listed five powerful forces in each of these two categories, as an indication of the opposing tensions. That's a sign of the general state of balance. If you think that some of these forces are more significant, or less significant, you may reach a different estimate of the probability for the success of the project. You may also wish to suspend your judgement until reviewing the major risks the project faces that I consider in the final chapter of this book, "Future uncertain".

The date 2040 will be the end of a sixth decade of work in rejuveneering, after its beginnings as a serious field for serious scientists in the 1980s. In that first decade, the number of such researchers was miniscule. But with an average tenfold increase each decade – a growth rate I believe to be credible and sustainable – there could be around one million people actively contributing valuable insights to the rejuveneering project by 2040. *Provided these insights can be organised in a useful way*, that level of input has a good chance of yielding rejuvenation therapies that are comprehensive, affordable, and reliable.

But there are many "ifs" lurking in this argument – assumptions and challenges that I'll do my best to highlight and explore in the chapters ahead.

Beyond "business-as-usual lifespan extension"

Q2: Is rejuveneering simply "more of the same" of previous healthcare enhancements?

The short answer is "no": there's a lot more to rejuveneering.

The longer answer starts by noting some data about the increase in human life expectancy over the last two centuries. From the 1840s until the present day, life expectancy for women has increased from around 45 to around 87, as measured in the country at the time with the highest such figure (this was Sweden in the 1840s, New Zealand in 1900, Norway in 1950, Iceland in 1980, and Japan in 2014[21]). As graphed[22] by longevity researchers James Vaupel and Jim Oeppen, this 42 year increase in life expectancy over the period of around 170 years broadly conforms to a steady progress line, with almost three months of additional life expectancy being added for each extra year that passed. It's a record of remarkable improvement.

If this trend continues, life expectancy for women, in at least some countries, will reach 100 by around 2065. That's what "more of the same" might be expected to deliver.

Vaupel and Oeppen comment that the increase in life expectancy has, several times, exceeded hard limits previously predicted by seemingly expert demographers:

> [Even] as the expectation of life rose higher and higher, experts were unable to imagine its rising much further. They envisioned various biological barriers and practical impediments.

For example, a report created in 1928 by Louis Dublin, Chief Actuary of the Metropolitan Life Insurance Company, quantified expert consensus of that time:

> Using U.S. life tables as a guide, [Dublin] estimated the lowest level to which the death rate in each age group could possibly be reduced. His calculations were made "in the light of present knowledge and without intervention of radical innovations or fantastic evolutionary change in our physiological make-up, such as we have no reason to assume." His

"hypothetical table promised an ultimate figure of 64.75 years" for the expectation of life both for males and for females.

That supposed "ultimate figure" was, however, nothing of the sort. It had already been exceeded in New Zealand, at the time when Dublin published his prediction. Indeed, forecasts of upper bounds for life expectancy have, Vaupel and Oeppen note[23], "been broken, on average five years after publication".

However, a significant part of the increase in life expectancy can be attributed to improvements in childhood health. In earlier times, large number of children died at young ages. Up to one quarter of all children died before reaching the age of one.

Happily, childhood diseases are an area where medicine has made remarkable progress. But when this factor is removed from the overall statistical analysis, the upward trend in life expectancy, whilst still notable, is less dramatic. Data from the Journal of the Royal Society of Medicine from 2008[24] track the total life expectancy in England and Wales of women who had reached the age of 15 (and who had therefore survived childhood diseases). This increased from 48.2 in the period 1480-1679, to 64.6 in the period 1780-1879, to 73.4 in 1951, and to 79.2 in 1989. In other words, we see an increase of around 15 years of "mature life expectancy" (from 64.6 to 79.2) over roughly the same 170 year time period as previously mentioned. That's a long way short of the figure of 42 years quoted earlier. And according to these figures, it may take at least another century before life expectancy reaches 100.

A similar note of caution emerges from data collected in another 2008 article in the same journal[25], by Judith Rowbotham and Paul Clayton, which compared life expectancy in 1840s Victorian London with that in the same city in modern times:

A common view remains that in the mid-Victorian era life was brutish and short: "The average life span in 1840, in the Whitechapel district of London, was 45 years for the upper class and 27 years for tradesman. Labourers and servants lived only 22 years on average". However, these figures rely too heavily on crude averages culled from registers of births and deaths which belie the reality of adult experience of old age...

Infant mortality rates were unquestionably high, and around 50% of all infant deaths at all levels of society was due to infectious diseases. In 1856,

Archbishop Tait lost five of his children in five weeks to scarlet fever. This was by no means exceptional...

Once the dangerous childhood years were passed, however, Victorian contemporary sources (including regional variables) reveal that life expectancy in the mid-Victorian period was not markedly different from what it is today. Once infant mortality is stripped out, life expectancy at age five was 75 for men and 73 for women. (The lower figure for women reflects the danger of death in childbirth or from causes that were mainly unrelated to malnutrition.) This compares favourably with present figures: life expectancy at birth, reflecting our improved standards of neo-natal care, currently averages 75.9 years for men and 81.3 years for women. Recent work has suggested that for today's working-class men and women (a group more directly comparable to the mid-Victorian population) this is lower, at around 72 years for men and 76 years for women. This relative lack of progress is striking...

Perhaps the most important conclusion from all these figures is that aging, *on this showing*, is *not* going to be abolished any time soon. Yes, people are living longer on the whole, but they still age. *Unless something significant changes*, there is no "longevity escape velocity" in sight, whereby the average life expectancy would rise by one year (or more) for each year that passes.

However, we need to contrast "business as usual lifespan extension" with the kinds of rejuvenation therapies I'll be discussing in this book. These therapies have the potential of a very different effect:

- With "business as usual", we'll see in coming decades increasing numbers of centenarians worldwide, and even an increase of supercentenarians (people aged 110+), but we cannot envision 150 year olds any time soon, and nor can we envision centenarians who are as active and sprightly as present-day 30 year olds

- With rejuveneering, on the other hand, both these last two goals become credible. Rejuveneering has the potential to enable major increases in healthy lifespan – people living to 150, 200, and beyond, whilst remaining in the full flower of health.

To be clear, the *methods* of rejuveneering grow out of the same disciplines and knowledge-set which have advanced the "business as usual" improvements in healthcare. Rejuveneering is enabled by science, technology, engineering, and entrepreneurial skills – the same as for medicine as a whole. Like medicine as a whole, rejuveneering benefits from improvements in miniaturisation, data analysis, software modelling, biochemical manipulation, pharmacological discovery, and so on. But whilst the broad methods of rejuveneering and traditional medicine overlap, there are two key differences between the two approaches:

1. The first key difference is in the *fundamental thinking* of the two approaches. As I'll explain in more detail shortly, whereas traditional medicine focuses on disease, rejuveneering focuses on aging itself

2. The second key difference is in the *degree of openness to disruptive new techniques* from outside the field of medicine. Rejuveneering anticipates and welcomes transformation from fields such as second generation artificial intelligence (deep learning), nanotechnology, and (more generally) an engineering mindset.

If successful, rejuveneering will bring about a kind of phase transition, similar to the way in which continuing to apply heat to water results first in the water becoming hotter, and secondly (the phase transition) in water turning into steam as it boils. Here, the application of heat is analogous to the application of general scientific, technological, and engineering principles. The first phase of outcome is the *retardation* of aging. The second phase is the *reversal* of aging.

The plasticity of aging

Q3: What's the scientific evidence that lifespans can be altered?

In recent decades, animal species as varied as yeast, nematode worms, fruit flies, and rodents, have had their lifespans significant extended by laboratory interventions. These interventions, which have included changes to diet and modifications to genetics, have increased not only the *average* lifespan of the animals concerned, but also their *maximum* lifespans.

For example, in experiments with fruit flies that have been running since 1981, Michael Rose of the University of California, Irvine, has used selection pressures (systematically picking the fruit flies that reproduced at later ages) to extend fruit fly lifespan, generation by generation. In the end, the project has quadrupled average lifespan[26], from around 50 days to approaching 200 days. Importantly, these longer lived flies also displayed many other characteristics of improved health[27], including increased fecundity, better resistance to acute stresses, and greater athletic performance.

This quadrupling of fruit fly lifespan involves multiple changes in genetic expression. Other experiments have confirmed that *single* genetic changes can increase lifespans of organisms:

- A mutation in a gene named "age-1" increased the average lifespan of the C. elegans nematode worm by 65%, and its maximum lifespan by 110% (this breakthrough 1988 finding[28] by Tom Johnson is described, in its context, in a comprehensive 2011 review article by Cynthia Kenyon, "The first long-lived mutants"[29])
- A mutation in a gene named "daf-2" was later (1993[30]) found to increase the average lifespan of the same organism by 100%
- A mutation in an apparently different gene, "PI3K-null", astonishingly resulted in a ten-fold increase in C. elegans lifespan[31]: median lifespan increased from around 16 days to around 160 days (and there was a similar increase in maximal lifespan).

Lifespan extension can also be achieved for various animals by:

- Putting these animals on a calorie restricted diet
- Treating them with drugs, such as rapamycin, which seem to trigger some of the same biological pathways as a calorie-restricted diet
- Injecting other drugs (known as "senolytic" drugs) which trigger the internal destruction of worn out ("senescent") cells in mice; in this last example, the mice lived 20%-30% longer than controls[32].

All these examples refute the idea that was prevalent in previous times that lifespans of species are fixed. Instead, they demonstrate at least some degree of *plasticity* of lifespan. It is this plasticity that rejuveneers intend to develop and enhance.

For more examples of "rejuveneering starting points", see Chapter 4.

We should also consider the question: What's the scientific evidence that *human* lifespans can be altered?

Experiments on the lifespans of humans are, by their nature, harder to carry out than experiments on the lifespans of shorter-lived organisms. A sceptic might assert that the growing evidence of plasticity of lifespan in worms, fruit flies, yeast, and mice, has no implication for human longevity.

However, that would be to hypothesise some fundamental differences in the cellular biology of humans, compared to that of other animals.

Of course, some biological pathways *do* vary between different species. Specific treatments that cure diseases for some animals, without known side-effects, often fail to have the same effect in humans. However, it would be a major leap of faith to assert that *all* the mechanisms for plasticity of lifespan in other animals will somehow fail to operate in humans.

As it happens, there's already preliminary evidence that human longevity can be altered by various drugs, including metformin, a drug in wide use to treat diabetes, and aspirin, a drug that has multiple existing uses. Rejuveneers see this preliminary evidence as just the beginning of a growing crescendo that they expect will become increasingly hard to ignore. For the reasons behind that conviction, read on.

Q4: Won't we need to wait many decades to know whether rejuveneering works?

Any claim that rejuveneering can extend healthy human lifespans to 150 and beyond is, by its nature, going to have to wait many decades before it can be fully vindicated. We'll have to wait until present-day centenarians (say) have lived another five decades.

Nevertheless, rejuveneers hope to be able to provide strong indications, well before anyone reaches the age of 150, that such outcomes have become feasible:

- The growing acceptance of particular "theories of aging", in which the decline in vitality and health at the whole body level is compellingly linked to breakdowns and complications at the molecular, cellular, and tissue levels in the body
- The growing acceptance of measurements of "biomarkers of age", obtainable from blood samples and by other means, as being reliable indicators of someone's overall biological health, and therefore as good proxies for their *effective age*
- Demonstrations that various treatments do reliably reduce someone's effective age, as measured by these biomarkers, without having any adverse effects that anyone can notice
- Demonstrations that people who have taken these treatments are showing remarkable health and fitness for their age, of an

unprecedented degree; for example, we may see repeated breakthroughs in the set of record performances[33] by athletes aged over 70, 80, 90, and beyond

- A significant decline in the incidence of all kinds of diseases, among cohorts of people who have taken these treatments, as compared to control groups.

Curing diseases

Q5: How does rejuveneering propose to address incurable diseases?

Before turning to incurable diseases, let's have a quick word about diseases caused by infection.

Medicine has made great strides in recent times in reducing the deadliness of former scourges such as smallpox, polio, malaria, typhoid, tuberculosis, influenza, cholera, syphilis, and the Black Death – diseases caused by infection. Some infectious diseases remain powerful threats in the present day, including Ebola, HIV/AIDS, mad cow disease (CJD), and emerging new forms of flu. Other infectious diseases might experience resurgence due to the evolution and spread of new variants of the infection that have become resistant to multiple antibiotics. Nevertheless, it is a credible projection that "more of the same" will continue to chip away at the risks of infectious diseases. These measures include better hygiene and sanitation, the control of mosquitos, early screening, improved vaccination programmes, and enhanced antibiotics.

As infectious diseases have been increasingly tamed, especially in the developed world, greater numbers of people are now dying, directly or indirectly, from what are sometimes called non-communicable diseases (NCDs) – diseases that (as far as we know) aren't spread by infection. NCDs include senile dementia (such as Alzheimer's), motor neuron disease, most cancers, respiratory diseases, heart diseases, stroke, asthma, diabetes, and sarcopenia (muscle degeneration). Progress in curing these diseases has been nothing like as comprehensive as for infectious diseases. It *would*, therefore, be wishful thinking to suppose that "more of the same" will eventually find good solutions for these diseases too. *Something different is needed.* As I'll explain, rejuveneering is that "something different".

One thing that NCDs have in common is that their prevalence – and their deadliness – increases as people become older. The older people become, the more likely they are to develop these diseases, and, once they have acquired an NCD, the more likely they are to die from it.

There are two broad approaches regarding this relationship between aging and non-communicable diseases:

- In the first approach, each of these diseases is viewed as having its own particular cause and its own course of development. Each disease therefore needs its own investigation and its own treatment. In this approach, aging is seen as an especially hard issue, which should be left to the end of the queue for research dollars, since it falls at the end of life, and appears intractable

- In the second approach, aging is seen as an underlying common cause and exacerbating agent of all sorts of disease (including NCDs). Addressing aging can be expected to reduce both the occurrence and the severity of these diseases.

The "Copernican revolution" of this second approach is what rejuveneering proclaims. Instead of having disease at the centre of our biomedical enterprise, we should give aging the prime role.

This approach depends upon the following assumptions:

1. The term "aging" involves a number of objective underlying biological conditions which are themselves treatable
2. Treating these conditions has the side-effect of reducing the impact of NCDs
3. The underlying conditions are sufficiently common between different NCDs; for example, treatments which reduce the likelihood of certain types of cancer can also reduce the likelihood of certain types of senile dementia.

Note that disease-specific research should, of course, continue to take place. However, these investigations should run in parallel with a much increased research initiative to prevent and reverse aging. It is the *combination* of "disease-first" and "aging-first" approaches that will likely prove decisive.

The biology underlying aging

Q6: What is the "aging" that rejuveneering proposes to prevent and reverse?

Evidently, people will still be growing *chronologically* older. That's not the kind of aging that rejuveneering proposes to reverse. Instead, the target for treatment is a number of biological characteristics. Dr. Felipe Sierra, Director of the Division of Aging Biology at the US National Institute on Aging, lists these characteristics in a short video[34] that describes the Trans-NIH GeroScience Interest Group:

- The decline in the ability of the body to regenerate cells from stem cells
- The adverse response of cells to stress
- The degree of inflammation in cells
- Degradation in proteostasis – the mechanisms whereby cells manage proteins
- Defects within metabolism – the chemical reactions which fuel motion and growth
- Macromolecular damage – damage to large molecules such as DNA, lipids, and proteins
- Problems with epigenetics and regulatory RNA – the systems which control gene expression.

Other writers include other factors, such as a decline in the performance of the immune system.

These factors are seen as the tangible connection between aging and disease. Address these factors, and the likelihood is that disease occurrence will reduce.

In similar vein, Dr Aubrey de Grey, the Chief Science Officer of SENS, outlines "seven major classes of such cellular and molecular damage", in his article "A Reimagined Research Strategy for Aging"[35]:

> Many things go wrong with aging bodies, but at the root of them all is the burden of decades of unrepaired damage to the cellular and molecular structures that make up the functional units of our tissues. As each essential microscopic structure fails, tissue function becomes progressively compromised – imperceptibly at first, but ending in the slide into the diseases and disabilities of aging.
>
> SENS Research Foundation's strategy to prevent and reverse age-related ill-health is to apply the principles of regenerative medicine to repair the damage of aging *at the level where it occurs*. We are developing a new kind of medicine: regenerative therapies that remove, repair, replace, or render

harmless the cellular and molecular damage that has accumulated in our tissues with time. By reconstructing the structured order of the living machinery of our tissues, these rejuvenation biotechnologies will restore the normal functioning of the body's cells and essential biomolecules, returning aging tissues to health and bringing back the body's youthful vigour.

Decades of research in aging people and experimental animals has established that there are no more than seven major classes of such cellular and molecular damage:

1. Cell loss, tissue atrophy
2. Cancerous cells
3. Mitochondrial mutations
4. Death-resistant cells
5. Extracellular matrix stiffening
6. Extracellular aggregates
7. Intracellular aggregates

Yet another characterisation of the biology underlying aging is contained in a 2013 paper in Cell, authored by Carlos López-Otín and colleagues. This paper describes in some detail nine "Hallmarks of Aging"[36]:

1. Genomic instability
2. Telomere attrition
3. Epigenetic alterations
4. Loss of proteostasis
5. Deregulated nutrient-sensing
6. Mitochondrial dysfunction
7. Cellular senescence
8. Stem cell exhaustion
9. Altered intercellular communication

Evidently, there's scope for disagreement over the most appropriate classification of these biological characteristics – whether described as "hallmarks" or "damage" or whatever. There's also scope for disagreement over some of these hallmarks potentially being more fundamental than others; for example, some researchers argue that the shortening of telomeres deserves the most attention. (I'll explore some of these disagreements in Chapter 7, "Runners and riders".) But the different classifications have one key idea in common – studying these characteristics, in order to find ways to reverse underlying biological decline, is likely to yield big impacts in curing (and even avoiding) NCDs.

Fixing the failures

Q7: How will rejuveneering handle the damage at the cellular and molecular levels?

The basic answer to this question is embedded in the above quotation from the SENS website:

> We are developing a new kind of medicine: regenerative therapies that remove, repair, replace, or render harmless the cellular and molecular damage that has accumulated in our tissues with time. By reconstructing the structured order of the living machinery of our tissues, these rejuvenation biotechnologies will restore the normal functioning of the body's cells and essential biomolecules, returning aging tissues to health and bringing back the body's youthful vigour.

Depending on the type of damage being addressed, different regenerative therapies will be needed. Until we have a fuller understanding of the pathways of causes and effects involved, extensive experiments with more than one type of therapy should be carried out, to determine which approaches are the most effective in different circumstances.

Potential damage-limitation and damage-reduction therapies range as follows:

- Regenerative mechanisms which already operate in healthy humans (especially in young healthy humans), and which could be encouraged to continue operating beyond the point when they ordinarily lose their potency
- Regenerative mechanisms which already operate in non-human animals, and which could be triggered, via ingenious processes, to operate in humans
- Brand new biological mechanisms, created via methods such as synthetic biology and genetic engineering, which have no direct parallel within any existing animals (human or otherwise)
- Brand new physical mechanisms at the macro-scale, for example involving mechanical replacement body parts
- Brand new physical mechanisms at the nano-scale, such as nano-surgery

- Combinations of the above.

The elixir of life?

Q8: Is rejuveneering the same thing as the search for the elixir of life?

Not really. Some people in bygone days did seem to think that a single substance could provide indefinite youthfulness. Such a substance, if discovered, would have been an elixir par excellence. Some investigators in modern times seem to think, in similar spirit, that a single drug, or a single genetic alteration, might do the trick. I see that as being unlikely. Aging is a complicated, multi-faceted process. Reversing aging is likely to involve a suite of different treatments.

Consider the modern motor car, or the modern smartphone. They're both the outcome of literally thousands of inventions and innovations, rather than a single breakthrough. It will almost certainly be the same with rejuveneering.

I don't deny that particular individual treatments might turn out to have great significance. Adding citrus fruit to the diet of sailors did wonders to ward off the disease scurvy, and therefore boosted healthy longevity in the British Navy in the 18th century. More recently, vaccinations have had a similar effect in the wider public. No doubt new treatments will provide significant additional boosts to life expectancy. But the rejuveneering programme expects that many new treatments will need to be developed and made available, before we can assert that aging has been abolished.

Q9: Isn't the idea of finding an elixir of life self-evidently naïve?

This question is representative of a wider class of criticism, which seek to throw doubts on rejuveneering by first narrowly identifying rejuveneering with a particular type of approach (such as the approach of hunting for a single potion that would, by itself, deliver comprehensive rejuvenation). If that approach can be discredited, the critic suggests that rejuveneering as a whole is discredited.

However, the better conclusion to draw, in such examples, is that rejuveneering would need to involve a broader set of remedies. Indeed, as covered in the previous answer, rejuveneering is working towards a suite of treatments, rather than a single potion, exercise regime, genetic modification, or whatever.

Entropy and other constraints

Q10: Don't principles of physics, such as entropy, render rejuveneering impossible?

The principle of entropy – the famous Second Law of Thermodynamics – says that a closed system cannot become more ordered. Left to itself, a closed system will eventually become more chaotic. This might suggest that all living organisms will inevitably be subject to decay.

However, living beings are far from being closed systems; they interact in multiple ways with their environment. Accordingly, there is nothing in the principle of entropy that prevents living beings from remaining indefinitely youthful, provided appropriate interactions with the environment take place. The hard part is to engineer these interactions. But just because the task is hard, it does not mean it is impossible.

Q11: Aren't there limits to how often human cells can divide?

In the early 1960s, the biologist Leonard Hayflick discovered a surprising limit to the number of times cells would divide. His experiments[37], repeated numerous times over the decades, concern cells extracted from foetuses and observed in culture (that is, in test-tubes or other laboratory conditions). Whether the cells came from lung, heart, skin, or muscle, they stopped dividing after about 40-60 divisions. The process could take different amounts of time – from one year to three years – depending on the concentration of nutrition made available to the cell culture. But in all cases, the number of divisions remained in the same range, before the cell became senescent.

This "Hayflick limit" may seem on first sight to rule out the possibility of indefinite healthy life extension. However, the following points should be noted:

- Cells within the body ("in vivo") can behave in different ways to cells in culture ("in vitro")
- The enzyme telomerase, when present in the biological environment, can allow cells to divide many more times; this is one of the mechanisms at play in cancerous growths
- Some types of cells – specifically, germline cells – can keep on dividing indefinitely; that's why a relatively old body, that is a human mother, can give birth to a baby consisting of young cells

- Even if some cells become senescent, their functionality can be taken over by new cells, made available from banks of stem cells or from other sources.

In summary, whilst the Hayflick limit is an important area of biology, it does not negate the possibility of extending healthy lifespans.

Q12: Aren't there natural limits to how long humans can live?

Nature appears to have some hard limits. For example, nothing can travel faster than the speed of light. Temperatures cannot be reduced below zero Kelvin (which is minus 273.15 degrees Celsius).

However, history is full of examples of limits being overcome. Think of the limit of "the four minute mile": some writers may have speculated that the human body would never be able to run a mile in less than four minutes, but Roger Bannister breached this limit in the famous race in 1954 in Oxford. Another example is the limit of 120 years of human life apparently given in chapter 6, verse 3, of the biblical book of Genesis: that limit was surpassed by Frenchwoman Jeanne Louise Calment when she turned 121 in 1996. As an aside, even the limit of zero degrees Kelvin now seems to have fallen[38], with a quantum gas composed of potassium atoms manipulated by lasers and magnetic fields.

The nearest thing that has been suggested, so far, to a hard limit on human aging, is the Hayflick mechanism mentioned earlier. But, as already reviewed, that mechanism is far from being absolute.

I therefore share the sentiment expressed by the distinguished science educator and Nobel prize-winning quantum physicist Richard Feynman, in his 1964 lecture "The role of scientific culture in modern society"[39]:

> It is one of the most remarkable things that in all of the biological sciences there is no clue as to the necessity of death. If you say we want to make perpetual motion, we have discovered enough laws as we studied physics to see that it is either absolutely impossible or else the laws are wrong.
>
> But there is nothing in biology yet found that indicates the inevitability of death. This suggests to me that it is not at all inevitable, and it is only a matter of time before the biologists discover what it is that is causing us the trouble, and that terrible universal disease or temporariness of the human's body will be cured.

Immortality

Q13: Does rejuveneering claim to convey human immortality?

Undoing the effects of aging is a separate matter from achieving the religious or philosophical notion of "immortality". That topic falls far outside the bounds of the rejuveneering project. Even once treatments are developed that routinely undo the bodily damage of aging, people will remain vulnerable to death in numerous ways:

- By being the victim of an accident, such as a transport collision, extreme weather, earthquake shocks, supervolcano explosion, meteorite impact, or the earth being struck by intense extra-terrestrial gamma rays
- The outbreak of war, in which people can be killed by numerous weapons
- Being murdered, as an act of terrorism, domestic rivalry, or criminal action
- New pathogens, which may kill a number of unfortunate people before medicine can respond with a new treatment.

It's true that other projects seek to address these causes of death. I'll come back in Chapter 12, "Radical alternatives", to the possibilities of, for example, cryonic suspension, exoskeletal protection, and mind-uploading. But these lie beyond the core focus of rejuveneering. Therefore the answer to this question is, No, rejuveneering does not claim to convey human immortality.

Instead of "immortality", a better word for what rejuveneering will provide might be "amortality", coined by Time writer[40] Catherine Mayer:

> The defining characteristic of amortality is to live in the same way, at the same pitch, doing and consuming much the same things, from late teens right up until death.

Rejuveneering will remove any need for people to slow down or take things easier, just because they are chronologically older.

Yet another word that can be suggested is "ageless" – as in the title of the very interesting book "The Ageless Generation: How Advances in Biomedicine Will Transform the Global Economy"[41] by Alex Zhavoronkov. (Personal note: Zhavoronkov's ideas have significantly influenced my own, after I hosted him speaking at a London Futurists event in 2013[42].)

Religious concerns

Q14: How relevant are religious ideas to the acceptance or rejection of rejuveneering?

Some readers will think that discussion of religious doctrines has no role in a book about rejuvenation biotechnology. But I disagree. Religious ideas have two levels of influence on the acceptance or rejection of rejuveneering:

- They have direct influence, in the minds of people who explicitly adhere to specific religious doctrines
- They have indirect influence, in the minds of people who have discarded traditional religious viewpoints, but whose underlying thinking still falls under the sway of religious concepts.

The next two questions fall under the first heading, and set the scene for the final question in this section, which falls under the second heading. You may view the first two questions as antiquated, but please bear with me.

Q15: Wouldn't rejuveneering interfere with the cosmic processes of karma and rebirth?

I'm no expert on the intricacies of religious notions of karma and rebirth. But I profoundly dislike any claims that, if people are suffering, or about to suffer death, this must be due to some moral misdeeds earlier in their life (or even in a previous life). That kind of philosophy could rationalise all manner of inaction. That philosophy would say: we should avoid action, because we'll be upsetting grander cosmic plans that we cannot comprehend.

In particular, that kind of philosophy would rationalise the termination of all research and deployment of medicine – that is, medicine of all kinds (not just the regenerative medicine that has a key role in rejuveneering). After all, all medicine is about taking action to interfere with biological processes.

To put things another way, if you think research to prevent aging is anti-karma, what do you think about research to prevent cancer? Or to prevent malaria? Wouldn't that research be anti-karma too?

But I have a confession. I introduced this question only as a step-up to the next one — a question which I consider equally objectionable, even though it is heard more often.

Q16: Wouldn't rejuveneering interfere with divine mandates about human death?

Some people prefer to search for their personal immortality in realms beyond the physical world. They see the physical world as an unworthy long-term home for their personality, and aspire to a new life beyond their earthly grave — a new life in which their essence will somehow be incorruptible and eternal. This aspiration for a "spiritual immortality" may be one that the person fully recognises and acknowledges, or it may remain subconscious and repressed. In either case, the aspiration may lead to hostility towards the rejuveneering programme described in this book.

The idea of spiritual immortality finds support, of course, in numerous holy books of different religions around the world. The same book of Genesis that set the maximum human lifespan at 120 years also contains a morbid curse upon humanity, from the mouth of the divine creator. From Genesis chapter 3, verses 17-19:

> To Adam he said, "Because you listened to your wife and ate fruit from the tree about which I commanded you, 'You must not eat from it,' cursed is the ground because of you; through painful toil you will eat food from it all the days of your life. It will produce thorns and thistles for you, and you will eat the plants of the field. By the sweat of your brow you will eat your food until you return to the ground, since from it you were taken; for dust you are and to dust you will return."

For dust you are and to dust you will return. But that's only part of the divine curse. In the preceding verse, there's additional punishment for women:

> To the woman he said, "I will make your pains in childbearing very severe; with painful labour you will give birth to children. Your desire will be for your husband, and he will rule over you."

That's the bad news. Later books of the Bible have apparent good news sections too, which promise that faithful believers can receive various kinds of resurrection and eternal life. Do such promises limit the options of true practitioners of these religions, to benefit from any rejuvenation therapies that modern medicine can provide? Would these therapies stand opposed to the divine instruction that "to dust you will return"?

Before answering, it's useful to make a brief remark about the associated biblical curse "I will make your pains in childbearing very severe; with painful labour you will give birth to children". When Britain's Queen Victoria was giving birth to her eighth and ninth children, in 1853 and 1857 respectively, she dispensed with advice given to her by her clerical advisors. Victoria had heard about the availability of chloroform as a pain-killer, to ease the experience of childbirth. The inventor of that technique, James Young Simpson, an Edinburgh obstetrician, had been verbally attacked by clergymen who denounced chloroform as "a decoy of Satan"[43]. That drug would, allegedly, "rob God of the deep earnest cries which arise in time of trouble for help". Victoria, however, exercised her queenly prerogative, and overruled her advisers. Her verdict[44] on the local anaesthetic: "blessed chloroform... soothing, quieting, and delightful beyond measure". Nowadays it is only the most extreme of religious faithful that would deny birthing mothers the comforts of painkillers.

The same principle that applies to the travails of childbearing can apply equally to the travails of growing old. People who remain keen to believe in a divine purpose behind death have numerous options to allow their beliefs to coexist with adoption of rejuveneering. For example, as mentioned earlier, the rejuveneering project cannot, by itself, make any promise of immortality. The religiously inclined can, therefore, reassure themselves that their hypothesised omnipotent divine overseer will find other ways to transport people from the world of the living to whatever spiritual hereafter has been prepared for them. That article of faith can fit alongside a practical desire to minimise and reduce the earthly pain of infirmity and bodily decline. There need be no conflict.

Q17: Isn't rejuveneering an attempt by humans to play god?

This question continues from where the last one left off: the book of Genesis – a book which is officially revered by three major world religions, and which therefore still casts a long shadow upon present-day ideas. In that story, the cause of the divine curse upon humanity was human hubris. The first humans sought access to knowledge and immortality independent of divine dictates:

> God commanded the man, "You are free to eat from any tree in the garden; but you must not eat from the tree of the knowledge of good and evil, for when you eat from it you will certainly die"...

> Now the serpent was more crafty than any of the wild animals God had made. He said to the woman, "Did God really say, 'You must not eat from any tree in the garden'?"...
>
> "You will not certainly die," the serpent said to the woman. "For God knows that when you eat from it your eyes will be opened, and you will be like God, knowing good and evil."
>
> When the woman saw that the fruit of the tree was good for food and pleasing to the eye, and also desirable for gaining wisdom, she took some and ate it. She also gave some to her husband, who was with her, and he ate it...
>
> And God said, "The man has now become like one of us, knowing good and evil. He must not be allowed to reach out his hand and take also from the tree of life and eat, and live forever." So God banished him from the Garden of Eden to work the ground from which he had been taken. After he drove the man out, he placed on the east side of the Garden of Eden cherubim and a flaming sword flashing back and forth to guard the way to the tree of life.

Nowadays fewer people give much conscious regard to an age-old tale of a talking serpent, an angry deity, and angelic cherubim positioned outside a primeval garden bearing a flaming sword to deter would-be Indiana Jones explorers from reaching a tree that could bestow eternal life. But the story retains a powerful influence over our collective unconscious. A message remains imprinted: *humans should beware reaching beyond their grasp, in defiance of ancient wisdom, for forbidden powers*. Such grasping will not end well. More briefly: *humans should not play god*.

That same message recurs in countless other works of fiction, both ancient and modern. One Greek legend features a brash youngster, Icarus, who failed to heed the wise advice of his father, Daedalus, and flew too close to the sun. The warmth of the sun's rays melted the wax in the fabricated wings worn by Icarus, who paid for his hubris when the wings fell apart, and he plummeted out of the sky into the sea below – to his death. The physics of the legend is wrong in multiple ways, but the moral strikes home: *high-flying ambition presages disaster*.

In Hollywood films of more recent times, characters that attain rejuvenation – the ability to remain young indefinitely – nearly all involve personality flaws. These characters are mean, self-absorbed, destructive, hurtful, and so on. Their pursuit of rejuvenation is shown to be a mistake.

They may gain immortality, but only at the price of unhappiness, boredom, and a loss of humanity.

However, the cry "don't play god" is a lazy use of words. Medical researchers play god every time they develop new cures. Engineers play god every time they create new tools, new vehicles, and new engines. Industrial chemists play god every time they construct new synthetic compounds. Breeders play god every time they select animals with special characteristics, to be the parents of the next generation. Doctors play god every time they triage patients, choosing which patients should receive scarce resources or expensive treatments. To be human is to "play god", every time we exercise creativity or choice.

There's nothing inherently wrong with ambition. Nor with the desire to extend healthy longevity. The problems arise when an ambition runs far ahead of capability, or when a creative desire cannot be served by the skills available.

So, yes, the rejuveneering project could be dangerous, if it consisted of false hopes, and expectations raised so high they could not be met. Whether that's a fair assessment of rejuveneering is the overall subject of this book. I'll argue that it's an unfair assessment: there is plenty of good science behind rejuveneering. I'll also argue that there's no inevitability for long-lived humans to demonstrate the nasty personality attributes beloved of Hollywood dystopia. The desire to live, abundantly and well, is a core part of the positive makeup of the human characteristic. Humans, therefore, ought to feel empowered to pursue that project, thoughtfully and diligently, without worrying about bringing down the wrath of cherubim and flaming swords.

Social concerns

Q18: Won't rejuveneering cause a dreadful population explosion?

If rejuveneering works, and is made widely available, people will die less often than before. Inevitably, that's going to have an impact on the global population. How much of a problem will this cause?

It is estimated that, currently, around 150,000 people die every day – which is around 55 million per year. If roughly two thirds of these deaths are related to aging, and if rejuveneering is made available to the whole world, the global population is going to grow by around 36 million additional people each year, compared to present-day trajectories. Within just 27 years, the population will be one billion higher than previously expected.

This calculation doesn't take account of potential changes in birth rate. This rate could change from present, because of side-effects of rejuvenation therapies. It's not only *healthy* lifespan that will be increased; *fertile* lifespan will likely increase too, with postponement of the menopause.

It's conceivable that birth rate will decline:

- Couples will be in less of a rush to interrupt their careers to have children
- Populations might accept social pressures to reduce the sizes of their families.

Equally, it's conceivable that birth rate will increase, because of the indefinite extension of the period in which child-bearing is possible.

Whether this is a real problem depends on whether society will be able to adequately feed and house larger populations. This can be broken down into four sub-questions.

The first sub-question: Is there room on the Earth to cope with several billion additional people? *Absolutely*. In fact, using data compiled by NASA, it is now known[45] that 50% of the present global population lives on just 1% of the Earth's land. As data visualizer Max Galka commented, the vast majority of the world's land area is actually very sparsely populated.

Let's carry out a simple thought experiment. The US state of Texas has an area just under 700,000 square kilometres. If we fitted 14 billion people into that area, split (on average) into, say, groups of two, each couple could be allocated a ground area of 10 metres by 10 metres, that is, 100 square metres. (Note: 14 billion is far larger than the current global population, which is between 7 and 8 billion.) That floor-space compares favourably with, for example, the figure of 76 square metres which is the average area of a UK house[46]. So the whole population of the earth could be accommodated, at a push, within the state of Texas.

You might ask: What about gardens, schools, recreational space, nature reserves, factory space, and so on? In this thought experiment, there's the rest of America – indeed, the rest of the world, for that. So we're not going to run out of living space any time soon.

I realise that many people find the result of this simple calculation counter-intuitive, even though they can follow the figures easily enough. The result clashes with our occasional experiences of seeing large crowds of people, and, sometimes, feeling bewildered and overwhelmed by such crowds. In such moments, we might think to ourselves, *there are too many people*. But the earth is also full of wide open spaces. Our intuition can lead us astray. The arithmetic of the matter is that the earth easily has sufficient room for, say, 100 billion people, especially when we consider stacking living space vertically, as in apartment blocks – which would provide even more living space.

The second sub-question is: What about feeding a larger population? From a pure technical point of view, there should be no issue. More than enough energy hits the earth from the sun every single hour[47] to meet the entire energy needs of the whole planet for an entire year. With sufficient political will, solar panels could cover one thousandth of the earth's surface. Even if they operated at only 25% efficiency, they would produce sufficient energy for human needs. That energy can also power modern seawater desalination facilities – such as have already made remarkable progress[48] in Israel, where 25% of fresh water is now created through desalination. Then a suite of modern agricultural techniques, including hydroponics, vertical farming, and synthetic biology, could turn large parts of that energy into healthy food.

Underlying this second sub-question there is a different concern. Critics can accept that there are technical solutions to providing good food for the entire global population, but they point out that there are political and social failures which are preventing this from happening in practice. Might not these political and social problems become worse, if the population increases? However, a larger population means more brains, as well as more mouths. It means more sources of innovation. It means more people who can work on solving the political and social aspects of feeding the global population, as well as on the technical angles.

The third sub-question is: What about the waste that a larger population will generate? That could be worrying, especially if the vast majority of the population adopts the same kind of affluent lifestyle that is practised in present-day North America. One particular worry is the increasing emission of greenhouse gases, such as carbon dioxide, as a by-product of burning fossil fuel.

This sub-question deserves careful attention. Indeed, I'll return to this topic in the final chapter of this book. But for now, I'll give the answer that the reprocessing of waste, into materials that can be re-used, is itself a technology which can be improved in numerous ways in the decades ahead. So as the population grows, there's no need for an *inevitable* increase in waste.

The fourth sub-question is: Can the above principles be extended, beyond the first few additional billion people of the next few decades, into indefinitely larger populations, as decades of healthy longevity turn into centuries of healthy longevity? What happens to questions of living space, food production, and waste recycling, once the human population reaches hundreds of billions? Will some form of compulsory euthanasia eventually become necessary, or some mandatory birth control? *Hardly.* In the centuries ahead, humans can build taller infrastructure, eventually moving that infrastructure into space. We can envisage huge numbers of new space stations, fashioned throughout the solar system – and even beyond – to operate as highly desirable living accommodation.

This discussion may strike some readers as fanciful. But the main point is this. Vague, far-off concerns, about the human population centuries in the future, ought not to constrain today's medical science from seeking ways to restore youthful powers to present-day humans. For as far ahead as we can dare to forecast the future with any confidence – a period, in reality, of less than a century – we can envision credible solutions to the modest incremental population growth that would result from successes of the rejuveneering project. Further afield, as the population growth increases cumulatively, there are plenty of potential solutions to consider.

The exceptions to this picture, as noted, are in the risk of potentially catastrophic side-effects from increased emissions of greenhouse gases, and in the risk of continuing political incompetence. These risks – of accelerated global warming and associated environmental and social upheavals – exist independently of the rejuveneering project, and need solutions in their own right. We'll review in later chapters how risks of civilizational decay co-exist with prospects for individual enhancement.

Q19: Won't long-lived people provide a brake on necessary societal change?

A different form of social concern is that, if people live indefinitely long, at the peak of their powers, this might make it much harder for new generations to gain positions of power and authority. It would no longer be possible simply to await someone's personal decline and death, in order to see progress take place.

This concern echoes the famous remark[49] from the late 1940s by German physicist Max Planck:

> A new scientific truth does not triumph by convincing its opponents and making them see the light, but rather because its opponents eventually die, and a new generation grows up that is familiar with it.

If people in authority no longer die, what scope is there for new fashions, new worldviews, new scientific understanding, and new winds of change?

The fear is heightened in the case of political dictators. Imagine if Stalin had never died, or Mao. Would their countries have continued indefinitely in a state of terror?

However, there are plenty of counter-examples:

- Government systems – such as in the United States – which limit the number of terms a president can serve, even if the president remains at the peak of health
- Dictators which were overthrown long before they became old and weak
- New scientific theories, such as Darwin's principle of natural selection, which were embraced by elderly scientists just as much as by youthful ones (contrary to the so-called "Planck principle")
- A new generation is frequently able to create and embrace a new fashion, despite disapproval from a previous generation that is still in the full flush of health.

Modest amounts of new rules governing society and organisations could relatively easily ensure that rotation of key positions occurs, without anyone hanging on to roles indefinitely.

Q20: In the absence of aging and death, what motivation will people have to get anything done?

Some critics hold that it is the prospect of aging and death that provides the impetus for people to make great efforts to rise above a state of lethargy and inertia. If rejuveneering succeeds, this could cause everyone to become indefinitely lazy. Why bother making Herculean efforts today, if there are potentially centuries ahead to make similar efforts? Procrastination will take a huge new boost.

One of the most notable upholders of the view of the necessity of aging and death, for the well-being of humanity, is Leon Kass, bioethics professor at the University of Chicago, and chairman of President George W. Bush's Council on Bioethics from 2001 to 2005. For example, here are some comments Kass made in an interview[50] in 2004:

> Time is a gift, but the perception of endless time or of time without bound in fact has the possibility of undermining the degree to which we take time seriously and make it count…
>
> If you push those limits back, if those limits become out of sight, we are not inclined to build cathedrals or write the B Minor Mass, or write Shakespeare's sonnets and things of that sort.

Kass also expressed this thought in an essay[51] in 2003:

> A flourishing human life is… ours only because we are born, age, replace ourselves, decline, and die — and know it. It is a life of aspiration, made possible by and born of experienced lack, of the disproportion between the transcendent longings of the soul and the limited capacities of our bodies and minds. It is a life that stretches towards some fulfilment to which our natural human soul has been oriented… It is a life not of better genes and enhancing chemicals but of love and friendship, song and dance, speech and deed, working and learning, revering and worshipping.

However, this criticism depends, frankly, upon a feeble assessment of human character. It's similar to the criticism that, if there is no God, then life becomes devoid of meaning. Both criticisms view humans as inherently small, weak, and dependent.

The answer to the second of these two criticisms is that humans can provide their own meaning. The purpose of life doesn't need to be handed down from any omniscient creator. The purpose of life is whatever humans decide it should be.

Likewise, the answer to the first criticism is that humans can find their own motivation for action. Indeed, young people already make plenty of Herculean efforts, even though they expect they will live for many decades longer. It's not the thought of their eventual death that makes them jump out of bed in the morning. There are many shorter-term deadlines which provide different sorts of motivation – hobbies they are pursuing, books they are enjoying reading, online games they are playing, people they are about to meet, work tasks they find fascinating, and so on.

Kass fails to acknowledge that greater health and longer lifespans are likely to increase many of the positives he lists as being fundamentally important to life – "love and friendship, song and dance, speech and deed, working and learning".

In any case, the style of thinking about technological interventions for better health, which Kass represents, has a poor track record. Kass himself was one of the most robust critics, in the 1970s and 1980s, of in-vitro fertilisation treatments for infertile couples. As Robin Marantz Henig wrote in the Washington Post[52] on the 25th anniversary of the birth of the first "test tube baby", Louise Brown:

> Listen, for example, to Leon Kass, a bioethics professor at the University of Chicago whose voice has been part of this debate for 25 years. "More is at stake [with IVF research] than in ordinary biomedical research or in experimenting with human subjects at risk of bodily harm," Kass testified before the federal government's Ethics Advisory Board shortly after Louise Brown's birth. "At stake is the idea of the humanness of our human life and the meaning of our embodiment, our sexual being, and our relation to ancestors and descendants."

It turned out, contrary to Kass's forecasts, that human society was more than capable of taking in its stride the opportunities provided by IVF technology. It ought to be the same with the opportunities provided by rejuvenation technology (though I'll return to this question in Chapter 11).

Q21: Won't the wealthy benefit disproportionately from rejuveneering?

Lurking behind many criticisms of rejuveneering, in my experience, is the apprehension that the benefits of that project will apply disproportionately to people with lots of wealth, power, or other social influence.

The redoubtable Guardian columnist George Monbiot raises the concern as follows[53]:

> Once it was a myth. Now it's a dream. And soon it will be an expectation. Suddenly the science of life extension is producing remarkable results. New papers hint at the possibility of treatments that could radically increase human longevity...

There are still plenty of missing steps, not least clinical trials and drug development, but there's a strong sense that we stand at an extraordinary moment. Who would not want this – to cheat the gods and mock the reaper? The benefits are so obvious that one recent article insists that political leaders who fail to provide sufficient funding for life-extension science should be charged with manslaughter. It's thrilling, dazzling, awe-inspiring. And rather alarming.

Here's what Monbiot finds alarming:

What if, beyond a certain point, longevity becomes a zero-sum game? What if every year of life extension for those who can afford the treatment becomes a year or more of life reduction for those who can't?

Already, on this planet of finite resources, rich and poor are locked into unacknowledged conflict, as hyperconsumption reduces the planet's capacity to sustain life. Grain is used to produce meat rather than feed people directly; the safe operating space for humanity is narrowed by greenhouse gases, industrial pollutants, freshwater depletion and soil erosion. It's hard, after a while, to see how this could produce any outcome other than a direct competition for the means of life, which some must win and others must lose. Perhaps the rich must die so that the poor can live.

The fact that rejuvenation treatments may reduce in price over time fails to reassure Monbiot:

It's true that the price of possible longevity treatments, which will be astronomical at first, would soon start to plummet. But this is a world in which many can't afford even antiseptic ointment; a world in which, even in the rich countries, universal access to healthcare is being slowly throttled by a selfish elite; in which a new era of personalised medicine coincides, by unhappy accident, with a new era of crushing inequality. The idea that everyone would soon have access to these therapies looks unfeasible. It's possible, as an article in Aeon magazine speculates, that two classes of people – the treated and the untreated – could pull inexorably apart, the first living ever longer, the second dying even younger than they do today…

Life-extension science could invoke a sunlit, miraculous world of freedom from fear and long-term thinking. Or a gerontocratic tyranny. If it's the latter, I hope I don't live long enough to see it.

In turn, the Aeon magazine article which Monbiot mentions – "The longevity gap"[54] by Linda Marsa of Discovery Magazine, states the issue as follows:

> The disparity between top earners and everyone else is staggering in nations such as the United States, where 10 per cent of people accounted for 80 per cent of income growth since 1975. The life you can pay for as one of the anointed looks nothing like the lot tossed to everyone else: living in a home you own on some upscale cul-de-sac with your hybrid car and organic, grass-fed food sure beats renting (and driving) wrecks and subsisting on processed junk from supermarket shelves. But there's a related, looming inequity so brutal it could provoke violent class war: the growing gap between the longevity haves and have-nots.
>
> The life expectancy gap between the affluent and the poor and working class in the US, for instance, now clocks in at 12.2 years. College-educated white men can expect to live to age 80, while counterparts without a high-school diploma die by age 67. White women with a college degree have a life expectancy of nearly 84, compared with uneducated women, who live to 73.

Marsa points out that the disparities are widening:

> The lives of white, female high-school dropouts are now five years shorter than those of previous generations of women without a high-school degree, while white men without a high-school diploma live three years fewer than their counterparts did 18 years ago, according to a 2012 study from Health Affairs.
>
> This is just a harbinger of things to come. What will happen when new scientific discoveries extend potential human lifespan and intensify these inequities on a more massive scale? It looks like the ultimate war between the haves and have-nots won't be fought over the issue of money, per se, but over living to age 60 versus living to 120 or more. Will anyone just accept that the haves get two lives while the have-nots barely get one?
>
> We should discuss the issue now, because we are close to delivering a true fountain of youth that could potentially extend our productive lifespan into our hundreds – it's no longer the stuff of science fiction.

Marsa foresees one cataclysmic outcome of a growing "longevity gap":

> The coming longevity gap might set us up for... a rage-filled conflagration that would make Occupy Wall Street, the US movement against the one per cent of top earners, pale. It could be grounds for revolution if the

wealthy lived twice as long while the poor died even younger than their parents did.

But Marsa emphasises, at the end of her article, that such an outcome is by no means inevitable:

Instead of allowing the wealth gap to turn into a longevity gap, perhaps we'll find a way to use everyone's talents and share the longevity dividend at all levels of income. This kind of sharing could leverage the wisdom of elders, forestall the economic collapse many have predicted when the grey tsunami picks up speed, and avoid an all-out revolt against the one or so per cent. We stand at the threshold of two distinct futures – one where we have a frail, rapidly aging population that saps our economy, and another where everyone lives much longer and more productive lives.

I write this book in the same spirit as that optimistic vision: rejuveneering can provide "healthy longevity for all", rather than a growing, divisive longevity gap.

Monbiot likewise concedes that there are many unknowns in the question of social implications of rejuveneering:

I don't know the answers to these questions, and I'm far from being able to propose solutions. It's all unknown from now on. But I do know that it's foolish to dismiss them.

For these reasons, the chapters ahead return to sociological and political questions on several occasions, in parallel to discussions of technology and engineering. Monbiot is right that it would be "foolish" to dismiss these questions – either by assuming these questions didn't matter, *or by assuming that these questions are somehow showstoppers against the rejuveneering project.*

Conflicting motivations

Q22: Isn't the field of rejuveneering full of cranks and charlatans?

It's easy to find examples of rejuvenation snake oil – potions and therapies that lacked sufficient evidence in their favour, but which were administered to eager adherents, often accompanied by razzmatazz publicity. In many cases the practitioners of these potions and therapies honestly believed in the value of their treatments, with a wishful leap of faith to cover the gaps in their knowledge.

These examples include:

- Charles-Édouard Brown-Séquard (1817-1894), who advocated the injection of material from the testicles of healthy young dogs and guinea pigs, as a treatment for human rejuvenation; one of the claims he made in support of this claim was his observation of his own "rejuvenated sexual prowess" after consuming a concoction of "extracts of monkey testis"

- Ilya Metchnikoff (1845-1916), who recommended drinking yoghurt to promote longevity, based on his theory that aging was caused by the action of toxic bacteria in the digestive tract

- Serge Voronoff (1866-1951), who surgically implanted testicles from youthful chimpanzees inside the scrotums of several hundred elderly human gentlemen, and gained temporary acclaim for his work in the 1920s (an Irving Berlin song in the Marx brothers film "The Cocoanuts" featured the line "If you're too old for dancing, get yourself a monkey gland")

- Linus Pauling (1901-1994), who endorsed long-term dietary supplementation with high doses of vitamin C for improved health and longevity, and to increase the survival time for patients with cancer.

As noted in a 2013 Atlantic article[55], Pauling declared in 1977 that:

My present estimate is that a decrease of 75% [of deaths from cancer] can be achieved with vitamin C alone… and a further decrease by use of other nutritional supplements.

He went on to predict:

Life expectancy will be 100 to 110 years, and in the course of time, the maximum age might be 150 years.

Sadly, Linus Pauling was to watch his wife of sixty years, Ava, battle stomach cancer for five years, before dying of the disease in 1981 – despite taking lots of vitamin C in the process. Pauling himself succumbed to prostate cancer fourteen years later.

None of these men were fools. Pauling is the only person to have twice won an undivided Nobel Prize. But in the above-mentioned Atlantic article, physician Paul Offit gave the following summary of his abilities:

[Pauling] was so spectacularly right that he won two Nobel Prizes and so spectacularly wrong that he was arguably the world's greatest quack.

If we look further back in history, we find similar examples. The first Chinese emperor, Qin Shi Huang, searched high and low throughout his new empire for elixirs of rejuvenation. He sampled numerous herbs and brews. Yet he died at the relatively young age of fifty. The cause of his death is still debated, but one theory blames the inclusion of lead and mercury in some of the potions he imbibed. If true, then rather than extending his life, these treatments shortened it.

Pioneering English scientist and philosopher Francis Bacon – the so-called "father of empiricism" – falls into the same category, of someone whose interests in life extension had the unintended side-effect of hastening his own death. At the age of 65, while travelling in the snow through Highgate in London, Bacon was apparently inspired to try an experiment into the possibility of using extreme cold to preserve flesh. With his companion, the king's physician, he stepped out of his carriage, and purchased a chicken from a woman living in a nearby house. Bacon asked the woman to kill the bird, and then proceeded to stuff the bird with snow. In the process, he developed a case of pneumonia, and was himself dead shortly afterwards. That's an ironic conclusion to the life of someone who frequently addressed in his writings the possibility of healthy life extension, describing it as "the most noble goal of medicine"[56]:

> The lengthening of the thread of life itself, and the postponement for a time of that death which gradually steals on by natural dissolution and the decay of age, is a subject of which no physician has handled in proportion to its dignity.

What should we conclude from this history? That the attempt to understand and apply principles of human rejuvenation is utterly flawed? That people who seek these treatments are misguided? That anyone who investigates life extension is to be mistrusted?

On the contrary, a broader perspective shows the following. Areas of science frequently involve many stumbles and mistakes, in parallel with the emergence of new insight. The modern field of chemistry emerged from the shadow world it shared with the wishful thinking of alchemy. Astronomy emerged from partnership with the wishful thinking of astrology. We can expect something similar for rejuveneering.

The examples listed above can be revisited, to witness the birth-pangs of legitimate new fields of research, alongside the over-exuberance of individual claims. For example:

- Charles-Édouard Brown-Séquard pioneered our understanding of what we now call hormones, and is one claimant to be called "the father of endocrinology"
- Ilya Metchnikoff conducted foundational research into the immune system, discovered macrophages, and led to the modern understanding that intestinal bacteria can indeed have significant effects on our health.

Writing as long ago as 1605[57], Francis Bacon gives a modern-sounding admonishment to any idea that there can be a quick fix to healthy longevity:

> Men should cease from trifling, nor be so credulous as to imagine that so great a work as this of delaying and turning back the course of nature can be effected by a morning draught or by the use of a precious drug, by potable gold, or essence of pearls, or such-like toys – but be assured prolongation of life is a work of labour and difficulty and consisting of a great number of remedies.

Indeed, rejuvenation depends on a spectrum of factors, which interact in subtle ways. Any focus on a single factor to the exclusion of other influences is likely a recipe for delusion. But whilst this criticism might apply to individual longevity researchers or physicians, who may be overly single-minded in their approaches, it's not a fair criticism to apply to the field of rejuveneering as a whole.

Q23: Why do some critics of rejuveneering pour undeserved scorn on the subject?

It's not just the proponents of the possibility of rejuveneering who sometimes overstep the mark of evidence, when they make exaggerated claims about the likely potency of their therapies. Critics of the field sometimes lapse into the opposite error. Seeing failures and mistakes by individual rejuveneers, they jump to the conclusion that the whole enterprise is inherently defective. Rather than just poking fun at instances of extreme behaviour, they uncritically extrapolate to pour scorn on the very idea of rejuvenation. *Why does this happen?*

The two sets of error have one aspect in common. They're both motivated, in part, by psychological factors. Yes, supporters of rejuvenation generally have strong personal commitments to the success of their projects. They passionately dislike the idea of people growing old and dying. That's why, on occasion, they overstate the chances of success of their research. Their internal psychological pressures override and subvert their rationality. But equally, as I'll explore further in Chapter 10, "Adverse psychology", opponents of rejuvenation can have their own personal demons that hinder clarity of thought. These opponents sometimes have their own deep-rooted reasons for antagonism to rejuveneering:

- Rejuveneering can offend their own personal religious creed (whether that creed operates at the conscious or subconscious level)
- Any support they express for rejuveneering would jeopardise their entrenched self-image as being someone who is publicly dedicated against hubris, social inequality, or the unchecked growth of the human population (and the planetary resources consumed by that population)
- Rejuveneering can threaten the stability of the protective mental infrastructure they have adopted – the infrastructure that reassures them that "death ain't too bad", and which shields them from being stricken incapable with terror about the impending annihilation of themselves and everyone they hold dear.

To be clear, these murky negative reasons often sit alongside commendable factors. Opponents of rejuveneering are in many cases motivated by constructive concerns as well as subterranean antagonism. They fear that the good name of medicine will be damaged by irresponsible statements and wild actions by rejuveneers who claim to speak with medical authority but who seemingly cut all kinds of corners. And they fear that legitimate business processes of responsible pharmaceutical companies will be undermined by fast-moving operators who disdain lengthy testing guidelines. These fears are understandable, but in my observation, they can sometimes lead critics to develop a kind of manic obsession. With their hearts on fire, smoke gets in their eyes.

Happily, science seeks to disentangle the question of *motivation* from the question of *assessment*. Just because someone has a questionable motivation for believing a certain statement, it does not mean the statement itself is invalidated. Just because we notice psychological flaws in the people speaking either for or against rejuveneering, that's not sufficient to settle the debate one way or another. We need to remain cool.

Indeed, the scientific endeavour recognises that individual scientists, writers, and researchers can have multiple motivations for the hypotheses they pursue. Science as a whole seeks to separate these motivations from the evidence for or against a hypothesis. The philosophy of science distinguishes "the context of discovery" – the circumstances which lead scientists to propose a theory, or which motivate them as individual human beings to be sympathetic to it – from "the context of justification" – the rules and principles governing whether scientists (as scientists) should accept the theory. For example, a chemist might have come up with an idea of a molecular structure while high on the drug LSD. We don't need to share the chemist's views on whether LSD should be legalised, before we check out whether the hypothesised molecular structure makes sense. So, yes, both proponents and critics of rejuveneering can have ulterior motives, which prompt them to the positions they articulate. But the existence of these ulterior motives should not damage the discussion of whether these positions, in the end, hold water.

Q24: Isn't it egocentric to pursue rejuveneering?

In January 2015, Microsoft founder Bill Gates responded to the following question[58] in an "Ask Me Anything" session held on Reddit:

> What do you think about life-extending and immortality research?

Putting into words a thought that is surely shared by large numbers of people, Gates replied:

> It seems pretty egocentric while we still have malaria and TB for rich people to fund things so they can live longer. It would be nice to live longer though I admit.

However, that same criticism could be raised against numerous medical research programmes – such as the programmes to cure cancer or heart disease. Fixing these diseases will extend lives too. But whilst people are still dying of malaria and TB (tuberculosis) – diseases that can be treated with relatively little expenditure – it might seem a displaced priority to put large amounts of money into looking for cures for cancer and heart disease. If the criterion really is to save the most lives by spending a given amount of money, perhaps it would be best to terminate our cancer research initiatives, and instead purchase more mosquito nets, ensuring they are distributed to all areas still suffering from malaria. *That argument shows that things are far from being black and white.*

In reality, the single biggest killer on the planet is neither malaria nor TB: it's aging. A successful rejuveneering project could, therefore, have the biggest payback of all. Pursuing that goal is far from being egocentric. It's not just the researchers (and those close to them) who will benefit from the programme. The benefits can reach out to everyone on the planet – including the people in the under-developed communities that are still suffering from outbreaks of malaria and TB. After all, people in these communities suffer from aging too.

The question of the financial effectiveness of different medical programmes hinges on two factors: the number of people who would benefit, and the costs to achieve these benefits. Someone who recognises the large benefits of rejuveneering could still, rationally, oppose the project, out of a belief that its costs will be vast and the timescales enormously extended. And that's the real crunch decision.

If you think it will be a very expensive project to bring about widespread rejuvenation, and if you think success with that project lies centuries into the future, you'll be inclined to view rejuvenation researchers as eccentric (mad) and/or egocentric (selfish). However, once you grasp the possibility that real progress could happen in the next few decades, for a cost-spend comparable to the amount of money that's currently being spent on, say, cancer alone, your assessment will change. You may start to view rejuveneers, not as eccentric, but as inspired; not as egocentric, but as heroic.

Timescales

Q25: Isn't the rejuveneering programme so inherently complicated it will require centuries of work?

As stated in the previous section, this is the crunch question. It deserves a full answer, which will occupy the remainder of this book. For now, I offer this short version of the answer: Technological progress is rapidly accelerating. Breakthroughs which would formerly have required centuries of effort can be anticipated to occur within the next few decades.

In turn, this speed up depends on:

- More and more people being educated, worldwide, to increasingly high standards

- More and more people being able to network together, to share ideas and solutions

- More and more techniques being understood and developed, ready for re-use in new circumstances

- More and more solutions being available to serve as building blocks for new solutions

- More open source, more information on wikis, more hardware that is readily accessible at low cost, more capabilities for people to design and manufacture materials, etc

- Wiser application of methods allowing positive collaboration, rather than a negative cacophony of interfering efforts.

A set of accelerating improvements, similar to those anticipated within the rejuvenation industry over the next few decades, took place in an earlier industry just over one hundred years ago. This earlier industry was the flight industry – an industry that, like rejuvenation, was long thought by critics to be hopelessly impractical.

As we'll see in the next chapter, these critics of the concept of powered flight included some of the most eminent thinkers of the time. But despite their eminence, these critics were blinkered. They failed to anticipate the full scope of human innovation and ingenuity. That's why they didn't see flight coming. And, in turn, that's a reason to maintain an open mind about the potential for rejuveneering to arrive sooner than eminent critics suppose.

3. From flight to rejuvenation

The quest for rejuvenation has a lot in common with the quest for flight. I find it illuminating to explore that comparison.

For countless millennia, dreamers pondered whether humans would ever be able to soar high through the skies, steering their own course, zigging and zagging like the birds – and living to tell the tale. Such a feat would defy the common observation that, once in the air, all humans quickly plummeted downwards – the observation that was given the name, in modern times, "the law of gravity". Only a fool would challenge that law. Many a fool did, attached to surrogate wings, feathers, and other contraptions – with deadly results.

Over these same countless millennia, dreamers have also pondered whether humans would ever be able to break free from another pervasive downward force – the force of declining physical health. Children gain strength and grow tall, but only for a moment in cosmic time, before weakness sets in and vigour dissipates. Mind and body, once proud and tough, dwindle in capacity, and soon turn into dust. Mythological creatures defied that law, according to poetic flights of fancy, but men and women in all walks of real life – in all ranks and stations in society – fell victim to what modern folk would call, grandly, "the second law of thermodynamics". This is the law of increasing entropy – the inevitability of growing chaos. Only a fool would challenge *that* law.

But thank goodness for fools. It's as George Bernard Shaw wrote in his play "Man and Superman"[59] in 1903:

> The reasonable man adapts himself to the world; the unreasonable one persists in trying to adapt the world to himself. Therefore all progress depends on the unreasonable man.

That same year, 1903, witnessed the first fitful instances of powered manned flight. The very first proper flight lasted only 12 seconds; later that day (14 December 1903), another flight lasted 59 seconds. The Wright brothers, Orville and Wilbur, were on their way to making history.

Criticism from all sides

The Wrights achieved success despite the prevailing folk wisdom common at the time:

> If God wanted man to fly, he would have made us with wings.

That fatalistic sentiment extended far beyond the religiously pious. Rear Admiral George W. Melville, with the exalted title as "engineer-in-chief" of the United States Navy, published his thoughts in the December 1901 edition of the North American Review, in an article entitled "The engineer and the problem of aerial navigation"[60]:

> There probably can be found no better example of the speculative tendency carrying man to the verge of the chimerical than in his attempts to imitate the birds, or no field where so much inventive seed has been sown with so little return as in the attempts of man to fly successfully through the air. Never, it would seem, has the human mind so persistently evaded the issue, begged the question, and, "wrangling resolutely with the facts", insisted upon dreams being accepted as absolute performance, as when there has been proclaimed time and again the proximate and perfect utility of the balloon or of the flying machine.

Melville's article thundered on for twelve pages, featuring choice words to describe the supporters of human flight: "purveyors of false hopes, mechanical moonshine, and downright charlatanism". The article particularly fretted about human flight *appearing* to become possible and attracting investments which would become ruinous:

> The worst thing that could happen would be a partial success for Aerial Navigation, in which case it would have all the insidious evil of a half-truth and be a commercial counterfeit susceptible of endless circulation. Companies would spring up like mushrooms, and thousands of people would lose the hoarded savings of years. The officers of a few of these companies would be self-deluded; but in the vast number of cases they would consist either of unprincipled promoters who take no personal risk, or else of veritable charlatans intent upon fleecing the public. In one or two instances, the treasuries of unwary Governments might be raided. All this without consideration of frequent and appalling catastrophe.

In summarising his article, and referring to himself in the third person ("he"), Melville wrote:

> He tries to approximate the evil and total up the injury that an engineering sham will bring to the nation. He denounces, in unmeasured terms, any

so-called mechanical device or unscientific pretension whose existence is a menace to the people's welfare.

Another critic of "aerial navigation" used more measured language, but was even more eminent. This critic was Sir William Thomson, better known as Lord Kelvin, the prominent British mathematical physicist, who is credited as defining the field of thermodynamics and discovering its second law. The absolute temperature scale is, for good reason, named after him. Kelvin, who in 1892 had become the first British scientist to be appointed to the House of Lords, received a request from Major Baden Baden-Powell (the brother of the founder of the Boy Scouts) that he should support an "Aeronautical Society". Writing under the letterhead "University of Glasgow" in December 1896, Kelvin declined Baden-Powell's request as follows[61]:

I am afraid I am not in the flight for "aerial navigation". I was greatly interested in your work with kites; but I have not the smallest molecule of faith in aerial navigation other than ballooning or of expectation of good results from any of the trials we hear of. So you will understand that I would not care to be a member of the aeronautical Society.

The problems of "aerial navigation" were to render even the Wright brothers deeply pessimistic from time to time. The challenges they faced in their trial flights included three kinds of balance and stability (roll, pitch, and yaw) as well as lift, power, and thrust. In 1901, in experiments at Kill Devil Hills, North Carolina, their glider span out of control on too many occasions. The elevator mechanism they had designed to regulate the pitch of the airplane was clearly ineffective. On the train journey back to their home in Ohio after six weeks of frustration, Wilbur remarked to his brother[62],

"Not within a thousand years would man ever fly."

The Wright brothers weren't the only ones who experienced bitter disappointments in their experiments. A few years earlier, Otto Lilienthal, the German flight pioneer who had initially made an encouraging series of (non-powered) aerial flights in gliders, lost control of his glider one time too many. Unable to pull his craft out of a steep dive, Lilienthal fell out of the glider from a height of around 15 metres to the ground. He died from his injuries two days later.

Someone else whose attempts to fly would end in striking failure was the American Samuel Langley. Langley carried out a number of experiments near to the Potomac River in Virginia, south of Washington DC. These would involve a "Langley Large Aerodrome A" airplane, and a brave human pilot, Charles Manly. Writer Carroll Gray reports what happened next[63]:

> Charles Manly was chosen to operate the Langley Large Aerodrome 'A' and plans for the first flight, in October of 1903, were made. This attempt was a dismal failure, caused by an improper balancing of the Aerodrome 'A'; it was nose-heavy and after leaving the launcher plunged into the Potomac River. Manly attempted to correct the problem by moving the tail, but the machine did not respond in time…
>
> After rebuilding the damaged Aerodrome 'A'…, another test was planned for December of 1903. On the 8th, the Aerodrome 'A' was again sent down the launching apparatus track, with Charles Manly again at the controls. Another, even more spectacular disaster resulted, as the Aerodrome 'A' reared-up into a vertical position, its propellers spinning and holding the craft momentarily in its vertical position, before it fell, yet again, into the Potomac River. This failure was caused, it was believed, by the tail snagging on the launching apparatus and then breaking.

As Gray reports, this double failure was received badly by public opinion:

> The newspapers were unforgiving of the failure, dubbing it "Langley's Folly," ridiculing the effort and railing about the expenditure of U.S. Army funds on the project. Manly believed that additional funds could have been secured to continue the experiments save for the negative press reports and blasting editorials. As for Langley, he was deeply disheartened by the failure (coming as it did as the last of the funds had been spent) and was also deeply hurt by the negative press. Hence, he decided it would not serve to request additional funding. Thus ended Langley's 16 years of aerial experiments.

Langley had received a total of $70,000 in funding from the US War Department and the Smithsonian museum. One of the critics of this high level of funding was the polymath Simon Newcomb, founding President of the American Astronomical Society. Newcomb's writings covered mathematics, statistics, physics, astronomy, and even political economy: he authored a book on that subject that would be praised by John Maynard Keynes[64]. As director of the Nautical Almanac Office, he initiated a major programme to verify the values of all major constants used in astronomy. Clearly he was no fool. But, as quoted in "When Hull Freezes Over"[65] by John Galluzzo, Newcomb wrote the following in October 1903, reflecting on the flying endeavours of Samuel Langley:

> May not our mechanicians… be ultimately forced to admit that aerial flight is one of the great class of problems with which man can never cope, and give up all attempts to grapple with it?...
>
> Imagine the proud possessor of the aeroplane darting through the air at several hundred feet per second. It is the speed alone that sustains him. How is he ever going to stop? Once he slackens his speed, down he begins to fall. He may, indeed, increase the inclination of his aeroplane. Then he increases the resistance to the sustaining force. Once he stops he falls a dead mass. How shall he reach the ground without destroying his delicate machinery? I do not think the most imaginative inventor has yet even put down upon paper a demonstrably successful way of meeting this difficulty.

In similar vein, an editorial in the New York Times on 10th December 1903 offered this advice[66] to Langley:

> We hope that Professor Langley will not put his substantial greatness as a scientist in further peril by continuing to waste his time and the money involved in further airship experiments. Life is short, and he is capable of services to humanity incomparably greater than can be expected to result from trying to fly… For students and investigators of the Langley type, there are more useful employments.

Two months earlier, the same venerable newspaper had given an enormous timescale[67] – "from one million to ten million years" – for the effort required to finally solve the problems of powered flight:

> The flying machine which will really fly might be evolved by the combined and continuous efforts of mathematicians and mechanicians in from one million to ten million years—provided, of course, we can meanwhile eliminate such little drawbacks and embarrassments as the existing relation between weight and strength in inorganic materials. No doubt the problem has attractions for those it interests, but to the ordinary man it would seem as if effort might be employed more profitably.

As for Langley, he remained assured that, sooner or later, these problems would find solutions – though not by him. One of his confidants was the writer Rudyard Kipling, who recalled the discussion in his 1937 autobiography[68]:

I met Professor Langley of the Smithsonian, an old man who had designed a model aeroplane driven—for petrol had not yet arrived—by a miniature flash-boiler engine, a marvel of delicate craftsmanship. It flew on trial over two hundred yards, and drowned itself in the waters of the Potomac, which was cause of great mirth and humour to the Press of his country. Langley took it coolly enough and said to me that, though he would never live till then, I should see the aeroplane established.

Gliding pioneer Otto Lilienthal also struck a philosophical attitude, on his deathbed in a Berlin hospital following his lethal fall from his out-of-control glider. It is recorded that his last words[69] to his brother Gustav were "Sacrifices must be made!" ("Opfer müssen gebracht werden!")

Lilienthal's fate was one of the topics that came up in an April 1902 newspaper interview[70] with powered flight sceptic Lord Kelvin. The interview appeared in the Newark Advocate, with the subtitle

The Master of Modern Science... Declares That Dirigibility of the Air Is Utterly and Absolutely Impracticable

The journalist asked Lord Kelvin: "Do you think it possible for an airship to be guided across the Atlantic Ocean?" Kelvin replied:

"Not possible at all...No motive power can drive a balloon through the air...

"No balloon and no aeroplane will ever be practically successful."

The journalist persisted: "But Lord Kelvin, you remember the experiments of the German, Lindenthal [sic], who used a gliding machine, starting from an elevation and riding down the slope of the air?"

Kelvin remained defiant in his views:

"Yes, but Lindenthal simply threw away his life. He was killed during his experiments, and later on another gentleman who had undertaken the same sort of flying also sacrificed his life. They both threw away their lives without any possibility of success in what they were undertaking to do."

Rapid breakthrough

What few observers could have foreseen at that time – regardless of their degree of enthusiasm or criticism towards the question of human flight – was *the rapid speed of progress* that would soon follow. The Wright brothers avoided publicity for the first few years after their December 1903 breakthrough, until they were satisfied they had sufficient patents in place to protect their ability to benefit financially from their hard-won engineering innovations. During this "stealth" period – to use a term from more modern times – the Wright brothers were happy to tolerate scepticism about whether their experiments had demonstrated anything of substance. The New York Herald's Paris edition in February 1906 alluded to a sentiment[71] that was widespread in aero-enthusiast circles in Europe at that time:

> The Wrights have flown or they have not flown. They possess a machine or they do not possess one. They are in fact either fliers or liars. It is difficult to fly. It's easy to say, "We have flown."

Indeed, the small number of initial photographs of the Wright brothers' flights could easily be interpreted as a craft skipping along the sands of Kitty Hawk, North Carolina, rather than as soaring through the air under its own power. It's akin to the photos allegedly showing Indian meditation gurus as levitating mid-air, as opposed to merely bouncing off their cushions.

It's on account of this initial clampdown on publicity that authority figures and apparent redoubtable experts continued to express profound scepticism about the prospect for powered flight. Simon Newcomb, the founding President of the American Astronomical Society mentioned earlier, wrote the following as late as 1906, in his book "Side-lights on Astronomy and Kindred Fields of Popular Science"[72]:

> The demonstration that no possible combination of known substances, known forms of machinery and known forms of force, can be united in a practical machine by which man shall fly long distances through the air, seems to the writer as complete as it is possible for the demonstration of any physical fact to be.

That same year, The Times in London offered this opinion[73], under the by-line of "Engineering Editor",

> All attempts at artificial aviation are not only dangerous to human life, but foredoomed to failure from the engineering standpoint.

In 1907, after witnessing some disappointing aeroplane experiments at Blair Atholl in Perthshire, Scotland, Lord Richard Haldane, the British Minister of War, stated baldly to colleagues[74] that

> The aeroplane will never fly.

All this scepticism vanished virtually overnight in August 1908, as Wilbur Wright made a series of public flights in France, including flying around a figure-of-eight. Less than a year later, one of the observers of Wilbur's flight, Louis Bleriot, flew across the English Channel from Calais to Dover, in a journey lasting 36 minutes. Within another ten years, John Alcock and Arthur Brown flew an airplane non-stop across the Atlantic – from St. John's, Newfoundland, in Canada, to Clifden in Ireland. After another fifty years, in 1969, Neil Armstrong and Buzz Aldrin landed on the moon. That journey to the moon fulfilled another long-cherished quest of human dreamers.

This ongoing series of subsequent breakthroughs surprised even the pioneers of the field with its unexpected speed. Wilbur Wright had expressed the following thoughts[75] in 1909:

> No airship will ever fly from New York to Paris. That seems to me to be impossible. What limits the flight is the motor. No known motor can run at the requisite speed for four days without stopping, and you can't be sure of finding the proper winds for soaring.

Four years later, in remarks carried at the time in the Washington state newspaper the Aberdeen Herald[76], Wilbur's brother Orville had reiterated the same scepticism:

> It is a bare possibility that a one-man machine without a float and favoured by a wind of, say, 15 miles an hour, might succeed in getting across the Atlantic. But such an attempt would be the height of folly. When one comes to increase the size of the craft, the possibility rapidly fades away. This is because of the difficulties of carrying sufficient fuel. On the basis of the figures which I have worked out, I find that no less than 53% of the entire load, including the weight of the machine itself and all, would have to be fuel... It will readily be seen, therefore, why the Atlantic flight is out of the question.

As we see, even the bold visionaries of a new technology sometimes fail to anticipate the speed at which subsequent improvements in that technology will dramatically exceed its initial capabilities.

More moonshine

It's not just the arena of air travel where eminent practitioners spectacularly underestimated the rapid pace of future engineering progress. To the remarkable list of over-pessimistic critics of aeroplane flight covered above

– critics that even, at times, included the Wright brothers themselves – we should add the names of physicists Robert Millikan, Ernest Rutherford, and Albert Einstein. In the case of these three outstanding scientists, however, the subject of their misplaced scepticism was an arena different from air travel. It was the arena of nuclear energy.

Robert Millikan is the person who, from 1909 onwards, first measured the charge on an electron, in an experiment which generations of high school students have repeated in advanced physics classes. A careful experimenter, Millikan also improved the accuracy of measuring Planck's constant, h, which has a fundamental importance in physics. But this pioneer of modern atomic physics was scornful of any idea that useful energy could be obtained from within the atom. In an address to the Chemists' Club in New York, as reported in the May 1929 edition of Modern Mechanics[77], Millikan opined as follows:

> There is no likelihood man can ever tap the power of the atom. The glib supposition of utilizing atomic energy when our coal has run out is a completely unscientific Utopian dream, a childish bug-a-boo. Nature has introduced a few fool-proof devices into the great majority of elements that constitute the bulk of the world, and they have no energy to give up in the process of disintegration.

Ernest Rutherford has an outstanding list of accomplishments to his name: the discovery that atoms have a small, dense nucleus; the principle of the half-life of radioactive compounds; the discovery of the proton; experiments in 1917 which were the first in which atomic nuclei were split (in this case, he split nitrogen atoms); and championing the idea that radioactivity involved the transmutation of elements (an idea that had long fascinated alchemists, but which now had rigorous scientific backing). On his death in 1937, he was buried in London's Westminster Abbey, a short distance from Isaac Newton and Charles Darwin. He was one of my childhood heroes, as I devoured books written about the history of science.

Given his accomplishments in nuclear physics, it might be expected that Rutherford would foresee the potential to extract vast amounts of energy from nuclear reactions. However, like Millikan, he frequently expressed scepticism about the prospects for practical net extraction of energy from such processes. For example, a lecture he gave to the British Association for the Advancement of Science in Leicester in September 1933 contained the following (as reported in the Times[78] the following day):

We might in these processes obtain very much more energy than the proton supplied, but on the average we could not expect to obtain energy in this way. It was a very poor and inefficient way of producing energy, and anyone who looked for a source of power in the transformation of the atoms was talking moonshine.

"Moonshine" – this word of contempt, used by Rutherford, was one of the insults hurled by Rear Admiral George W. Melville in his twelve page article in 1901 that, as mentioned above, scoffed at people who had aspirations for flying machines.

The energy that might be released by a nuclear reaction would be described by the famous equation $E=mc^2$ of Albert Einstein. Einstein's breakthrough accomplishments in physics – the quantum theory of light, special relativity, general relativity, and lots more – leave even those of Ernest Rutherford in the shade. Yet Einstein shared with Rutherford (and Millikan) the view that it would remain impractical to extract useful energy from any nuclear reaction. Talking to reporters in Pittsburgh after a lecture in 1934, Einstein remarked[79] that:

Splitting the atom by bombardment is something akin to shooting birds in the dark in a place where there are only a few birds.

The newspaper that reported these remarks, the Pittsburgh Post-Gazette, summarised the interview with this headline:

Atom Energy Hope Is Spiked by Einstein

In this regard, Einstein was being true to an opinion he had expressed on several previous occasions. For example, in a discussion at a reception in a physics laboratory in Prague in 1921, Einstein was confronted by a questioner eager to press the suggestion that the equation $E=mc^2$ would enable the creation of weapons with massive destructive power – an idea that had already featured in a 1914 novel written by HG Wells, "The World Set Free". Einstein dismissed the idea[80], saying that

Its foolishness is evident at first glance.

Someone who was strongly influenced by reading Wells' novel "The World Set Free" was another physicist, the Hungarian Leo Szilard. Szilard gave a lot of thought to the possibilities of nuclear weaponry. There's a famous story that he read the report in the Times about Rutherford's dismissal the idea of nuclear energy as "moonshine", the day after Rutherford's lecture, and almost immediately conceived of a specific mechanism that invalidated Rutherford's conclusion. Biographer Gene Dannen explains[81]:

> Irritated by Rutherford's remarks, Szilard brooded on the subject while walking through the streets of central London. He thought especially about the recently discovered neutron, which had no electric charge and could enter the atomic nucleus without resistance.
>
> Looking up at a stoplight at the corner of Southampton Row, it suddenly occurred to him that if an element existed that released two neutrons after being struck by one neutron, the result would be a neutron chain reaction.
>
> It would spread automatically, multiplying from one atom to the next, liberating energy with each step, liberating neutrons, more energy, more neutrons. If left uncontrolled, in a mass above a certain critical size, it could explode with incredible force.
>
> Such a discovery would mean not only atomic energy, but also atomic bombs. H.G. Wells had predicted exactly that in his 1914 novel "The World Set Free". The book was fresh in Szilard's mind from reading it only a year earlier. In Wells' story, the discovery of atomic energy led to a war fought with "atomic bombs" that almost destroyed civilization. Finally, wiser minds prevailed to form a world government.
>
> In fiction, or in fact, it was obvious that the discovery of atomic energy would change the world. It would be one of the most important discoveries in history.

Szilard went to bed that evening with a profound apprehension of the future he had conceived. Some years later, Szilard persuaded Albert Einstein to put his name to a letter requesting US President Roosevelt to commence what became the Manhattan Project, to ensure that the US created the atomic bomb ahead of Hitler. As a mark of a true scientist, Einstein had reversed his previous view that the concept of nuclear weaponry was "foolishness", on being presented with new ideas. The new principle of a nuclear chain reaction had made tangible the previously fanciful idea of nuclear energy.

As noted[82] by artificial intelligence researcher Stuart Russell,

> The interval of time between Rutherford's confident assertion that atomic energy would never be feasibly extracted and Szilard's invention of the neutron-induced nuclear chain reaction was less than twenty-four hours.

It was just over a decade later that the principle of nuclear chain reaction saw its awful realisation in the bombs dropped on Hiroshima and

Nagasaki. That's a measure of how quickly a major engineering project can deliver an outcome that was previously thought to be impossible – provided there is sufficient political will behind the project.

Desiring more life

The powered flight of the Wright brothers was preceded, as I mentioned, by the glider of Otto Lilienthal. And before there were any successful gliders, there were balloons – some filled with hot air, others with hydrogen. There's a fascinating account[83] of one reaction to the first manned hot-air balloon flight:

> [A] French noblewoman, a duchess in her eighties…, on seeing the first ascent of Montgolfier's balloon from the palace of the Tuilleries in 1783, fell back upon the cushions of her carriage and wept. "Oh yes," she said, "Now it's certain. One day they'll learn how to keep people alive forever, but I shall already be dead."

The lamentations of this venerable French noblewoman echo through the ages. *One day they'll learn how to keep people alive forever, but I shall already be dead.* If engineers could figure out a way to solve the age-old problem of raising humans safely high into the air, and then back again, it was a strong hint that other engineers would eventually be able to figure out a way to solve another age-old problem, namely the problem that people age, become old, and then die.

Let's compare the two projects. Human rejuvenation defies the law of entropy, in the same way that human flight defies the law of gravity. Human rejuvenation defies the biblical curse "For dust you are, and to dust you shall return", just as human flight defies the common saying that "If God wanted man to fly, he would have made us with wings". The prospect of human rejuvenation has attracted many naïve, flawed, snake-oil theories – but so did the prospect of human flight.

The comparison goes further. There were many different approaches to human flight, including ideas involving balloons, gliders, feathers, cannons, rockets, and steam engines. It wasn't obvious in advance which approach would turn out to be the most promising. (The Wright brothers took special advantage of the unique insights they had developed in their professional business of bicycle engineering – such as the importance of balance and stability. They also filled notebooks with their careful observations of birds in flight.) Likewise, there are many different approaches to human rejuvenation, including a focus on genetics, telomeres, stem cells, hormones, the immune system, reducing cell inflammation, and nanotechnology. It's not clear, a priori, which approach will prove the most successful.

The rejuveneering project claims, in effect, that the comparison extends one more step: the core problems of the project are engineering ones, and there is likely to be fast progress after some key breakthroughs – similar to the remarkably swift progress made in flight after the Wrights gave public demonstrations of what they had accomplished.

In this analysis, the main difference between solving human flight and solving human rejuvenation is simply a matter of difficulty. Let's use the letter 'N' to denote how many times more complicated the human rejuvenation project is than the human flight project. For example, N might be one hundred, one thousand, one million, or even one billion.

Might N be infinity? That is, might the human rejuvenation project be completely outside the scope of what humans will ever be able to accomplish? The next chapter looks at the case against that extreme conclusion. As we'll see, the argument has the following components:

- Nature already features many important examples of rejuvenation
- Various interventions by scientists and engineers have already used the same underlying biological processes to stunning effect, creating new or extended examples of rejuvenation
- These interventions can become even more dramatic when combined with non-biological technologies
- There is no evidence of any fundamental limit to what can be accomplished by clever new combinations of these and other innovative engineering interventions.

4. Rejuveneering starting points

How much effort will the rejuveneering project require? A commonly held view is that the task will be incredibly hard, and will therefore require one or more centuries of continuous endeavour. I have *some* sympathies for that argument, but I'm going to postpone discussion of these points until the next chapter. First, I want to consider a more extreme view. This holds that the task is, for all practical purposes, impossible. Even with centuries of effort, rejuveneering will, in this view, make little progress – therefore there's no point even in trying.

This "practically impossible" view is similar to the opinions frequently expressed around the year 1900 (as covered in the previous chapter) that powered flight would be impossible.

This chapter provides counters to the extreme "practically impossible" view. These counters will also serve as starting points for the considerations in subsequent chapters as to why the hard, hard task of rejuveneering might, nevertheless, be solved within as little as twenty five years.

Rejuvenation in nature

Living organisms may frequently wither and die, but there's more to nature than decay. Indeed, nature features impressive cases of rejuvenation, even before human rejuveneers set to work.

Let's start with the everyday phenomenon of childbirth – though perhaps we should call it the "everyday miracle". A body consisting of comparatively aged cells – the body of the mother – generates a body consisting of youthful cells – the body of the baby. The old gives rise to the new.

The youthful cells that are earmarked for the next generation have a special origin, which is the so-called "germline" of cells, stored in ovaries and testes. Other cells (that is, apart from the germline) are known as somatic cells, meaning "body" cells. Germline cells retain their vitality from generation to generation, even as the surrounding somatic cells become old. Special biological processes protect the germline cells. That's rejuvenation at work, courtesy of nature.

What prevents the engineering of processes that will protect somatic cells too? Is there a principle of nature that would fundamentally rule out such protection? I see no evidence of any such principle. Indeed, what we'll see throughout this book is examples of biological processes that do enable the renewed vitality of somatic cells, in lots of different circumstances. We'll also see examples of the replacement of these cells by new ones, enabling rejuvenation at the level of organs rather than cells. These examples are the building blocks from which rejuveneers can, step by step, assemble practical therapies for human rejuvenation.

A dramatic example of regeneration takes place in the organism that has been nicknamed the "immortal jellyfish". The scientific name for this creature is *turritopsis dohrnii*. Its lifecycle can be compared to that of the caterpillar and butterfly, in that it passes through several stages. Born as a free-swimming larva, it becomes attached to the seafloor and transforms into a colony of polyps (small tentacles). In turn, jellyfish form as buds on the polyps, and become separated, swimming off. This might appear to be the final form of the creature – in the way that the butterfly is the final form of a caterpillar. In this stage, the jellyfish can give birth to new larvae, starting a new generation, seemingly confirming the impression of the jellyfish being the end of this particular lifecycle. But that's not the whole story. Remarkably, in stressful situations, including sickness or impending old age, this jellyfish can re-attach itself to the seafloor, at which time it undergoes another metamorphosis, back to the polyps stage. New York Times writer Nathaniel Rich describes the process[84] as follows:

> In other... species, the [jellyfish] dies after it spawns. A turritopsis jellyfish, however, sinks to the bottom of the ocean floor, where its body folds in on itself, assuming the jellyfish equivalent of the foetal position. The bell reabsorbs the tentacles, and then it degenerates further until it becomes a gelatinous blob. Over the course of several days, this blob forms an outer shell. Next it shoots out stolons, which resemble roots. The stolons lengthen and become a polyp.

This is as if a butterfly reverted to being a juvenile caterpillar, rather than dying. Even more remarkable is that the whole process has been observed to repeat numerous times: adult to juvenile to adult to juvenile to adult...

To be clear, the adjective "immortal" in the nickname "immortal jellyfish" is misleading, since these creatures frequently do die, by being eaten by predators such as sea slugs. And of course, the reversion to a foetal status or gelatinous blob is hardly something to which we humans would aspire. However, the species still deserves our close attention, on account of its dramatic metamorphic powers. The low-level molecular processes that are taking place inside these jellyfish, during their remarkable transformation, could become key parts of new therapies with human applicability.

The Japanese researcher Shin Kubota has undertaken a thorough investigation of the creature and has, as Times writer Rich notes, high hopes for what might be uncovered by further research. Kubota expresses his vision in this way:

> Turritopsis application for human beings is the most wonderful dream of mankind. Once we determine how the jellyfish rejuvenates itself, we should achieve very great things. My opinion is that we will evolve and become immortal ourselves.

What happens at the cellular level during this metamorphosis is a process known as transdifferentiation: somatic cells in the jellyfish change their type, as if a skin cell would become a nerve cell, and so on. Controlling the transdifferentiation of cells in new circumstances could be very useful for human rejuveneering. Once we understand them better, the biological processes trail-blazed by the immortal jellyfish could be put to dramatic new usage.

Repairs and replacements

A different mechanism of repurposing cells lies at the basis of the powerful repair mechanisms which are another of the toolbox of techniques that exist in nature. In these cases, animals can regenerate new replacement limbs, extra sets of teeth, and so on. One star performer is the salamander – an amphibian – which can grow a new leg to replace one that has been cut off, without any evidence of scarring. These animals can also grow new tails, new eyes, new jaws, and even new spinal cords. When their hearts are damaged, they can in some cases regenerate the parts that are missing.

Whilst falling far short of the self-repair capabilities of the salamander, humans demonstrate *some* elements of bodily regeneration:

- The liver can repair itself, if part of it (perhaps as much as three quarters) is lost to disease

- If someone loses the end of a fingertip, with a clean cut, the tip will grow back in some cases
- People sometimes grow a third set of teeth, rather than just the two standard sets.

Other animals display regenerative powers that are intermediate in capability: various species of fish have the ability to repair a broken spinal cord, and young rats have been observed to grow a new leg to replace one they have lost.

What is it about the salamander that gives it such a remarkable ability to repair damage that arises? That's a lively field of research. It seems that there's a particular biological pathway that's active inside salamander cells – a pathway known as "ERK" – which enables the regeneration of cells. Can a similar pathway be enabled in other animals? It would be a foolhardy scientist who would state categorically that this mechanism is irretrievably restricted to just one organism.

UCL News recently reported[85] some findings in this regard from lead researcher Dr Max Yun of UCL's Institute of Structural & Molecular Biology:

> The secret of how salamanders successfully regrow body parts is being unravelled by UCL researchers in a bid to apply it to humans.
>
> For the first time, researchers have found that the ERK pathway must be constantly active for salamander cells to be reprogrammed, and hence able to contribute to the regeneration of different body parts.
>
> The team identified a key difference between the activity of this pathway in salamanders and mammals, which helps us to understand why humans can't regrow limbs and sheds light on how regeneration of human cells can be improved.
>
> The study… demonstrates that the ERK pathway is not fully active in mammalian cells, but when forced to be constantly active, gives the cells more potential for reprogramming and regeneration. This could help researchers better understand diseases and design new therapies.

The report quoted Dr Yun as follows:

> "While humans have limited regenerative abilities, other organisms, such as the salamander, are able to regenerate an impressive repertoire of complex structures including parts of their hearts, eyes, spinal cord, tails, and they are the only adult vertebrates able to regenerate full limbs.

"We're thrilled to have found a critical molecular pathway, the ERK pathway, that determines whether an adult cell is able to be reprogrammed and help the regeneration processes. Manipulating this mechanism could contribute to therapies directed at enhancing regenerative potential of human cells."

If Nature's own regenerative mechanisms cannot be precisely duplicated from salamanders into humans, human ingenuity has the option to create novel biochemical pathways with similar outcomes. These pathways may involve the practice of stem cell engineering, featuring "pluripotent" stem cells that are capable of turning into numerous types of mature cell. For example, a recent trial at Melbourne Stem Cell Centre involving 70 patients with damaged knee cartilage has been said to show "stunning results"[86]:

Stem cells are being used to regrow damaged knee cartilage in world-first Melbourne trials it is hoped will make many joint replacements and other surgery unnecessary.

Doctors have halted damage caused by degenerative conditions, and even reversed it, in one of the first studies to use stem cells to rebuild cartilage in humans.

In initial results, half of those treated at Melbourne Stem Cell Centre saw a three-quarters reduction in pain and vastly improved knee function.

A different research team in Melbourne – this time at Monash University – has recently reported progress in manipulating cells from one type to another without passing through an intermediate stem cell status. The team at Monash use the same "transdifferentiation" mechanism as occurs in the immortal jellyfish. Writing in the Australian, John Ross describes the breakthrough[87]:

An Australian breakthrough could turn regenerative medicine on its head by taking the stem step out of stem cell therapies.

Melbourne biologists have teamed up with British mathematicians to devise a computerised recipe for reprogramming adult cells. The new program... eliminates the need to rewind cells to their "pluripotent" or embryonic stage before using them to fight diseases.

Senior author Jose Polo said the approach would massively accelerate research and treatment by taking the guesswork out of producing regenerative tissues. "Every cell has the potential to become another cell," said Dr Polo, a stem cell biologist at Monash University. "But now it will be much easier to go from one mature cell type to another, without going through that (pluripotent) stage."

The article goes on to explain how the team's new method is an improvement on a much slower process that was previously used:

> Scientists have long known that it is possible to switch adult cells from one type to another... But the field has moved slowly, largely because it is difficult to coax stem cells to develop or "differentiate" into the desired type of mature cells. Researchers have tried to shortcut the process by directly converting adult cells, in a procedure called "trans-differentiation".

> This involves the addition of proteins, known as "transcription factors", which stimulate cell changes. But with some 2000 such proteins to choose from, the process has proven exhaustive.

> Dr Polo said the handful of successful attempts at trans-differentiation so far had required about five years of trial and error. He said the new approach reduced this to just four or five months, by outlining exactly which transcription factors to use...

> Dr Polo said the technique could be used to treat conditions ranging from burns, diabetes and Parkinson's disease to congenital problems in the heart and brain. He said it was theoretically possible to change cell types within the body, producing tissue grafts internally and eliminating the need to inject regenerative cells.

Negligible senescence

Immortal jellyfish are far from being the only sea creatures of interest to rejuveneers. The rockfish and the turtle both attracted the attention in the late 1980s of Caleb Finch, a professor in the biology of aging at the University of Southern California. Some species of rockfish and turtles seemed not to age at all. Finch coined the term "negligible senescence" to describe what he observed. Members of a species are said to display negligible senescence if, as they become chronologically older, the creatures:

- Show no increase in the rate at which they die (their "mortality rate")
- Show no decrease in their reproductive fertility
- Show no decline in the functionality of their somatic cells
- Are able to completely regenerate somatic cells.

To be clear, humans do *not* display negligible senescence. Human mortality rates follow an empirical law, named the Gompertz Law, after

British actuary and mathematician Benjamin Gompertz, who published his observations back in 1825. Every extra eight years that we live, past the age of around 35, we become twice as likely to die within the next year. We go from having a one in a thousand chance of dying in the next year, when aged 35, to having a one in ten chance of dying in the next year, when aged around 85. *Our mortality grows exponentially.* In contrast, studies of rockfish and turtles show no such increasing propensity for the animals to die. They can also remain reproductively active throughout their lives. Finch noted in a review article[88] in 2009:

> Long lifespans exceeding 100 years are accepted for some species of deep-dwelling marine fish (groundfish) by combinations of radio-isotope and growth ring measurements... The maximum age recorded is for rougheye rockfish, 205 years... The greatest ages are recorded for fish caught in the deepest waters... These ages underestimate the maximum lifespan because of sampling issues and because the individuals caught were healthy fish in natural habitats. No gross organ degeneration has been seen; tumours are very rare ($< 0.1\%$)...

It's worth re-emphasising these last two points: For these rougheye rockfish, "No gross organ degeneration has been seen; tumours are very rare ($< 0.1\%$)".

There are various ways of calculating the lifespan of individual sea creatures. One bowhead whale captured by Eskimos at Barrow, Alaska, in May 2007, had embedded inside it fragments of a harpoon from a previous attack earlier in its life. That particular type of harpoon is known to have been used for only a short period of time after it was introduced, back in 1879. This suggests[89] that whale was at least 115 years old when it died. Analysis of amino acids in the eye lenses of bowhead whales points to some whales living more than 200 years.

Even higher lifespans have been recorded. An enormous quahog clam dredged from the ocean floor north of Iceland in 2006 has had its age ascertained as 507 years[90], from careful counting of the annual growth lines on its shell. This age was confirmed by carbon-14 testing. Had the clam not been plucked from the ocean floor and then frozen for storage (killing it in the process, alas), it might well still be alive and strong today, as negligibly senescent as ever.

Negligible senescence is not restricted to sea creatures. It is displayed, at least in part, by a number of long-lived birds, including the albatross and the petrel. A poignant series of photographs exist, showing Aberdeen University Professor George Dunnet on the Orkney island of Eynhallow, accompanied each time by a bird known simply as "Fulmar 57". The first photograph is from 1951, when Dunnet was in his twenties. The next is from 1984[91], and the last one is from 1992[92], shortly before Dunnet died of a stroke (an aging-related disease). The bird, identified by ring markers on its leg, retained all the signs of youthfulness, including regularly breeding, whilst the human professor noticeably aged over the decades. Fulmar 57 outlived the professor and reached at least the age of 50[93] before, presumably, dying of predation or an infectious disease out of sight of scientist observation, away from the island.

More recently, an albatross named "Wisdom" has reached the age of 60 on a wildlife refuge in Hawaii. That news was reported as follows in 2011 in the New York Times[94]:

> Wisdom, a Laysan albatross who lives in the Midway Atoll National Wildlife Refuge in the Pacific northwest of the main Hawaiian island, is 60 years old...
>
> The miracle of Wisdom is not only that she is alive, but that she is breeding. Birds that live that long often (but not always) have years without reproduction, said Bruce Peterjohn, the chief of the geological survey's North American bird banding program. But Wisdom not only does not look her age, he said, she has also produced another healthy chick...
>
> Wisdom also nested in 2008, 2009 and 2010. Officials said she probably has raised 30 to 35 babies in her lifetime.

Elements of negligible senescence are also displayed by one very interesting land-dwelling mammal: the naked mole-rat. As the 'mole' part of their name suggests, naked mole-rats live in networks of underground tunnels. This animal has a lifespan much shorter than the turtle or the rockfish – 28 years, in comparison to upwards of a century for the sea creatures. However, that lifespan is considerably larger than what would be expected from the small physical size of the mole-rat. (Normally, the smaller the physical size of an animal species, the shorter is its average lifespan.) What's more, it seems that very few instances of cancer have ever been found in that species, despite the bodies of several thousand animals being examined. Their arteries show no sign of stiffening, and the animals remain reproductively active throughout their adult life.

Other species that suffer very little from cancer[95] include elephants (as few as one in twenty elephants die of the disease), the bowhead whale, the red sea urchin, and various long-lived seabirds.

The extended youthfulness of all these animals seems to depend on repair mechanisms operating at the level of individual cells and individual organs. These mechanisms maintain the youthfulness of the animal. This is an area of real interest to rejuveneers.

As a further sign of what already happens in nature, consider the 2001 research[96] by Kristina Connor and Ronald Lanner into the variation in vitality with age of the long-lived Great Basin bristlecone pine tree:

> Great Basin bristlecone pine growing on high-elevation sites age very slowly. Lanner and Conner tested several parameters of plant aging (vascular system function, photosynthetic balance, and mutation loads in pollen, seed, and seedling progeny) in Great Basin bristlecone pines on the Inyo and Dixie National Forests. Tree ages ranged from 23 to 4,713 years. None of the parameters had a statistically significant relationship to tree age. The authors concluded "the concept of senescence does not apply to these trees."

In simple terms: although these trees grew chronologically older – and had the tree rings to prove it – there was no decline in any of the metrics of tree health. If trees could talk, one might say to another, "You're how old? 4,000? You don't look a day over 400!"

Senescence involves the accumulation of bodily damage as time passes. Negligible senescence involves the operation of repair mechanisms to undo any bodily damage that arises, or to prevent any such damage occurring in the first place. With skilful engineering, similar mechanisms ought in principle to be capable of being developed and applied in humans, turning us, too, into creatures with negligible senescence. What nature can do, human intervention (with sufficient skill and knowledge) can improve.

Or can it? It's time to look at one important contrary argument – an argument that held considerable sway among biologists for half a century. This is an argument advanced by one of the most prominent evolutionary thinkers of the 20th century: George C. Williams.

Out-smarting evolution

The New York Times carried an obituary[97] on 13 September 2010 for evolutionary biologist George Williams:

George C. Williams, an evolutionary biologist who helped shape modern theories of natural selection, died Wednesday at his home in South Setauket on Long Island, near Stony Brook University, where he taught for 30 years. He was 83.

The cause was Parkinson's disease, said his wife, Doris Williams...

He is "widely regarded by peers in his field as one of the most influential and incisive evolutionary theorists of the 20th century," said Douglas Futuyma, a colleague and the author of a leading textbook on evolution.

Dr. Williams laid out his ideas in 1966 in his book "Adaptation and Natural Selection." In it, he seized on and clarified an issue at the heart of evolutionary theory: whether natural selection works by favouring the survival of elements as small as a single gene or its components, or by favouring those as large as a whole species...

The importance of Dr. Williams's book was immediately recognized by evolutionary biologists, and his ideas reached a wider audience when they were described by Richard Dawkins in his book "The Selfish Gene" (1976).

Williams's ideas were not only responsible for inspiring the "selfish gene" idea which subsequently launched Richard Dawkins to international attention. A 1957 article Williams authored in the academic journal "Evolution" also had far-reaching influence – this time, in the field of the study of aging.

That article was entitled "Pleiotropy, Natural Selection, and the Evolution of Senescence"[98]. The word 'Pleiotropy' means that a single gene can have more than one effect. A famous example is that a variant of a particular gene (the HbS variant of the HBB gene) can, in some circumstances, increase resistance to malaria, but in other circumstances, makes a carrier prone to sickle-cell anaemia. The first effect is good for the individuals carrying that gene, whereas the second is bad. Another example is the p53 gene which interrupts the proliferation of cancer cells, but which may also interfere with the regeneration of stem cells.

The fact that a gene can have more than one function – one good, the other bad – explains why genes with bad effects persist in populations. For example, even though some carriers of the HbS gene variant die from sickle cell anaemia, other carriers gain the advantage of being resistant to malaria.

Now consider the question: what happens to such a gene if it has a good side effect when the carrier is young, but has a bad side effect when the carrier is old? Williams argued in his article as follows: natural selection will typically result in the increase of such a gene within the population. This will happen if the gene improves the health of an organism up to and including the time of child-bearing, even if it has other effects that reduce the health of the organism after the time when it has successfully reproduced. In other words, genes that result in senescence later in life will become more numerous in a population, *despite their detrimental effects*, provided they also have beneficial effects (via pleiotropy) earlier in the organism's life. The fact that older individuals in the population grow weak and die will not matter from the point of view of the gene; what matters is that the gene is spread to larger numbers of the next generation – and subsequently to yet more new generations.

Williams summarised this insight as follows:

> Natural selection may be said to be biased in favour of youth over old age whenever a conflict of interests arises... Natural selection will frequently maximize vigour in youth at the expense of vigour later on and thereby produce a declining vigour (aging) during adult life.

So far, so good. Next, Williams took this insight further. Old age, he proposed, arose due to a combination of factors applying to multiple different subsystems in the biological body. It's not just one kind of bodily damage that gradually renders organisms weaker and more decrepit, but many. As we get older, more and more subsystems in our body demonstrate aspects of failure: dementia, muscle mass decline, arthritic joints, atherosclerotic plaque build-up, immune system problems, failing eyesight, etc. Now suppose that a genetic variation could alter the impact of aging in one of these subsystems, such as arthritic joints. Would this variation tend to be the subject of evolutionary pressure, into subsequent generations?

Williams argued that it would depend on the age at which the effect of the gene applies. The older the individual is when the associated change in healthiness would kick in, the lower the chance that genetic variation will be positively selected. For example, if the organism typically dies of other factors by the age of 30 years, and a genetic variation could improve the organism's health from the age of 50 years onwards, there will be little evolutionary pressure for that new variation to be adopted. Equally, if a genetic variation would *diminish* the organism's health from 50 years onwards – potentially catastrophically – there will be little evolutionary pressure for that new variation *not* to be adopted. If that same variation also, via pleiotropy, has *good* effects at, say, 10 years of age, evolution *will* select this variation and, as a consequence, will conspire to store up late-life problems for any descendants of that organism that happen, through changed circumstances, to eventually become able to approach 50 years in lifespan.

In other words, any genetic changes that might potentially increase lifespan, by their effect on a biological subsystem, will be effective only if that subsystem impacts individuals' healthiness ahead of the onset of aging in other subsystems. Health improvements due to genetic changes will take place only up to the point when the subsystem in question is no longer an "outlier" – that is, up to the point when that subsystem is no longer the first to be causing death by aging. From then on, there is no point in evolution enabling that subsystem to remain healthy for longer, since the individual will in any case be dying at that time of other forms of old age. The result is that an individual in a species accumulates aging damage in different bodily subsystems roughly in parallel. Evolution can bring about changes in subsystems that are outliers (causing aging ahead of the pack of other causal factors), but it cannot bring about changes in the pack as a whole.

This is how Williams expresses it:

> If adverse genic effects appeared earlier in one system than another, they would be removed by selection from that system more readily than from any other... If, for example, degenerative changes in the endocrine glands were the primary cause of human senescence, there would be little selection against the deterioration of other organs.... This selection and the accumulation of random genetic effects in other systems would cause the senescence rate of the other systems to approach that of the endocrine glands.

Williams then draws a zinger of a conclusion:

> Basic research in gerontology has proceeded with the assumption that the aging process will be ultimately explicated through the discovery of one or a few physiological processes... Any such small number of primary physiological factors is a logical impossibility if the assumptions made in the present study are valid. This conclusion banishes the "fountain of youth" to the limbo of scientific impossibilities, like the perpetual motion machine... Such conclusions are always disappointing, but they have the desirable consequence of channelling research in directions that are likely to be fruitful.

Here, then, is a serious argument that the rejuveneering project – dubbed the "fountain of youth" by Williams – is in fact beyond the grasp of engineering, in much the same way as a perpetual motion machine is rendered impossible (in that case, by the second law of thermodynamics).

Williams points out that his theory fits with some observed failures of previous rejuveneering projects:

> Formerly it was believed that mammalian senescence was largely a hormonal phenomenon. Miraculous rejuvenation was anticipated from the implantation of young gonads into aged people, but the miracles were never realised. It was also thought by some that a deterioration in the nervous system was the primary cause of senescence in certain insects... however there is little evidence for these beliefs.

Nearly two decades later, in 1978, another leading professor in the field of aging, George M. Martin of the University of Washington, reiterated the view that single changes in genes would not be able to significantly impact the longevity of organisms. Martin is cited as follows in the book by Wall Street Journal science writer David Stipp, "The Youth Pill: Scientists at the Brink of an Anti-Aging Revolution"[99]:

> "It is naïve to believe that a mutation at a single [gene] could be responsible for the determination of life-span and the various debilities of aging."

In his 1978 paper, "Genetic syndromes in man with potential relevance to the pathobiology of aging"[100], Martin suggested that as many as 7,000 different genes were associated with the pace of human aging.

These blanket statements – "the limbo of scientific impossibilities", and "naïve to believe" – recall the denouncements, from the previous chapter, made by apparently expert critics about the possibility of powered human flight. For example, from Simon Newcomb:

> May not our mechanicians... be ultimately forced to admit that aerial flight is one of the great class of problems with which man can never cope, and give up all attempts to grapple with it?...

And from Lord Kelvin,

> I have not the smallest molecule of faith in aerial navigation.

To be clear, we now know that all these apparently expert views are wrong – both as regards the impossibility of powered flight, and as regards the impossibility of humans to improve on the exertions of natural selection. These views all underestimate the potential for human creativity, innovation, and engineering prowess.

The mistake in the case of the analysis by George Williams is in thinking too highly of natural selection – thinking:

- That natural selection will always find the best solutions to given biological problems
- That natural selection has been able to try out all possible solutions
- That human engineering will not be able to accomplish anything beyond the solutions that natural selection has been able to explore.

This is akin to thinking that since natural selection did not put wings on humans, humans would never be able to fly.

On the contrary, natural selection is limited to solutions that:

- Can be reached in a step-by-step evolutionary manner from previous solutions
- Reflect the particular history of the environment experienced by the population.

What's more, the biological mechanism known as "epigenetics" (that has become better understood only in the last few decades) can selectively enable or disable the function of a gene at different stages in an organism's life. A pleiotropic gene with a positive impact earlier in life can be epigenetically disabled later in life, so that its subsequent deleterious effects on health are switched off. Treatments applied as part of rejuvenation therapies can augment this epigenetic effect, beyond the extent to which it operates naturally.

In their 2002 review article "Evolutionary Theories of Aging and Longevity"[101], husband and wife co-authors Leonid and Natalia Gavrilova lamented the consequences of Williams' strong pronouncement that attempts to reverse aging should be banished "to the limbo of scientific impossibilities, like the perpetual motion machine". As the Gavrilovas expressed it, with heavy irony:

> Evolutionary biologists were always very generous with gerontologists in providing advice and guidance on how to do aging research "in directions that are likely to be fruitful". Surprisingly, this generous intellectual assistance proved to be extremely injurious for aging studies in the past. This happened because evolutionary theory was interpreted in such a way

that the search for single-gene mutations (or life-extending interventions) with very large positive effects on lifespan was considered a completely futile task, destined for failure for fundamental evolutionary reasons. Researchers were convinced by the forceful evolutionary arguments of George Williams...

As a result of this triumphant evolutionary indoctrination, many exciting research opportunities for lifespan extension were squandered for half a century until the recent and astonishing discovery of single-gene mutants with profoundly extended longevity was ultimately made, despite all discouraging predictions and warnings based on evolutionary arguments.

The review paper by the Gavrilovas goes on to list three cases of single gene mutations that had recently been discovered, that, contrary to the predictions of the biological establishment (led by people like Williams and Martin), caused significant extensions, not only in lifespan, but in *healthy* lifespan:

Recent discoveries of lifespan-extending mutations are spectacular. A single-gene mutation (daf-2) more than doubles the lifespan of nematodes [worms], keeping them active, fully fertile..., and having normal metabolic rates. Another single-gene mutation, called methuselah, extends the average lifespan of fruitflies by about 35%, enhancing also their resistance to various forms of stress, including starvation, high temperature, and toxic chemicals. Finally, a single-gene mutation was found in mice extending their lifespans by about 30% and also increasing their resistance to toxic chemicals.

After pointing out these counterexamples to the viewpoint that had long prevailed within the field, the Gavrilovas sagely concluded their review as follows:

Gerontologists will have to learn a lesson from the damage caused by decades of misguided research, when the search for major life-extending mutations and other life-extension interventions was equated by evolutionary biologists to a construction of perpetual motion machine. Perhaps some wisdom from this lesson can be found in the title of a recent scientific review on the evolution of aging: "Evolutionary theories of aging: handle with care."

Examples of successful engineering

To recap: the first part of the argument that rejuveneering will *eventually* be possible (in other words, that the task is not *infinitely* hard) is that nature provides human scientists with a rich set of building blocks from which we can fashion new solutions. These building blocks have been reviewed above, and include:

- The birth of a body made up of new cells, from a body made up of old cells
- The rejuvenation of the body of one creature – the "immortal jellyfish" – back to a more youthful state, even after that creature has given birth to a new generation of jellyfish larvae
- The transdifferentiation of somatic (body) cells from one (mature) type to new types, that make up a rejuvenated body
- The apparent "negligible senescence" (to varying degrees) of diverse organisms such as rockfish, turtles, bowhead whales, clams, albatrosses and petrels, naked mole-rats, and (most impressively) bristlecone pine trees
- The regeneration of new limbs, tails, jaws, spinal cords, and parts of the heart, in salamanders.

What's more, scientists keep finding additional natural mechanisms in cases where, previously, it seemed that biology had hit a dead end. For instance, it was widely thought for many decades that some key parts of the body lacked the ability for cellular regeneration. The brain was singled out as a particular example: it was commonly said that, once a brain had grown to its full size, in an adult body, there would be no new cells created in it. As explained by psychiatrist Norman Doidge, author of the book "The brain that changes itself"[102]:

> For four hundred years... mainstream medicine and science believed that brain anatomy was fixed. The common wisdom was that after childhood the brain changed only when it began the long process of decline; that when brain cells failed to develop properly, or were injured, or died, they could not be replaced. Nor could the brain ever alter its structure and find a new way to function if part of it was damaged. The theory of the unchanging brain decreed that people who were born with brain or mental limitations, or who sustained brain damage, would be limited or damaged for life. Scientists who wondered if the healthy brain might be improved or preserved through activity or mental exercise were told not to waste their time.

A neurological nihilism—a sense that treatment for many brain problems was ineffective or even unwarranted—had taken hold, and it spread through our culture...

But in more recent years, contra to what Doidge labels "the doctrine of the unchanging brain", overwhelming evidence has arisen that the adult brain features many elements of neurogenesis (the creation of new brain cells) and neuroplasticity (the transformation of functions of parts of the brain). It's another sign that biology is capable of greater amounts of regeneration than first appears to be the case. It's another sign that sceptics ought to become more open-minded about the prospects for rejuveneering.

Accordingly, nature provides many tools to aspiring rejuveneers. The next part of the argument, against the view that even huge amounts of science and technology will fail to deliver practical rejuveneering, is the growing evidence of ways in which engineering interventions are utilising, modifying, and re-combining these tools, to extend and amplify the results already observed in nature.

Let's start with the ability to regenerate a new head. Some animals possess the remarkable ability to regrow their heads – or, at least, their brains – if the original is removed. This includes tadpoles (but not adult frogs), salamanders, zebrafish, and *some* species of flatworms.

The worm with the scientific name *Schmidtea mediterranea* has excellent regeneration capabilities. As noted in July 2013[103] by research group leader Jochen Rink of the Max Planck Institute of Molecular Cell Biology and Genetics in Dresden:

We can cut the worm to 200 pieces, and 200 new worms will regenerate from each and every piece.

However, other species of worm lack this capability. The flatworm *Dendrocoelum lacteum* cannot regenerate a new head, if cut into two. The article from the Max Planck Institute continues,

Even though it is a close cousin of the regeneration master *Schmidtea mediterranea*, this species had been reported to be incapable of regenerating heads from its posterior body half. "What's the salient difference between the two cousins?" the researcher asked.

What might it take, to enable *Dendrocoelum lacteum* worms to be able to grow a new head too? Because of the seemingly hugely complicated task of rebuilding a head – including a brain, eyes, and nerve connections in between – Rink's team had expected it would take a great deal of genetic manipulation in order to support this functionality in other worms. However, genetic engineering confounded expectations:

> Together with researchers from the Center for Regenerative Therapies Dresden, Rink's team searched for an answer amongst the genes of the two species, focusing on the so-called Wnt-signalling pathway. Like a cable link between two computers, signalling pathways transmit information between cells. The Dresden researchers inhibited the signal transducer of the Wnt pathway with RNAi and thus made the cells of the worm believe that the signalling pathway had been switched to 'off'. Consequently, *Dendrocoelum lacteum* were able to grow a fully functional head everywhere, even when cut at the very tail.

The research article concludes as follows:

> Jochen Rink is stunned: "We thought we would have to manipulate hundreds of different switches to repair a regeneration defect; now we learned that sometimes only a few nodes may do". Will this knowledge soon be applicable to more complex organisms – like humans, for example? "We showed that by comparisons amongst related species we can obtain insights into why some animals regenerate while others don't – that's an important first step".

Next, let's look at a different example of what genetic engineering can accomplish, in terms of improved rejuvenation capabilities. In this case, the animal in question is a mammal – a strain of lab mouse. In November 2013, the Scientific American reported the work[104] of George Daley of Children's Hospital Boston and Harvard Medical School. He was experimenting with a set of lab mice, in which a gene known as Lin28a remains active after birth. (This gene normally shuts down when a mouse is born, but in this line of mice, genetic engineering resulted in its continued expression.) These mice, exceptionally, have the ability to repair holes in their ears, tips cut off their toes, and portions of their fur that have been waxed off.

But that's only the start of the story. Having noticed the effect, Daley's team found they could obtain the same result even in mice that lacked this genetic change, by means of administering certain drugs:

> The team found they could replicate the healing abilities of the engineered mice by giving nongenetically altered ones drugs that help activate certain metabolic processes—the same pathway Lin28a stimulates—revving up and energizing cells as if they were much younger.

That example highlights an important general principle:

- Certain biological capabilities tend to lie dormant, non-activated, within organisms
- In some cases, genetic changes can trigger these capabilities, resulting in body repair mechanisms
- Once a biological repair mechanism has been understood, it can often be duplicated – or even improved – by means of other sorts of engineering intervention.

Consider growing a new heart – something that is of immense interest to doctors who lack sufficient numbers of donated hearts for transplant purposes. Several thousand patients in the USA alone are on the waiting list for a heart transplant[105]. It has been possible for over a decade to grow groups of heart cells, from a starting point of embryonic stem cells, into a mass of cells in a lab dish that can beat in synchrony. What's harder is ensuring the right structure for these cells to operate as a new heart, and the right network of embedded capillaries to remove waste products and to supply nutrients and oxygen. Two possible options involve:

- 3D printing, with micro-control over location of added elements
- Using an existing heart structure – taken from someone who is dead, or even from a different animal (such as a pig) – to provide the framework for the new cells to grow.

The latter procedure is described in a July 2013 article in Nature[106], written by Brendan Maher, describing the work of Doris Taylor from the Texas Heart Institute in Houston:

> Taylor is in the vanguard of researchers looking to engineer entire new organs, to enable transplants without the risk of rejection by the recipient's immune system. The strategy is simple enough in principle. First remove all the cells from a dead organ — it does not even have to be from a human — then take the protein scaffold left behind and repopulate it with stem cells immunologically matched to the patient in need. *Voilà!* The crippling shortage of transplantable organs around the world is solved...
>
> The leading techniques for would-be heart builders generally involve reusing what biology has already created. One good place to see how this is done is Massachusetts General Hospital in Boston, where Harald Ott, a surgeon and regenerative-medicine researcher, demonstrates a method that he developed while training under Taylor in the mid 2000s.

Suspended by plastic tubes in a drum-shaped chamber made of glass and plastic is a fresh human heart. Nearby is a pump that is quietly pushing detergent through a tube running into the heart's aorta. The flow forces the aortic valve closed and sends the detergent through the network of blood vessels that fed the muscle until its owner died a few days before. Over the course of about a week, explains Ott, this flow of detergent will strip away lipids, DNA, soluble proteins, sugars and almost all the other cellular material from the heart, leaving only a pale mesh of collagen, laminins and other structural proteins: the 'extracellular matrix' that once held the organ together.

To be clear, this engineering process involves solving hard problems:

The tricky part, Ott says, is to make sure that the detergent dissolves just the right amount of material. Strip away too little, and the matrix might retain some of the cell-surface molecules that can lead to rejection by the recipient's immune system. Strip away too much, and it could lose vital proteins and growth factors that tell newly introduced cells where to adhere and how to behave.

But it's the nature of engineering to have to solve difficult issues of quantification and control. Teams led by Ott and Taylor have already produced some encouraging early results with new hearts for rats.

Other replacements for failing human organs might depart further from the original biological template. This is especially the case for organs that serve more than one purpose. For example, the kidney filters waste from the body, as well as regulating the concentration in the body of various ions such as potassium, sodium, and phosphate. Gabor Forgacs, Professor of Biological Physics at the University of Missouri-Columbia, is a pioneer of 3D bio-printing. In a 2011 interview with PopTech[107], Forgacs explained his thinking about creating synthetic replacements for human organs such as the kidney:

We don't have to reproduce exactly the same kidney that you have in your body, which ... is the result of many millions of years of evolution. The kidney is a complex organ but one of its major functions is to rid the body of toxins. If we just concentrate on that function, I see no reason why we would not be able to build from the patient's own cells a structure that can perform the same function. This structure will not look like a kidney and it will not mimic or resemble 100% that kidney that we carry in our body...

If I can come up with a structure from your own cells – so I put it in your body and there is no immunological reaction and that structure performs the same function as far as ridding the body of toxins – then I accomplished my goal. It's a very important realization that that's what we'll be able to do in the future. Maybe not in the too distant future. Don't ask me when exactly because I don't know. But this is my vision of regenerative medicine.

Forgac has founded a company, Organovo, to carry out that vision. As an important intermediate step, the company is providing its services to the pharmaceutical industry, to accelerate the process of determining whether new drugs might prove toxic to human organs. As reported by Caitlin McCabe in the Wall Street Journal[108] in February 2015:

Every year, the pharmaceutical industry spends more than $50 billion on research and development. But the path to drug approval by the Food and Drug Administration is laden with abrupt failures in late-phase testing. Only one in 5,000 drugs will make it to market, according to one estimate.

One small biology company believes it has a solution to the pipeline problem: 3-D printing.

At San Diego-based Organovo Holdings Inc., the idea is to predict the toxicity of a drug in its earliest days by testing it on real, living human liver tissue—created at the click of a button with a 3-D printer. For 42 days the slivers of tissue will respond to drugs the same way a full-size human liver would. According to Organovo, this trumps current methods of early-stage drug trials, including petri dishes of cells—which stop functioning like livers after a few days—and animals, which don't consistently react to drugs as a patient would.

Examples of hybrid engineering

Yet another engineering technique which can advance over the unaided mechanisms of nature is to use the healthy services of one animal to develop or repair cells from a different animal. As far back as 1998, John Critser of Purdue University collected a batch of ovarian tissue from some African elephants that had recently been killed. The tissue was frozen, transported to labs, and, a year later, it transplanted into specially bred lab mice – mice which had been selected to be tolerant to foreign tissue. The result in at least one case was that a mouse produced an elephant egg[109] (although the egg was not viable to develop into an actual elephant). One implication of this research is that, when trying to create new young animals from an endangered species, it could be sufficient to start with ovarian tissue, rather than an egg (which is often harder to obtain).

Mice can also be used to help grow replacement human cornea (the white of an eye). In good health, the cornea is kept transparent by the operation of certain kinds of stem cells within the eye – limbal stem cells. But if the eye is damaged, by disease, by spillage of chemicals, or by burning, a shortage of these stem cells can result in cloudy vision, other visual distortions, and even blindness. Research published in July 2014[110] by the Massachusetts Eye and Ear Institute, along with other partners, reported on a breakthrough in treating this condition. Thanks to an improved technique to identify limbal stem cells within the eyes of deceased human donors, these cells can now be collected efficiently and transplanted into mice. The recipient animals then grew fully functioning human corneas, ready for transplant back into humans awaiting corneal reconstruction.

The longer-term goal in all these cases is to avoid the need for intermediate lab animals altogether. This should become possible once the relevant biological processes have been more fully understood. It remains an open question to which extent replacement tissues need to have a biological origin as opposed to a mechanical origin (such as a replacement hip, a replacement knee, or a replacement eye lens).

Along similar lines, there is evidence[111] that transfusing blood from younger animals into older animals can, on occasion, produce renewed vigour in the older animal. These experiments initially involved the technique of parabiosis, in which two animals (one young, and one old) have parts of their skin surgically stitched together, obliging the animals (typically rats) to move around together, akin to Siamese twins. Blood from the old animal flows into its young partner, and vice versa. The result, in experiments that have been carried out from the 1950s onwards, is that aspects of the old rat, when studied under a microscope, appeared rejuvenated

- Their livers and muscles looked younger
- Their hearts were stronger
- Their sense of smell improved
- Their memory was sharper, indicating improvements in the brain, too.

Unfortunately for the younger rats, they, conversely, prematurely aged.

A 2014 letter to Nature, with lead author Saul Villeda of the University of California San Francisco, entitled "Young blood reverses age-related impairments in cognitive function and synaptic plasticity in mice"[112], reported on recent breakthroughs in understanding some of the mechanisms involved:

> Our data demonstrate that exposure to young blood counteracts aging at the molecular, structural, functional, and cognitive levels in the aged hippocampus [part of the brain]... Cognitive improvements elicited by young blood may not be limited to neurogenesis but may also be due to enhancements in synaptic plasticity.

The letter expressed due caution at extrapolating these results from rodents to human, but recommended continued experiments:

> It is important to consider that the results of this study are currently limited to aged mice; however future studies are warranted in aged humans and potentially those suffering from aged-related neurodegenerative disorders.

Examples of nano-engineering

Something else that can be repurposed for positive results, by medical engineering, is the set of viruses which, in previous eras, caused numerous dreadful diseases. With cunning alterations, these viruses can now be used to attack, not the body as a whole, but cancerous growths. For example, molecular biologist Matthias Gromeier at Duke University has altered the polio virus, removing a genetic sequence so that the virus can no longer reproduce in normal cells. However, that virus still does reproduce *inside cancerous growths*, thereby weakening the cancer to the point that the patient's immune system is spurred to recognise the danger and to finish the task of defeating the tumour. Using this technique, Duke University has achieved spectacular results[113] in the treatment of glioblastoma, a particularly nasty form of brain cancer. It's a stunning vindication of the engineering approach.

A different use of specially re-engineered DNA is as a packaging vehicle for a medical payload, such as a drug that needs to be delivered to a specific target location. In this case, the technique has been called "DNA origami", since the DNA sequence is chosen in order that the molecule folds (upon heating and cooling) in a particular way. It is also an example of nano-engineering, since the engineering takes place at the nanometre scale.

A news article[114] from the Ohio State University describes an encouraging application of DNA origami to overcome drug resistance:

> Researchers at The Ohio State University are working on a new way to treat drug-resistant cancer that the ancient Greeks would approve of—only it's not a Trojan horse, but DNA that hides the invading force.
>
> In this case, the invading force is a common cancer drug.
>
> In laboratory tests, leukaemia cells that had become resistant to the drug absorbed it and died when the drug was hidden in a capsule made of folded up DNA.

The article quoted the two researchers from that university who led the cross-disciplinary investigation, mechanical engineering professor Carlos Castro and haematology director John Byrd:

> The study involved a pre-clinical model of acute myeloid leukaemia (AML) that has developed resistance against the drug daunorubicin. Specifically, when molecules of daunorubicin enter an AML cell, the cell recognizes them and pumps them back out through openings in the cell wall...
>
> "Cancer cells have novel ways of resisting drugs, like these pumps, and the exciting part of packaging the drug this way is that we can circumvent those defences so that the drug accumulates in the cancer cell and causes it to die," said Byrd... "Potentially, we can also tailor these structures to make them deliver drugs selectively to cancer cells and not to other parts of the body where they can cause side effects."
>
> "DNA origami nanostructures have a lot of potential for drug delivery, not just for making effective drug delivery vehicles, but enabling new ways to study drug delivery. For instance, we can vary the shape or mechanical stiffness of a structure very precisely and see how that affects entry into cells," said Castro.

To be clear, in this technique, the chosen string of DNA serves a purpose only through its three-dimensional structure – not via any biological interactions (such as creating proteins). The biological interaction is due to the payload which has been carried along inside the DNA packaging.

This example is part of a growing move towards more extensive use of "nano-machines" and "nano-surgery". Another recent example[115] is from the laboratory of Professor Hendrik Dietz at the Technical University of Munich:

Dietz lab's latest DNA nanomachines demonstrate dynamics and precision: Nanoscale rotor and gripper push DNA origami to new limits

Scientists at the Technical University of Munich (TUM) have built two new nanoscale machines with moving parts, using DNA as a programmable, self-assembling construction material. In the journal Science Advances, they describe a rotor mechanism formed from interlocking 3-D DNA components. Another recent paper, in Nature Nanotechnology, reported a hinged molecular manipulator, also made from DNA. These are just the latest steps in a campaign to transform so-called "DNA origami" into an industrially useful, commercially viable technology.

Inspired by nature's nanomachines – such as the enzyme ATP synthase and the motor-driven flagella of bacteria – physicists in Prof. Hendrik Dietz's lab at TUM keep expanding their own design and construction repertoire. They have systematically developed rules and procedures for creating self-assembled DNA origami structures with ever greater flexibility and control. Moving from DNA basepair matching to shape-complementary building techniques – with a variety of interlocking "bricks" – the researchers' toolkit has advanced steadily in the direction of higher-level programming and modular assembly.

Striking medical uses of even smaller nanomachines were reviewed in a 2015 TEDx talk by Sabine Hauert[116], a lecturer in robotics at the University of Bristol. The talk, entitled "Swarming Nanomedicine"[117], provides intriguing examples of the application of principles of "swarming" as demonstrated by flocks of birds. Similar principles can be used to control the collective migration of huge numbers of nano-particles inside biological tissue.

All the signs are that medical nano-engineering is a field with a great future ahead of it.

Examples of better genetics

The final set of engineering solutions that will be noted here refer to the field which biologist George Williams was convinced would be impossible: changes in genes that, in turn, have big effects, not only on longevity, but in healthspan. Evidence has been accumulating in the last few decades about numerous so-called "gerontogenes" – genes that, when altered, can extend the lifespan of members of a species beyond the normal limits for that species. Such genes have been positively identified in yeast, earthworms, fruitflies, mice, and rats. Within humans, a gene known as FOXO3 is found unusually often in centenarians. A 2008 article in the Proceedings of the National Academy of Sciences[118], with lead author Bradley Willcox of Queen's Medical Center, Honolulu, was entitled "FOXO3A genotype is strongly associated with human longevity". According to the paper, people with two copies of a particular variant of this gene are three times as likely to live to the age of one hundred. Here's the conclusion of the paper:

> In summary, we found that common, natural genetic variation within the FOXO3A gene was strongly associated with human longevity and was also associated with several phenotypes of healthy aging. Further study of FOXO genes and aging phenotypes is warranted in other populations.

Another example is in a species of mice known as the Ames Dwarf Mouse. A single genetic change affects the operation of the pituitary gland, reducing the amount of growth hormone produced by the animal. As a result, the animals are smaller than their littermates, but live 40%-60% longer. This additional longevity seems to be independent of the diet fed to the animals.

A different kind of genetic change in a mouse is when the animal creates more than usual of an enzyme known as telomerase. This enzyme in turn extends the "telomeres" – the ends of chromosomes – during cell division. This allows cells to divide a greater number of times, rather than this process of division stopping due to the telomeres becoming too short. A team led by Maria Blasco at the Centro Nacional de Investigaciones Oncológicas, Madrid, shared some results in 2012, in a paper entitled "Telomerase gene therapy in adult and old mice delays aging and increases longevity without increasing cancer"[119]:

> A major goal in aging research is to improve health during aging. In the case of mice, genetic manipulations that shorten or lengthen telomeres result, respectively, in decreased or increased longevity. Based on this, we have tested the effects of a telomerase gene therapy in adult (1 year of age) and old (2 years of age) mice…

The genetic change is administered via an "adeno associated virus". As the paper noted, this change

> …had remarkable beneficial effects on health and fitness, including insulin sensitivity, osteoporosis, neuromuscular coordination and several molecular biomarkers of aging. Importantly, telomerase- treated mice did

not develop more cancer than their control littermates... Finally, telomerase- treated mice, both at 1- year and at 2- year of age, had an increase in median lifespan of 24 and 13%, respectively...

Together, these results constitute a proof- of- principle of... delaying physiological aging and extending longevity in normal mice through a telomerase- based treatment, and demonstrate the feasibility of anti- aging gene therapy.

It is for good reason that blogger Dave Woynarowski, known as "Dr Dave", responded with great enthusiasm[120] to these results:

OK, the BIG BANG study of the year is Dr Blasco's latest study and it is gigantic for several reasons.

First, it uses telomerase therapy and markedly extends the life spans of adult mice (24% longer lived) and old, old mice (14% longer lived) with a single (yep, that is one time) injection of telomerase therapy. Next, it uses viral transfection, to insert the telomerase gene, a method that had heretofore, increased the risk of cancer. Now, it can be done with no risk of increasing cancer...

It is important to note that the mice were allowed to accumulate the damage of aging to adult and old age, before they were treated. Then, when they were already "damaged by aging" they were treated and got better!

The mention of the increased risk of cancer, often associated with increased telomerase, is a reminder of the set of "trade-off" arguments that can be advanced that rejuveneering is an inherently doomed enterprise. These arguments state that any changes in genes which improve longevity are very likely to have some drawbacks – otherwise natural selection would have favoured these changes earlier in biological history:

- Genes that express more telomerase are likely, other things being equal, to cause an increase in cancer
- Genes that cause Ames dwarf mice to be able to live longer in laboratory conditions also make these rodents significantly smaller, and therefore potentially more vulnerable to environmental hazards.

However, as noted above, there seem to be ways around these trade-offs. The mice studied by Maria Blasco avoided falling victim to cancer, despite having more telemorase. And there are some gerontogenes, such as FOXO3 as studied by Bradley Willcox, which appear to result in positive health benefits without any known drawbacks. Even if drawbacks do occur, in new circumstances, it will be the task of engineering to address any such side-effects. This is in line with the general formulation of rejuveneering as characterised in this book: it will involve a suite of different therapies, rather than a single intervention.

More than marginal improvements

It is worth briefly considering one further counter-argument as to the technical feasibility of rejuveneering. In this view, each innovative medical intervention might only gain a marginal improvement. One treatment – one, say, which mimics the effect of the FOXO3 gene – might push up healthy life expectancy by three to five years. Another treatment might conceivably push it up another 12 to 18 months. These treatments would be welcome, for all kinds of reason, but they might have limited cumulative effect. Rather than enabling indefinite rejuvenation, they might enable the maximum human lifespan to reach, say, 130 years, and no more.

My response is to say: I see no such inherent limit in nature. If the rougheye rockfish can live for 205 years with negligible senescence, why not humans? If the bristlecone pine can live for 4,713 years with negligible senescence, why not humans? If the naked mole-rat can live without cancer, why not humans?

Of course, there are many practical differences in the biology of these different species, but the evidence of the engineering success stories listed above (and which form only a fraction of what a longer view of recent research would show) is that human biology is malleable. We can, in principle, re-engineer our biology, improving its operation, so that regeneration operates much more widely.

The remaining question is: what is the *scale* of the research and development required, to create the requirement treatments? Although the complexity multiplication factor (N) may not be infinite, it could be very large. That is, the effort to enable indefinitely repeatable rejuvenation might be one million, or even one billion, times harder than the effort to enable human powered flight. In which case, won't it take a million, or even a billion, times longer to complete that project?

We'll pick up that argument in the next chapter. But first, let's reflect on one final notable intersection between the two great projects of human flight and human rejuvenation. That intersection is in the person of Charles Lindbergh.

The legacy of a pioneer of flight

Charles Lindbergh was catapulted into public fame in May 1927, when, in his airplane *Spirit of St. Louis*, he became the first person to fly single-handedly across the Atlantic. The effort took 33 and a half hours, and considerable bravery: six aviators had already lost their lives in earlier attempts to win the "Orteig" prize of $25,000 for the pilot of the first non-stop flight made in either direction between Paris and New York. Crowds of motor cars which travelled from all around Paris to the airfield, some seven miles outside the city, to observe Lindbergh landing, caused what has been described as "the largest traffic jam in Parisian history".

The 25-year old Lindbergh received numerous honours for his pioneering flight, including the *Légion d'honneur* from French President Gaston Doumergue, and the Distinguished Flying Cross from American President Calvin Coolidge. He was also the first person named by *Time* magazine as their person of the year (in 1927) – and he remains, to the present day, the youngest person to receive that nomination. The aviation industry owed him a large debt, with public confidence in the fledgling industry receiving a huge boost from all of Lindbergh's publicity. After Lindbergh, no-one could deny the reality of powered human flight. To be sure, it remained a dangerous mode of travel, but everyone could see that great strides of progress were being taken – in a technology area which, just two decades earlier, had been widely derided by the experts of that time as a bogus fantasy.

Five years later, Lindbergh experienced the horror of having his infant son kidnapped. The child's body was discovered, dead, two months later. The resulting detective investigation and criminal trial generated huge publicity. In view of the public interest, newspapers dubbed the case "The crime of the century". Newspaper critic H.L. Mencken went one step further, describing the episode as "the biggest story since the Resurrection".

Conquering a widespread cause of death was, as it happens, a passionate and long-standing interest of Lindbergh – one that pre-dated the kidnapping of his son. Mencken may not have known it, but the subject of "resurrection" was never too far away from Lindberg's mind. One trigger for Lindbergh's interest was the persistent heart problems experienced by

Elisabeth, the elder sister of his wife, Anne Morrow. As Lindbergh recounted in his book "Autobiography of values"[121], published posthumously:

> My experimental interests were channelled, as so often happens, by a chance development of life—by the illness of my wife's older sister, Elisabeth. She had contracted rheumatic fever as a secondary complication of pneumonia. A lesion had developed in her heart, restricting her activities until her doctor recommended a year of complete rest in bed. Since a remedial operation of the heart was impossible, he said, her life would be limited both in activity and length. I asked him why surgery would not be effective. He said the heart could not be stopped long enough for an operation to be performed because blood had to be kept circulating through the body. I asked why a mechanical heart could not maintain the blood circulation temporarily while the heart was being operated on. He replied that he did not know. He had never heard of a mechanical heart being used.

Lindbergh's interest in a mechanical pump was aligned with his personal observation of the extraordinary wonders that engineering could accomplish. He had been the first person in history to be in New York on one day and in Paris the next. He had designed his own plane, *Spirit of St. Louis*, taking account of the need to carry huge amounts of fuel for his globe-striding voyage. The plane had skimmed across the Atlantic, sometimes only a few feet above the crests of the wave, repeatedly defying the ancient downward pull of gravity, until the very end of his journey, when he had landed to rapturous acclaim.

More specifically, Lindbergh had long personal experience with valves, pumps, and filters, dating back to his childhood days on the family farm, when he regularly used to repair his father's car – which he also drove far and wide on the open road. The precocious driver-mechanic was only twelve years old at that time. The young Lindbergh had also learned about synthetic replacements of body parts from his maternal grandfather, who was a pioneering dental surgeon. Why, he wondered, couldn't bio-engineering facilitate improvements to the valves, pumps, and filters inside the human body?

Lindbergh's earlier flying career had been fraught with difficulties. Several times he had to parachute out of mail airplanes he was piloting, to live to fly another day, as the planes crashed to the ground. By human fortitude, and by taking smart advantage of the output of science and engineering, Lindbergh had overcome all these difficulties. Wrestling with weak human organs, such as a failing heart, would be a difficult challenge too, no doubt, but Lindbergh was not someone to easily accept 'No' for an answer.

Lindbergh kept asking medical professionals about his idea for a mechanical heart. The night in 1930 his wife Anne gave birth to their first child – the boy who would be tragically murdered just twenty months later – Lindbergh quizzed the anaesthetist who was attending to his wife. Was the anaesthetist aware of anyone who could act on Lindbergh's ambitious ideas? In this way, Lindbergh came to be introduced to 1912 Nobel prize-winner Alexis Carrel (the first American to have been awarded a Nobel Prize). The two men found they had a common intuition that smart machinery could reverse the ravages of disease and aging. They were ready to view the human body as something which engineering could improve: organs that stopped working properly could be repaired by mechanical intervention. They commenced a long partnership, based at the Rockefeller Institute in Manhattan, New York.

As reported in a 2008 BBC News Magazine article, "Lindbergh's deranged quest for immortality"[122]:

> At the Rockefeller lab, Lindbergh and Carrel... made some extraordinary breakthroughs.
>
> Lindbergh created something that Carrel's team had singularly failed to: a perfusion pump that could keep a human organ alive outside of the body. It was called the "Model T" pump. In later years, Lindbergh's pump was further developed by others, eventually leading to the construction of the first heart-lung machine.

The BBC article goes on to quote David Friedman, the author of a fascinating book on Lindbergh and Carrel, "The Immortalists: Charles Lindbergh, Dr. Alexis Carrel, and Their Daring Quest to Live Forever"[123]:

> Friedman says Lindbergh considered himself a "superior being". "Let's not forget that, as a pilot, he felt he had escaped the chains of mortality. He had had a god-like experience. He flew amongst the clouds, often in a cockpit that was open to the elements. Flying was such a rare experience back then. In taking to the skies, he did something humans have dreamt of for centuries. So it is perhaps not surprising that he ended up trying to play god in a laboratory."

By some measures, Lindbergh's project to address the problems of weak hearts must be judged a failure. His sister-in-law Elisabeth died, from complications arising from her weak heart, in 1934. She was just 30 years old. The heart-lung machine that was inspired by Lindbergh's work came far too late for her.

We can say that Lindbergh misjudged the time-scale required for the project he and Carrel envisaged: synthetic replacements for failing human organs. His precipitous rise to success in the world of air flight was not to be matched by an equally fast impact in the world of human rejuvenation. The two great projects have a lot in common, but they are poles apart in terms of the scale of effort required. Whereas human flight was a hard, hard problem to solve, human rejuvenation is a hard, hard, hard, hard… hard, hard, hard problem.

There might even be a million dots in the expanded version of that last sentence. In the next chapter, I'll argue that, nevertheless, there's a reasonable chance that the second problem will have been largely solved in just 25 years' time.

5. Scaling up

As we've seen, the rejuvenation project has powerful tools at its disposal:

- Regenerative techniques that are already used in nature, and which can be applied in new circumstances
- New biological pathways that nature can be coaxed into following
- Small-scale and large-scale add-ins, ranging from nanobots to 3D-printed structures.

New food supplements, genetic reprogramming, improved synthetic organs, repurposing of viruses – these are all part of the expanding arsenal of the growing international community of rejuveneers. Moreover, new *kinds* of tools are regularly being discussed which would give even more capability to the arsenal. Momentum seems to be building.

Is it, therefore, only a matter of time before the rejuveneering project achieves its vision, with the creation of a suite of affordable treatments that will allow everyone to roll back the onset of aging, as many times as they wish?

There are three main responses to that question. The first response is that, *yes*, we can extrapolate relatively straightforwardly from the medical advances of the last century, which have doubled life expectancy in many areas of the world. Science has worked wonders in the recent past, and will continue to work wonders over the next few decades.

The second response is that, *no*, all the low-hanging fruits of this project have already been picked: childhood vaccinations, improved hygiene, campaigns against smoking, better nutrition, the invention of antibiotics, and so on. Therefore we cannot extrapolate from the past improvements – impressive though they are – to a near-future time in which life expectancy doubles again. That next phase of progress will require *much* more effort than in the past. It's not something we're likely to see for, say, at least a hundred years.

The third response, as I'll explain in this and the following chapter, is a kind of combination of both the previous viewpoints. It's the one I think is correct. In this view, the next stage in extending healthy lifespan will indeed be much harder than the progress that has already been achieved: perhaps even one million times harder. (To that extent, the second response is correct.) But that doesn't mean it will take one million times as long. Instead, progress will accelerate, in line with the general exponential trends which are doing so much to speed up the flow of new inventions. Rather than taking centuries, the required breakthroughs may be with us within just a few decades. (To that extent, the second response is incorrect, and the first is closer to the truth.)

Indeed, history is accelerating. If, hypothetically, someone had fallen into a deep coma in, say, the year 900AD, and woke up in 1400AD, five whole centuries later, he or she wouldn't notice much that was different. There would probably be a few differences in accent or language, but comparatively few changes in technology, in social structure, and in prevailing patterns of thought. In contrast, if someone had fallen asleep in 1966 and woke up in 2016 – five *decades* later – what a difference they'd notice. There are big, flat, electronic screens everywhere, displaying video advertising. There are small screens everywhere, with people regularly consulting them. Supermarkets have been transformed, with self-service checkouts operated by a kind of robot. Same-sex marriages are widely tolerated. The UK has had a woman prime minister. The US "first family", in the White House, is black.

Exponential progress

Let's look at some additional examples of exponential change and the acceleration of history.

The earliest known surviving photograph dates from 1826. Taken by Nicéphore Niépce, who had earlier held an officer's position inside Napoleon's army, it bears the name *View from the Window at Le Gras*. For many decades, photography was a time-consuming, labour intensive practice. It was only after the invention of the easy-to-operate Kodak "Brownie" camera in 1900 that the habit of photography became more widespread. By the 1930s, one hundred years after Niépce's pioneering photographs, the number of photographs taken each year had risen to around one billion, due to low cost of cameras, and a popular culture which took delight in photographs of babies, children, weddings, and other family settings.

A naïve extrapolation of that trend would predict that it might take another hundred years to reach the figure of two billion photographs being taken each year – and perhaps one thousand years to reach ten billion per year. Instead, it is estimated[124] that ten billion photographs were being taken each year *by as early as 1970*.

Jump forward to 2014, and the report on Internet trends[125] issued by Mary Meeker of KPCB. This report gives the number of photos that were uploaded *every day* to Facebook, in 2012, as 300 million. That's one hundred billion per year. By 2013, taking into account uploads by other applications, like Instagram, Snapchat, and WhatsApp, the daily figure had soared four-fold – to 1.2B photo uploads every day. And by May of 2014, when Mary Meeker issued her report, the daily figure was 1.8B uploads.

Expressed another way, people nowadays take as many photographs, every two minutes, as the total number of photographs taken in the entire 1800s.

In broad terms, this growth follows an exponential curve. Numbers which previously already seemed to be large – one billion photos taken in a year by 1930 – shrink into comparative insignificance as more time passes. The reasons for the dramatic rise in the number of photographs taken are that:

- Previous complications with the photography process are eliminated – especially with the transition from analogue (film) to digital (electronic) photography
- Photography capabilities have been included in devices – smartphones – that more and more people, all over the world, carry with them wherever they go
- These devices make it easy, not only for people to take photos (at only a moment's notice), but also to share them with friends and colleagues; this instant shareability is another factor encouraging people to take many photographs.

As for photography, so also for many other trends. Cooper's Law[126] – named after Martin Cooper, one of the pioneers of the mobile phone industry – describes the increasing efficiency with which technology enables transmission of information (whether voice or data) by wireless protocols over the air. The number of low-level data "conversations" that can take place in a given area, over radio spectrum, has consistently doubled, doubled, and doubled again, ever since Marconi's experiments in the south of England in 1895. The average doubling period works out to around 30 months. That's equivalent to a million-fold improvement over 50 years –

and to a trillion-fold improvement over 100 years. Similar improvements also apply to the computational efficiency of integrated circuits, under what is known as Moore's Law. This time, the doubling period turns out to be 18 months. That's a billion-fold improvement over the 50 years since the first statement of Moore's Law (in 1965).

In both cases – Cooper's Law and Moore's Law – the steady improvements reflect the conjunction of three phenomena:

1. The physical possibility of further improvements in the hardware
2. The willingness and capability of large companies to invest growing numbers of highly skilled resources in research to incrementally improve our engineering grasp of the hardware possibilities
3. The desire of the marketplace to purchase goods which take advantage of improved hardware.

For another example of exponential growth, consider the growth in the number of trained software developers in the world. Ada Lovelace, the mathematician daughter of the English poet Lord Byron, is generally credited as being the world's first software developer: in 1843 she published an algorithm for the Analytic Engine of Charles Babbage to calculate a set of mathematical numbers known as Bernoulli numbers. By 2013, according to a report[127] issued by the research firm IDC, there were 18.5 million software developers in the world, consisting of 11 million professional developers and another 7.5 million hobbyists. This growth from one to 18.5 million was far from being linear (constant-paced), but had many exponential aspects:

- When the world had very few computers, there was little need for software developers
- As the number of computers has grown, the number of software developers has increased in parallel
- The spread of books, magazines, online training courses, and knowledgeable instructors, means that it has become increasingly easy for people to acquire skills in software development
- With the help of software tools, the effectiveness of single software developers has jumped upwards: small teams can nowadays create huge software programmes.

Growing numbers of rejuvenation engineers

As for software engineers, so also for rejuvenation engineers. With a potential ten-fold increase each decade in the number of rejuvenation engineers, starting from (say) 1980, an accumulated million-fold increase could be attained after six decades – that is, by 2040. There may well be millions of people working in that field in the run up to 2040. That's how, in principle, a problem that is one million times harder might be solved within sixty years from the start of serious work on it.

Where might all these millions of rejuvenation engineers come from? It's the same as with the growth of software engineers: they'll come from many, many sources – from the many, many industries that could be impacted (for better or for worse) by the new technology.

Specifically, increasing numbers of people from the following sectors are likely to become at least part-time rejuvenation engineers:

- The cosmetics industry – as companies seek to extend the effectiveness of their products, from just making people *look* younger (on the outside), to making people *actually* younger (on the inside as well as on the outside)
- The military – to help the swift recuperation of injured soldiers
- The food industry – to answer consumer demands for food that not only tastes good but which demonstrably has positive side-effects on health
- The sports industry – to keep sportspeople at the peak of their physical performance for longer
- The pharmaceutical industry – to apply rejuvenation treatments for specific diseases, as well as for general healthcare
- The IT industry – as more and more parts of healthcare become recognised as challenges for information technology (such as big data analytics).

It won't only be full-time professionals who become involved in this burgeoning sector. At least as many people, again, will be active as "citizen scientist rejuveneers". These are people who:

- May be retired, semi-retired, or unable to find full-time work
- Pursue study of regenerative medicine for personal reasons, rather than as part of their main career

- Can benefit from the quickly growing set of online resources by which they can learn more and more of the relevant science and engineering
- Take part in online discussions, reviews, and projects
- Publish their own findings, including verifications and critiques of work done by others, and their own original research.

What lies behind this potential swift growth in the number of rejuvenation engineers will be a combination of four factors:

1. The recognition that the underlying science is tractable – there are no firm limits to the possibility of rejuveneering
2. The recognition that progress is actually happening, step-by-step, rather than being a far-off dream
3. The recognition that there are strong moral and financial arguments in favour of accelerating progress on rejuveneering
4. The recognition that there are concrete ways in which new participants in the field can make a significant net positive difference to the rate of progress.

The first of these points was the subject of the previous chapter. The second point has been illustrated by a number of examples already in this book, and there will be many more in the pages ahead. The third point – the moral and financial arguments – will be the subject of later chapters. For now, let's dig into possibly the most controversial of the four claims – the last one.

The reason it's a controversial claim is because there are many examples when having more people working in a field actually slows down overall progress, rather than speeding it up. This observation is captured in the common proverb "Too many cooks spoil the broth". It's also referred to as "Brooks' Law", after Fred Brooks, the author of the classic volume of reflections on software engineering, "The Mythical Man-Month"[128].

Brooks worked for many decades at computing giant IBM from the 1950s onwards. "The Mythical Man-Month", published in 1975, summarises Brooks' observations from his experiences leading development of IBM's System/360 family of computers, as well as its OS/360 software support package. The statement which has come to be known as Brooks' Law is that

Adding manpower to a late project makes it later.

After all, the more people who work in a field, the greater is the effort needed to:

- Coordinate between everyone involved – keeping communications up-to-date

- Train newcomers (without distracting the people who are presently doing the "real work")

- Identify the valuable "signal" in research findings, which is at risk from being swamped by huge amounts of low-quality work.

Famously, Brooks pointed out in "The Mythical Man-Month" that the nine months period of pregnancy experienced by a mother-to-be cannot be shortened by dividing up the task of pregnancy between the mother and a number of would-be assistants. Nine mother-months cannot be sped up into a single month via the cooperation of nine mothers.

This thought raises the following spectre. Although there might, conceivably, be a million times as many people working on rejuveneering in 2040 as in 1980, the amount of *useful* work being done by that vast cadre of people in 2040 might be only, say, a hundred times as much as that done by the much smaller band of rejuveneering pioneers in 1980. If that's true, the timescale to achieve significant progress with rejuveneering would revert to centuries rather than decades.

But there are ways around Brooks' Law.

Surmounting Brooks' Law

Renowned software development consultant Steve McConnell, author of classic texts such as "Code Complete" and "Rapid Software Development", shared his own observations about Brooks' Law in a 1999 article "Brooks' Law Repealed?"[129]:

> For more than 20 years, industry experts have been reciting Brooks' Law as gospel: Adding people to a late software project is like pouring gasoline on a fire--it just makes it later…
>
> When junior project managers try to rescue a late project by adding more staff, wizened project managers and consultants intone the mantra: "Mustn't add people to a late project; adding people will make the project later."
>
> I have evangelized this well-worn software engineering chestnut many times myself, but I no longer think it's true.

McConnell summarises the logic behind Brooks' Law:

> Brooks' Law is based on the idea that communications overhead is a significant factor on software projects, and that work on a software project is not easily partitioned into isolated, independent tasks. Ten people can pick cotton ten times as fast as one person because the work is almost perfectly partitionable, requiring little communication or coordination. But nine women can't have a baby any faster than one woman can because the work is not partitionable. Brooks argues that work on a software project is more like having a baby than picking cotton. When new staff are brought into a late project, they aren't immediately productive, and they must be trained. The staff who must train them are already productive, but they lose productivity while they're training new staff.

However, there's an important contrast between "chaotic" projects and "controlled" projects:

> Controlled projects are less susceptible to Brooks' Law than chaotic projects. Their better tracking allows them to know when they can safely add staff and when they can't. Their better documentation and better designs make tasks more partitionable and training less labor intensive. They can add staff later in the project with less risk to the project.

What's more, modern software development practices such as continuous integration and test-driven development add to the ease with which the efforts of additional staff can be absorbed.

And even when a project is chaotic, the likelihood is that additional staff will still improve the ultimate speed at which it operates. McConnell offers this advice:

> Go ahead and add staff. You'll have time for them to become productive. Your project will still be later than your plan, but that's not a result of Brooks' Law. It's a result of underestimating the project in the first place. The additional people will help, not hurt.

In his celebrated 1998 essay "The Cathedral and the Bazaar"[130], open source software enthusiast Eric Raymond also highlighted limitations of Brooks' Law:

> In *The Mythical Man-Month*, Fred Brooks observed that programmer time is not fungible; adding developers to a late software project makes it later. He argued that the complexity and communication costs of a project rise with the square of the number of developers, while work done only rises linearly. This claim has since become known as "Brooks' Law" and is

widely regarded as a truism. But if Brooks' Law were the whole picture, Linux would be impossible...

Linux is the open source operating system that was initially created by Linus Torvalds in the 1990s. With Torvalds acting as a "benign dictator" in control of the vision and the evolution of the software, a vast community of software developers contributed to the development of new releases. The Linux operating system today lies at the heart of the Android mobile devices which are used by over one billion people worldwide.

Raymond's essay continues as follows:

> The history of Unix should have prepared us for what we're learning from Linux (and what I've verified experimentally on a smaller scale by deliberately copying Linus' methods). That is, that while coding remains an essentially solitary activity, the really great hacks come from harnessing the attention and brainpower of entire communities. The developer who uses only his or her own brain in a closed project is going to fall behind the developer who knows how to create an open, evolutionary context in which bug-spotting and improvements get done by hundreds of people.

Raymond proposed one counter to Brooks' Law, which he christened "Linus' Law", after Linus Torvalds:

> Given enough eyeballs, all bugs are shallow

In other words, with more and more people helping the project – supplying eyeballs – and provided these project members are suitably coordinated (more on that below), problems that would previously have been viewed as insurmountable become "shallow". As Raymond explained,

> Linus was keeping his hacker/users constantly stimulated and rewarded – stimulated by the prospect of having an ego-satisfying piece of the action, rewarded by the sight of constant (even daily) improvement in their work.
>
> Linus was directly aiming to maximize the number of person-hours thrown at debugging and development, even at the possible cost of instability in the code and user-base burnout if any serious bug proved intractable. Linus was behaving as though he believed something like this:
>
> *Given a large enough beta-tester and co-developer base, almost every problem will be characterized quickly and the fix obvious to someone.*
>
> Or, less formally, "Given enough eyeballs, all bugs are shallow." I dub this: "Linus' Law".
>
> My original formulation was that every problem "will be transparent to somebody". Linus demurred that the person who understands and fixes

the problem is not necessarily or even usually the person who first characterizes it. "Somebody finds the problem", he says, "and *somebody else* understands it. And I'll go on record as saying that finding it is the bigger challenge." But the point is that both things tend to happen quickly.

What is the difference between a chaotic crowd and an engaged community? In which circumstances do the individual contributions tend to drown each other out, and in which do they positively reinforce? Raymond identified two key factors:

- Powerful communications mechanisms (such as the Internet)
- Inspirational leadership without coercion, which can motivate participants to align their efforts.

In more detail on the first point:

Linux was the first project to make a conscious and successful effort to use the entire world as its talent pool. I don't think it's a coincidence that the gestation period of Linux coincided with the birth of the World Wide Web, and that Linux left its infancy during the same period in 1993-1994 that saw the takeoff of the ISP [Internet Service Provider] industry and the explosion of mainstream interest in the Internet. Linus was the first person who learned how to play by the new rules that pervasive Internet made possible.

And on the second point:

While cheap Internet was a necessary condition for the Linux model to evolve, I think it was not by itself a sufficient condition. Another vital factor was the development of a leadership style and set of cooperative customs that could allow developers to attract co-developers and get maximum leverage out of the medium.

But what is this leadership style and what are these customs? They cannot be based on power relationships - and even if they could be, leadership by coercion would not produce the results we see...

The "severe effort of many converging wills" is precisely what a project like Linux requires – and the "principle of command" is effectively impossible to apply among volunteers in the anarchist's paradise we call the Internet. To operate and compete effectively, hackers who want to lead collaborative projects have to learn how to recruit and energize effective communities of interest.

As Raymond points out, this effectiveness of this form of cooperation can puzzle some observers:

Many people (especially those who politically distrust free markets) would expect a culture of self-directed egoists to be fragmented, territorial, wasteful, secretive, and hostile. But this expectation is clearly falsified by (to give just one example) the stunning variety, quality and depth of Linux documentation. It is a hallowed given that programmers hate documenting; how is it, then, that Linux hackers generate so much of it?...

By properly rewarding the egos of many other hackers, a strong developer/coordinator can use the Internet to capture the benefits of having lots of co-developers without having a project collapse into a chaotic mess. So to Brooks' Law I counter-propose the following:

Provided the development coordinator has a medium at least as good as the Internet, and knows how to lead without coercion, many heads are inevitably better than one.

Slow progress before fast progress

The example of the Linux operating system shows what's possible: huge numbers of people cooperating from all over the world, collectively making faster progress than had previously been thought feasible.

A similar example is the way in which the open-source product Firefox overtook Microsoft Explorer as the market-leading web browser (before itself eventually being overtaken by another product based on open source, namely Google's Chrome browser). Firefox showed that open source software cooperation can create a product that has high degrees of user-friendliness in addition to rich functionality, good security, and robust performance.

Firefox is interesting in one other way. In an earlier part of its life, that project seemed to be going nowhere for a long time, and many observers thought it ought to be abandoned. Firefox had its roots in the Netscape browser, created in the mid-1990s by a team led by Marc Andreessen. Under powerful competition in the late 1990s from Microsoft's Internet Explorer (IE), Netscape took what proved to be a bold, imaginative decision: to release significant parts of their software as open source. In parallel – partly because of the constraints of the rules of open source – a major architectural rewrite was commenced. The rewrite ended up taking *much* longer than expected. The Wikipedia article for Netscape 6.0[131] gives some of the details:

In March 1998, Netscape split off most of the Communicator code and put it under an open source license. The project was dubbed Mozilla. It was estimated that turning the gutted source code (all proprietary elements had to be removed) into a new browser release might take a year, and so it was decided that the next release of the corporate Netscape browser, version 5.0, would be based on it...

Later that year it was quite evident that development on Mozilla was not proceeding quickly, so Netscape reassigned some of its engineers to a new Communicator 4.5 release. This had the result of redirecting part of the browser effort into a dead-end branch while Internet Explorer 5.0 was still building momentum.

The version 5 of the browser was skipped, at the time when Internet Explorer 5.0 had been available for a year and a half. There were plans to release an almost-ready version 5.0 based on the 4.x codebase, but this idea was scrapped. The Mozilla engineers decided to scrap the Communicator code and start over from scratch. All resources were bound to work on the Mozilla-based Netscape 6.0 release, which some Netscape employees still deem one of the bigger mistakes in the company's history.

Things did not look good:

The first public builds of Mozilla two years later were rather disappointing, with many mid-level PCs too slow to run the larger codebase...

Versions 6.1 and 6.2, released in 2001, addressed some stability problems and were more respected, but still had a relatively small number of users and was facing new competition from Internet Explorer 6.0, released in the summer of 2001.

Software industry insider Joel Spolsky – well known for his articles "Joel on software" – poured scorn on the efforts, in an April 2000 article entitled "Things You Should Never Do, Part I"[132]:

Netscape 6.0 is finally going into its first public beta. There never was a version 5.0. The last major release, version 4.0, was released almost three years ago. Three years is an *awfully* long time in the Internet world. During this time, Netscape sat by, helplessly, as their market share plummeted.

It's a bit smarmy of me to criticize them for waiting so long between releases. They didn't do it *on purpose*, now, did they?

Well, yes. They did. They did it by making the *single worst strategic mistake* that any software company can make:

They decided to rewrite the code from scratch.

Spolsky identified psychological reasons which prompt software programmers to want to rewrite code anew:

> We're programmers. Programmers are, in their hearts, architects, and the first thing they want to do when they get to a site is to bulldoze the place flat and build something grand. We're not excited by incremental renovation: tinkering, improving, planting flower beds...

But then he lamented the very practical downsides of undoing old, time-worn software:

> When you throw away code and start from scratch, you are throwing away all that [historical] knowledge. All those collected bug fixes. Years of programming work.
>
> You are throwing away your market leadership. You are giving a gift of two or three years to your competitors, and believe me, that is a *long* time in software years.
>
> You are putting yourself in an extremely dangerous position where you will be shipping an old version of the code for several years, completely unable to make any strategic changes or react to new features that the market demands, because you don't have shippable code. You might as well just close for business for the duration.

Given the criticisms heaped onto it by observers – and given its tumbling market share 1999-2001 – the Netscape browser gave many impressions of being doomed. It had taken the project a *long* time to achieve what appeared to be comparatively small increments in its functionality. However, behind the scenes, the attempts to attain a more powerful, future-proof architecture paid off handsomely. The new platform enabled more and more features to be integrated quickly. By June 2003, Spolsky had much more positive things[133] to say about the software (known at the time as "Mozilla Firebird", ahead of being rebranded as "Firefox"):

> Today... for the first time, the Mozilla Firebird browser has finally caught up with Internet Explorer. After downloading virtually every Mozilla release over the last three years, this is the first browser I'm actually going to make my default web browser. All the little problems are fixed. It loads fast. It's not ugly and clunky. My beloved Alt+D/Ctrl+Enter work perfectly. NT challenge/response authentication is supported. And there are new features, too: tabbed browsing, which is better than it sounds. Incremental search, which is brilliant and I already can't live without. Text size adjustments that always work. A download manager. Excellent cookie management...
>
> Bravo! Now with a good code base to build upon, Firebird is likely to soar past IE [Internet Explorer] in functionality and performance.

I draw the following general conclusion: progress with major technological projects often goes through slow periods. Yes, sometimes these delays prove terminal, and the project is unable to recover. But when sound foundations are laid for a new phase of growth, progress can accelerate in ways that are surprisingly impressive.

That's why it's hazardous to look at a project from the outside, notice lots of activity with little external outcome, and to conclude that the project is doomed. The right conclusion is: *future progress depends on whether or not a sound architecture is being created.*

More than once in my life, I worked in an office next to a building site. For what seemed like an age, there was little change in the appearance of the building site. It looked like there was no progress at all. But once the foundations had been laid, the project went into a new phase, and the building in question shot up quickly.

A similar set of events happened with the smartphone software company, Symbian, which was founded in June 1998, with me as one of the co-founders. At that time, our business plan projected it would take us until 2001 – three years – to become profitable. In reality, it took far longer than we (and our investors) had hoped, for improvements to take place in both the hardware and software of advanced mobile phones (and in the wireless networks used by these phones). It therefore took us until 2005 to become profitable. By the following year, 2006 – eight years from our formation – we passed the milestone of 100 million phones running our software. Another 100 million phones were shipped in just 18 more months – so whereas it took Symbian 96 months to reach the first 100 million, it took less than 96 *weeks* to double that performance. Within another three years, the accumulated shipments reached half a billion. (For the full story of the rise and fall of Symbian – and for lessons that can be drawn from that rollercoaster experience – see my 2014 book "Smartphones and beyond"[134].)

Android – which would displace Symbian as the world's most widely used smartphone operating system – had a similar long gestation. Andy Rubin, the brains behind the creation of that platform, spoke about his vision[135] as early as August 2003:

> There is tremendous potential in developing smarter mobile devices that are more aware of its owner's location and preferences.

128

> If people are smart, that information starts getting aggregated into consumer products.

After some near-death financial experiences, Android was purchased by Google in August 2005. It's tempting to say "and the rest is history". However, it took seven long years from the formation of Android (2003) until ten million smartphones were using that platform (2010).

These cases have in common a growth pattern with, broadly speaking, an exponential shape:

- Initially, progress seems disappointing – it takes longer than expected to improve the platform to meet market expectations
- However, provided the platform has sound internal qualities, growth in capability can become highly disruptive
- What fuels the subsequent growth is that more and more contributions can be included into the platform (and/or in the products enabled by the platform)
- A period in which it seems that "too many cooks spoil the broth" is replaced by a period in which "many hands make light work".

We can explain this by returning to the wording used by Steve McConnell in his description of Brooks' Law. The initial groundwork can transform a platform in which the key tasks cannot be partitioned, into one in which subsequent key tasks *are* partitionable. Sequential, bottlenecked effort can be replaced by parallel effort. More people can become involved in the project, making it progress significantly faster, rather than significantly slower.

Frameworks for collaboration

Despite the above examples, I don't mean to imply that it's somehow easy to enable large groups of people to collaborate. On the contrary, it's probably more usual for would-be large-scale collaboration projects to fail than to succeed.

Collaboration efforts can fail for all kinds of reasons:

- Lack of agreed standards, common working methods, or shared processes to integrate good work from multiple people
- The standards, common working methods, and shared processes that *are* agreed, turn out not to be fit for purpose for use in large

projects: they stifle innovation, rather than enabling it to flourish; they prevent participants from pursuing the lines of research that seem most promising to them

- Different subgroups within the overall project have goals and objectives that are radically misaligned from each other, resulting in project chaos rather than project cohesion
- Lack of effective quality control means that good work is drowned out by increasing tides of poorer quality work – for example, by work that has strong political sponsorship but lacks intrinsic underlying merit
- The visible leadership of the project fail to command deep respect, and end up alienating would-be contributors due to an unwarranted air of privilege or self-importance.

However, just because large-scale collaboration is hard, this does not mean it is impossible. Over time, sectors of research and development gradually develop the skillsets and platforms (including tools, databases, investment processes, and sets of programming interfaces) that enable larger amounts of collaboration.

The progress of what can be called "collaboration platforms" mirrors some elements of the progress of the underlying technology which the sector is trying to develop:

- There can be periods of slow progress ahead of periods of fast progress – that is, periods of weak collaboration mechanisms ahead of periods of stronger collaboration mechanisms
- Wise observers can learn from failures as much as from successes, and mould their activities accordingly
- The winning collaboration platforms can expand their influence rapidly, once they reach a certain tipping point
- Individual collaboration platforms often eventually run out of scope for further improvement, and reach their own bottlenecks, but at such times, the industry sector can transition to a new platform, with improved methods – a platform which can learn from awareness of the restrictions of the previous platform
- Transitions from a previous platform to a new platform can take a lot of time, and appear chaotic as they are underway, but (all being

well) a new phase of improved performance will emerge from the transition.

Ultimately it does not matter if many would-be large-scale collaboration platforms fail, so long as at least some succeed. The ones that succeed will sweep around the world, fulfilling the purpose that the other platforms also intended – enabling larger and larger number of project participants to build upon each other's contributions, usefully and powerfully.

Dynamics of that sort played out in the smartphone industry. The very first smartphones and mobile communicators – such as the Nokia 9000 (1996), the Ericsson GS 88 (1997), and the Motorola TimePort P1088 "map phone" (2000) – used operating systems that turned out to have many technical limitations. Moreover, these platforms posed fundamental difficulties to any third party developers who wanted to write applications for these phones. After a period of turmoil, the Symbian platform became established as a better basis for more powerful mobile devices and for application developers who could produce remarkable add-on software for these devices. As mentioned above, some 500 million smartphones using Symbian were sold around the world from 2001-2010. But throughout that period, manufacturers and developers, alike, increasingly ran up against limitations of the Symbian platform. Accordingly, dozens of alternative platforms were trialled – usually with very limited success – whilst, in parallel, the Symbian camp made numerous upgrades to that platform.

Eventually, from around 2008 onwards, the smartphone industry found alternative platforms which did meet their requirements for yet more powerful devices and accompanying add-on software. These new platforms – iOS by Apple and Android by Google – managed to sidestep key limitations that had become apparent with the Symbian platform. The new platforms made it easier for application developers to create, distribute, and benefit from the software they wrote. In the case of Android, the platform was also significantly easier for new phone manufacturers to work with (compared to Symbian), allowing teams of developers in these companies to more quickly become productive in their projects to create and customise new phones. In the case of iOS, the platform soon had widespread consumer recognition ("there's an app for that") in a way that never happened for Symbian; consumer interest helped drive more funding to the platform and provided the financial incentive for innovative new partnership models between Apple and network operators such as Verizon,

AT&T, Vodafone, and Telefonica. In both cases, the new platform brought industry collaboration to higher levels than previously thought possible.

Similar dynamics can play out – though in different contexts and facing different challenges – in the medical field, and, in particular, for the field of rejuvenation. Once again, the way progress will be achieved won't just be because of breakthroughs in technology. It will happen because of breakthroughs in collaborative platforms – breakthroughs in ways of working together in larger teams around the world.

That's the general principle of how improved collaboration can work. In the next chapter, let's look at how these general principles can work in the specific field of rejuveneering.

6. Collaborative rejuveneering

It's time to see how the general principles of collaboration frameworks, introduced in the previous chapter, can apply to the field of rejuveneering – despite some initial impressions to the contrary.

Accelerating genetic analysis

For a striking example of a phase change of collaborative progress in the medical field, consider the task of sequencing an entire human genome. The information that is buried within the three billion DNA base pairs in a human genome can in principle forecast the susceptibility of that person to given diseases. Critically, it can also predict their responsiveness to specific drug treatments, thereby enabling personally tailored treatments, known as "personalised medicine".

These future possibilities were included in an essay written in 2002 by famous biologist Richard Dawkins. The essay was Dawkins' contribution to a book entitled "The next fifty years"[136], edited by John Brockman. Dawkins drew attention to the declining cost of sequencing segments of DNA. A cost of around £1,000 per base-pair in 1965 had declined to about £10 per base-pair in 1975, £1 in 1995, and £0.10 in 2000. Simple extrapolation would predict that an entire human genome, with three billion base pairs, could be sequenced for £1,000 by somewhere around 2040. (Yes, that's a date still more than two decades into the future – and nearly four decades from the time when Dawkins was writing.) The essay by Dawkins drew out some of the far-reaching implications, for improved healthcare and other fields.

Astutely, Dawkins proposed the name "The son of Moore's Law" for the trend of declining sequencing costs. The steady year-by-year improvements in genetic sequencing methods mirrored similar continuous improvement in the computational powers of the latest semiconductor chips (the subject of the original Moore's Law).

The trend is confirmed by graphs released on the US government website http://www.genome.gov/sequencingcosts/ by the National Human Genome Research Institute. These graphs provide, for comparison, a benchmark line labelled "Moore's Law", showing the rate of progress experienced for semiconductor chip performance. The improvements in genetic sequencing match that rate until the beginning of 2008. But from that time onwards, there's a dramatic change in the improvement rate. Instead of it taking around two years to halve the cost, it now only took around five months to achieve that improvement:

- Total genome sequencing costs of $100M in 2001 had declined to $10M by 2007 – a tenfold improvement in six years
- The costs plummeted to just $10k in 2011 – a thousand-fold improvement in four years.

The US government site contains the following explanatory comment:

Note… the sudden and profound out-pacing of Moore's Law beginning in January 2008. The latter represents the time when the sequencing centres transitioned from Sanger-based (dideoxy chain termination sequencing) to 'second generation' (or 'next-generation') DNA sequencing technologies.

These "second generation" technologies were the collective product of numerous companies and organisations that had become aware of the huge commercial potential of the field. As a result, large additional amounts of funding were invested into different laboratories around the world.

Professor George Church of Harvard used to maintain a list of "Next generation DNA sequencing technologies" on his website[137]. By September 2014, the list had reached a total of 71 technologies recorded.

In March 2016 came the announcement of a service by Veritas Genetics[138] to sequence someone's entire genome for the cost of $1,000 – and to include, for no extra charge, an interpretation of the data and genetic counselling on any issues arising. The 2040 future had arrived, 24 years early.

This example fits a general pattern. Expectations from potential users (and from people who saw they could supply products and services to meet these expectations) drove a dramatic acceleration in the rate of technological progress. As these expectations increase, there is more incentive for clever companies and research labs to find new solutions to long-standing engineering problems.

There's a wider principle here. One important way to speed up progress towards a desirable future outcome is to raise expectations in the public mind as to the feasibility and the attractiveness of that outcome. The change in public mood can lead to alterations in the overall climate in which research and development takes place:

- The press will highlight encouraging stories about early results and future possibilities
- More scientists, engineers, entrepreneurs, and researchers will see the field as something they should personally prioritise
- Funding bodies and other sources of investment will become more likely to support research in the field
- Politicians will become more likely to alter legislation in order to support the field.

To be clear, the declining costs of human genome sequencing tell only part of what is a more complicated story about the potential benefits for personalised healthcare. Even as a dramatic acceleration was occurring in the technologies underlying personal genomics, many within medicine were disappointed at the slow rate at which it was possible to develop medical cures based on that technology. The connection between someone's genome and their phenotype (their body, behaviour, and other physiological properties) turns out to be considerably more complicated than some enthusiasts had initially supposed. It will take a great deal more work to create the practical applications that had been envisaged. That work is covered throughout this book. The pace of that work is likely to change in the same way:

- Key breakthroughs, when they occur, will receive encouraging coverage in press
- More scientists, engineers, entrepreneurs, and researchers will find themselves inspired to redouble their efforts in the field – with support from funding bodies and politicians
- Progress is likely to move from one speed (relatively slow) to another (considerably faster), akin to the change in the rate of progress in genomic sequencing from 2008 onwards
- Diseases of all sorts will lose their potency, in the face of new clinical treatments
- Rejuvenation will stop being a theoretical idea, but will be a practical reality.

I make these claims despite being well aware of the phenomenon known as Eroom's Law – a phenomenon that challenges my claim of acceleration in medical progress.

Eroom's Law

Eroom's Law was introduced in a 2012 article in Nature[139], which drew attention to increasing complications with medical research:

> ### Diagnosing the decline in pharmaceutical R&D efficiency
>
> Jack W. Scannell, Alex Blanckley, Helen Boldon & Brian Warrington
>
> The past 60 years have seen huge advances in many of the scientific, technological and managerial factors that should tend to raise the efficiency of commercial drug research and development (R&D). Yet the number of new drugs approved per billion US dollars spent on R&D has halved roughly every 9 years since 1950, falling around 80-fold in inflation-adjusted terms.

In other words, although Moore's Law describes a relatively steady rate of increase in computational power, Eroom's Law describes a relatively steady *decrease* in the effectiveness of research and development within the pharmaceutical industry.

By the way, Eroom isn't a person: it's "Moore" spelt backwards.

The Nature article continues:

> There have been many proposed solutions to the problem of declining R&D efficiency. However, their apparent lack of impact so far and the contrast between improving inputs and declining output in terms of the number of new drugs make it sensible to ask whether the underlying problems have been correctly diagnosed. Here, we discuss four factors that we consider to be primary causes, which we call the 'better than the Beatles' problem; the 'cautious regulator' problem; the 'throw money at it' tendency; and the 'basic research–brute force' bias…

Derek Lowe, a chemist who works in the drug discovery area, writes the influential "In the pipeline" blog, in which he summarised[140] some of the issues covered in the Nature article:

> Eroom's Law indicates that powerful forces have outweighed scientific, technical and managerial improvements over the past 60 years, and/or that some of the improvements have been less 'improving' than commonly thought. The more positive anyone is about the past several decades of progress, the more negative they should be about the strength of

countervailing forces. If someone is optimistic about the prospects for R&D today, they presumably believe the countervailing forces — whatever they are — are starting to abate…

Readers of much of what has been written about R&D productivity in the drug industry might be left with the impression that Eroom's Law can simply be reversed by strategies such as greater management attention to factors such as project costs and speed of implementation, by reorganizing R&D structures into smaller focused units in some cases or larger units with superior economies of scale in others, by outsourcing to lower-cost countries, by adjusting management metrics and introducing R&D 'performance scorecards', or by somehow making scientists more 'entrepreneurial'. In our view, these changes might help at the margins but it feels as though most are not addressing the core of the productivity problem.

Techonomy biosciences writer Catherine Arnst reviews the explanations[141] as to why drug discovery has slowed down:

[There] is the widely-held "low hanging fruit" theory of the drug drought: the easier disease targets, such as high cholesterol, asthmatic airway passages, migraines, and ulcerous digestive systems, have been met. Complex diseases such as cancer and neuro-degenerative conditions are much harder to solve.

But Scannell and his colleagues [in the Nature article] also laid out four additional, interlocking arguments that may explain the decline in R&D output:

1. **The 'better than the Beatles' problem**: Imagine how hard it would be to come up with a successful pop song if any new song had to be better than the Beatles. Unlike cars, or electronics, with drugs there's no interest in novelty for its own sake. And there's no point in creating something that's only just as good as what's already available, especially since today's hit drug is tomorrow's inexpensive generic.

2. **The 'cautious regulator' problem**: The progressive lowering of risk tolerance, particularly after the pain treatment Vioxx was removed from the market in 2004 for safety reasons, raises the bar on safety for new drugs, which makes R&D both costlier and harder.

3. **The 'throw money at it' tendency**: The tendency to just keep pouring more money and resources into a research project or a widely-held theory until something sticks. Could also be called throwing good money after bad.

4. **The 'basic research-brute force' bias**: The industry's tendency to overestimate the probability that advances in basic research and large scale screening processes will show a molecule safe and effective in clinical trials.

I don't mean to belittle these problems. The statistics tell their own, bleak story. As Arnst recounts:

Drugs approvals by the US Food & Drug Administration (FDA) have plunged 40% since 2005, while spending on research and development almost doubled during the same period, according to a December 2011 report by consultancy Oliver Wyman ("Beyond the Shadow of a Drought"). The number of new drug approvals averaged 22 per year between 2005 and 2010, compared with 36 per year from 1996 to 2004. That's Eroom's Law in action.

However, I see four important trends which, combined, have the potential to dramatically accelerate the pace of medical discoveries:

1. An increased readiness to reflect on past failures and to seek new ways of working
2. An openness to consider changes in the regulatory and testing frameworks
3. Testing new drugs using extensive human cell banks
4. Advanced computer models and data analytics which speed up new discovery and testing options, especially in the area of personalised medicine.

These trends are, in turn, accelerated by the fact that there are significantly greater numbers of people seeking to work in the field, willing to experiment collaboratively with new technologies, new working methods, and new business models.

In the remainder of this chapter, let's look more closely at these four trends. Together, they provide the methods to accelerate medical progress in the next 10-25 years, in spite of the decades-long slowdown in drug development.

Note: all four trends are weighty, but of the four, it is the last one whose impact may be the greatest. Accordingly, I give most space to it in the remarks that follow.

Learning from failures

First, the pharmaceutical industry is becoming increasingly open to admit, discuss, and share details of its failures. Out of frank analysis of these failures, R&D processes can be altered to become more successful. The coining of the term "Eroom's Law" is an important step in this direction. Defining a problem is the first step to solving it.

In her Techonomy article about Eroom's Law, Catherine Arnst comments:

> Scannell and his co-writers suggest that that each drug company should create a Chief Dead Drug Officer (CDDO) responsible for figuring out the reasons behind a drug failure at every stage of the R&D process, and publish the results in a scientific journal. Today, companies rarely publish the results of failed clinical trials or experiments. Consequently, scientists keep trying to invent the same broken wheel.
>
> It seems unlikely a drug company will appoint a dead drug officer anytime soon, but the idea does highlight an important point—from failure can come great learnings. Pharmaceutical companies know their R&D process needs to change, but it is hard for billion dollar enterprises with proud histories of life-saving drug discoveries to change their ways, and to admit failure.

The suggestion to honestly review failures is important. Project managers in multiple industries have long upheld the principle of performing a "lessons learned" retrospective at the end of any major project. In such a retrospective, project participants are encouraged to objectively consider questions such as "what went well, and why?" and "what went badly, and why?" Books such as "Bad Pharma: How Drug Companies Mislead Doctors and Harm Patients"[142] by Ben Goldacre are playing a broadly similar role within the pharmaceutical industry, challenging the industry to look more searchingly at its persistent flaws. In each case, the intent is to enable:

- A broader appreciation of the *messiness* of how technology actually progresses in the real world
- A recognition of how established practice has developed various counter-productive aspects as well as some productive ones
- Fruitful discussions as to how future developments can avoid needlessly repeating the same kinds of failure.

Chas Bountra, Professor of Translational Medicine in the Nuffield Department of Clinical Medicine at the University of Oxford, and the Chief Scientist at Oxford SGS, made a number of specific suggestions along these same lines in his keynote address to the SENS "RB2015" rejuvenation biotech conference in San Francisco in August 2015. His presentation was entitled "Transforming the Discovery of New Medicines"[143].

In his presentation, Bountra advocated what he called a "complete transformation of how we discover new medicines", away from a culture of "too much secrecy and too much competition", into a culture of greater openness and greater collaboration. The unhappy outcome of the present culture, Bountra said, is that development of new medicines is too costly, too risky, and too slow:

- Regarding costliness, Bountra pointed to analysis recently carried out by Forbes magazine[144], into costs incurred by large pharmaceutical companies as they research and develop new drugs. This analysis showed, for example, that it cost AstraZeneca an average of close to $12 billion expenditure to develop each new drug they launched. Even the company with the lowest average cost among those analysed, Amgen, spent the huge sum of $3.5 billion for each new drug launched.

- Regarding risk: out of 529 compounds being researched around the world for potential use against cancer in 2003, spread across the various phases of clinical studies trials, only 45 had made it to the market by 2014; 95 were still in development at that time; and the other 389 had been terminated. From wider surveys, it seems that a drug that reaches phase one of clinical studies has only a 7.5% chance of reaching the market. Drugs that reach phase three still only have a 33% chance of being launched. The whole process is, accordingly, fraught with risk.

- Regarding slowness: the time between initial data indicating that a molecule could be useful in cancer treatment, and the clinical use of that molecule, typically varies from six to thirty years.

Bountra commented that researchers across multiple different companies and academic institutes are often working in parallel on the same small number of ideas, without being aware of what each other are doing. This duplication of effort takes place largely in secret, due to the operation of confidentiality regimes and the tight guarding of intellectual property.

The fact that one company has already found major problems with a given potential treatment is often not made public; therefore many other companies can waste huge resources eventually coming to the same conclusion. Sadly, these later companies spend years exposing trial patients to drugs that earlier groups already know are destined to failure.

In other words, at least part of the cause of the costliness, riskiness, and slowness of development of new medicines lies in *organisational issues* – how the industry organises itself. Recognising this fact is the start of fixing it.

This wasted duplication of effort can be reduced by industry players pooling resources and sharing more of their findings about the problems encountered by various initiatives. As a step in this direction, the UK-based Wellcome Trust charity has provided £16 million pounds for a consortium supported by ten large pharmaceutical companies, including GSK, Pfizer, Novartis, and Merck. The intent is to stimulate a greater degree of risk-sharing and collaborative development. Details of interim outputs from this work – such as the characteristics of promising new compounds – are being published openly, allowing other companies to take these ideas further. This follows the principle of successful open source software development, in which innovations are made available to anyone who wants to utilise them for their own purposes.

The resulting transparency engenders greater trust among potential collaborators, allowing the network of research labs to grow in size, and become collectively more engaged and collectively more intelligent. It's enabling the promise of "crowdsourced medicine" to start to become a reality.

As one practical outcome from this more open approach to drug development, Bountra described work that started six years earlier on a family of epigenetic proteins known as bromodomains. At that time, it was widely thought to be too hard to create drugs that could target these proteins. That's one reason Bountra picked the area, and called for research collaborators.

A candidate drug molecule was identified after two years of collaborative research with a number of academic teams. Details were published in Nature of experiments showing beneficial application to types of cancer. Since that time, that drug molecule has been given to more than one thousand labs worldwide, for trials with a large range of different cancers, as well as in other disease circumstances. There have now been more than 300 publications on the applications of this drug. Further, six of the pharmaceutical companies in the consortium have adapted the drug in various ways, and are presently involved in 14 separate clinical studies. That's powerful progress, in a relatively short period of time, for a family of proteins which had been previously thought to be too difficult to target. All this progress resulted from the fact that the initial research was, contrary to common practice, made publicly available.

In the end, many promising drugs will still hit problems in the phase of human trials. That reflects the complicated interactions between drugs and the rich biochemistry of the human body. But Bountra made the following appeal at the close of his keynote presentation: *Rather than twenty different companies testing essentially the same drug in twenty different clinical trials, in parallel and in secret, let's do the experiment once, well, with the result being shared.* That will allow a quicker identification of the nine in ten initially promising drugs that fail the final testing hurdle. As a result, the small proportion of truly promising drug molecules can receive more attention more quickly.

Changing regulations

The second trend which has the potential to speed up medical innovation is that of an increased focus on the need for regulatory reform.

Government regulations that apply to the development and deployment of new medical treatments are designed to:

- Avoid patients being misled by exaggerated claims about treatment efficacy
- Reduce the incidence of damaging side-effects from treatments
- Prevent medical companies from carelessly cutting corners in a quest to bring risky or unproven products to market more quickly.

However, legislation often becomes bogged down in inertia. Legislation that made good sense at one period in an industry's evolution may make less sense subsequently. It may discriminate against smaller newcomers. It may presuppose some overall technical framework which no longer fully applies. It may fail to keep up with the possibilities offered by new approaches. Unfortunately, it takes time for regulations to change – especially when there's pressure in favour of the status quo from companies who have a vested interest in minimising radical change.

In short, legislation can stand in the way of the kinds of creative destruction which actually have the potentially to lead, in due course, to radically better solutions. However, the good news is that this unwelcome outcome is now increasingly recognised. For example, consider the subtitle of the 2013 book "The Cure in the Code"[145] by Peter Huber, senior fellow at the Manhattan Institute for Policy Research:

How 20th Century Law is Undermining 21st Century Medicine

The description of the book on Amazon.com conveys the flavour of the analysis it contains:

Never before have two revolutions with so much potential to save and prolong human life occurred simultaneously. The converging, synergistic power of the biochemical and digital revolutions now allows us to read every letter of life's code, create precisely targeted drugs to control it, and tailor their use to individual patients. Cancer, diabetes, Alzheimer's and countless other killers can be vanquished—if we make full use of the tools of modern drug design and allow doctors the use of modern data gathering and analytical tools when prescribing drugs to their patients.

But Washington stands in the way, clinging to outdated drug-approval protocols developed decades ago during medicine's long battle with the infectious epidemics of the past. Peter Huber, an expert in science, technology, and public policy, demonstrates why Washington's one-size-fits-all drug policies can't deal with diseases rooted in the complex molecular diversity of human bodies. Washington is ill-equipped to handle the torrents of data that now propel the advance of molecular medicine and is reluctant to embrace the statistical methods of the digital age that can. Obsolete economic policies, often rationalized as cost-saving measures, stifle innovation and suppress investment in the medicine that can provide the best cures at the lowest cost.

There's a lot of anti-government rhetoric in Huber's book. But he does point to some positive examples of what might be possible when government finds reason to bypass its normal regulations:

In the 1980s, an AIDS diagnosis was a death sentence, until the FDA loosened its throttling grip and began streamlining and accelerating approval of life-saving drugs. *The Cure in the Code* shows patients, doctors, investors, and policy makers what we must now do to capture the full life-saving and cost-saving potential of the revolution in molecular medicine.

Writing in March 2015 with one of his Manhattan Institute colleagues, Paul Howard, Huber addressed the specific opportunities of "precision medicine" to accelerate cures for diseases. The article[146] confirmed that flawed regulatory standards were impeding that progress:

> Precision medicine—tailoring treatments to the biochemistry of individual patients—has the potential to cure countless diseases. Molecular biomarkers are the foundation of this approach. Many doctors—notably, oncologists—routinely prescribe drugs in ways that best fit each patient—biomarker profile. The Food and Drug Administration (FDA), however, has been slow to incorporate biomarkers into the regulatory procedures for drug approval and, as a result, has significantly slowed the development of safe and effective treatments for many diseases.
>
> Realizing the full potential that biomarkers offer to revolutionize modern medicine will require substantive and clear regulatory standards, now lacking, for incorporating biomarkers into the drug-approval process, as well as a more transparent, predictable, and timely FDA process for reviewing biomarker submissions...
>
> Precision medicine is the future of medicine. But it is also the antithesis of the FDA's long-standing one-size-fits-all drug-approval process. Top officials at the FDA have publicly acknowledged this for over a decade, but the agency has been very slow to develop consistent and transparent standards for using biomarkers in drug trials. The absence of such standards has sharply reduced industry incentives to make the large investments needed to develop new targeted drugs or seek formal approval of new uses for existing drugs.

In the UK, CASMI – the Centre for the Advancement of Sustainable Medical Innovation – was established in 2012 as a partnership between Oxford University and UCL. The stated goal of CASMI is "to develop new models for medical innovation". Their website[147] gives more details:

> The centre aims to address the issues that have led to current failures in the translation of basic bioscience into affordable and widely adopted new treatments.

One of the initiatives advocated by CASMI matches that championed by Peter Huber in the US: a more flexible, adaptable approach in the regulation of experimental new medical treatments. In March 2014, the European Medicines Agency announced[148] that it would launch a pilot study to explore an adaptive licensing approach with real medicines in development:

> The European Medicines Agency (EMA) is inviting companies to participate in its adaptive licensing pilot project. Companies who are

interested in participating in the pilot are requested to submit ongoing medicine development programmes for consideration as prospective pilot cases...

The adaptive licensing approach, sometimes called staggered approval or progressive licensing, is part of the Agency's efforts to improve timely access for patients to new medicines. It is a prospectively planned process, starting with the early authorisation of a medicine in a restricted patient population, followed by iterative phases of evidence gathering and adaptations of the marketing authorisation to expand access to the medicine to broader patient populations.

The Agency acknowledged that any changes in regulation will require careful collaboration:

As a holistic approach, adaptive licensing requires the involvement of all stakeholders who have a role in determining patient access, including the EMA, the industry, health technology assessment (HTA) bodies, organisations issuing clinical treatment guidelines and patient organisations. All discussions will take place in a 'safe harbour' environment to allow free exploration of the strengths and weaknesses of all options for development, assessment, licensing, reimbursement, monitoring, and utilisation pathways in a confidential manner and without commitment from either side.

"With the adaptive licensing pilot project we intend to explore with real medicines in development a progressive licensing approach that would allow timely access for patients to new medicines that address serious conditions with unmet medical needs," explains Hans-Georg Eichler, the Agency's Senior Medical Officer.

As noted in a CASMI August 2014 press release[149], the approach being taken by the FDA towards the Ebola outbreak embodied the adaptive process favoured by CASMI:

FDA uses 'adaptive' approach championed by CASMI for experimental Ebola treatment

The US Food and Drug Administration (FDA) this month announced that they were lifting the hold on the experimental Ebola drug, TKM-Ebola, to allow 'fast-tracked' safety and efficacy studies to go ahead.

This decision was made in light of the Ebola outbreak in West Africa, which health experts are declaring as an emergency situation.

CASMI has been campaigning for the adoption of this flexible approach to medicine licensing in response to unmet clinical need. There are currently no licensed drugs or vaccines targeting the Ebola virus, so this is a clear instance where Adaptive Pathways and Licensing are crucial to get innovative medicines to patients more quickly and efficiently.

We welcome the FDA's decision to modify the restriction in the hope that more victims of the deadly disease can be saved.

The perception of an emergency can do wonders to focus minds, and to dislodge people from their previous intransigence. However, to be prepared for such emergencies, it's important for groups such as CASMI to proactively explore alternative methods in advance. Then when the emergency strikes, flustered officials will have the benefit of careful scenario analysis that has already taken place, which weighed up the pros and cons of possible changes. After all, some "quick fixes" that might come to mind, in the midst of a medical emergency, might actually makes things worse, not better.

The key word in the preceding paragraph is "perception". People are ready to take decisive action when they *perceive* they are facing a crisis. My view, which I'll reiterate in the following chapters, is that we are already in the midst of a much wider emergency concerning aging and infirmity. But because people don't see how this can be fixed, they avoid admitting to themselves the seriousness of the situation.

New methods of testing new medicines

The developments discussed in the last two sections will increase the speed at which patients can receive promising new treatments:

- By working in a more *collaborative* spirit, companies will waste less effort in the needless duplication of trials of drugs that are already known, by other parts of the industry, to have adverse effects on humans; this will allow greater effort on drugs that have a higher likelihood of success
- By working in a more *adaptive* spirit, treatments can be released earlier for patient trials than is possible when following a rigid one-size-fits-all approvals process.

Even so, many initially promising treatments will still have deeply disappointing effects when applied in large groups of patients. These undesirable outcomes range from ineffectiveness through to death, with all kinds of adverse side-effects in between. As previously mentioned, this reflects the vastly complicated interactions between drugs and the rich biochemistry of the human body. Critically, human biochemistry often differs in unexpected ways from those of the animals, such as rodents, dogs, or monkeys, in which drugs were tested at an earlier stage in trials.

Medicine has a long history of trialling new drugs on animals. To the extent that human response to drugs matches that of various animals, then complications and disappointments in the treatment of human patients can be reduced. However, it's hard to know in advance whether the responses of humans will indeed match that of specific animals. Human diseases frequently have new characteristics, when compared to the corresponding diseases in other species.

One alternative, of course, is to carry out tests of the drugs on human cell cultures which have been created in vitro (for example, in a test tube). But, again, the responses of human cells in vitro can differ markedly from the responses when these cells are part of a complete living, breathing organism ("in vivo").

But here's what's changing: banks of human cells can now be grown, that provide a fuller emulation of the behaviour these cells would manifest in vivo. Testing compounds on these banks of cells can provide timely new insight, without the drawbacks of side-effects on real human subjects.

These techniques involve the use of pluripotent stem cells, which can be coaxed into turning into other types of cell, including banks of heart cells. This allows a more reliable method of, for example, testing whether anti-inflammatory drugs might have adverse side effects on the performance of the heart. This method was described[150] by a team of researchers at Stanford University School of Medicine, led by Joseph Wu:

> Researchers at the Stanford University School of Medicine describe a "clinical trial in a dish" using patient-specific induced pluripotent stem, or iPS, cells to predict whether a drug will dangerously affect the heart's function. The technique may be more accurate than the current in vitro drug-safety screening assays used by pharmaceutical companies, say the researchers, and may better protect patients from deadly side effects of common medications.
>
> The technique allows scientists for the first time to test drugs directly on cells with mutations that cause hereditary cardiac diseases…
>
> The use of patient-specific iPS cells may help drug designers winnow heart-safe medications from those like the blockbuster anti-inflammatory

drug Vioxx, which was withdrawn from the market because of unanticipated adverse cardiovascular events...

"Right now, the first time any drug sees a human heart cell is in a phase-1 clinical trial," said Andrew Lee, a Stanford medical student and one of three lead authors of the study. "If adverse effects are seen, it can result in patient deaths, as in the case of the anti-inflammatory drug Vioxx or with cisapride, a drug previously used to treat digestive problems in people with diabetes..."

The researchers anticipate that the technique, if adopted, could save millions of dollars and thousands of lives by streamlining the drug-testing process and increasing its sensitivity.

Both Vioxx and cisapride caused enormous damage because their fatal cardiotoxic side-effects were found only after these drugs were in wide use by patients worldwide. By the time of the withdrawal of Vioxx in 2004, more than 38,000 deaths[151] were related to its usage in America alone. Merck, the manufacturer of Vioxx, is facing compensation lawsuits totalling around eight billion dollars – and that's on top of three billion dollars of development costs for the drug.

Stephen Minger, Chief Scientist of GE Healthcare Life Sciences, addressed this same topic in his presentation "The future of regenerative medicine"[152] at London Futurists in January 2015. Minger discussed the response of GE Healthcare to a challenge posed by its customers within the pharmaceutical industry, namely, to find better ways to identify cardiotoxicity of drugs under development.

GE developed an industrial-scale process that, starting with human embryonic stem cells, created human adult heart muscle cells (cardiomyocytes), over a period of just 28 days. The resulting culture spontaneously beats, in the same way as a real human heart, at a rate of around 70 beats per minute. Electrophysiological analysis of the culture shows that different types of heart muscle cells are present in the same quantities as in a real heart: 80% ventricular, 18% atrial, and 1-2% nodal. This provides confirmation that the industrial process used to create these cells successfully mimics what occurs in development of a human foetus inside the womb.

More significantly, these cells have their electrophysiological properties altered by various known cardiotoxic drugs, even at low drug dosage levels. These drugs each cause the same distinctive types of irregular heart beat (arrhythmia) in the GE heart culture as happens when real human hearts are exposed to the same drugs. Crucially, similar arrhythmia does *not* occur for tests of these drugs on standard preparations created from animal hearts, unless an abnormally high dosage is applied. As Minger explains in his presentation, "We're not dogs, we're not rabbits, we're not mice, we're not rats: we're human. And humans respond very differently to these drugs."

These cultures derived from human stem cells therefore open the way for much earlier testing of new drugs for cardiotoxicity. As a result, huge amounts of expenditure can be avoided, in the development of drugs which would never be able to succeed in human usage.

To be clear, this is still early days for this new approach to drug testing:

- The banks of heart cells don't yet include the structural elements which would turn them from a beating mass of cells into an operational heart
- Attempts to create similar banks of human adult liver cells, starting from stem cells, have so far not been successful
- More complicated medical interactions between different organs cannot yet be emulated.

However, given the potential benefits – both commercially and clinically – this is a field which can be expected to blossom in the decades ahead. It's another solid reason why the present trend of Eroom's Law is unlikely to persist.

From in-vitro and in-vivo to in-silico

As we've seen, each different approach to testing new drugs has its own drawbacks:

- Tests in animals cannot cope with the many cases of divergent animal and human responses to specific drugs
- Tests in live humans have the drawback that many humans can be harmed – even lethally – by inappropriate drugs
- Tests in human cell cultures cover only a fraction of the full range of dynamic interactions of a complete living human.

The drawbacks of the third case are gradually being reduced, by the use of increasingly sophisticated fabrication and construction techniques, such as the stem cell methods just mentioned. But in this section, let's consider yet another transformation that is underway. Rather than testing in-vitro or in-vivo, this aims to test *in-silico*. That is, it involves progressively more powerful computer models of aspects of human biochemistry.

One successful recent example of a computer model of part of the humanity anatomy involves the same clinical requirement as featured in the previous section: anticipating the response of the heart to drugs that might trigger arrhythmia (irregular heartbeat). In this case, the analysis used a three dimensional dynamic computer model of the heart known as UT-Heart, created by the Super Computational Life Science department at the University of Tokyo (UT). The UT-Heart model involves 170,000 tetrahedrons connected in what's known as a finite element model. As is vividly illustrated in a video[153] on the UT Super Computational Life Science department's YouTube channel, the model includes:

- Arteries, veins, and valves, as well as the main chambers of the heart
- Variations of thickness of the heart wall and inner structures
- Electrical activity throughout the heart
- Detailed blood flow and local energy consumption.

The model incorporates information from physics, chemistry, medicine, and physiology. As such, it can generate a realistic electrocardiogram (ECG), of the sort that is studied by doctors to determine the health of a patient's heart. Significantly, the ECG output can be studied as the UT-Heart model is altered by the incorporation of different drugs at varying concentration levels. A team of University of Tokyo researchers led by Jun-ichi Okada studied the performance of the model with twelve separate drugs, including some drugs with cardiotoxic properties and others that served as experimental controls. They reported the successful outcome of their work in Science Advances[154]:

> Each drug induced a concentration-dependent characteristic type of ventricular arrhythmia, whereas no arrhythmias were observed at any dose with drugs known to be safe.

Their conclusion:

> We have shown that our system combining in vitro and in silico technologies can predict drug-induced arrhythmogenic risk reliably and efficiently.

Other in-silico models can be used to predict, not only adverse reactions, but positive interactions. That is, this technology has value not only in *drug safety evaluation*, but also in in *drug discovery* – specifically, in discovering potential uses of existing drugs in new clinical areas.

Many existing drugs were developed with one clinical application in mind, but could conceivably have useful effects for markedly different medical conditions. This is similar to the way that[155] Viagra was originally created, under the name "UK-92480", as a potential treatment for angina (a chest pain caused by insufficient flow of blood to the heart), before its unexpected usage for erectile dysfunction was serendipitously discovered. Another example is Ritalin, which is widely used nowadays to treat Attention Deficit Hyperactivity Disorder (ADHD), but which was developed, fifty years earlier, as a potential treatment for depression. Again, the common painkiller aspirin keeps having beneficial new uses discovered.

But can we accelerate this process of discovering potential new uses for existing drugs? The company Insilico Medicine was founded on the assumption that artificial intelligence systems are reaching a level of sophisticated that makes this possible. In an interview[156] given to Doug Black of Enterprise Tech in December 2015, Insilico Medicine CEO Alex Zhavoronkov explains the vision of the company:

> Discovering cures for cancer, for Alzheimer's, for multiple sclerosis, for Parkinson's, for the halting and reversing of aging itself, may not require the development of new drugs. It may mean discovering properties and therapies in drugs already developed and used for other diseases.
>
> That's the principle driving bioinformatics start-up Insilico Medicine, a Baltimore-based company utilizing GPU-accelerated NVIDIA advanced scale computing to power deep learning neural nets using massive datasets for drug repurposing research that targets aging and age-related diseases.
>
> Drug re-targeting is not new. One of the best known cases is rapamycin, a drug originally thought to be an antifungal agent before it became widely used in in organ transplantation and then as a cancer fighter. Other companies have pursued drug re-purposing as a development strategy, but Dr. Alex Zhavoronkov, Insilico CEO, said his company using big data analytics to scale the strategy to a level never previously attempted.
>
> Insilico researchers not only generate their own data, they "scavenge" existing datasets that pharmaceutical companies and research institutions have retired because they were too small, in themselves, to provide much research value. Aggregated and analyzed, the data is providing Insilico, its

pharmaceutical partners and physicians with insights into how medications designed and approved for one ailment can be redirected to attack another.

Zhavoronkov explained what's particularly new about the Insilico approach. In short, Insilico utilises the open source software framework Hadoop to enable sophisticated data collaboration (Zhavoronkov uses the medical term 'suture', meaning to stitch together):

> "We've found a way to suture together our data with many other databases," said Zhavoronkov, "and then it starts making sense." Altogether, Insilico has 3 million gene expression samples amounting to hundreds of terabytes of data. "The breakthrough is combining so many pieces of the puzzle in one particular place," he said, explaining that Hadoop has been instrumental to harmonizing large amounts of unstructured, weakly related data, and then running Insilico's drug scoring algorithms against it.
>
> Of course, drug discovery is an endeavour prone to high hopes and false starts. Many new drugs are found early in the development process to have toxicities that cause unacceptable side effects. But Insilico's approach has the advantage of focusing on 20,000 medications worldwide already in use, drugs that have been approved (either in the U.S. or in other countries) and whose side effects are known.

Understanding "exceptional responders"

Yet another breakthrough possibility involving powerful AI data-crunching techniques is that drugs can be tied more reliably to characteristics of individual patients, in ways that predict the circumstances in which a drug will have a good impact on that patient.

These distinctions between individual patients can be likened to the differences between various blood types, such as A, B, AB, and O. Blood transfusions should not take place until the blood type of the recipient is clearly known. Likewise, there are many other biochemical variations between patients that determine which kind of reactions a drug will have inside someone's body. These variations include genetics (personal genome), epigenetics (variations in the expression of the genome due to environment), and microbiota (the set of bacteria in our digestive system). Whereas the significance of blood type variation is widely understood, the full significance of these other variations remains to be determined. That is where big data analytics can play a big role. And, in turn, drugs which were formerly withdrawn, due to unpredictable bad side-effects on a portion of patients, can now be re-introduced, with a greater understanding of which patients can tolerate these drugs.

The anti-cancer drug Iressa provides an important example. In 2003, the FDA approved Iressa for use against lung cancer, as one of the first applications of what was called an "accelerated approval" program. This program allowed drugs for serious diseases to be made available to patients after only partial evidence of effectiveness, so long as the initial tests were followed up by wider clinical trials. As such, the "accelerated approval" program looked like an important process innovation. However, two years later, the FDA withdrew approval for Iressa, because the follow-up trials had failed to provide more systematic evidence that the drug was effective. Writing in the New York Times[157], Andrew Pollack explained what happened:

> The Food and Drug Administration stopped just short of withdrawing the lung cancer pill Iressa from the market yesterday, restricting access to the drug to existing or previous users and to patients in clinical trials.
>
> The action follows the failure of the drug, developed by AstraZeneca, to prolong lives in two clinical trials.
>
> This is the first time the F.D.A. has restricted use of a cancer drug that had received so-called accelerated approval...
>
> Patient advocacy groups say the program speeds desperately needed drugs to patients. But some critics have said the program can allow ineffective or risky drugs on the market.
>
> Representative Edward J. Markey, a Massachusetts Democrat, recently issued a report stating that drug companies often do not do the promised follow-up studies. Questions were also raised when the multiple sclerosis drug Tysabri, which received accelerated approval last November, was withdrawn from the market three months afterward when it was linked to deadly brain infections.

Pollack's article went on to give more details about the Iressa trials:

> Iressa was approved in 2003 based on a small trial showing that it shrank tumours in about 10% of patients who had run out of other therapy options. There were some examples of near miraculous improvements. But subsequent larger trials showed it did not prolong lives in the lung cancer population as a whole...
>
> Some patient groups expressed dismay about the decision.

"What about a new patient who has washed out of all other options?" asked Laurie Fenton, president of the Lung Cancer Alliance. "Why should Iressa not be made available to them?"

The answer to this question is that all drugs cost money, and all drugs risk adverse side-effects. The FDA has to apply a targeted approach, in which focus is given to the drugs that show best evidence of positive potential. Drugs whose impact cannot be distinguished from statistical noise fall down the priority order.

Pollack's article ended with an indication that further twists in the story could be expected:

There is… evidence that Iressa works best in Asians, non-smokers, and people whose tumours have particular mutations. If such observations are verified, the drug may be approved for particular groups.

"The science just needs to catch up in order for Iressa to have another chapter," said Mary Lynn Carver, a spokeswoman for AstraZeneca.

Peter Huber's testimony to the US Senate[158] in July 2015, ten years later, covers what happened next:

In 2003 and 2004 the FDA granted accelerated approval to two drugs, Iressa and Tarceva, on the strength of their dramatic therapeutic effects in about one in ten non-small-cell lung cancer patients. Over the course of the next two years the drugs were prescribed to many patients whom they didn't help, and several follow-up clinical trials seemed to indicate that the drugs didn't work after all…

In early 2005 Iressa became the first cancer drug to be withdrawn from the U.S. market after the required follow-up trials failed to confirm its worth to the FDA's satisfaction. After further trials failed to establish that Iressa extends average patient survival, and serious side effects surfaced in some patients, the manufacturer halted further testing in the United States.

We do however know that Iressa survival times and side effects vary widely among patients. And we have a pretty good idea why. As Bruce Johnson, a researcher at Boston's Dana-Farber Cancer Institute and one of the doctors involved in the original Iressa trials, remarked in 2005, "For us as investigators, at this point, there are at least 20 different mutations in the EGF [Epidermal growth factor] receptors in human lung cancers, and we don't know if the same drug works as well for every mutation…"

When the FDA rescinded Iressa's license, it allowed U.S. patients already benefiting from its use to continue using it. One such patient who started on Iressa in 2004, when he had been given two to three months to live, was still alive eight years later, and walking his dogs several miles daily.

Huber highlights the significance of these "exceptional responder" individual cases, where response to drugs differs from that of the larger population:

> Rare cases like his have no influence at the FDA but are of great interest to doctors and researchers. In 2013, the National Cancer Institute (NCI) announced its Exceptional Responders Initiative. Four major research institutions are analyzing tissue samples, collected during clinical trials of drugs that failed to win FDA approval, to identify biomarkers that distinguished the minority of patients who did respond well, from the majority who did not. The analysis of roughly a decade of prior trials in the first year of the study identified about 100 exceptional responders.
>
> As of March 2015, more than 70 cases have been provisionally accepted for further analysis, with hundreds more anticipated. Accepted tumour tissue samples "will undergo whole-exome, RNA, and targeted deep sequencing to identify potential molecular features that may have accounted for the response." When the molecules that distinguish the exceptional responders align with what the drug was designed to target, these findings could well lead to the resurrection of drugs that might have helped many patients over the last decade.
>
> In one such trial the drug failed to help over 90% of the bladder cancer patients to whom it was prescribed. But it did wipe out the cancer in one 73-year old patient. A genetic analysis of her entire tumour revealed a rare mutation that made her cancer sensitive to the molecular pathway that the drug modulates. Similar mutations were found in about 8% of the patients, and the presence of the mutation correlated well with the cancer's sensitivity to the drug. Similar analyses of a decade of other trials have identified about 100 exceptional responders and could well lead to the re-examination and approval of drugs that could have started saving many lives years ago.

Detailed analysis of what makes "exceptional responders" different will benefit from increased computational power, smarter algorithms, and larger data sets. Later in his testimony to the US Senate, Huber highlights the role of software giants Google and Amazon in this effort:

> New devices now make it quite easy to collect large amounts of genetic and other medically relevant data from many people. Amazon and Google are reportedly in a race to build the largest medically focused genomic databases. According to Google's genomic director of engineering, Google

aims to provide the best "analytic tools [that] can fish out genetic gold—a drug target, say, or a DNA variant that strongly predicts disease risk—from a sea of data." Academic and pharmaceutical research projects are currently the company's biggest customers, but Google expects them to be overtaken by clinical applications in the next decade, with doctors using the services regularly "to understand how a patient's genetic profile affects his risk of various diseases or his likely response to medication."

Google and Amazon are by no means the only giants of the computing industry that are making significant contributions towards accelerating medical discoveries. IBM's "Watson" supercomputer looks set to catalyse important breakthroughs as well.

IBM's medical discovery initiative

The Watson supercomputer gained its initial fame by its performance on the US general knowledge quiz show "Jeopardy". This show features questions[159] such as:

- "It can mean to develop gradually in the mind or to carry during pregnancy" (answer: "gestate")
- "A 15-ounce VO5 moisture milks conditioner from this manufacturer averages a buck online" (answer: "Alberto")
- "Maurice LaMarche found his inner Orson Welles to voice this rodent whose simple goal was to take over the world" (answer: "Brain")
- "William Wilkinson's 'An Account of the Principalities of Wallachia and Moldavia' inspired this author's most famous novel" (answer: "Bram Stoker").

In a specially arranged contest in 2011, Watson out-performed the two highest-scoring human players from the long-running history of the game, Ken Jennings and Brad Rutter. During this contest, Watson was disconnected from the Internet, but could carry out real-time analysis of 15 terabytes of information it had previously gleaned from numerous data sources – including Wikipedia, the complete works of Shakespeare, the Internet movie database IMDb, the medical encyclopaedia "Gray's Anatomy", and much more. This analysis ran in parallel[160] on 2,880 processor cores. What's particularly significant is that none of the reference sources had been designed to be read and understood by computers. The intended users were humans.

Watson's breakthrough was in its ability to understand natural language. Subsequent to the Jeopardy contest, IBM have pointed Watson at a different set of reference material – that from medicine. The scale of the challenge of keeping on top of relevant new medical reports was described in an August 2014 article[161] by Joab Jackson of IDG News Service:

IBM continues to make the case for the nascent field of cognitive computing, showing off some Watson prototypes Thursday that could help speed scientific discovery in the medical field, by scanning large volumes of literature and data far more quickly than humans can, and suggesting possible leads…

In the presentations on Thursday, IBM senior vice president Mike Rhodin pointed to how Watson could speed literature searches and analysis for a particular field, a process that is increasingly becoming too unwieldy for even the largest research teams to complete.

The medical field serves as a good testing ground for these capabilities.

IBM executives outlined the accelerating pace of growth of medical information, and how their Watson software is able to cope in response:

Medical information doubles every three years and by 2020 will double every 73 days, Rhodin said. As a result, a doctor can no longer rely solely on their own medical training, even with voracious reading of the latest medical journals. "We are human, and there are limits to what we can learn," he said.

Watson can do the background work necessary to narrow down the information to a smaller set of possibilities, Rhodin suggested. "Watson is not bound by volume or format."

In one presentation, IBM showed how it helped the Baylor College of Medicine more quickly identify possible treatments for a protein linked to many cancers, called p53.

More than 70,000 scientific papers have been written about p53. "It is just impossible for a single researcher to read all that. Yet there could be very critical facts in that evidence they can't get access to," said Scott Spangler, an IBM Research manager overseeing analytics. He referred to this under-read material as the "dark literature problem" of the medical community.

The Watson service was able to comb through papers and suggest a number of other proteins that could control p53 activity. Using Watson's analysis, researchers found seven proteins within a few weeks that could lead to possible treatment. Typically, the medical community finds about one new protein-based treatment a year.

Jackson's article went on to describe usage of Watson by Johnson & Johnson:

> Another organization testing Watson has been Johnson & Johnson, which also put the cognitive computing service to work ingesting and analyzing scientific papers, this time to compare the effectiveness of various drugs and other treatments, looking for those with the best results and the fewest side-effects.
>
> For example, for back pain, a quick scan of the medical literature turns up published results of over 3,000 trials, describing the effectiveness of 27 different treatments. No one doctor can read all of these documents, said Soledad Cepeda, Johnson & Johnson director of epidemiology.

Lauren Friedman gave a further update in May 2015, in a Business Insider article "IBM's Watson computer can now do in a matter of minutes what it takes cancer doctors weeks to perform"[162]:

> Fourteen US and Canadian cancer institutes will use International Business Machines Corp.'s Watson computer system to choose therapies based on a tumour's genetic fingerprints, the company said on Tuesday, the latest step toward bringing personalized cancer treatments to more patients.
>
> Oncology is the first specialty where matching therapy to DNA has improved outcomes for some patients, inspiring the "precision medicine initiative"...
>
> But it can take weeks to identify drugs targeting cancer-causing mutations. Watson can do it in minutes and has in its database the findings of scientific papers and clinical trials on particular cancers and potential therapies...
>
> IBM is positioning Watson for exactly this task: an area of medicine where humans can see the vast potential, but can't begin to wrangle the data needed to achieve it. "Genomics is the secret to unlocking personalized medicine," said Steve Gold, a Vice President of the IBM Watson Group, at a press conference on Tuesday...

As the article emphasised, there's still a great deal of work ahead, but there are encouraging signs of important progress happening:

> The scientists directly involved with Watson aren't making any promises, but they're hopeful they can slowly begin to make a difference in the world of cancer treatment, which today leaves a great number of patients without many good options.
>
> "Traditional cancer treatments are moderately effective, associated with moderate toxicity, and many patients still succumb to the disease," said

Lukas Wartman, assistant director of Cancer Genomics at Washington University and a leukaemia survivor, at Tuesday's press conference. "There's been a lot of pessimism among those [fighting] cancer, and Watson offers an opportunity to fight back against that pessimism."

One reason to be encouraged is because of some general principles regarding the insights that can be drawn from "big data". Let's look at these next.

The unreasonable effectiveness of big data

Three factors can improve the performance of computer analysis of a field of data:

1. When the underlying computer hardware becomes more powerful
2. When the algorithms become smarter
3. When the data becomes larger.

The first case includes faster clock speed, more memory, and larger banks of parallel processors. The second case involves better software. But it is the third case where the improvement can be most surprising.

This point was made as long ago as 2001 by two Microsoft researchers, Michele Banko and Eric Bell, in a publication entitled "Scaling to Very Very Large Corpora for Natural Language Disambiguation"[163]. This took one particular language problem as an example: can software learn which word from a set that are commonly confused (for example, "to", "too", and "two"; or "principle" and "principal") is the right choice for a given sentence? That is, given a number of examples of correct word selection, how accurately can algorithms infer the correct word to use in new phrases that are similar (but not identical) to the training set?

Banko and Brill considered four different algorithms, with names such as "Naïve Bayes", "Perceptron", and "Winnow". In each case, the algorithm was shown sets of sentences demonstrating the correct use of confusable words, before being tested on new sentences.

When the training sets comprised around one million examples, the algorithms proved successful at the subsequent tests with scores varying around 75% to 83%. In other words, some algorithms are better than others. No doubt, more sophisticated algorithms might push the success score higher again. However, the researchers repeated the experiment with ever larger training sets. With ten million sentences, all four algorithms were performing better than even the best had done with just one million sentences. The same improvements happened again, moving up to 100 million training sentences, and yet again, moving up to one billion. By this time, all four algorithms were clustered around 95% success on new sentences.

Banko and Brill state their conclusion:

> In this paper, we have looked into what happens when we begin to take advantage of the large amounts of text that are now readily available. We have shown that for a prototypical natural language classification task, the performance of learners can benefit significantly from much larger training sets.

In other words, for at least some computer learning problems, finding larger sets of learning data can provide better improvements than refining the algorithms used.

The theme was developed in a 2010 presentation by Peter Norvig, Director of Research at Google. The presentation has the memorable title "The Unreasonable Effectiveness of Data"[164]. Norvig's presentation looked at two classes of problem:

- Manipulating text – for example, translating text from Chinese into English
- Manipulating graphical images – for example, removing parts of a photo which were deemed to intrude on the main content, and filling in these areas with content that fits the rest of the photo.

Norvig described a huge database made available by Google, which includes over one trillion words, forming 95 billion sentences, collected from the worldwide web. The database has 13 million unique words. The value of the database comes from tracking the relative occurrences of different "bigrams" (pairs of words next to each other), "trigrams", "fourgrams", and so on. For example, out of the 1.3 billion distinct fourgrams in the database, the sequence "serve as the independent" occurs 794 times, whereas "serve as the index" occurs 223 times, and "serve as the indication" occurs 72 times. Another database gives the probability of a given short phrase in one language being translated into various short phrases in another language, and so on. Relatively simple algorithms, which refer to these massive databases, have produced better results for computer-driven translation than previous algorithms which sought to embody complex rules for grammar and pronunciation. Other algorithms made an impressive job of manipulating graphical imagery, by taking advantage of large online databases of pictures.

In order to benefit from this "unreasonable effectiveness of big data", it's necessary to be able to assemble the data in the first place, potentially from diverse sources and in multiple formats. It's also necessary to identify and remove poor quality elements from the data – such as persistent misspellings, or texts that were created by a low calibre translation algorithm (and which might cause a propagation of mistranslations if they were included in new training data). However, clever software can help with such tasks. A Google Research blogpost from March 2015 by Patrick Riley, Dale Webster, and Bharath Ramsundar, "Large-Scale Machine Learning for Drug Discovery"[165] gives details of how this can work in the area of medical data. Here's the problem statement from the article:

> Discovering new treatments for human diseases is an immensely complicated challenge; Even after extensive research to develop a biological understanding of a disease, an effective therapeutic that can improve the quality of life must still be found. This process often takes years of research, requiring the creation and testing of millions of drug-like compounds in an effort to find a just a few viable drug treatment candidates. These high-throughput screens are often automated in sophisticated labs and are expensive to perform.

And here's the solution developed by the Google Research team, with its ability to combine medical data from multiple different diseases to provide additional insight:

> Recently, deep learning with neural networks has been applied in virtual drug screening, which attempts to replace or augment the high-throughput screening process with the use of computational methods in order to improve its speed and success rate. Traditionally, virtual drug screening has used only the experimental data from the particular disease being studied. However, as the volume of experimental drug screening data across many diseases continues to grow, several research groups have demonstrated that data from multiple diseases can be leveraged with multitask neural networks to improve the virtual screening effectiveness.
>
> In collaboration with the Pande Lab at Stanford University, we've released a paper titled "Massively Multitask Networks for Drug Discovery", investigating how data from a variety of sources can be used to improve the accuracy of determining which chemical compounds would be

effective drug treatments for a variety of diseases. In particular, we carefully quantified how the amount and diversity of screening data from a variety of diseases with very different biological processes can be used to improve the virtual drug screening predictions.

The solution illustrates the power that can be obtained from systems that can assemble and analyse large amounts of diverse data:

Using our large-scale neural network training system, we trained at a scale 18x larger than previous work with a total of 37.8M data points across more than 200 distinct biological processes. Because of our large scale, we were able to carefully probe the sensitivity of these models to a variety of changes in model structure and input data. In the paper, we examine not just the performance of the model but why it performs well and what we can expect for similar models in the future…

One encouraging conclusion from this work is that our models are able to utilize data from many different experiments to increase prediction accuracy across many diseases. To our knowledge, this is the first time the effect of adding additional data has been quantified in this domain, and our results suggest that even more data could improve performance even further.

Machine learning at scale has significant potential to accelerate drug discovery and improve human health. We look forward to continued improvement in virtual drug screening and its increasing impact in the discovery process for future drugs.

This provides another indication that larger number of teams of people, working in the field of rejuvenation biotechnology, can produce net positive results, rather than (as some might fear) an accumulation of noise:

- More teams will tackle different hypotheses and different lines of enquiry
- The various pieces of data created by these teams can be collected into sophisticated unified databases
- Data analysis will indicate the most promising results that deserve further exploration
- This data analysis will be conducted, in part by human researchers, and in part by powerful software.

The same kinds of dramatic improvement characterise ongoing work in image manipulation and language translation can be expected, accordingly, to be seen in swifter drug discovery and drug testing.

The further growth of deep learning

In case there's any doubt about the potential over the next 10-25 years for deep learning methods to dramatically accelerate research across multiple fields – including rejuveneering – let's briefly note a few additional points about deep learning.

Deep learning can be called "second generation artificial intelligence":

- In the first generation – lasting from the 1950s until the present day – software is given sets of rules by human programmers, and then applies these rules to convert input data into output data
- For deep learning, the operation, in a sense, goes the other way round: software is given matching sets of input and output data (such as corresponding sets of Chinese and English sentences), and infers the rules by which the output can be generated from the input.

Deep learning has existed, in various forms, just as long as standard artificial intelligence. But it's only in the last 10-15 years that it has achieved significant results – aided by much more powerful computers, and larger data sets, than were previously available.

The recent book "The master algorithm"[166], by University of Washington professor of computer science and engineering Pedro Domingos, provides a helpful survey of the remarkable progress being made across the entire field of deep learning. The book is subtitled "How the quest for the ultimate learning machine will remake the world".

As Domingos explains, there are currently five different "tribes" within the overall machine learning community. Each tribe has its origin in a different field of academic research, and also its own idea for the starting point of the (future) master algorithm:

- "Symbolists" have their origin in logic and philosophy; their core algorithm is "inverse deduction"
- "Connectionists" have their origin in neuroscience; their core algorithm is "back-propagation"
- "Evolutionaries" have their origin in evolutionary biology; their core algorithm is "genetic programming"
- "Bayesians" have their origin in statistics; their core algorithm is "probabilistic inference"

- "Analogizers" have their origin in psychology; their core algorithm is "kernel machines".

What's likely to happen over the next decade or two is that a single master algorithm will emerge that unifies all the above approaches – and, thereby, delivers great engineering power. Domingos suggests a comparison with the progress made by physics as the fundamental forces of nature have gradually been unified under a single theory.

With that universal learning machine at hand, new solutions are likely to emerge to problems which have long held up scientific progress For example, given sets of biochemical reactions of various drugs on different cancers, the universal learning machine would infer an algorithm to suggest the best treatment for any given cancer.

Something that may "accelerate the acceleration" of the unification of deep learning is the way in which major software companies are releasing parts of their respective machine learning toolkits as open source, ready for other researchers to use, adapt, and improve.

For example, Facebook has open-sourced modules for its Torch deep learning system. This includes "tools for training convolutional neural networks"[167]. More recently, Facebook have released the design of the "Big Sur" hardware platform that runs their AI software. This move was hailed[168] by Steven Max Patersson of Ars Technica, as "the start of the deep learning revolution":

Collaboration is the key to building the machine learning boat and getting it to water.

A few days ago, Facebook open-sourced its artificial intelligence (AI) hardware computing design. Most people don't know that large companies such as Facebook, Google, and Amazon don't buy hardware from the usual large computer suppliers like Dell, HP, and IBM but instead design their own hardware based on commodity components. The Facebook website and all its myriad apps and subsystems persist on a cloud infrastructure constructed from tens of thousands of computers designed from scratch by Facebook's own hardware engineers.

Open-sourcing Facebook's AI hardware means that deep learning has graduated from the Facebook Artificial Intelligence Research (FAIR) lab into Facebook's mainstream production systems intended to run apps created by its product development teams. If Facebook software developers are to build deep-learning systems for users, a standard hardware module optimised for fast deep learning execution that fits into and scales with Facebook's data centres needs to be designed, competitively procured, and deployed.

Announcing this release, Facebook commented[169]:

Although machine learning (ML) and artificial intelligence (AI) have been around for decades, most of the recent advances in these fields have been enabled by two trends: larger publicly available research data sets and the availability of more powerful computers — specifically ones powered by GPUs. Most of the major advances in these areas move forward in lockstep with our computational ability, as faster hardware and software allow us to explore deeper and more complex systems.

At Facebook, we've made great progress thus far with off-the-shelf infrastructure components and design. We've developed software that can read stories, answer questions about scenes, play games and even learn unspecified tasks through observing some examples. But we realized that truly tackling these problems at scale would require us to design our own systems. Today, we're unveiling our next-generation GPU-based systems for training neural networks, which we've code-named "Big Sur"...

Facebook has a culture of support for open source software and hardware, and FAIR has continued that commitment by open-sourcing our code and publishing our discoveries as academic papers freely available from open-access sites. We're very excited to add hardware designed for AI research and production to our list of contributions to the community.

We want to make it a lot easier for AI researchers to share techniques and technologies. As with all hardware systems that are released into the open, it's our hope that others will be able to work with us to improve it. We believe that this open collaboration helps foster innovation for future designs, putting us all one step closer to building complex AI systems that bring this kind of innovation to our users and, ultimately, help us build a more open and connected world.

As another example, in November 2015, Google released its "TensorFlow" software library – described as "an open source software library for machine intelligence". On that website, Google state and answer the question "Why Did Google Open Source This?"[170]

If TensorFlow is so great, why open source it rather than keep it proprietary? The answer is simpler than you might think: We believe that machine learning is a key ingredient to the innovative products and technologies of the future. Research in this area is global and growing fast, but lacks standard tools. By sharing what we believe to be one of the best machine learning toolboxes in the world, we hope to create an open standard for exchanging research ideas and putting machine learning in products. Google engineers really do use TensorFlow in user-facing products and services, and our research group intends to share TensorFlow implementations alongside many of our research publications.

Analysis by Matthew Mayo of KDnuggets, highlights that the use[171] of deep learning within Google is growing exponentially:

DistBelief, Google Brain's first generation deep learning research project, started in 2011... As recently as Q3 2013, there were comparatively few deep learning projects at Google, estimated... to be in the double digits at said point in time.

Growth has since exploded, and continues exponentially, with an approximate 1200% increase between Q3 2013 and Q3 2015... Google is clearly and aggressively harnessing deep learning as we move into the future.

This corporate emphasis is confirmed by remarks made by Google CEO Sundar Pichai as he reported the company's financial performance in October 2015. His remarks were analysed[172] by Jillian D'Onfro of Business Insider:

During CEO Sundar Pichai's prepared remarks, he went out of his way to point out that investments in machine learning and artificial intelligence were a continued priority for the company moving forward.

Pichai even went as far as to say that Google was "re-thinking" all of its products to include more AI and machine learning.

In the words of Stanford University's Rob Schapire, the goal of machine learning is "to devise learning algorithms that do the learning automatically without human intervention or assistance."

Those smart algorithms already power Google's voice search and translation, its Photos product, and the new service Now On Tap which anticipates what information you might need before you ask for it...

"Machine learning is a core, transformative way by which we're re-thinking how we're doing everything," Pichai said on the call... "We are thoughtfully applying it across all our products, be it search, ads, YouTube, or Play. And we're in early days, but you will see us — in a systematic way — apply machine learning in all these areas."

In these remarks, Pichai drew no direct attention to two other companies under the "Alphabet" umbrella of one-time Google companies

– Calico and Verily. Both these companies have a healthcare focus, and both can be expected to be ready to apply Google's deep learning technology (as well as deep learning technology from other sources) to accelerate their business goals.

Incidentally, the difference between Calico and Verily was described[173] by Verily head Andrew Conrad in an interview with Stephen Levy in October 2014, at a time when Verily was known as "Google X Life Sciences":

> The mission of Google X Life Sciences is to change healthcare from reactive to proactive. Ultimately it's to prevent disease and extend the average lifespan through the prevention of disease, make people live longer, healthier lives.
>
> *Levy: It sounds like that mission overlaps a little with another Google health enterprise, Calico. Are you working with them?*
>
> Let me give you the subtle difference. Calico's mission is to improve the maximum lifespan, to make people live longer through developing new ways to prevent aging. Our mission is to make most people live longer, getting rid of the diseases that kill you earlier.
>
> *Levy: Basically you're helping me live long enough for Calico's stuff to kick in.*
>
> Exactly. We're helping you live long enough so Calico can make you live longer.

Factoring complexity

Google's separation of companies – into Verily, Calico, the (new, smaller) Google, and potentially a whole alphabet of others – under the new Alphabet overseeing entity, is in line with one final principle that I wish to discuss in this chapter. It's one more principle for dealing with the issues when a field of research (such as the field of rejuveneering) becomes overly complicated. The principle can be summarised as "divide and conquer".

Harvard professor Clayton Christensen emphasises that point in his book "The innovator's prescription: a disruptive solution for health care"[174]. The book was co-authored by Jerome Grossman and Jason Hwang. The book addresses the question: *How can we find ways to allow technological breakthroughs to reduce the spiralling costs of healthcare?*

One of the prevailing themes of "The innovator's prescription" is the need to restructure complex systems:

While indeed there are economies of scale, there are countervailing costs of complexity – the more product families that are produced, the higher the overhead burden rates.

One example examined by Christensen and his co-authors – an example outside the field of healthcare, but with important lessons for healthcare – describes a manager analysing a manufacturing plant which was struggling with overhead costs. At this plant, 6.2 dollars were spent in overhead expenses for every dollar spent on direct labour:

> These overhead costs included not just utilities and depreciation, but the costs of scheduling, expediting, quality control, repair and rework, scrap maintenance, materials handling, accounting, computer systems, and so on. Overhead comprised all costs that were not directly spent in making products.

The quality of products made at that plant was also causing concern:

> About 15% of all overhead costs were created by the need to repair and rework products that failed in the field, or had been discovered by inspectors as faulty before shipment.

However, it didn't appear to the manager that any money was being wasted:

> The plant hadn't been painted inside or out in 20 years. The landscaping was now overrun by weeds. The receptionist in the bare-bones lobby had been replaced long ago with a paper directory and a phone. The manager had no secretarial assistance, and her grey World War II vintage steel desk was dented by a kick from some frustrated predecessor.

Nevertheless, this particular plant had considerably higher overhead burden rates than the other plants from the same company. What was the difference?

The difference was in the complexity. This particular plant was set up to cope with large numbers of different product designs, whereas the other plants (which had been created later) had been able to optimise for particular design families.

The original plant essentially had the value proposition,

> We'll make any product that anyone designs.

In contrast, the newer plants in the same organisation had the following kind of value proposition:

> If you need a product that can be made through one of these two sequences of operations and activities, we'll do it for you at the lowest possible cost and the highest possible quality.

Further analysis, across a number of different plants, reached the following results:

> Each time the scale of a plant doubled, holding the degree of pathway complexity constant, **the overhead rate could be expected to fall by 15%.** So, for example, a plant that made two families and generated $40 million in sales would be expected to have an overhead burden ratio of about 2.85, while the burden rate for a plant making two families with $80 million in sales would be 15% lower (2.85 x 0.85 = 2.42). But every time the number of families produced in a plant of a given scale doubled, **the overhead burden rate soared 27%.** So if a two-pathway, $40 million plant accepted products that required two additional pathways, but that did not increase its sales volume, its overhead burden rate would increase by 2.85 x 1.27, to 3.62…

This is just one aspect of a long and fascinating analysis by Christensen and his co-authors. Modern day general purpose hospitals support huge numbers of different patient care pathways, so high overhead rates are inevitable. The solution is to allow the formation of separate specialist units, where practitioners can then focus on iteratively optimising particular lines of healthcare. We can already see this in firms that specialise in laser eye surgery, in hernia treatment, and so on. Without these new units separating and removing some of the complexity of the original unit, it becomes harder and harder for innovation to take place. The innovation becomes stifled under conflicting business models.

In short: reducing overhead costs isn't just a matter of "eliminating obvious inefficiencies, spending less time on paperwork, etc". It often requires initially painful structural changes, in which overly complex multi-function units are simplified by the removal and separation of business lines and product pathways. Only with the new, simplified set up – often involving new companies, and sometimes involving "creative destruction" – can disruptive innovations flourish.

Indeed, new technology often requires associated changes in business model and in product design before it can be successful. Creative destruction often involves near-simultaneous innovations in all three of these dimensions. Thankfully, with ever larger numbers of talented, educated, thoughtful people becoming involved in the field of rejuveneering, we can expect these innovations to be forthcoming, for all the reasons I've listed in this chapter. And together, these innovations have a great chance to reverse the trend of Eroom's Law, en route to reversing aging itself.

The CRISPR game-changer

I started this chapter with one example of dramatic acceleration in a technology highly relevant to the rejuveneering project: the ability to analyse large DNA sequences. I'll end with one more example: the ability to *synthesise* DNA sequences. Just as the cost to read DNA has plunged downwards in the last few years, the cost to *write* DNA has likewise improved. And for writing (or editing) DNA, it's not just that the cost has dropped; the ease of use has jumped forwards too.

Up until 2012, DNA editing was typically carried out with the help of proteins known as zinc finger nucleases and TALENs. However, since then, a new technology known as CRISPR has become much more widely used.

Since its first use in 2012 to edit strings of DNA, CRISPR has exceeded expectations, time and again, regarding its scope and utility. The location of a DNA alteration can now be much more tightly controlled, reducing the risk of unpredictable side effects of gene edits (effects where edits took place in locations other than the ones intended).

In December 2015, the staff of Science magazine picked CRISPR as their choice for "breakthrough of the year" (across *all* branches of science). Science writer John Travis explains[175]:

> It was conceived after a yogurt company in 2007 identified an unexpected defence mechanism that its bacteria use to fight off viruses. A birth announcement came in 2012, followed by crucial first steps in 2013 and a massive growth spurt last year. Now, it has matured into a molecular marvel, and much of the world—not just biologists—is taking notice of the genome-editing method CRISPR, Science's 2015 Breakthrough of the Year.
>
> CRISPR has appeared in Breakthrough sections twice before, in 2012 and 2013, each time as a runner-up in combination with other genome-editing techniques. But this is the year it broke away from the pack, revealing its true power in a series of spectacular achievements…

The biomedical applications of CRISPR are just starting to emerge. Clinical researchers are already applying it to create tissue-based treatments for cancer and other diseases. CRISPR may also revive the moribund concept of transplanting animal organs into people. Many people feared that retroviruses lurking in animal genomes could harm transplant recipients, but this year a team eliminated, in one fell swoop, 62 copies of a retrovirus's DNA littering the pig genome. And [a recent] international summit saw many discussions of CRISPR's promise for repairing genetic defects in human embryos...

Referring to one of the co-discoverers of the power of CRISPR, Emmanuelle Charpentier of the Max Planck Institute for Infection Biology in Berlin, Travis highlights the remarkable potential of the technique:

It's only slightly hyperbolic to say that if scientists can dream of a genetic manipulation, CRISPR can now make it happen. At one point during the human gene-editing summit, Charpentier described its capabilities as "mind-blowing." It's the simple truth.

Here's part of what's "mind-blowing". CRISPR is making it increasingly easy for diverse medical research teams to explore potential new biochemical mechanisms. The application of techniques borrowed from the world of "conventional" (silicon-hosted) software is already having an additional impact. Writing in a February 2016 article "Software Helps Gene Editing Tool CRISPR Live Up to Its Hype"[176] in IEEE Spectrum, Emily Waltz explains this software crossover:

New algorithms make CRISPR as easy as point-and-click

Biotechnologists are jumping at the chance to use the revolutionary gene-editing tool known as CRISPR. The molecular gadget can be programmed to accurately tweak the DNA of any organism, but scientists need software algorithms to hasten the programming process. Dozens of teams are developing such software...

Traditional [pre-CRISPR] genome modification techniques involve shuttling DNA into cells without knowing where in the genome it will stick. Editing with CRISPR is like placing a cursor between two letters in a word processing document and hitting "delete" or clicking "paste." And the tool can cost less than US $50 to assemble.

CRISPR, therefore, is itself a notable example of collaboratively produced technology, which in turn facilitates additional collaboration. It is enabling precise experimentation with a huge new set of potential rejuvenation therapies, which were previously too complicated even to consider. And as such, it illustrates one additional way in which the slow-down effects of Eroom's Law can be circumvented: game-changing technical breakthroughs can inject explosive new waves of energy that overcome the weary inertia of previous systems.

7. Runners and riders

Rejuveneers form a broad spectrum. They can agree on the desired end goal of their research, namely the availability of therapies to slow down, prevent, and ultimately reverse biological aging. They can also agree on the general set of rejuvenation building blocks from which these therapies might be constructed – building blocks that potentially include:

- Genetic manipulations
- Drugs to be administered
- Changes in lifestyle (such as diet)
- Cell transformations (including stem cell engineering)
- Nanoscale interventions (such as roving nanobot repair mechanisms)
- Larger-scale interventions (such as synthetic replacements for organs)
- Other biological transformations (such as altering aspects of human biochemistry).

However, different groups of rejuveneers emphasise different possible routes forward. It's not yet clear which approaches are going to prove the most effective to develop rejuvenation therapies that are practical and comprehensive. This chapter compares and contrasts a representative sample of the major runners and riders in this race.

Living long enough to live indefinitely

Rejuvenation treatments vary in their ambition level. Some treatments would merely slow down the onset of aging, rather than reversing it. A treatment that provides, say, only two or three more years of healthy life expectancy, may still be well worth pursuing and adopting. That's because this additional period of time might provide the bridge to the availability of new, more powerful rejuvenation therapies. The application of a series of different therapies, several years apart, each more powerful than the previous one, might keep individuals alive and healthy until such time as the full abolition of aging is possible.

This sentiment is expressed in the heroic phrase "Live long enough to live forever" which features as the subtitle of the 2004 book "Fantastic voyage"[177] co-authored by futurist Ray Kurzweil and medical practitioner Terry Grossman. That book talks about three main "Bridges" to reaching an indefinitely long life. The idea is introduced by analogy[178] between the lifetime of a human being and the lifetime of a house:

> How long does a house last? The answer obviously depends on how well you take care of it. If you do nothing, the roof will spring a leak before long, water and the elements will invade, and eventually the house will disintegrate. But if you proactively take care of the structure, repair all damage, confront all dangers, and rebuild or renovate parts from time to time using new materials and technologies, the life of the house can essentially be extended without limit.
>
> The same holds true for our bodies and brains. The only difference is that while we fully understand the methods underlying the maintenance of a house, we do not yet fully understand all of the biological principles of life. But with our rapidly increasing comprehension of the human genome, the proteins expressed by the genome (proteome), and the biochemical processes and pathways of our metabolism, we are quickly gaining that knowledge. We are beginning to understand aging, not as a single inexorable progression but as a group of related biological processes.
>
> Strategies for reversing each of these aging progressions using different combinations of biotechnology techniques are emerging. Many scientists, including the authors of this book, believe that we will have the means to stop and even reverse aging within the next two decades. In the meantime, we can slow each aging process to a crawl using the methods outlined in this book.
>
> In this way, the goal of extending longevity can be taken in three steps, or Bridges. This book is intended to serve as a guide to living long enough in good health and spirits – Bridge One – to take advantage of the full development of the biotechnology revolution – Bridge Two. This, in turn, will lead to the nanotechnology-AI (artificial intelligence) revolution – Bridge Three – which has the potential to allow us to live indefinitely.

I believe this three-step framework to be essentially sound. Most of what I am writing about in this book fits into the "Bridge Two" of Kurzweil and Grossman, although I believe that step will be significantly aided by the twin technologies of nanotechnology and AI which these authors attribute as coming into their own in the subsequent "Bridge Three".

Kurzweil and Grossman have something rather different in mind for the third step – developments that are more radical, to which I'll return in the penultimate chapter of my own book. These developments are intended to bridge the gap between "living agelessly – but still subject to death from numerous accidents" to "living indefinitely – safe not only from aging but from almost every other threat to life".

Lifestyle changes

Before any of us can benefit from either Bridge Two or Bridge Three, we need to keep ourselves sufficiently healthy in the short term. Books such as "Fantastic Voyage" provide large amounts of advice on that score.

Actually the word "vast" would be better than "large". Advice on healthy living is an enormous industry. Some items of advice from this vast mix are uncontroversial, such as to stop smoking, to avoid becoming obese, not to spend too much time sunbathing, and not to drive while intoxicated. Many other items of advice, available in numerous health books and magazines, are more contentious. For example, some writers swear by a vegan diet (usually augmented with some mineral supplements), whereas others swear by a "paleo" diet with plenty of meat. Other writers conflict on the optimal forms of exercise (e.g. high-intensity versus low-intensity).

Looking down the long, long list of recommendations on the Fantastic Voyage website[179], it's hard for a layperson reader to known how much confidence to place on recommendations such as:

- Replace coffee, which is quite acidic, with less acidic beverages such as tea.

- In general, unfiltered tap water should not be drunk. Filtered tap water or ideally filtered, alkalinized water should be drunk instead. (Purified alkaline water can be produced from tap water by using an alkalinizing water machine: see recommended products listing).

- Minimize exposure to hair dryers, electric shavers, etc. Reduce your total cell phone usage and use "hands free" connection with air tube, ferrite choke, and external antenna.

- Do not use aluminium cookware or aluminium foil. Replace aluminium containing antiperspirants with non-aluminium containing products (available at natural food stores).

The reference to the possibility of purchasing an alkalinizing water machine – available from a company recommended by Kurzweil and Grossman – highlights one of the complications of health advice: such advice frequently comes from people who have something to sell. In some cases, what's being sold is an actual product, such as an alkalinizing water machine, antiperspirants free from aluminium, or sets of mineral supplements. In other cases, what's being sold is a message. Either way, the objectivity of the advice is called into question.

Worse, the advice from people who are honestly seeking to improve our health is frequently drowned out by waves of marketing from well-funded corporations who have unhealthy products to sell. Like the tobacco companies who at one time implied that smoking actually conveyed health benefits (for example, via the 1940s advertising slogan "More doctors smoke Camels than any other cigarette"[180]), many present-day corporations imply that their sugary, high-carbohydrate foods are, somehow, good for us. These cross-currents of information (and, sometimes, misinformation) make it all the harder for the layperson to distinguish reliable advice from unreliable advice.

There are similar conflicting currents of claims and counterclaims about the health benefits of yoga (ably reviewed by William Broad in "The science of yoga: the risks and the rewards"[181]), meditation, positive thinking, red wine, so-called "detox" treatments, and numerous organic compounds.

Anecdotal evidence in this field is particularly suspect. People can unwittingly benefit from the placebo effect if they earnestly believe that particular lifestyle changes will boost their health. They can also mislead themselves via selective recall, and by jumping to wrong conclusions about the causes of changes in their health. (Health changes can take place independent of whatever modifications in lifestyle are being trialled at the time.)

I say all this, not to let any of us off the hook as regards our obligation to understand and then follow the components of improved lifestyles. Hoping to coast through to Bridge Two, without making any effort to look after our health in the meantime, might prove to be the height of naivety. Anyone who wishes the abolition of aging, for themselves or for loved ones, needs to be mindful that there's great uncertainty about the date at which effective rejuvenation therapies will become available. Steps that will provide an extra few years of healthy longevity could well turn out to make all the difference between us reaching – or missing – a subsequent set of bridge steps towards indefinitely long healthiness.

My recommendations for people who wish to set out on this "Bridge One" journey are that we should:

- Avoid travelling alone. Seek out like-minded fellow-travellers, to pool learnings and insight from the latest research they have found

- Collectively guard against wishful thinking and other cognitive biases which could lead to the misguided adoption of lifestyle changes that end up doing more harm than good

- Search for evidence that could disconfirm our current favoured theories

- Be ready to revise our opinions, as soon as better evidence or better arguments become available

- Avoid being overly influenced by pronouncements from figures with apparent authority, but who may be as prone as the rest of us to occasional lapses in judgement. Indeed, just because someone is relatively expert in one field (for example, chemical bonds), it is no reason to assume they will be relatively expert in a different area (such as healthy lifestyles).

But the most important recommendation for Bridge One travellers is this: realise that Bridge One – the set of longevity improvements from changes in lifestyle – isn't, by itself, going to abolish aging. Without the biomedical interventions of Bridge Two, we're all going to become aged and infirm. The onset of these infirmities might be delayed by a few decades (in optimistic estimates), but a spiralling downhill fate still awaits us.

In short, any therapies that might be described as "natural" – changing what we eat, how we exercise, how we sleep, how we breathe, how we think, and similar – are going to run out of steam, sooner or later. If rejuveneering restricts itself to natural remedies, it's going to fail.

Any apparent evidence to the contrary – claims of lifespans of 120 or more for Indian gurus or yoghurt-eating country folk from Georgia, or whatever – has failed to withstand the scrutiny of investigators. What investigators have found, instead, is:

- Evidence of gullibility, on the part of people passing on news stories of exceptional longevity

- Reasons why people might have wanted to falsify their ages: to gain greater respect from their contemporaries, to become exempt from obligations of military service, and so on.

Extra supplements

It's worth spending a few minutes discussing a special case of the ideas from the previous section. This is the idea that certain substances that are ordinarily found in relatively small quantities in our diets could usefully be taken in much larger quantities, with significant effect on our healthspans.

Two versions of this idea were mentioned in Chapter 2, "Rejuveneering 101":

- Ilya Metchnikoff recommended drinking yoghurt to promote longevity
- Linus Pauling endorsed long-term dietary supplementation with high doses of vitamin C.

In each case, there was a "theory of aging" behind the idea of the supplement:

- Metchnikoff believed that aging was caused by the action of toxic bacteria in the digestive tract – bacteria that could be combatted by yoghurt
- Pauling believed that aging was caused by adverse stress effects in cells of chemicals variously known as "oxidants", "free radicals", or "reactive species" – chemicals whose impacts could be reduced by others known as "antioxidants", such as vitamin C.

Both these theories of aging have fallen out of favour in the intervening years. These factors are no longer seen as the *primary* or *single* causes of aging.

Vitamin C, along with other antioxidants, may well still have a role to play in diminishing the risk of diseases. The institute which Pauling founded in 1973 and which bears his name, the Linus Pauling Institute, recently issued the following analysis[182] of the vitamin, urging that the daily RDA (Recommended Dietary Allowance) for this compound be increased from 60mg to 120mg:

Vitamin C is an important dietary antioxidant ... a substance in foods that significantly decreases the adverse effects of reactive species, such as reactive oxygen and nitrogen species, on normal physiological function in humans. The adverse effects of these reactive species are oxidative damage to biomolecules, such as lipids, DNA, and proteins. Such oxidative damage has been implicated in chronic diseases, including heart disease, stroke, cancer, and cataract...

Based on our review of the literature, we conclude that the RDA for vitamin C should be 120 mg/day for optimum risk reduction of heart disease, stroke, and cancer in healthy individuals.

Their recommendations were based, they said, on:

a rigorous review of over 200 research articles on the health benefits of vitamin C.

Their recommendations extended to two other antioxidants, namely vitamin E and selenium. Their overall conclusion was as follows:

Since heart disease, stroke, and cancer are the three top killers in the U.S., causing about 1.3 million deaths per year, the potential of an adequate vitamin C nutriture, as well as vitamin E and selenium..., to benefit public health and reduce the economic and medical costs and concomitant suffering associated with these chronic diseases is substantial.

Pauling himself had taken up to 18,000 mg of vitamin C per day – some 300 times the RDA. As noted in Chapter 2, Pauling died at the age of 93, of cancer – a disease he had hoped would be tamed by such large ingestion of vitamin C. Although a ripe old age by conventional standards, 93 was some way short of the figures of 100 to 110 years (and in due course 150 years) which Pauling had included in his writings.

And of course, the mere fact that Pauling lived as many as 93 years, having taken large doses of vitamin C, is no proof that this intake was *responsible* for his longer-than-average lifespan. What are needed are larger trials, involving many more people. However, contrary to the expectations expressed by Pauling, such trials of antioxidants have generally shown no effect or, worse, an *adverse* effect. Some key results are summarised in a 2013 article[183] in The Atlantic written by Paul Offit. Here are just two of many examples quoted:

- In a trial of 29,000 men in Finland, known to be at high risk of cancer and heart disease (since they were all long-term smokers aged over 50), the group taking vitamins had an *increased* likelihood of dying from heart disease or lung cancer

- Researchers from the University of Copenhagen found that mortality rates from intestinal cancer were 6% *higher* in groups taking antioxidant supplements than in controls who did not.

Offit quotes Steven Nissen, chairman of cardiology at the Cleveland Clinic:

"The concept of multivitamins was sold to Americans by an eager nutraceutical industry to generate profits. There was never any scientific data supporting their usage."

Reflecting on the results, Offit comments:

Given that free radicals clearly damage cells – and given that people who eat diets rich in substances that neutralize free radicals are healthier – why did studies of supplemental antioxidants show they were harmful?

The most likely explanation is that free radicals aren't as evil as advertised. Although it's clear that free radicals can damage DNA and disrupt cell membranes, that's not always a bad thing. People need free radicals to kill bacteria and eliminate new cancer cells. But when people take large doses of antioxidants, the balance between free radical production and destruction might tip too much in one direction, causing an unnatural state in which the immune system is less able to kill harmful invaders. Researchers have called this "the antioxidant paradox." Whatever the reason, the data are clear: high doses of vitamins and supplements increase the risk of heart disease and cancer.

At the very least, we have to give the following assessment to the idea that it is free radicals which causes aging: *things are more complicated than that*. Antioxidants such as vitamin C may well be beneficial in some circumstances, but can only form a partial subset of any comprehensive suite of rejuvenation therapies.

A broader principle deserves attention. Some aspects of damage at the cellular level are, by themselves, perfectly compatible with ongoing health at the larger, organic level. The body can continue to thrive despite the damage caused by oxidative stress to molecules such as lipids, DNA, and proteins: either the cells repair this damage themselves, or the body generates new cells to take the place of these cells, or the cells can continue to function with the damage in place. What's more, specific biochemical interventions designed to address that damage could have unexpected side-effects. In short, it may well be better *not* to intervene to try to prevent or remove that damage.

This, however, is by no means the end of the free radical theory of aging. The theory lives on, in evolved forms. Here are two examples:

- The *mitochondrial theory of aging* highlights one particular kind of oxidative stress damage as having particular significance, namely damage to the DNA of the mitochondria powerhouses that exist within the body of cells (outside the cell nucleus)

- The *metabolic stability theory of aging* accepts that free radicals have many positive effects in the body, and suggests that ill effects only occur when the concentration of free radicals in cells grows in an unstable way.

But in neither case does the new theory claim to be the single, comprehensive theory of aging. For that, we have to widen our gaze.

Dealing with damage

These ideas that aging is due to various sorts of cellular damage from oxidative stress caused by free radicals are part of a broader conception of aging. In this broader conception, aging at the organic (body) level is due to the runaway accumulation of several types of damage at the cellular and molecular level, which in turn hinders the normal functioning of the body. Examples of this damage include:

- The growth in number of crosslinks known, by a convenient acronym, as AGEs – advanced glycation end-products. AGEs involve proteins or lipids which are part of the normal functioning of cells, except that they have become "glycated", meaning the molecules have bonded with sugar molecules (glucose). AGEs tend to cross-link to each other, resulting in stiffening, and in turn, to an increased propensity to numerous diseases, including diabetes and Alzheimer's disease

- The decline in power of the lysosomes within cells that would ordinarily break down waste products within the cell for subsequent reuse. One consequence is that specific cells known as macrophages can no longer perform their function of swallowing and recycling the toxic by-products of cholesterol. This results in arterial disease such as atherosclerosis. Another consequence is macular degeneration (a form of eyesight loss); yet another is the onset of neurodegenerative disease

- The accumulation of senescent cells, which are cells that have suffered some internal damage, and which would normally have their contents recycled by the body, except for the fact that the cell refuses to die, and continues in existence, zombie-like, in an abnormal state that can cause inflammation of the immune system or other degradation of nearby tissue
- The decline in the ability of pools of stem cells within the body to generate new cells to replace those which are lost during the normal processes of metabolism; as a result, organs shrink, muscles weaken, the brain loses cognitive powers, and the immune system becomes compromised
- Damage to mitochondrial DNA, caused by action of free radicals as described in the previous section; this diminishes the ability of the cell to generate energy and therefore to function as normal
- Cells that start dividing too often, due to damage in their nuclear DNA, resulting in cancerous growths
- The accumulation of extracellular amyloid – misfolded, adhesive proteins – which disrupt the normal healthy function of nearby organs and tissues; amyloid can contribute to Alzheimer's disease, diabetes, Parkinson's disease, heart disease, and numerous other diseases.

To address this multiplicity of types of damage, rejuveneers have two different approaches they can consider:

1. Pluralist: Accept that there are many distinct types of molecular and cellular damage, and seek to create a suite of multiple rejuvenation therapies, each designed to handle one type of damage. Rejuvenation will, in this case, involve a cocktail from these different therapies

2. Fundamentalist: Identify some types of damage as being more fundamental than others, in that fixing the more fundamental damage will automatically result in (or simplify the search for) fixes for the other categories of damage.

In later sections of this chapter, I'll look at a number of examples of theories of the fundamentalist type. First, let's look at perhaps the best-known example of the pluralist approach. This is the SENS programme devised by Aubrey de Grey, which first featured in an academic publication in 2002: "Time to Talk SENS: Critiquing the Immutability of Human Aging"[184].

SENS envisages and supports seven different research initiatives, proceeding in parallel, targeting the seven types of damage listed earlier. These initiatives are, respectively:

- GlycoSENS: "Breaking extracellular crosslinks"[185]
- LysoSENS: "Clearing waste accumulations out of cells"[186]
- ApoptoSENS: "Removing dysfunctional cells"[187]
- RepleniSENS: "Replacing lost cells"[188]
- MitoSENS: "Preventing damage from mitochondrial mutations"[189]
- OncoSENS: "Making cancerous mutations harmless"[190]
- AmyloSENS: "Removing junk from between cells"[191].

SENS has been running public conferences since 2003 at which longevity researchers have debated aspects of the SENS proposals. I attended portions of the events in 2007, 2011, and 2013 (all held in Queens' College Cambridge) as well as a larger event in San Francisco in 2014. Additionally, de Grey has featured as a guest presenter at London Futurists events on around half a dozen occasions, where audience members have asked him numerous questions. I've had plenty of opportunity to evaluate the progress of the project.

Progress towards SENS

SENS is an abbreviation for "Strategies for Engineered Negligible Senescence". SENS can be evaluated from a variety of perspectives. Here are my responses:

- *Does the basic SENS framework withstand scrutiny? Is it useful to conceive and address aging as a number of different sorts of molecular and cellular damage?* Yes, I see this programme as being intellectually robust and well worth support

- *Is SENS likely to prove the most effective approach to rejuveneering?* It strikes me as desirable for different research teams within the overall research community to variously pursue both pluralist and fundamentalist approaches, and to share their findings. The question as to which approach will turn out to be the most effective will be answered in the years ahead (I'll have more to say about it later in this chapter)

- *Are there additional types of damage that need to be considered, beyond the ones listed by SENS?* That remains an open question. It's possible that one or more of the classes listed will need, in time, to be split into two, with two different sets of therapies being needed to handle them. But the basic classification has already withstood analysis for well over a decade

- *Are the SENS recommendations, for dealing with each kind of damage, all likely to be turned into practical therapies?* The identification of a category of damage is a separate matter from identifying the best set of interventions to deal with that damage. If it turns out that one of the specific SENS research initiatives becomes bogged down, and a different approach proves more fruitful to address that particular type of damage, that's no indication of a mistake in the original SENS seven-fold classification of damage

- *Does SENS, with its portfolio of diverse research initiatives, offer any advantage over traditional medical approaches to the varieties of diseases of old age?* Absolutely. In the traditional disease-first approach, there are many, many more than seven different lines of enquiry that need to be pursued. Moreover, treatments for single diseases have diminished efficacy as the patient suffers simultaneously from other diseases due to the ongoing accumulation of cellular and molecular damage. But in the SENS aging-first approach, the number of lines of enquiry is much reduced. To the extent that any of these lines of research is successful, there will benefits arising for scores of different diseases.

When I first learned about SENS, it was an organisation that was full of ideas, and which regularly asked people to make donations to support further research into these ideas. I sometimes heard it criticised for just being a fundraising endeavour. However, since that time, SENS has become increasingly recognised for the research it has carried out or sponsored.

For example, the organisation's 2015 annual report[192] provides details of SENS-sponsored research being carried out at:

- Albert Einstein College of Medicine ("Epimutations: Targets or Bystanders for Rejuvenation Biotechnology?")
- The Babraham Institute ("Target Prioritization of Adventitious Tissue Crosslinking")
- University of California, Berkeley ("Rejuvenation of the Systemic Environment")
- Buck Institute for Research on Aging ("Death-Resistant Cells: From Inhibiting SASP to Geroprotector")
- Harvard University and Brigham & Women's Hospital ("Novel Diagnostics for Transthyretin Amyloid")
- University of Oxford, Centre for the Advancement of Sustainable Medical Innovations ("Rebalancing Risk:Benefit Appraisal in Clinical Trials")
- Rice University ("Clearance Therapeutics Against Lipofuscin")
- SENS Research Foundation Research Center ("Engineering New Mitochondrial Genes to Restore Mitochondrial Function" and "Identification of the Genetic Basis of ALT")
- University of Texas-Houston Medical School ("Catalytic Antibodies Targeting Transthyretin Amyloid")
- Wake Forest Institute for Regenerative Medicine ("Cell Therapy for the Intestinal Tract" and "Tissue-Engineered Thymus")
- Yale University ("Glucosepane Crosslinks and Routes to Cleavage").

As the report clarifies, all of this work is in line with the SENS analysis:

Foundation-funded research includes teams which are:

- Developing a regenerative medicine approach to treating inflammatory bowel disease, creating underlying technologies vital for future approaches to cancer
- Creating therapeutic approaches to intracellular aggregates which build up over time and compromise the functioning of cells in the brain, heart, and muscles
- Engineering healthy new tissue for the thymus, helping to restore the vigorous immune response of youth
- Engineering new mitochondrial genes to restore function to damaged mitochondria—a source of age-related disease and currently incurable inherited disorders

- Exploring non-invasive approaches to the diagnosis and monitoring of certain underdiagnosed forms of heart disease – avoiding the need for cardiac biopsy – and identifying ways to remove aggregates which lead to impaired heart function

- Understanding the genetic basis of certain cancers which rely on a mechanism called ALT (alternative lengthening of telomeres), to pave the way for new cancer treatments

- Developing the tools needed to create therapies which reduce hypertension, stroke and kidney disease by breaking molecular crosslinks which cause arteries to stiffen with age.

The report also highlights news about emerging business models to accelerate aspects of SENS research and development. For example, regarding the LysoSENS initiative:

CASE STUDY: technology transfer: Human Rejuvenation Technologies, Inc.

SENS Research Foundation's LysoSENS program had been investigating methods of removal of unwanted intracellular aggregates since 2009. One project focused on aggregates that are the key drivers of the damage underlying plaque formation in atherosclerosis. Removing these aggregates from the immune cells that they disable would reduce plaque formation and dramatically lower the prevalence of heart disease. The project had successfully identified a non-human enzyme that was effective at eliminating some of these aggregates.

It became clear that the research was at a stage where significant further investment could greatly accelerate progress, and that such investment could be achieved by transferring the research into a private company. This was done in 2014, when Jason Hope – himself a long-term supporter of the Foundation – formed Human Rejuvenation Technologies, Inc. (HRT). The technologies developed by the Foundation were transferred to HRT in return for a 10% stake in the company.

And here's an update related to ApoptoSENS:

CASE STUDY: seed funding: Oisin Biotech

SENS Research Foundation was considering the creation of an internal project to investigate novel rejuvenation biotechnology solutions to the ablation of senescent cells…

Instead we helped in the creation of Oisin Biotech, providing seed funding along with the Methuselah Foundation. Oisin is using licensed liposome technology matched with their own patent-pending DNA construct to perform apoptosis-induced eradication of senescent cells. They have demonstrated that their construct can selectively target senescent cells *in vitro*.

To keep everything in context, the CEO of the SENS Research Foundation, Mike Kope, provided the following personal introduction to the report:

As I write, my grandmother is being kept alive by medical intervention. She is ninety-seven, and very sick. A pacemaker forces her ailing heart to beat. Her muscles are withered from sarcopenia, her bones are brittle from osteoporosis. She can scarcely leave her bed. Alzheimer's has been devastating: she cannot remember the family and friends who visit her every day, and so she lives in loneliness, even though surrounded by those who love her. Medical costs mount, savings are quickly being exhausted, and there is little more that can be done.

Her suffering is far from unique. It is a depressing reality of the world in which we live.

Every year sees the announcement of new and ever-more sophisticated ways to treat disease. But when it comes to the diseases of aging, the world needs equally sophisticated ways to preserve health, to prevent these diseases from ever taking hold. We *can* reimagine how we treat age-related disease. As a society, we *must*.

So now, imagine a world free from sarcopenia, osteoporosis, heart disease and Alzheimer's.

SENS Research Foundation is working to create that world…

Against my grandmother's inexorable decline I set the knowledge that we are on a journey to end the suffering of age-related disease for countless others.

The report concludes with an appeal for donations, to accelerate that journey to end the suffering of age-related diseases:

Every donation matters to us, whatever the amount. They cover equipment costs, or allow a researcher to attend a conference, or fund a Summer Scholar, or, well, everything you find within these pages is made possible by our generous supporters…

Help us continue our journey to "reimagine aging".

Please donate to SENS Research Foundation.

Every single dollar takes us closer to the end of age-related disease. You can help at sens.org/donate[193].

It's a powerful plea. But out of the different approaches to rejuveneering, how might the pluralist approach of SENS compare to those of some of its competitors? It's time to look at several of the competing, fundamentalist, approaches.

Telomere theory of aging

Michael Fossel, professor of clinical medicine at Michigan State University for almost 30 years, has written extensively on the role of telomeres in human aging – including his recent book "The Telomerase Revolution: The Enzyme That Holds the Key to Human Aging, and Will Soon Lead to Longer, Healthier Lives"[194].

Telomeres are the regions right at the end of chromosomes, consisting of thousands of repetitions of a short sequence of nucleotide base pairs. (For humans – indeed, for all vertebrates – the sequence that is repeated is TTAGGG: two thymine nucleotides, one adenine nucleotide, and three guanine nucleotides.) Ordinarily, when a cell divides, and copies are made of the chromosomes it contains, the length of the telomere decreases each time. This reduction is a consequence of how the duplication mechanism works. The duplicating engine is not able to proceed right to the end of the original chromosome.

After a certain number of duplications, the telomere has become so short that no other duplications are possible. Cell division therefore stops. This fact lies behind the Hayflick number mentioned in previous chapters – the observed limit in the number of times that cells can duplicate. This fact also forms the centrepiece of the telomere theory of aging. Fossel expresses that theory in a single sentence as follows:

Cells divide, telomeres shorten, gene expression changes, cellular repair and recycling slow down, errors slowly accumulate, cells fail, tissues fail, organs fail, and we fail.

Cells with shorter telomeres are less able to take part in the normal processes that repair and recycle the damage that naturally accumulates as a by-product of organic metabolism. Writing on his blog[195], Fossel explains his thinking:

In aging organisms, it's neither the genes nor the damage, but the slowing rate of recycling and repair that results in old cells, old tissues, old organisms, and age-related diseases.

Bizarrely and ironically, most people still look at biological systems and ignore the fact that they are alive, that they are dynamic, that they are constantly in flux. We look at a particular molecule – whether beta amyloid, collagen, GDF-11, or a thousand others – and we ignore the fact that these molecules are constantly being created, broken down, and replaced, but instead, we blindly focus on the damage itself. It's true that as an organism ages any given pool of molecules shows an increase in damage – such as the aggregates of beta amyloid in early plaque formation – but the key is not the damage, the key is the slowing of the metabolic turnover. An accumulation of damage is not static and passively accumulative; it occurs because the rate of turnover falls as a result of changes in the pattern of gene expression. Whether we look at tau proteins, elastin, or any other molecular pool you want to look at, the key to the problem lies not in any particular gene nor in any particular source of damage. The key lies in the rate at which both anabolism and catabolism are replacing those molecules.

In summary:

We don't age because we accumulate damage; we accumulate damage because aging permits damage to accumulate.

And in this theory, the factor underlying aging is the decrease in telomere length. What's more, the theory proposes that aging can be reversed by finding ways to extend telomere length again. This involves the enzyme telomerase – an enzyme which is already active in certain aspects of cell division:

- Telomerase is used in the division of germ cells (sperm and ova), to maintain the full length of telomeres for the cells that will provide the starting point for the next generation of life
- It is also used in some cancers, so that the cancerous cells keep on duplicating far beyond their Hayflick limit (with, unfortunately, bad consequences for the organism as a whole).

If telomerase can be introduced in the division of normal somatic (non-germ) cells, these cells, likewise, could in principle keep on dividing indefinitely, with no loss of function. Without cellular aging, the organism as a whole will also be freed from aging – according to this theory.

Fossel's first book on the telomere theory of aging was published in 1996: "Reversing Human Aging"[196]. The core ideas of that book were subject to clinical investigation by Calvin Harley and his colleagues at Geron Corporation, first in cell culture, and then in tissues. Fossel reports[197] that his ideas received good support:

> Harley showed that when telomerase was used to reset telomere length in an old cell to a length typical in a young cell, the old cell became indistinguishable from a young one...

> In 1999, Geron's scientists published a history-making paper in which they showed that when you reset telomere lengths in old human cells, you reset not only their Hayflick Limit, but also the pattern of gene expression as well. Old human cells looked and acted like young cells once again. Aging was no longer an immutable fact of life. Cell aging could now be reset at will. It was only in cells, not in patients, but it was the first time that cell aging was ever reversed, and it was the first important step toward clinical therapy.

That initial research was in cell culture (groups of cells). The second step was to repeat the experiments in human tissues:

> In the few years immediately following the turn of the century, several experiments – at Geron and in academic labs as well – showed that researchers could reverse aging both in cells and in the tissues made from those cells. For example, if you take the most common types of human skin cells (fibroblasts and keratinocytes) from an old person and allow them to grow together, these cells form skin tissue that is thin, friable, and typical of the skin we see in an old person. If you do the same with cells from a young person, the skin tissue that forms is thick, complex, and typical of the skin seen in a young person. But if you take skin cells from an old person and reset their telomere lengths, then the skin tissue that forms is typical of young human skin. In short, we could reverse aging in old skin cells and thereby grow young skin.

> Similar results occur with human vascular cells, using old cells to grow young vascular tissue and using old human bone cells to grow young bone tissue. In all cases, when we restore telomere lengths to the lengths seen in young cells, we can grow young cells from old cells: tissue that looks and functions like young tissue.

So far, so good. After experiments in cell culture and in cell tissues, the next step is for *in-vivo* experiments in whole organisms. There's some encouraging work to report here too. Maria Blasco and her colleagues at the

Centro Nacional de Biotecnología in Madrid have published some intriguing results for mice, including the 2011 article in Aging Cell, "The telomerase activator TA-65 elongates short telomeres and increases health span of adult/old mice without increasing cancer incidence"[198]. Using different techniques, Ronald DePinho, a cancer geneticist at the Dana-Farber Cancer Institute and Harvard Medical School, has achieved similar results. DePinho's research was described by Ewen Callaway, in a Nature article entitled "Telomerase reverses ageing process"[199]:

> **Dramatic rejuvenation of prematurely aged mice hints at potential therapy.**
>
> Premature ageing can be reversed by reactivating an enzyme that protects the tips of chromosomes, a study in mice suggests.
>
> Mice engineered to lack the enzyme, called telomerase, become prematurely decrepit. But they bounced back to health when the enzyme was replaced. The finding, published online today in Nature, hints that some disorders characterized by early ageing could be treated by boosting telomerase activity.
>
> It also offers the possibility that normal human ageing could be slowed by reawakening the enzyme in cells where it has stopped working, says Ronald DePinho... who led the new study...

Callaway explained the experiment:

> When mice are engineered to lack telomerase completely, their telomeres progressively shorten over several generations. These animals age much faster than normal mice – they are barely fertile and suffer from age-related conditions such as osteoporosis, diabetes and neurodegeneration. They also die young. "If you look at all those data together, you walk away with the idea that the loss of telomerase could be a very important instigator of the ageing process," says DePinho.
>
> To find out if these dramatic effects are reversible, DePinho's team engineered mice such that the inactivated telomerase could be switched back on by feeding the mice a chemical called 4-OHT. The researchers allowed the mice to grow to adulthood without the enzyme, then reactivated it for a month. They assessed the health of the mice another month later.
>
> "What really caught us by surprise was the dramatic reversal of the effects we saw in these animals," says DePinho. He describes the outcome as "a near 'Ponce de Leon' effect" – a reference to the Spanish explorer Juan Ponce de Leon, who went in search of the mythical Fountain of Youth.

Shrivelled testes grew back to normal and the animals regained their fertility. Other organs, such as the spleen, liver and intestines, recuperated from their degenerated state.

The results extended to an arguably even more important organ:

The one-month pulse of telomerase also reversed effects of ageing in the brain. Mice with restored telomerase activity had noticeably larger brains than animals still lacking the enzyme, and neural progenitor cells, which produce new neurons and supporting brain cells, started working again.

Despite these results, the telomere theory of aging faces a number of questions.

Questions about telomeres

The first question about telomeres is whether the provision of extra telomerase might result in greater numbers of cancers. In this viewpoint, the limited operation of telomerase in unmodified humans may represent a hard-fought natural balance between two competing problems:

- Too little telomerase means cells stop dividing too early, and become dysfunctional, triggering some of the diseases of aging
- Too much telomerase means that cells are prone to dividing too often, resulting in an increase in the incidence of cancer.

However, an alternative viewpoint – championed by researchers such as Michael Fossel – is that the causation of cancer needs to be broken into two stages:

1. Some original damage in a cell causes mutations, and the start of a small tumorous growth
2. If these mutations result in the generation of additional telomerase, or indeed an alternative mechanism for telomeres to be indefinitely lengthened (this mechanism is known as "ALT"), the growth becomes malignant.

In this alternative analysis, it is better to prevent the first of these two stages. This can be accomplished by ensuring that cells continue to replicate and repair themselves properly. To this end, longer telomeres will be very helpful. If on the other hand, telomeres become too short, damage will occur, which can then spiral out of control via the multiple mutations that can subsequently take place.

This analysis finds support in various experiments, such as the one by Peter Willeit and colleagues reported in JAMA (the Journal of the American Medical Association) in July 2010. The abstract of the paper[200] gives the conclusion:

> Telomeres are essential to preserve the integrity of the genome. Critically short telomeres lead to replicative cell senescence and chromosomal instability and may thereby increase cancer risk.

This research is usefully summarised in a Scientific American review article[201] by Jalees Rehman:

> [The] study collected blood samples and measured the mean telomere length of white blood cells in 787 participants and followed them for 10 years to see who would develop cancer. Telomere length was inversely correlated with likelihood of developing cancer and dying from cancer. The individuals in the shortest telomere group were three times more likely to develop cancer than the longest telomere group within the ten year observation period!

Further evidence for this viewpoint can be found in the experiments already mentioned by Maria Blasco and her colleagues. The title of that paper emphasises that longevity improvements were obtained for middle-aged mice, by providing more telomerase, *without increasing the incidence of cancer.*

Despite this evidence, many researchers remain unconvinced. In the Scientific American review article already quoted, Jalees Rehman goes on to assert that the correlation between longer telomeres and a lower incidence of cancer does not imply any cause-and-effect connection:

> Increasing telomerase levels ought to lengthen telomeres but in the case of cancer, too much telomerase can be just as bad as too little telomeres. Too much telomerase can help confer immortality onto cancer cells and actually increase the likelihood of cancer, whereas too little telomerase can also increase cancer by depleting the healthy regenerative potential of the body. To reduce the risk of cancer we need an ideal level of telomerase, with not a whole lot of room for error.

Rehman concludes:

> This clarifies that "telomerase shots" are not the magical anti-aging potion that Faust and so many other humans have sought throughout history.

One reason for caution here is a second major question that can be raised about telomeres: how much is it credible to extrapolate, from the experiments carried out on mice, regarding the implications for humans?

Bear in mind that the mice on which Ronald DePinho experimented had been specially modified to lack telomerase. They were far from being standard mice. Ewen Callaway, in his Nature article about these experiments, quotes this observation from David Harrison, a researcher into aging from Jackson Laboratory in Bar Harbor, Maine:

"They are not studying normal aging, but aging in mice made grossly abnormal."

Even to the extent that similar experiments may be carried out, successfully, on standard mice, there remains uncertainty as to how similar experiments would fare with humans. Although humans and mice share many aspects of genetics and metabolism, there is a long, sad history, across many aspects of medicine, of experiments in mice failing to convert straightforwardly into positive results in humans. What's more, even if human patients appear rejuvenated for an initial period of time, following the deployment of telomerase, we cannot easily rule out the possibility of longer-term drawbacks.

The right thing to do here is to continue carrying out scientific research and developing engineering solutions. Additional experiments will yield additional data which can then be fed into evolved and improved models of the relevant biochemical interactions underlying diseases of aging. We cannot be sure of the answers in advance, but we should remain open to the possibilities of new surprises.

This brings us to a third question: can the telomere theory of aging be extended to give good accounts of aspects of aging that, on first sight, seem not to involve the diminished capabilities of cells to divide? In response to this question, the telomere theory of aging distinguishes between direct aging and indirect impacts. It's worth quoting Michael Fossel at some length[202] on this matter:

Almost invariably, someone will argue that telomeres couldn't possibly cause heart disease or Alzheimer's dementia. Usually, this argument comes from a perfectly rational academic scientist whose grasp of biology is magisterial, but whose grasp of clinical pathology is much less so.

In the case of heart disease, they point out that heart muscle cells, cardiomyocytes, almost never divide, and so heart disease can't possibly result from telomere shortening.

But the pathology is more complex. Saying that telomere loss can't cause heart attacks because heart muscle cells don't lose telomeres is like saying cholesterol can't cause heart attacks because heart muscle cells don't accumulate cholesterol.

It's not changes to the cardiomyocytes that lead to heart disease, but changes in the coronary arteries – the vascular endothelial cells – which lose telomeres and accumulate cholesterol. The underlying pathology lies in the arteries, not in the muscle. The fact that cardiomyocytes don't divide is irrelevant to the pathology of heart disease.

The same criticism – with a similar misunderstanding of pathology – is used in regard to Alzheimer's dementia: neurons almost never divide, so Alzheimer's dementia can't possibly be due to telomere shortening.

While it is roughly accurate to say that adult neurons don't divide, the microglial cells that surround and support those neurons divide continually, and their telomeres certainly do shorten with age. Microglial telomere shortening correlates with Alzheimer's disease and appears to precede the onset of several hallmarks of dementia, including beta amyloid deposition and the formation of Tau protein tangles.

Hence the distinction between direct and indirect impacts of telomere shortening:

It is useful to make a rough distinction here between direct age-related pathology and indirect age-related pathology. Alzheimer's and heart disease are examples of indirect pathology, where neurons and the cardiomyocytes are "innocent bystanders." Direct aging means that aging cells cause pathology in their own tissue; indirect aging means that aging cells cause pathology in a different tissue, or different cell type.

This line of argument is further developed throughout Fossel's recent book, which provides analysis of how telomere shortening increases the likelihood of numerous diseases. It's an impressive piece of work. The mechanisms outlined have a good degree of plausibility, and can be investigated by experimentation. What's still unclear, however, is whether telomere shortening is *the sole underlying cause* of these diseases, or whether there are other fundamental aspects of aging which need their own separate treatment. Moreover, it's unclear to what extent lengthening of telomeres might have undesirable consequences in the longer term, such as the potential for increased cancer already mentioned. In other words, it's still unclear how much of an impact on aging can be expected from a singular focus on telomeres, or whether a more plural approach will prove to be needed (as pursued by, for example, the SENS Research Foundation).

The shortest fuse?

Another long-time advocate of the telomere theory of aging, Bill Andrews, uses the metaphor that aging is caused by a number of separate sticks of dynamite inside the body (that is, a number of potentially faulty biochemical mechanisms), each with a fuse burning towards the point of catastrophic failure. However, if one type of stick has a significantly shorter fuse than the others, that is the cause which needs to be tackled most urgently. According to Andrews, telomeres should be understood in that light. In a 2011 Popular Science extended profile article entitled "The man who would stop time"[203], the idea is described as follows:

> Andrews likens the underlying causes of aging, free radicals and the rest, to sticks of dynamite, with truncated telomeres being the stick with the shortest fuse. "I believe there's a really good chance that if we defuse that stick," he says, "and the person doesn't smoke and doesn't get obese, it wouldn't be surprising if they lived to be 150 years old. That means they're going to have 50 more years to be around when somebody solves the other aging problems."

Andrews has made major personal contributions to the biology of telomeres, including his work at Geron in the 1990s leading the team that was the first to identify the human version of the gene for telomerase. For a quick summary of his ideas, see his 20-page pamphlet, "Curing aging"[204], which is available online as a free PDF file. Andrews also appears, along with Aubrey de Grey of SENS, in the 2014 film "The Immortalists"[205]. Most of his work is devoted to one final key question about telomeres: what is the *practical* method whereby appropriate amounts of telomerase can be activated in the bodies of living humans? That is the same question which preoccupies Michael Fossel.

In his blogpost "Four ways to lengthen telomeres"[206], Fossel reviews various options:

- Directly add the telomerase protein to cells
- Add the mRNA (messenger RNA) for telomerase
- Modify the cell's DNA to add a new gene to create telomerase

- Activate the telomerase gene that is already present in cells (but which is usually disabled)

Some approaches will involve patients taking oral compounds – potentially even food supplements, known as "nutraceuticals" by analogy with "pharmaceuticals". Some approaches involve injections of drugs. Yet others – including the method favoured by Fossel – involve gene therapy, administered via a different type of injection. Fossel envisages that a single injection of a viral vector could have a beneficial effect for a period of ten years:

- The injection would trigger the spread of new genes throughout the body, where they would create sufficient telomerase to reset telomeres to the lengths characteristic of youthful cells
- The genes would subsequently dissolve, avoiding excess telomerase being present in the body over a long period of time (and thereby reducing the risk of incidence of cancer)
- The treatment could be repeated ten years later.

Elizabeth Parrish, CEO of BioViva Sciences, submitted herself in September 2015 as a test subject[207] for a treatment very similar to this. A press release in April 2016 conveyed the initial results, "First gene therapy successful against human aging"[208]:

American woman gets biologically younger after gene therapies

In September 2015, then 44 year-old CEO of BioViva USA Inc. Elizabeth Parrish received two of her own company's experimental gene therapies: one to protect against loss of muscle mass with age, another to battle stem cell depletion responsible for diverse age-related diseases and infirmities.

The treatment was originally intended to demonstrate the safety of the latest generation of the therapies. But if early data is accurate, it is already the world's first successful example of telomere lengthening via gene therapy in a human individual. Gene therapy has been used to lengthen telomeres before in cultured cells and in mice, but never in a human patient…

The press release went on to explain how the telomere lengths had been measured:

In September 2015, telomere data taken from Parrish's white blood cells by SpectraCell's specialised clinical testing laboratory in Houston, Texas, immediately before therapies were administered, revealed that Parrish's telomeres were unusually short for her age, leaving her vulnerable to age-associated diseases earlier in life.

In March 2016, the same tests were taken again by SpectraCell revealed that her telomeres had lengthened by approximately 20 years, from 6.71kb to 7.33kb. This implies that Parrish's white blood cells (leukocytes) have become biologically younger. These findings were independently verified by the Brussels-based non-profit HEALES (HEalthy Life Extension Company), and the Biogerontology Research Foundation, a UK-based charity committed to combating age-related diseases...

Bioviva will continue to monitor Parrish's blood for months and years to come. Meanwhile, BioViva will be testing new gene therapies and combination gene therapies to restore age related damage. It remains to be seen whether the success in leukocytes can expanded to other tissues and organs, and repeated in future patients. For now all the answers lie in the cells of Elizabeth Parrish, 'patient zero' of restorative gene therapy.

As I write these words, it's too early to tell what the longer-term impact of this treatment will be, either on Parrish, or on the overall rejuveneering project. Science is, rightly, cautious about reading too much into the experience of a single patient. But provided there are no significant adverse effects, it is likely that further experiments will take place on other human subjects – particularly in cases where patients already have advanced cases of diseases of old age, such as Alzheimer's.

Interestingly, the treatment undergone by Parrish involves *two* separate genetic changes. Writing in Technology Review[209], Antonio Regalado describes the two treatments:

Parrish says she had received two forms of gene therapy produced under contract with a commercial laboratory, which she did not identify, outside the United States. In one treatment, she says, she received injections into her muscles containing the gene follistatin, which in animal experiments is shown to increase muscle mass by blocking myostatin, itself an inhibitor of muscle growth. She says she also received an intravenous dose of viruses containing genetic material to produce telomerase, a protein that extends telomeres...

BioViva appears to have taken its inspiration, and its basic genetic recipes, from research published by mainstream labs. The idea for extending life span using telomerase, for instance, is based on work by the laboratory of Maria Blasco, a Spanish scientist who in 2012 showed that telomerase gene therapy could extend the life span of mice by as much as 20%.

Parrish says the second treatment she received was "very similar" to a study of a follistatin gene therapy under way in boys with muscular dystrophy at Nationwide Children's Hospital in Columbus, Ohio.

This second treatment, to prevent muscles from weakening, shows that BioViva don't (yet) accept the view that all other aspects of aging are secondary to that caused by shortening telomeres. As Parrish says, "aging probably doesn't have just one angle". Indeed, presentations by Parrish, such as one delivered at Mar A Lago[210], list as many as seven separate types of targets from gene therapy under consideration by the company:

- Lengthening telomeres
- Reversing atherosclerosis
- Clearing misfolded proteins
- Removing senescent cells
- Strengthening muscles
- Boosting the immune system
- Increasing cell signalling.

My own view is that it remains unclear how many of these (and other) aspects of aging are genuinely independent. I therefore applaud all sincere attempts to make progress on either a theoretical or experimental level. As more researchers become involved in rejuveneering, our collective understanding is set to improve.

Genomic stability

One person whose opinion on longevity extension deserves attention, surely, is the person described as the "current world record holder in life extension for model animals"[211] – on account of the ten-fold extension he engineered in the lifespan of nematode worms. The researcher in question is Robert Shmookler Reis, a professor in the Department of Geriatrics at the University of Arkansas for Medical Sciences. Professor Reis is the author of over 100 papers in genetics, bioinformatics, and cancer research. For example, in his 2009 paper "Extreme-Longevity Mutations Orchestrate Silencing of Multiple Signaling Pathways"[212] he describes many experiments with remarkable results, including the following:

A single-gene mutation in the nematode C. elegans was recently shown to increase adult survival by tenfold, exceeding the previous record by a factor of at least three. Median lifespan was boosted from around 16 days at 20°C, to over 5 months, with comparable effects on mean and maximal (90th percentile) lifespan. Four- to six-fold extensions of nematode lifespan had been achieved previously through a combination of two or three interventions. Similarly, a ten-fold increase in yeast lifespan was recently attained by combining three interventions: two mutations plus severe caloric restriction. These results suggest that in both taxa [both nematodes and yeast], several parallel mechanisms curtail normal lifespan, and that the benefits of subverting them are "additive" – meaning that their combined effect is roughly the sum of those seen for individual factors.

At the end of that review article, Reis and his co-authors struck a note of caution, in a section with the headline question "If this were translated to mammals, could humans (like Methuselah) surpass 900 years?"

A two-fold or ten-fold increase in nematode lifespan may not, however, translate to a proportional enhancement of human survival. Extrapolation from worms to mammals is risky at best, and it cannot be assumed that interventions will result in comparable life extension factors. Longevity gains from dietary restriction, or from mutations studied previously, yield smaller benefits to Drosophila [flies] than to nematodes, and smaller still to mammals. This is not unexpected, since mammals have evolved to live many times the worm's lifespan, and humans live nearly twice as long as the next longest-lived primate. From an evolutionary perspective, mammals and their ancestors have already undergone several hundred million years of natural selection favouring traits that could directly or indirectly favour increased longevity, and may thus have already settled on gene sequences that promote lifespan...

Even if tenfold life extension, realized in nematodes and yeast, proves to be unattainable in humans, there is still ample room for pharmacological extension of healthy human life beyond present levels, and even beyond what could be achieved by dietary restriction... Substantial improvements in healthy lifespan may be achievable, but will require striking a delicate balance between two opposing cell states, replication and quiescence.

A more recent line of research undertaken by Reis and his colleagues suggests a new angle on possible extension of healthy lifespans, as engineered by genetic changes. This work, published in Nature in August 2015[213], starts with some observations about animals that display negligible senescence:

A growing number of animal species are recognized to exhibit what is called negligible senescence, i.e. they do not show measurable reductions with age in their reproductive ability or functional capacities. Death rates in negligibly senescent animals do not increase with age as they do in senescent organisms.

One possible example is the ocean quahog clam, which may live as much as 400 years in the wild and is the longest-living non-colonial animal. Its extreme longevity is associated with increased resistance to oxidative stress in comparison with short-lived clams. No noticeable signs of aging were found in a few turtle species, such as Blanding's turtle, whose lifespan is over 75 years, and the painted turtle, which was documented to live at least 61 years. Studies indicated no differences between the mortality rates and reproductive outputs of young and old painted turtle, which is consistent with the negligible-senescence hypothesis. The best-known (and arguably best-studied) example of negligible senescence is the naked mole rat, which has been documented to live in captivity for at least 28 years with no signs of increasing mortality, little or no age-related decline in physiological functions, sustained reproductive capacity over the period of observations, and resistance to common age-related diseases such as cancer, throughout their lifespans - which are at least 7 times those of mice or other rodents of comparable size. These phenotypic observations accord well with exceptional resistance of naked mole rat tissues to diverse genotoxic stresses.

The key observation refers to the stability of gene expression, over an organism's lifespan, for animals that display negligible senescence, as compared to animals that display so-called "normal" (or "exponential") aging:

In contrast, aging in most species studied leads to an exponential increase of mortality with age, commonly characterized by the Gompertz or Gompertz-Makeham laws, which may be a direct consequence of underlying instability of key regulatory networks. Recent studies of gene expression levels in the naked mole rat and long-lived sea urchin showed that the number of their genes exhibiting expression changes with age is lower than in other animal species.

The conclusion drawn:

Therefore, the lifelong stability of the transcriptome may be a key determinant of longevity, and improving the maintenance of genome stability may be a sound strategy to defend against numerous age-related diseases.

This is backed up by some mathematical models developed in the course of the research:

We show that... there exist two distinctly different classes of aging dynamics, separated by a sharp transition depending on the genome size, regulatory-network connectivity, and the efficiency of repair systems. If the repair rates are sufficiently high or the connectivity of the gene network is sufficiently low, then the regulatory network is very stable and mortality is time-independent in a manner similar to that observed in negligibly senescent animals. Should the repair systems display inadequate efficiency, a dynamic instability emerges, with exponential accumulation of genome-regulation errors, functional declines and a rapid aging process accompanied by an exponential increase in mortality.

The onset of instability depends on the gene-network properties only, irrespective of genotoxic stress levels, and as such can be viewed as being hard-wired in the genome of the species. The two regimes also show dramatically different dynamics of stress-resistance with age: stable genetic networks are more robust against noise, and the efficacy of stress defences does not decline with age. In contrast, the ability of "normally aging" animals to cope with stresses deteriorates with age. Moreover, the lack of stability of the gene regulatory networks may prevent complete recovery of organisms experiencing strong stresses, as can be shown by careful investigation of life histories of animals, such as fruit flies, surviving traumatic damage early in life.

The article ends as follows:

Since gene networks stability is naturally related to aging and can be favoured in multiple ways, further research has the clear potential to create novel therapies to protect against the most morbid age-associated diseases, and perhaps even against aging itself.

In an IEET article "Genome Stability Leads to Negligible Senescence"[214], longevity researcher Maria Konovalenko commented on this research as follows:

What would you say if I told you that aging happens not because of accumulation of stresses, but rather because of the intrinsic properties of the gene network of the organism...?

We all know that some animals just don't care about time passing by. Their mortality doesn't increase with age... The paper [by Reis et al] explains what it is exactly that makes these animals age so slowly – it's the stability of their gene networks.

What does network stability mean then?... If the DNA repair mechanisms are very efficient and the connectivity of the network is low enough, then this network is stable. So, normally aging species, such as ourselves, have unstable networks… But there is a way to overcome this problem, according to the proposed math model…

So what does this paper mean to all of us? It means that if we analyse transcriptome data theoretically would be able to understand how we can transform a normally aging organism into a negligibly aging one.

The idea here is that rejuveneering might best proceed, not by multiple interventions to seek to periodically remove and repair damage within the body, but by altering the human genome to increase its stability. With greater genomic stability, the organism will be able to remove and repair normal "wear and tear" damage by itself, regardless of how long it has lived. The self-repair capacity it has at youth will be maintained indefinitely, throughout its lifespan. As such, the organism will display negligible senescence.

This theory has a point of overlap with the telomere theory of aging covered in the previous sections. According to that theory, if telomeres are regularly lengthened throughout the body of the organism – for example, by genetic modification so that telomerase is expressed more often – then the body will be able to repair and heal itself. Therefore, the modification to the human genome to increase the expression telomerase might result in what the genomic stability theory of aging desires, namely a genome that remains stable even as the organism ages. Indeed, it has been reported[215] that some long-lived species of birds have telomeres which decline in size comparatively slowly. In one case, the particularly long-lived Leach's storm-petrel, the telomeres actually grow longer over time. Nevertheless, other long-lived animals, with slow rates of aging, have telomeres that can actually shrink in length from one generation to another, without any noticeable consequences[216] for the lifespans of the different generations.

Therefore, the genomic stability theory of aging is open to a wider, more complex set of genomic changes being applied, rather than just looking at the production of telomerase. These changes could impact major metabolic pathways, including the ones involving energy efficiency, sensitivity to insulin, responses to perceived shortage of food, and speed of growth – pathways which have each been linked to the pace of aging.

Note also that insight from understanding genomic pathways can be applied, not just by seeking to modify human genetics, but also by introducing or modifying proteins or other biological molecules within the body. These proteins would have been the products of transformed genes, but manipulating the genes is by no means the only way to alter the presence of these proteins in cells.

Investigating genetic variation

Consider the long-running study carried out by endocrinologist Jaime Guevara-Aguirre into a group of 99 individuals from Ecuador who suffered from Laron syndrome – a genetic mutation which stunts growth, by preventing the body from responding to growth hormone. People with this syndrome are typically less than three and a half feet tall, and are commonly called "dwarves". However, over the 24 years of the study, none of these individuals died of cancer, and only one of them experienced a cancerous growth (which turned out to be non-malignant). None experienced diabetes either. In contrast, other similarly-aged individuals from the same region who ate the same diet but who lacked the genetic mutant did suffer from cancer (17%) and diabetes (5%). The lack of diabetes among the individuals with Laron syndrome was particularly striking, given that many of them were obese (a factor that ordinarily makes diabetes more likely).

The results were reported in a 2011 article in Science Translational Medicine, "Growth Hormone Receptor Deficiency Is Associated with a Major Reduction in Pro-Aging Signaling, Cancer, and Diabetes in Humans"[217]. The article concludes as follows:

> Our results provide a foundation for further investigation into the role of drugs blocking the GHR [growth hormone receptor] and downstream conserved pro-aging pathways to prevent or reduce the incidence of cancer, diabetes and other age-related diseases including inflammatory disorders, stroke, and neurodegenerative diseases.

In an article entitled "Ecuadorean Villagers May Hold Secret to Longevity"[218], New York Times science writer Nicholas Wade points out connections between the genetic changes in Laron syndrome and similar genetic changes associated with greater longevity in roundworms and rats:

> The Laron patients' mutation means that their growth hormone receptor lacks the last eight units of its exterior region, so it cannot react to growth hormone. In normal children, growth hormone makes the cells of the liver churn out another hormone, called insulin-like growth factor, or IGF-1, and this hormone makes the children grow. If the Laron patients are given doses of IGF-1 before puberty, they can grow to fairly normal height.

> This is where the physiology of the Laron patients links up with the longevity studies that researchers have been pursuing with laboratory animals. IGF-1 is part of an ancient signaling pathway that exists in the laboratory roundworm as well as in people. The gene that makes the receptor for IGF-1 in the roundworm is called DAF-2. And worms in which this gene is knocked out live twice as long as normal...

Wade then mentions related findings for mice and rats:

> A strain of mice bred by John Kopchick of Ohio University has a defect in the growth hormone receptor gene, just as do the Laron patients, and lives 40% longer than usual...
>
> Andrzej Bartke, a gerontology expert at Southern Illinois University, said that the new result was "very important" and that the authors had done a fine job in following the patients and generating high-quality data. "This fits in with what we are learning from studies in animals about the relationship of growth hormone to aging, because both cancer and diabetes are related to aging," Dr. Bartke said.
>
> The longest-lived mouse on record is one studied by Dr. Bartke. It had a defect in its growth hormone receptor gene, just as do the Laron patients. "It missed its fifth birthday by a week," he said. The mouse lived twice as long as usual and won Dr. Bartke a prize presented by the Methuselah Foundation (which rewards developments in life-extension therapies) in 2003.

Nevertheless, despite these interesting connections, the safest thing to say about the effects of variations in human genetics on the likelihoods of long lives is "it's complicated". In at least some cases, reduction in the likelihood of some causes of death may turn out to be tied with increases in likelihood of other causes of death. For example, the Ecuadoran individuals with Laron syndrome have rates of death from alcoholism and from accidents that are considerably higher than usual.

The GenAge Database of Aging-Related Genes[219], developed and maintained by Joao Pedro de Magalhaes and colleagues, already lists over 1,500 genes which are known to have an effect on the aging and/or lifespan of organisms studied in laboratories. The number of genes listed is steadily increasing. It is an active field of research to understand:

- The individual biochemical mechanisms involved
- Interactions between the different genes

- Options to take advantage of these insights in treatments that • might extend human healthy longevity – whether by stabilising the overall genome, or by other means.

The 2013 book by science writer Ted Anton, "The longevity seekers: science, business, and the fountain of youth"[220] contains a great deal of interesting background material about a number of the genes and genetic pathways that have been studied for their effect on aging. Usefully, Anton's book also:

- Provides biographical accounts of many of the key scientists and researchers involved – including how their thinking evolved over several years and (in some cases) decades
- Chronicles the growth of the field from a mere handful of isolated researchers in the mid 1980s to hundreds of different labs in the early 2010s
- Describes changes in the way research was conducted under the influence of commercial interest, as scientists formed companies to convert their R&D insight into potential blockbuster drug treatments, and as some of the normal scientific processes (including careful peer review) were sometimes sidestepped in the rush to publicise results in favourable ways.

(Note: despite the book's title, which suggests a wide survey of all the different approaches to extending human longevity, the book only really covers the study of the genetics of aging; it has little to say about several of the other approaches that I include in the present book.)

Three prevailing themes emerge from the history as surveyed by Anton:

- The transition of the idea of human longevity genes from being fringe and disreputable into something recognised as a proper subject matter within the mainstream of scientific research
- A recurring series of disappointments, as potential treatments that seemed promising on first investigation failed to fully live up to initial expectations; for example, treatments based on resveratrol (as contained in red wine) turned out not to extend lifespans in organisms in the ways suggested in the popular media stories that heralded the first experiments as having revolutionary implications. (These stories helped boost the commercial valuation of the company involved, Sirtris Pharmaceutical, to stratospheric heights:

the company was acquired by GlaxoSmithKline for $720 million in 2008, but the unit was shut down by its new parent[221] five years later.)

- Despite progress not happening as quickly as some supporters wished – and despite the instances when experiments proved difficult to replicate in other labs – the overall body of knowledge did accumulate, at increasing rates.

Anton brings his survey to a close by describing the research being undertaken in 2013 by many of the researchers who had featured in previous chapters of his book. It's a wide range of interesting science, which builds on previous work. Anton comments as follows:

> It is the beginning of the new science of the molecular genetics of aging. The longevity genetics tools developed in the 2010s launched a young science into its adolescent age. "The next decade", promised Brian Kennedy [President and CEO of the Buck Institute for Research on Aging], "is going to be amazing".

Disruption from deep learning

Anton's book was published ahead of the 2014 formation of the very interesting company Human Longevity Inc (HLI), and therefore excludes coverage of HLI. Co-founded by genomics pioneer Craig Venter and Singularity University executive chairman Peter Diamandis, HLI is one of a number of new companies that are following a different approach to making sense of the connection between genetics and the diseases of aging. As Venter and Diamandis explained during a discussion at the Milken Institute Global Health Conference in April 2015[222], the basic ideas of the company include the following:

- Individual genes tend to have multiple effects at different times in life
- Genes which are correlated with particular diseases – such as the BRCA gene variation which increases the likelihood of breast cancer – have their effects overridden in at least some cases by other factors (so that not everyone with a faulty BRCA gene develops breast cancer)
- Many of these mechanisms are currently not understood

- Better insight is likely to emerge only from analysis of much larger data sets
- The computing power capable of carrying out the required level of analysis has only recently become feasible
- The content of the data sets to be analysed by HLI will include up to one million complete genomic sequences, information about the microbiome and metabolome of the same individuals, and numerous other points about the physiological characters of these individuals.

Note: the HLI website[223] explains what is meant by "microbiome" and "metabolome":

> The microbiome consists of all the microbes that live in and on the human body that contribute to health and disease status of an individual. By better understanding a person's microbiome (gut, oral, skin, lung, and other body sites), the company anticipates developing improved probiotics and other advanced diagnostic and therapeutic approaches to improve health and wellness.
>
> Along with the microbiome data, HLI will capture and analyze each individual's metabolomic data. The metabolome is the full complement of metabolites, biochemicals and lipids circulating throughout the human body... Metabolomics is important because quantifying and understanding the full picture of circulating chemicals in the body can help researchers get a clearer picture of that individual's health status, and provide markers and pathways associated with drug action.

HLI state that they expect to observe correlations between the various pieces of genomic, microbiome, and metabolome data, on the one hand, and the performance of stem cells on the other. To this extent, they prioritise understanding how to repair damage within the stem cells throughout the human body:

> The company will be embarking on an ambitious multi-pronged effort utilizing stem cell therapy advances to enhance and improve the healthy life span. HLI's work is premised on the theory that as the human body ages many biological changes occur, including substantial changes and degradation to the genome of the differentiated, specialized cells found in all body tissues. There is also a depletion and degradation of healthy regenerative stem cell populations in the body over time. HLI will monitor the genomic changes which occur during stem cell differentiation, normal aging, and in association with the onset of disease.

What's potentially significant about HLI, compared to the other researchers who have been looking into similar areas, is that HLI expect new patterns to become visible in the data, not from painstaking human observation and theorising, but from the emerging discipline of machine learning. Brad Perkins, chief medical offer at HLI, listed four trends at a Wired Health conference in April 2015[224] that he expected to transform genomic analysis:

- The reduction in the cost of genome sequencing (from $100M per genome in 2000, to just over $1,000 in 2014)
- The vast improvement in computational power
- The development of large-scale machine learning techniques
- The wider movement of health care systems towards 'value-based' models.

The result which Perkins expected:

This "supercharged" approach to human genome research could see as many health breakthroughs made in the next decade as in the previous century.

To help drive their research, HLI have hired Franz Och as their chief data scientist. Och previously worked at Google on the Google Translate project which provides automated translations[225] between over 100 human languages. The way in which Google Translate out-performed previous machine translation software is notable:

- Previous translation algorithms included lots of complex hand-crafted rules for grammar, diligently inserted the software by human linguistic experts
- Google Translate is an example of "deep learning" in which the software infers, by its own observation, which rules are important for transforming from one language to another.

In the same way, HLI expects to infer connections between genomics data and stem cell performance – or other important connections amongst the vast data it collects – that differ from those suggested by current scientific concepts. Given the impressive track record of deep learning, especially over the last few years, I can share the optimism of HLI that important new correlations will, indeed, emerge from the data sets accumulated by the company. These correlations may well, in turn, suggest new therapies that can be used to reduce or even remove the threat of various aging-related diseases.

But it's an open question as to whether genetic changes, potentially coupled with regular direct introduction of biomolecules in lieu of certain other genetic changes, will prove to be a practical route to *comprehensive* human rejuveneering. Advocates of pluralist damage theories of human aging – such as the SENS Research Foundation – suggest, instead, that the human genome will prove to be too complex to manipulate in ways that *indefinitely* extend healthy lifespan without introducing deleterious side-effects. As such, these theories recommend that research programmes continue in place to devise ever better ways to intervene to remove accumulated cellular and molecular damage on a regular basis.

What can be envisioned, therefore, is a combination of two approaches:

A. Human biology can be *modified* so that innate mechanisms of repair and renewal operate more comprehensively, without degradation over time; this could be arranged by, for example, making the human genome more stable, and/or by adding extra telomerase to the body so that telomeres are regularly extended

B. Human biology can be *augmented* by a suite of new mechanisms for repair and renew which deal with damage that cannot be tackled by the first approach.

Time will tell which of these two approaches will perform the lion's share of the task. Evidently, the second approach has greater scope and flexibility. However, the first method may prove very useful at providing a *partial* extension of healthspan. As such, the modification method can be seen as "Bridge 2A", and the augmentation method can been seen as "Bridge 2B" – to return to the conceptual framework of three (now four) bridges from earlier in this chapter:

- Bridge 1: Lifestyle modifications and food supplements, in order to stay alive and healthy long enough to benefit from later bridges
- Bridge 2A: Modifications to human biology, to slow down aging in a more significant way
- Bridge 2B: Augmentation of human biology, repairing damaging and renewing functionality primarily by non-biological means, allowing people to live agelessly

- Bridge 3: Modifications to the human condition to ensure survival even of more extreme accidents (see Chapter 12 for further discussion of this Bridge).

Incidentally, many of the researchers covered in Anton's book would very likely state that there are limits to what genetic modifications can achieve. These researchers hope to enable an extension of healthy longevity, but doubt that any *indefinite* extension is feasible by such means. Such a conclusion is consistent with the view I have just expressed, that more radical engineering interventions will probably be needed, before the latter aim can be reached.

To be clear, the insights from analysing the data sets from HLI may well inform Bridge 2B solutions as well as Bridge 2A solutions.

Evolution and rejuveneering

I'll draw this chapter towards a close by reviewing the work of a longevity researcher who sees himself as opposed to the "repairing damage" view of rejuveneering.

I am referring to Professor Michael Rose, of the Department of Ecology and Evolutionary Biology at the University of California, Irving. Rose has been researching aging since his doctoral studies at the University of Sussex, England, from 1976-1979. Books that he has written include[226] "Evolutionary Biology of Aging" (1991), "The Long Tomorrow: How Advances in Evolutionary Biology Can Help Us Postpone Aging" (2005), and "Does Aging Stop" (2011). When I met him at a conference in Cambridge a few years ago, he introduced himself by saying "I'm Michael Rose, and I'm going to defeat aging" (or words to that effect). His online biographies often include the following claim[227]:

> His 1991 book *Evolutionary Biology of Aging* offered a view of aging that was a complete departure from the views that had dominated the aging field since 1960. The scientific journal *Evolution* subsequently described the field of gerontology as having become "after Rose."

Rose's stated disagreement with what he calls the "molecular biology" analysis of aging therefore merits attention.

Rose's thinking is described on the website "Michael Rose's 55 Theses – A New Context for Health"[228], which contains a PDF "The 55: A First Introduction"[229]. It contains strong claims:

The genomic revolution has shown us that genome sequences, gene regulation, and gene function are vastly more complex than previously thought. The conceit that we could unravel, dissect, and explain most biological functions in terms of simple molecular-genetic pathways is defunct. What we are facing instead is complex networks of many genes, still more transcripts, and exponentially more molecular interactions underlying each significant feature of development, function, and pathophysiology...

The crude syllogistic tools of traditional biological reductionism are wholly inadequate to make sense of such data...

Traditional models for pharmaceutical development and clinical medication are now in tatters...

The time has arrived for biology to re-found itself, just as it has four times already, about once each half-century. In this re-founding, the principles of complexity and quantitative analysis have to be accepted. As in the re-founding of physics at the start of the 20th Century, after Einstein's 1905 publications, we have to give up the traditional intuitive concepts of biology, just as physics gave up the simple certitudes of Newtonian physics.

Rose is particularly critical of the theory that aging is due to cumulative damage at the cellular and molecular level. He writes as follows (in Thesis 22):

One of the basic theories of aging that has enjoyed popularity among cell and molecular biologists is that aging is due to cumulative damage at the cellular and molecular level. Taking this particular reductionist theory as gospel, the charismatic Aubrey de Grey has proposed that we can solve the problem of aging simply by repairing all such damage. In his somewhat Panglossian view, there are only seven types of cell/molecular damage, and there are relatively straightforward ways to repair that damage, he says...

Even if we take this "aging is cumulative damage" theory on its own terms, well-trained pathologists would naturally point out that cumulative damage can also occur at the organ and systemic levels. Those addicted to running assiduously pound away on their joints if they run regularly on concrete and other paved surfaces. After the early twenties, our joints no longer re-grow cartilage, so such running can literally wear away the connective tissue that sustains joint function, progressively hobbling us. The acids in our stomach frequently reflux up into our esophagi, eating away at their tissues, leading to degraded esophageal function, which we experience as heartburn and difficulty swallowing. And this list goes on.

Damage occurs at every level of our bodily machinery. Yes, it always involves changes to molecules and cells, but the causes of cumulative damage are not confined to those levels. Furthermore, the widespread turnover of cells and molecules throughout much of the human body suggests that our bodies already have fairly good machinery for dealing with damage at these lower levels: get rid of damaged cells and replace them with new ones that have not yet been damaged.

Thus, even on their own terms, molecular damage theories of aging do not necessarily lead to elegant technological solutions to the problems of aging, because there are many types of damage that may require repair, some well above the level of individual cells functioning in isolation.

I've already mentioned in Chapter 2 Rose's remarkable experiments that quadrupled the lifespan of fruit flies. These experiments involved replicating the effect of natural selection. From each generation of fruit flies, the individuals selected to continue the experiment into subsequent generations were the offspring of parents that had reproduced late in life. As a result, generations started living longer, and longer, whilst retaining key aspects of health and vitality. Average fruit fly lifespan increased from around 50 days to around 200 days.

Rose sees this experiment as an example of the power of the "evolutionary biology" viewpoint which he contrasts with that of "molecular biology". In his view, aging occurs only because evolutionary pressures have not had the opportunity to prioritise changes in genetic makeup that will keep an animal's body well adapted to its environment beyond the age at which organisms typically die of other causes. This lack of adaptation is called "detuning". Thus Rose's Thesis 20:

A single pharmaceutical or nutritional substance will never cure aging, for aging is not a simple physiological disease or dysfunction, but the detuning of adaptation with adult age.

And Thesis 21:

Multiple pharmaceutical substances or nutritional supplements will only ameliorate aging to the extent that they achieve genome-wide tuning similar to that which natural selection achieves when its forces are strengthened at later ages.

The positive recommendations that Rose makes are as follows:

1. Humans will experience less of the diseases of aging if they eat and exercise (especially in later life) in a way similar to that experienced by their ancestors for most of human evolutionary history; he states that "No one who has any alternative should sustain an industrial diet of heavily processed, highly sweetened, pre-packaged foods"
2. Further insight into aging will emerge from additional experiments in modifying selection pressures, for creatures closer to humans than fruit flies
3. Modern information processing tools will enable a more sophisticated understanding of the complex network effects in the causation of chronic diseases.

On the last point, he writes:

> Solving non-trivial scientific problems in biology will depend on the use of bioinformatic tools to process vast arrays of genomic, transcriptomic, metabolomic, and still other omic data. The characteristic feature of such data is its sheer magnitude.

However, although Rose time and again insists his perspective is at marked variance with those of other rejuveneers, I see many points of commonality. For example, his advice on changing lifestyle, by taking account of insight about the evolutionary circumstances of our forebears, slots straightforwardly into the first phase of a Bridge 1, Bridge 2, Bridge 3 model of the abolition of aging. Moreover, advocates of the "repairing damage" theory of aging are open to two points that Rose makes:

- Important ways for bodily damage to be repaired or removed may be to stimulate and augment the various biological processes which are, to various extents, already operational within nature
- The repair and removal of this damage may have to take place at several different levels, that is, not just at the molecular and cellular levels.

Here's a summary of Rose's position, taken from his description of the 55th of his 55 theses:

> In the previous ten theses, I have presented the scientific case for a particular type of dietary and lifestyle intervention that, I contend, should give some health benefits to a large number of middle-aged and possibly

older adults. In the case of those with hunter-gatherer ancestry, the benefits from this switch could be spectacular.

But even so, this is only the start of a revolution in human health that I expect to occur during this century. The cold grey grip of the reductionist biomedical establishment will be progressively weakened by the onslaught of reductionism-killing genomic data. That establishment is like the Aristotelian natural philosophers who were mainstays of the Catholic establishment during the Renaissance, full of power, prestige, and support. But dead wrong, even as they received funding for their indulgences. As the Procrustean dogmas of twentieth century cell biology are killed off, we will be able to transform human health using tools afforded to us by the burgeoning new biology, a biology that is better equipped to handle the exponentially-growing onslaught of "omic" data, whether genomic, proteomic, transcriptomic, metabolomic, or other-omic.

This new biology will be founded on formal theoretical tools, especially an upgraded evolutionary genetic theory that has been refined and strengthened by access to the genome-wide data that it has long needed.

With the new genomic biology, we will discover how our metabolisms need to be retuned in order to slow our aging and even end it earlier. With further advances in stem-cell technology and nanotechnology, we will become steadily better at replacing cells and repairing tissue matrices that have become worn or acutely damaged. Larger-scale structures, like livers or spleens, will be re-built from our own stem cells, so that they can be replaced without long-sustained immune suppression.

Over time, the chronic diseases that make our later lives so miserable will become as controlled and limited as contagious disease is in our time... Death from aging-associated disease will seem as unusual as death due to infection now is in affluent industrialized countries.

Rose emphasises this this outcome will be possible only if a change in mindset first takes place:

Achieving this salubrious outcome will require that the presently entrenched forces of the biomedical establishment be overthrown. Overthrown not by the naïve or the self-deluding, but by those who see clearly the scientific failure of the twentieth century biomedical reductionism which fuels the prestige and the profits of the medical-pharmaceutical industrial complex.

I fully agree with the importance of a prior change in mindset, which can re-orient and re-energise the medical, pharmaceutical, and healthcare industries. But I disagree that the needed change is best described as a transition from "molecular biology" to "evolutionary biology". Nor that it's a change from "reductionism" to "network complexity". Rather, I describe the change as moving from "accepting aging" to "anticipating rejuvenation". It's also a change:

- From seeing diseases as relatively independent to aging, with each disease deserving its own separate investigation and requiring its own separate course of treatment
- To seeing aging as the root underlying cause of multiple diseases, and as something that can be slowed or reversed in its own right, with numerous parallel benefits regarding these diseases.

Within that broader transition, the question of whether a "molecular first" or an "evolution first" approach will prove to be most effective becomes a matter of tactics. I have no doubt that evolutionary studies can provide important new insight into the constraints and possibilities of biological systems. However, the best use of that new insight may well be to design new engineering interventions which have a greater impact on healthy longevity than anything that could be achieved even by thousands of human generations of evolutionary modifications.

But what options are there to accelerate that broader transition of mindset? That's the subject of the next few chapters.

If that broader transition does accelerate – that is, if more and more people become convinced of both the possibility and the desirability of the abolition of aging – we can look forward to an exponential surge in the number of researchers contributing new data, and associated new theories, into the field. These new approaches are likely to involve novel combinations of the various ideas discussed in this chapter, and, probably, some fundamentally new concepts.

The next phase of the race

If I were to rewrite this chapter in, say, five years' time, much of its content could be significantly different, with new runners and riders taking the lead. I cannot anticipate, now, exactly who the new leaders will be in that race at that time. But I do anticipate that the race will have moved on substantially.

Very possibly, that retelling of this chapter would include companies and organisations based in countries that have featured little in what I've written above – perhaps China, India, Korea, Singapore, Russia, or up-and-coming powerhouses in Africa, Latin America, the Gulf States, or the former Commonwealth of Independent States. Public officials, and others who control large sources of funding, may be more amenable in those countries to the change of mindset from *accepting aging* to *anticipating rejuvenation*. They may see the opportunities more clearly than their opposite numbers in other countries, and seize the leadership role in response.

8. Changing minds

For debates where both sides have deep mental and social roots, it can be hard work to change opinions. That's certainly the case with the debate whether to accept the inevitability of aging, or instead to embrace the possibility to create a "humanity+" society free from aging. But we can find some encouragement – and draw some lessons – from examples of similar seemingly intractable debates which did, in the end, move forwards. That's what I'll review in this chapter.

We're all familiar with visual illusions which can be perceived in two different ways. For example, a picture can be either a duck or a rabbit[230], depending on how we look at it. Another picture can represent either a vase, or two faces looking at each other[231]. Yet another picture – this time, one that animates[232] – can, disturbingly, be seen either as a ballerina rotating clockwise, or as the same ballerina rotating anti-clockwise.

In all these examples, what's impossible is to accept both viewpoints simultaneously. Our brains can jump from one perspective to the other, but cannot hold both at once.

Something similar happens on occasion in the progress of science, although in that case, the effort to move from one perspective to the other can be even harder. Here, the two conflicting perspectives are two different scientific theories in a given field of knowledge. For example, consider the clash in the sixteenth century between the prevailing Aristotelian principle that bodies left to themselves would tend to come to rest, and the new idea, championed by Galileo, that the natural state of affairs was for bodies to continue travelling in straight lines at constant speed. Or consider the clash in the twentieth century between the once-dominant theory that continents have been fixed in place throughout the history of the earth, and the rival new theory that South America and Africa once jostled next to each other, in a long-ago reconfiguration of the continents, before that supercontinent broke up and individual continents drifted apart.

We'll shortly look at some examples of clashing scientific paradigms within the medical sphere, and then we'll return in the next chapter to the clash between the "accepting aging" paradigm and the rival "anticipating rejuvenation" paradigm. But first, let's look more closely at the intriguing and illuminating case of the theory of continental drift. The hostility shown by mainstream geologists towards the "too large, too unifying, too ambitious" theory of continental drift seemed, at the time, to be amply justified. That fact should give modern-day critics of rejuveneering reason to pause, before they dismiss that theory as being (likewise) "out of the question".

Scientific hostility to continental drift

Which child growing up in the twentieth century, looking at a world map, did not wonder to themselves about the similarity of the outlines of South America and Africa? Could these two giant continents once have been part of an even larger whole, somehow split asunder? The same naïve imagination could also chuckle at the thought that, in a similar way, the eastern coastline of North America broadly matched the western coastlines of Northern Africa and Europe. Was this a strange coincidence, or an indication of something more profound?

Mainstream geologists resisted such an idea. To them, the earth was fixed and solid. Ideas to the contrary could be held by naïve school children, but not (they said) by serious scientists.

Even when contrarian writers like Alfred Wegener (from 1912 onwards) and Alex du Toit (from 1937) assembled more data supportive of the idea that continents must have somehow drifted apart from a prehistoric unified landmass, orthodoxy shrugged off the evidence. Wegener and du Toit pointed to surprising similarities of fossils of flora and fauna along the different edges of continents which were now far apart, but which (they suggested) must have been adjacent in bygone times. Moreover, even the rock strata at the edges of these continents matched in surprising ways; for example, rocks in parts of Ireland and Scotland are very similar to those in New Brunswick and Newfoundland, Canada.

But Wegener was an outsider. His doctorate was in astronomy, and his profession was meteorology (weather forecasting). He had no specialist background in geology. Who was he to upturn conventional thinking? Indeed, his lecturing position, at Marburg University, was unpaid – this was seen as another sign that he lacked authority.

Wegener's detractors found plenty to criticise:

- Careful cardboard cut-outs of the edges of continents showed that the alleged match was far from snug; the coincidence was by no means as compelling as per first glance
- Wegener's background as an Artic explorer and a high-flying balloonist resulted in jibes that he suffered from "wandering pole plague" as well as "moving crust disease"
- There was no clear mechanism for how continents could actually drift, as part of an earth that was assumed to be solid throughout.

Rollin Chamberlin, an orthodox geologist from the University of Chicago, thundered at a meeting of the American Association of Petroleum Geologists[233] in New York in 1926 that

> If we are to believe Wegener's hypothesis we must forget everything which has been learned in the last 70 years and start all over again.

At the same meeting, Chester Longwell, a geologist from Yale University, exclaimed that

> We insist on testing this hypothesis with exceptional severity, for its acceptance would mean the discarding of theories held so long that they have become almost an integral part of our science.

Richard Conniff, writing in the Smithsonian magazine in an article entitled "When Continental Drift Was Considered Pseudoscience"[234] noted that, for decades afterwards,

> Older geologists warned newcomers that any hint of an interest in continental drift would doom their careers.

Eminent English statistician and geophysicist Harold Jeffreys – whose textbooks were still in use in Cambridge when I was a mathematics undergraduate there in the late 1970s – was another strong opponent of the theory of continental drift. His view was that continental drift was "out of the question", since no force could be sufficient to move continental slabs over the surface of the globe. This was no idle surmise. As explained on the biographical page for Jeffreys[235] on the Penn State University website, Jeffreys had extensive calculations to back up his opinions:

> His main issue with the theory was Wegener's idea about how the continents moved. Wegener stated that the continents simply ploughed through the oceanic crust when they moved. Jeffreys calculated that the Earth is simply too rigid for that to have happened. According to Jeffreys'

calculations that if the Earth was weak enough for plates to move through the oceanic crust then mountains would crumble under their own weight.

Wegener also stated that the continents moved in a westward direction due to tidal forces affecting the interior of the planet. Again, Jeffreys' calculations show that tidal forces that strong would stop the rotation of the Earth within a year. Basically, according to Jeffreys, the Earth is simply too rigid to allow for any significant movement of the crust.

The opponents of continental drift offered their own suggestions for how, in some cases, the flora and fauna of far-separated continents could manifest remarkable similarities. For example, the continents in question may at one time have been connected by slender land bridges, similar to that which used to connect Alaska and Siberia across the Bering Strait. One opponent – Chester Longwell, mentioned earlier – even made the desperate suggestion[236] that:

> If the fit between South America and Africa is not genetic, surely it is a device of Satan for our frustration.

In short, there were two clashing opinions – two competing paradigms. Each paradigm faced questions which it could not answer in any fully satisfactory way – questions of coincidence, and questions of mechanism. In such a case, the opinions adopted by leading scientists depended at least in part on their background philosophies of life, rather than on the intrinsic significance of any one piece of evidence. Science historian Naomi Oreskes points to a couple of factors[237] that were particularly significant for at least some leading American geologists:

> For Americans, right scientific method was empirical, inductive, and required weighing observational evidence in light of alternative explanatory possibilities. Good theory was also modest, holding close to the objects of study… Good science was anti-authoritarian, like democracy. Good science was pluralistic, like a free society. If good science provided an exemplar for good government, then bad science threatened it. To American eyes Wegener's work was bad science: It put the theory first and then sought evidence for it. It settled too quickly on a single interpretive framework. It was too large, too unifying, too ambitious. In short, it was seen as *autocratic*…
>
> Americans [also] rejected continental drift because of the [principle] of uniformitarianism. By the early twentieth century, the methodological principle of using the present to interpret the past was deeply entrenched in the practice of historical geology. Many believed this the only way to

interpret the past, that uniformitarianism made geology a science, for without it what proof was there that God hadn't made the Earth in seven days, fossils and all?... but according to drift theory, continents in tropical latitudes did not necessarily have tropical faunas, because the reconfiguration of continents and oceans might change matters altogether. Wegener's theory raised the spectre that the present was not the key to the past—that it was just a moment in Earth history, no more or less characteristic than any other. This was not an idea Americans were willing to accept.

Changing minds on moving continents

Deep Learning pioneer Geoffrey Hinton provides one additional account of the entrenched resistance to the idea of continental drift. He explains about the experience of his father[238], who was an entomologist (a specialist in the study of insects):

> My father was an entomologist who believed in continental drift. In the early '50s, that was regarded as nonsense. It was in the mid-50s that it came back. Someone had thought of it 30 or 40 years earlier named Alfred Wegener, and he never got to see it come back. It was based on some very naive ideas, like the way Africa sort of fit into South America, and geologists just pooh-poohed it. *They called it complete rubbish, sheer fantasy.*

> I remember a very interesting debate that my father was involved in, where there was a water beetle that can't travel very far and can't fly. You have these in the north coast of Australia, and in millions of years, they haven't been able to travel from one stream to another. And it came up that in the north coast of New Guinea, you have the same water beetle, with slight variations. The only way that could have happened was if New Guinea came off Australia and turned around, that the north coast of New Guinea used to be attached to the coast of Australia. It was very interesting seeing the reaction of the geologists to this argument, which was that 'beetles can't move continents.' *They refused to look at the evidence.*

The above descriptions may lead to the conclusion that an unresolvable impasse had been reached, with people in different paradigms unwilling even to look at the evidence they couldn't explain. Indeed, an impasse persisted for several decades. Then, thankfully, good science prevailed. Despite the stubbornness of a number of individual scientists, the science community as a whole remained open to the possibilities of significant new evidence; and significant new evidence emerged.

First, in the 1950s, geologists started paying more attention to the emerging field of paleomagnetism[239]. That field looks at the orientation of magnetic material in rocks or sediment. This orientation was seen to vary in prehistoric rocks from that of more recent rocks, with interesting patterns of variation that became apparent due to improved measurement techniques. Scientists were led to conclude: either the earth's magnetic poles were in a different location when these rocks were formed, or the rocks may have moved over large parts of the earth in the intervening aeons of time. The more closely geologists looked at this data, the more support they found for the principle of continental drift. For example, rock samples from India strongly suggested that India had previously lain south of the equator (whereas nowadays it is entirely north of that line).

Second, examination of the trenches on the ocean floor, along with deep thermal vents and submarine volcanoes, provided further evidence of significant subterranean fluid activity. This helped establish the concept that continental plates were propelled apart by the sea-floor spreading. What decided the matter, for many scientists, was the result of a particular test that was proposed. Oreskes takes up the story:

> Meanwhile, geophysicists had demonstrated that the earth's magnetic field has repeatedly and frequently reversed its polarity. Magnetic reversals plus sea-floor spreading added up to a testable hypothesis...: If the sea floor spreads while the Earth's magnetic field reverses, then the basalts forming the ocean floor will record these events in the form of a series of parallel 'stripes' of normal and reversely magnetized rocks.
>
> Since World War II, the United States Office of Naval Research had been supporting sea-floor studies for military purposes, and large volumes of magnetic data had been collected. American and British scientists examined the data, and by 1966 the... hypothesis had been confirmed. In 1967-68, the evidence of drifting continents and the spreading sea-floor was unified into a global framework.

In the end, scientific consensus changed relatively quickly, as more and more data was linked with refined, more sophisticated models of sea floor spreading and the resulting continental drift.

In parallel, the strong philosophical positions which had previously predisposed some scientists to oppose the theory of continental drift – positions such as a preference for "modest" theories, and the preference for uniformitarianism over any sort of catastrophism – had lost their vigour.

These philosophies were recognised as being, perhaps, useful general guides, but lacking the universality to strike down theories which had strong explanatory and predictive powers of their own.

Washing hands

The principles that applied in the case of continental drift also applied in the case of hand disinfection in hospitals. If Alfred Wegener was the sad victim in the first case – dying in obscurity in Greenland, in 1930, long before the merit of his hypothesis was widely recognised – then Ignaz Semmelweis was similarly the victim in the second case.

Semmelweis had gathered experimental data in favour of improved sanitation in hospitals, but his theories found little respect at the time. He became severely depressed, and was confined to a mental institution where he was beaten by guards and confined in a straitjacket. He died within two weeks of entering the institute, aged only 47[240].

Some twenty years earlier, in 1846, the young Semmelweis had been appointed to an important medical assistance role in the maternity department of Vienna's General Hospital. The hospital had two maternity clinics, and townspeople already knew that the mortality rate at one of these clinics (10% and upwards) was considerably higher than at the second (4%). Large numbers of women in the first clinic were dying from puerperal fever (childbed fever) after giving birth. Semmelweis put a lot of effort into trying to understand this variance. He finally observed that medical students working at the first clinic frequently also performed autopsies on cadavers, before visiting the maternity ward and examining women there; no such students worked in the second ward. It was a keen piece of empirical observation.

Based on his observations, Semmelweis surmised that some kind of microscopic material from dead bodies, carried on the hands of trainee doctors, was the cause of the high mortality rate in the first clinic. He introduced a system of rigorous hand-washing, using chlorinated lime. This process removed the odour of dead bodies from doctors' hands, in a way not accomplished by conventional washing with soap and water. The death rate plummeted, reaching zero within one year.

From our modern standpoint, we are inclined to say "Of course!" We find ourselves astonished at the prior lack of hand-washing. However, all this took place several decades before Louis Pasteur popularized the germ theory of disease. At that time, it was commonly thought that diseases were spread by "bad air" (miasma). Indeed, lacking any awareness of germs, the medical orthodoxy of the time resisted the advice of Semmelweis that rigorous hand-washing be introduced more widely.

In an echo of criticisms that were to be applied one hundred years later to Alfred Wegener, the ideas of Semmelweis were seen as being too all-encompassing: too far-reaching, and too disruptive. Semmelweis claimed that one single cause – poor cleanliness – was responsible for a large proportion of hospital illnesses. That flew in the face of prevailing medical doctrine, which held that each individual case of illness had its own unique causes, and therefore needed its own tailored investigation and treatment. Blaming everything on poor hygiene was too singular an idea.

The practice of painstaking hand-washing was also something that, it seems, offended at least some doctors, who were affronted by the idea that their normal gentlemanly levels of personal hygiene might somehow be substandard. They could not accept that they, personally, were responsible for the deaths of the patients they examined.

Semmelweis lost his position at Vienna's General Hospital in 1848, the year of many revolutions throughout Europe. The head of the department was politically conservative, and increasingly distrusted Semmelweis, some of whose brothers were actively involved in the movement for Hungarian independence from Austria. This political difference exacerbated an already fraught personality conflict. Semmelweis left the hospital and was replaced in his role by Carl Braun. Remarkably, Braun undid much of the progress in the clinic. Braun later published a textbook that listed thirty different causes of childbed fever. The mechanism identified by Semmelweis, poisoning from microscopic material from corpses, featured as number 28 on the list[241], with little prominence. Maternal death rates rose again in the clinic, as focus on proper hygiene was replaced by a predilection for improved ventilation systems – a predilection that fitted the prevailing miasma ("bad air") paradigm for the cause of many diseases.

Therefore even at the hospital where the breakthrough insight had occurred, the heavy weight of orthodox tradition resulted in numerous women subsequently dying needless deaths. Similar dismal patterns were followed throughout Europe, until such time as independent evidence in favour of the germ theory of disease had accumulated, through the work of (among others) John Snow, Joseph Lister, and Louis Pasteur. By 1880s, thorough antiseptic washing had become standard practice, and the miasma paradigm had been overturned by the germ theory one.

Not for the first time – and not for the last – established practice within the medical profession, therefore, fell far short of the founding principle of the occupation: *first, do no harm*. Faulty thinking by doctors led to poor hygiene and therefore to an avalanche of unnecessary harm. This departure from the Hippocratic Oath was in part due to lack of knowledge (lack of the germ theory of disease) but also due to the overhang of prior habits and prior styles of thinking.

To my mind, the *accepting-aging* paradigm fits the same pattern. It persists in part due to lack of knowledge (the progress made by rejuvenation biotechnology), but also due to the overhang of prior habits and prior thinking styles. Those who are immersed in that paradigm tend to see things differently, of course.

Medical paradigm shifts, resisted

Ignaz Semmelweis is often identified as a key pioneer of the broader principle of "evidence-based medicine". He tested his hypotheses about the causes of childbed fever by varying the practice of medical staff and observing the subsequent changes in mortality. His observations had previously ruled out a number of potential causes of the differences in mortality in the two clinics – different socio-economic status, different physical positions adopted by the mothers while giving birth, and so on. When the new antiseptic hand-washing routine was introduced, the results were dramatic.

As we've seen, however, this evidence failed to make sense from inside the competing paradigm which viewed "bad air" as the more likely cause of diseases. Supporters of that paradigm reinterpreted the changed mortality rates as likely having different causes – such as improved ventilation. Unfortunately, no rigorous tests were carried out to distinguish between these different theories. The principles that we nowadays expect to apply to trials of medical efficacy were not yet understood at that time, despite the insight of Semmelweis. These principles include:

- Control: patients receiving a new treatment are compared with a "control" set who don't receive that treatment (they may receive a placebo instead), but who are otherwise as alike as possible to the first group

- Randomisation: the assignment of patients between the two groups, control and treated, takes place randomly, to prevent biases (conscious or unconscious) in the selection that would undermine the result
- Statistical significance: the design of tests to avoid being misled by the chance deviations that naturally occur from time to time; in particular, tests with small sample sizes have little value
- Reproducibility: repetition of trials, with different sets of clinical practitioners involved each time; if the same results arise, this gives a greater indication of the underlying reliability of a proposed treatment.

Indeed, the term "evidence-based medicine" is only a few decades old. The first academic paper[242] published about it was in 1992. The term was introduced in distinction to the prevailing practice of "clinical judgement", which refers to doctors taking decisions on potential treatments based upon their own hunches and intuitions – hunches and intuitions that have in turn been schooled by the long experiences of individual doctors. An alternative term for "clinical judgement" commonly in use was "the art of medicine".

The drawbacks of reliance on "clinical judgement" were forcibly underlined in a 1972 book "Effectiveness and Efficiency: Random Reflections on Health Services"[243] by Scottish doctor Archie Cochrane. Cochrane was passionately critical about much of the thinking and practice of his fellow medical professionals. He pointed out that:

- A significant part of the earlier improvement in public health was due to improvement in environmental factors, such as hygiene, rather than medical treatments in their own right
- Doctors are under great pressure from their patients to provide them a prescription or some other treatment, and may well do so, even though there's no clinical evidence for the effectiveness of that treatment
- The fact that some patients recover after being treated by a particular course of treatment is no proof of the effectiveness of that treatment; the recovery might instead be caused by other

factors (including the body's tendency to get better of its own accord, in time)

- The fact that patients believe a course of treatment has done them good is, again, no proof of the effectiveness of that treatment.

Cochrane noted[244] that culture in general, at the time he wrote his book, was more likely to be impressed by "opinion" than by "experiment":

There still seems to be considerable misunderstanding amongst the general public and some medical people about the relative value of opinion, observation, and experiment, in testing hypotheses.

Two of the most striking changes in word usage in the last twenty years are the upgrading of 'opinion' in comparison with other types of evidence, and the downgrading of the word 'experiment'. The upgrading of 'opinion' has doubtless many causes, but one of the most potent is, I am sure, the television interviewer and producer. They want everything to be brief, dramatic, and black and white. Any discussion of evidence is written off as lengthy, dull, and grey. I have seldom heard a television interviewer ask anyone what his evidence was for some particular statement. Fortunately it does not usually matter; the interviewers only want to amuse (hence the interest in pop singers' views on theology), but when they deal with medical matters it can be important.

The fate of 'experiment' is very different... It has been taken over by journalists and debased... and is now being used in its archaic sense of 'action of trying anything', hence the endless references to 'experimental' theatres, art, architecture, and schools.

Cochrane had plenty of good things to say about medical practice. He described some positive examples which could serve as templates for future investigations – for example, the development of effective treatments for tuberculosis, which involved wide usage of randomised control trials in the years after the Second World War. He praised doctors for being far ahead of other professionals, such as judges and headmasters, in organising experimental controlled trials of different "therapeutic" or "deterrent" treatments. However, as Cochrane pointed out, medical history is full of examples where strongly prevailing opinion was eventually demonstrated, via careful experiments, to be incorrect:

- Tonsillectomy, especially for children, was once thought to be a near-panacea, and was practised widely, but following a critical review of the evidence in 1969 (in an article entitled "Ritualistic surgery – circumcision and tonsillectomy"), it is now undertaken much less often

- The gold-based compound sanocrysin became popular in America in the 1920s as a treatment for tuberculosis; one doctor published in 1931 the results of a trial with 46 patients in which he declared that the drug was "outstanding". However, that trial contained no controls; all 46 patients received the drug. In the same year, other doctors, from Detroit, trialled the drug on a randomly chosen subset of 12 out of 24 tuberculosis sufferers. The other patient in each pair instead received an injection that just contained sterile water, unbeknown to them. The result this time was decisive: the control patients were the ones more likely to survive. Sanocrysin, previously acclaimed as a wonder drug, was shown to be nothing of the sort

- Enforced bed rest was another treatment for tuberculosis that was long popularised, until tests in the 1940s and 1950s showed that such a regime was actually harmful rather than beneficial: patients that lied supine had extra complications from their coughs. Sanatoria around the world were closed in the wake of this research.

In parallel, Cochrane demonstrated instances where supposed clinical expertise was nothing like as infallible as its practitioners claimed. Druin Burch recounts the following episode in his 2009 book "Taking the Medicine: A Short History of Medicine's Beautiful Idea, and our Difficulty Swallowing It"[245]:

Electrocardiograms (ECGs) are recordings of the heart's electrical activity… Cardiologists claim skills in reading them that are beyond the measure of other doctors. Cochrane took randomly selected ECGs and sent copies to four different senior cardiologists, asking them what the tracings showed. He compared their opinions and found that these experts agreed only 3 per cent of the time. Their confidence in being able to look at the tracings and see the 'truth' did not seem justified. At least ninety-seven times out of a hundred, someone was getting something wrong.

When Cochrane performed a similar test with professors of dentistry, asking them to evaluate the same mouths, he found that there was only a single thing that their diagnostic skills consistently agreed on: the number of teeth.

After his death in 1988, Cochrane's surname was incorporated in 1993 in the name of the newly founded Cochrane Collaboration[246]. The collaboration describes its work as follows:

Cochrane exists so that healthcare decisions get better.

During the past 20 years, Cochrane has helped to transform the way health decisions are made.

We gather and summarize the best evidence from research to help you make informed choices about treatment...

Cochrane is for anyone who is interested in using high-quality information to make health decisions. Whether you are a doctor or nurse, patient or carer, researcher or funder, Cochrane evidence provides a powerful tool to enhance your healthcare knowledge and decision making.

Cochrane contributors – 37,000 from more than 130 countries – work together to produce credible, accessible health information that is free from commercial sponsorship and other conflicts of interest.

The Cochrane Collaboration, in fulfilling the vision of evidence-based medicine that was trail-blazed by Archie Cochrane and others, is nowadays recognised as performing an extremely important task. By 2009, Cochrane Reviews were being downloaded[247] from their website at the rate of one every three seconds. Among the currently most popular downloads[248] are reviews on the evidence in subjects such as:

- Acupuncture for tension-type headache
- Midwife-led continuity models versus other models of care for childbearing women
- Interventions for preventing falls in older people living in the community
- Vaccines to prevent influenza in healthy adults.

These are all areas where intuitive "clinical judgement" is very usefully supplemented by a careful survey of the experimental evidence – evidence which often confounds expert expectations.

Without being aware of the history, it would be difficult to imagine how much hostility the concept of evidence-based medicine engendered before it became more widely accepted. The original criticism of clinical judgement was widely resisted:

- Senior medical professionals feared that their hard-won tacit knowledge would become under-valued by the movement towards black-and-white evidence-based medicine
- These same professionals often insisted that patients needed to be treated as individuals, rather than being forcibly fit into one of a small number of stereotypes as featured in new medical textbooks.

Bloodletting

Let's look at one final telling example. Bloodletting – the removal of blood from a patient's body, often by use of leeches – was widely advocated as a medical treatment for more than two thousand years. It was recommended for a huge string of medical conditions, including acne, asthma, diabetes, gout, herpes, pneumonia, scurvy, smallpox, and tuberculosis. Early prominent supporters included Hippocrates of Kos (460-370BC) and Galen of Pergamum (129-200AD). The practice had its occasional prominent critics over the centuries, including William Harvey, the person who had in the 1620s discovered the path of the circulation of blood around the body, but it continued in wide use. DP Thomas, writing in 2014 in the Journal of the Royal College of Physicians Edinburgh[249], notes that:

> The fervour with which physicians in earlier times carried out bloodletting seems extraordinary today. Guy Patin (1601–1672), Dean of the Paris Medical Faculty, bled his wife 12 times for a 'fluxion' of the chest, his son 20 times for a continuing fever, and himself seven times for a 'cold in the head'. Charles II (1630–1685) was bled following a stroke, and General George Washington (1732–1799), suffering from a severe throat infection, was bled four times in a matter of a few hours. The amount of blood taken from him has been variously estimated at between five and nine pints. Strong man though he was, even his constitution could not withstand the misguided efforts of his physicians, and it seems likely such treatment hastened his end.

Thomas goes on to mention the case of Benjamin Rush:

> Benjamin Rush (1746–1813), a distinguished American physician and signer of the Declaration of Independence, was convinced that bleeding his patients was the best treatment... During the yellow fever epidemic in Philadelphia in 1793 Rush bled and purged his patients...

Rush's approach is a salutary reminder of the dangers of sincerely held beliefs in the value of traditional methods, and highlights the need for a critical, evidence-based assessment of all forms of treatment.

Systematic evidence on the effect of bloodletting started to be gathered in the nineteenth century. Frenchman Pierre Charles Alexandre Louis analysed data in 1828 from 77 patients suffering pneumonia, showing that bloodletting had, at best, little effect on the prospects for recovery. However, many practising physicians pushed his results aside, preferring to rely on what they *thought* their own personal experience confirmed, and to trust the weight of venerable tradition running all the way back to Hippocrates and Galen.

In the second half of the nineteenth century, John Hughes Bennett at Edinburgh University reviewed additional data on survival rates in hospitals in American and in Britain. He pointed out that, for example, over an 18 year period at Edinburgh Royal Infirmary, out of 105 standard cases of pneumonia that he himself treated, without any bloodletting, not one patient died. In contrast, at least one third of the patients who did receive bloodletting, under treatment from other physicians at the hospital, subsequently died. But despite this data, Hughes Bennett faced fierce criticism from within his own profession. DP Thomas comments:

From today's perspective, perhaps the most surprising aspect of the pioneering work of Louis and Hughes Bennett was how slow the medical profession was to accept their strong evidence, especially in relation to the treatment of pneumonia. Hughes Bennett was attempting to introduce a more scientific approach to identifying and treating disease, involving both laboratory observations and statistical analysis of results. However, this approach came into conflict with that of more traditional clinicians who continued to rely on their own experience, based solely on clinical observation. Despite growing scepticism of the treatment, the controversy about bloodletting continued throughout the latter half of the nineteenth century, and indeed well into the twentieth.

Writing in the British Columbia Medical Journal[250] in 2010, Gerry Greenstone reflects on the question as to why bloodletting continued for so long:

We may wonder why the practice of bloodletting persisted for so long, especially when discoveries by Vesalius and Harvey in the 16th and 17th centuries exposed the significant errors of Galenic anatomy and physiology. However, as IH Kerridge and M Lowe have stated, "that bloodletting survived for so long is not an intellectual anomaly—it resulted from the dynamic interaction of social, economic, and intellectual pressures, a process that continues to determine medical practice."

With our present understanding of pathophysiology we might be tempted to laugh at such methods of therapy. But what will physicians think of our current medical practice 100 years from now? They may be astonished at our overuse of antibiotics, our tendency to polypharmacy, and the bluntness of treatments like radiation and chemotherapy.

Never mind "100 years from now". In my view, it's likely that within 10-20 years, physicians will be looking back at present-day practice with astonishment that the phenomenon of aging received so little attention, and that rejuvenation biotechnology was such a minority interest.

But as I said, paradigms have deep effect. The phrase from IH Kerridge and M Lowe quoted above puts the same sentiment in other words: medical practice arises "from the dynamic interaction of social, economic, and intellectual pressures". It is to the economic pressures that we now turn.

9. Money matters

One thing that worries many people about the idea of longer lifespans is the possibility that these longer lifespans will involve large additional expense – especially due to the infirmities and diseases of old age. It's a concern that deserves to be taken seriously.

This sentiment has been expressed in forthright tone on a couple of occasions by Taro Aso, a distinguished Japanese politician. Aso, the grandson of a previous Japanese prime minister, was himself prime minister from September 2008 to September 2009. During that time, Aso was the first overseas political leader to visit US President Barack Obama in the White House. Also during that time, in remarks that ricocheted around the globe, Aso complained[251] about the cost of taxes to pay for healthcare for pensioners who need frequent medical attention:

> I see people aged 67 or 68 at class reunions who dodder around and are constantly going to the doctor. Why should I have to pay for people who just eat and drink and make no effort?

Aso commented, not unreasonably, that these people, who were aged the same as him, ought to be putting more effort into looking after themselves, such as by taking a daily walk, rather than relying on state handouts.

In December 2012, after a period in which his political party was out of office and he resigned the party leadership, Aso was appointed to the twin roles of Deputy Prime Minister and Finance Minister. One month later he returned to the topic of the costs of an aging population, in remarks reported by Justin McCurry in the Guardian[252]:

> Taro Aso, the finance minister, said on Monday that the elderly should be allowed to "hurry up and die" to relieve pressure on the state to pay for their medical care.
>
> "Heaven forbid if you are forced to live on when you want to die. I would wake up feeling increasingly bad knowing that [treatment] was all being paid for by the government," he said during a meeting of the national council on social security reforms. "The problem won't be solved unless you let them hurry up and die…"
>
> Rising welfare costs, particularly for the elderly, were behind a decision last year to double consumption (sales) tax to 10% over the next three years…

To compound the insult, he referred to elderly patients who are no longer able to feed themselves as "tube people". The health and welfare ministry, he added, was "well aware that it costs several tens of millions of yen" a month to treat a single patient in the final stages of life.

McCurry also reported Aso's plans for what should happen in the case of his own ill-health:

The 72-year-old, who doubles as deputy prime minister, said he would refuse end-of-life care. "I don't need that kind of care," he said in comments quoted by local media, adding that he had written a note instructing his family to deny him life-prolonging medical treatment.

On both occasions, 2009 and 2012, political correctness quickly obliged Aso to amend his public comments. His advisors worried, with good reason, that he might lose the support of the sizeable proportion of the Japanese electorate who are elderly. Saying that they were "doddering around" was too blunt. Therefore Aso apologised, insisting that he had not meant to hurt the feelings of anyone who was ill. Instead, he was trying to draw attention to surging medical costs arising from diseases that were exacerbated by poor lifestyle. Whilst individual lifestyle choices need to be respected, the medical costs arising from these choices could not be allowed to rise indefinitely. It's a fair point.

Aso's comments in Japan resonated with those expressed a couple of decades earlier, in 1984, by US Governor Richard Lamm at a public meeting in Denver, Colorado. Lamm's views were reported in the New York Times[253]:

Elderly people who are terminally ill have a "duty to die and get out of the way" instead of trying to prolong their lives by artificial means, Gov. Richard D. Lamm of Colorado said Tuesday.

People who die without having life artificially extended are similar to "leaves falling off a tree and forming humus for the other plants to grow up," the Governor told a meeting of the Colorado Health Lawyers Association at St. Joseph's Hospital.

"You've got a duty to die and get out of the way," said the 48-year-old Governor. "Let the other society, our kids, build a reasonable life."...

Lamm's underlying concern was the same as Aso's:

The costs of treatment that allows some terminally ill people to live longer [are] ruining the nation's economic health.

As a society, we take collective decisions to impose limits on personal freedoms. For example, we insist everyone wears safety belts in cars, in part to reduce the medical costs arising from injuries from car crashes. But what about the medical costs arising from people living increasingly long lives? Do individuals really have the right to keep on living, longer and longer, if social costs keep rising as a result?

Hoping that people will die quickly

The argument that it would be better for the elderly to "hurry up and die" has been made, not just by various politicians, but also (in more careful words) by eminent American medical writer Ezekiel Emanuel. In October 2014, Emanuel wrote an article in The Atlantic[254] which bore the subtitle

> An argument that society and families—and you—will be better off if nature takes its course swiftly and promptly.

The main title of the article was even more striking than the subtitle. Emanuel, who was born in 1957, chose the headline phrase "Why I Hope to Die at 75". In other words, Emanuel anticipates dying, without fuss, sometime around 2032:

> Seventy five.
>
> That's how long I want to live: 75 years.
>
> This preference drives my daughters crazy. It drives my brothers crazy. My loving friends think I am crazy. They think that I can't mean what I say; that I haven't thought clearly about this, because there is so much in the world to see and do. To convince me of my errors, they enumerate the myriad people I know who are over 75 and doing quite well. They are certain that as I get closer to 75, I will push the desired age back to 80, then 85, maybe even 90.
>
> I am sure of my position. Doubtless, death is a loss. It deprives us of experiences and milestones, of time spent with our spouse and children. In short, it deprives us of all the things we value.
>
> But here is a simple truth that many of us seem to resist: living too long is also a loss. It renders many of us, if not disabled, then faltering and declining, a state that may not be worse than death but is nonetheless deprived. It robs us of our creativity and ability to contribute to work, society, the world. It transforms how people experience us, relate to us, and, most important, remember us. We are no longer remembered as vibrant and engaged but as feeble, ineffectual, even pathetic.

Emanuel has impressive credentials. He is:

- Director of the Clinical Bioethics Department at the U.S. National Institutes of Health
- Head of the Department of Medical Ethics & Health Policy at the University of Pennsylvania
- Vice Provost of the University of Pennsylvania
- Author of the well-regarded book "Reinventing American Health Care: How the Affordable Care Act will Improve our Terribly Complex, Blatantly Unjust, Outrageously Expensive, Grossly Inefficient, Error Prone System"[255] which provides a thorough defence of the healthcare initiatives of President Obama.

Emanuel clearly has a great deal of knowledge. As such, he is a notable proponent of the accepting-aging paradigm. His viewpoint deserves attention.

He builds his argument by referring to the case of his father, Benjamin Emanuel, who was a doctor too:

> My father illustrates the situation well. About a decade ago, just shy of his 77th birthday, he began having pain in his abdomen. Like every good doctor, he kept denying that it was anything important. But after three weeks with no improvement, he was persuaded to see his physician. He had in fact had a heart attack, which led to a cardiac catheterization and ultimately a bypass. Since then, he has not been the same.
>
> Once the prototype of a hyperactive Emanuel, suddenly his walking, his talking, his humour got slower. Today he can swim, read the newspaper, needle his kids on the phone, and still live with my mother in their own house. But everything seems sluggish. Although he didn't die from the heart attack, no one would say he is living a vibrant life. When he discussed it with me, my father said, "I have slowed down tremendously. That is a fact. I no longer make rounds at the hospital or teach."

Emanuel's conclusion:

> Over the past 50 years, health care hasn't slowed the aging process so much as it has slowed the dying process… the contemporary dying process has been elongated.

The point is that that greater lifespans have brought extended periods of ill-health at the end of life. Emanuel references quantitative data that backs up this viewpoint:

Over recent decades, increases in longevity seem to have been accompanied by increases in disability—not decreases. For instance, using data from the National Health Interview Survey, Eileen Crimmins, a researcher at the University of Southern California, and a colleague assessed physical functioning in adults, analyzing whether people could walk a quarter of a mile; climb 10 stairs; stand or sit for two hours; and stand up, bend, or kneel without using special equipment. The results show that as people age, there is a progressive erosion of physical functioning. More important, Crimmins found that between 1998 and 2006, the loss of functional mobility in the elderly increased. In 1998, about 28% of American men 80 and older had a functional limitation; by 2006, that figure was nearly 42%. And for women the result was even worse: more than half of women 80 and older had a functional limitation.

The prospect for misery in old age is compounded by some statistics about stroke:

Take the example of stroke. The good news is that we have made major strides in reducing mortality from strokes. Between 2000 and 2010, the number of deaths from stroke declined by more than 20%. The bad news is that many of the roughly 6.8 million Americans who have survived a stroke suffer from paralysis or an inability to speak. And many of the estimated 13 million more Americans who have survived a "silent" stroke suffer from more-subtle brain dysfunction such as aberrations in thought processes, mood regulation, and cognitive functioning. Worse, it is projected that over the next 15 years there will be a 50% increase in the number of Americans suffering from stroke-induced disabilities.

Then there's the challenge of dementia:

The situation becomes of even greater concern when we confront the most dreadful of all possibilities: living with dementia and other acquired mental disabilities. Right now approximately 5 million Americans over 65 have Alzheimer's; one in three Americans 85 and older has Alzheimer's. And the prospect of that changing in the next few decades is not good. Numerous recent trials of drugs that were supposed to stall Alzheimer's—much less reverse or prevent it—have failed so miserably that researchers are rethinking the whole disease paradigm that informed much of the research over the past few decades. Instead of predicting a cure in the foreseeable future, many are warning of a tsunami of dementia—a nearly 300% increase in the number of older Americans with dementia by 2050.

The cost of aging

The viewpoint defended by Emanuel echoes a position outlined in 2003 by Francis Fukuyama, faculty dean and professor of international political economy at the School of Advanced International Studies at Johns Hopkins. Fukuyama was speaking in a SAGE Crossroads debate on "The future of aging"[256]. Here's what he had to say:

> Life extension seems to me a perfect example of something that is a negative externality, meaning that it is individually rational and desirable for any given individual, but it has costs for society that can be negative.

He backs up this view with an account of his own mother's demise:

> At the age of eighty-five, something like fifty percent of people develop some form of Alzheimer's, and the reason you have this explosion of this particular disease is simply that all of the other cumulative efforts of biomedicine have allowed people to live long enough to where they can get this debilitating disease...

> I had a personal experience with this; my mother was in a nursing home for the last couple of years of her life and if you see people caught in that situation it's really a fairly morally troubling thing because nobody wants their loved ones to die, but these people are simply caught in a situation where they have lost control.

In their 2004 report "The Lifetime Distribution of Health Care Costs"[257], researchers Berhanu Alemayehu and Kenneth E Warner surveyed how much of an individual's spending on healthcare (adjusted for inflation) occurred at different ages. They analysed healthcare expenditure by nearly four million members of the Blue Cross Blue Shield of Michigan health insurance scheme, as well as data from the Medicare Current Beneficiary Survey, the Medical Expenditure Panel Survey, the Michigan Mortality Database, and Michigan nursing home patient counts.

They showed that, if someone was still living at the age of 85, 35.9% of their lifetime healthcare costs still lay in the future. If someone was still living at the age of 65, an astonishing 59.6% of their healthcare costs lay ahead of them.

The greater health expenditure of people who are elderly can be understood as resulting from a number of factors:

- As people age, they become liable to suffer from more than one ailment at the same time – this is called "comorbidity"

- Patients with comorbidities already consume the lion's share of national health expenditure, due to the complex interactions between different medical conditions
- Even without an explicit comorbidity, an elderly person is less likely to respond quickly to standard medical treatments, since their bodies are weaker and less resilient
- As their health deteriorates, medical science can keep people alive for longer than in the past, though at the cost of treatments that are prolonged and therefore expensive.

This pattern fits into a broader one, sometimes called the "demographic crisis":

- Families are having fewer children
- Senior citizens are living longer
- The proportion of people in work, compared to those who have left the workforce and who are likely to generate larger healthcare bills, continues to rise
- Unless major changes occur, national economies risk being bankrupted on account of the growing demands for healthcare expenditure.

It is in this context that Ezekiel Emanuel proposes his solution: at least some people should voluntarily commit to a date in the future when they will no longer accept expensive healthcare. That could be a date when their lives have already passed through three generations – such as the age of seventy five picked for himself by Emanuel.

To be clear, Emanuel is no supporter of euthanasia, assisted suicide, or the like. He has a long history of strongly opposing these causes. That's not what he has in mind. Instead, this is what he proposes:

> Once I have lived to 75, my approach to my health care will completely change. I won't actively end my life. But I won't try to prolong it, either. Today, when the doctor recommends a test or treatment, especially one that will extend our lives, it becomes incumbent upon us to give a good reason why we don't want it. The momentum of medicine and family means we will almost invariably get it.
>
> My attitude flips this default on its head. I take guidance from what Sir William Osler wrote in his classic turn-of-the-century medical textbook, The Principles and Practice of Medicine: "Pneumonia may well be called

the friend of the aged. Taken off by it in an acute, short, not often painful illness, the old man escapes those 'cold gradations of decay' so distressing to himself and to his friends."

My Osler-inspired philosophy is this: At 75 and beyond, I will need a good reason to even visit the doctor and take any medical test or treatment, no matter how routine and painless. And that good reason is not "It will prolong your life." I will stop getting any regular preventive tests, screenings, or interventions. I will accept only palliative—not curative— treatments if I am suffering pain or other disability.

He goes on to spell out some consequences:

This means colonoscopies and other cancer-screening tests are out—and before 75. If I were diagnosed with cancer now, at 57, I would probably be treated, unless the prognosis was very poor. But 65 will be my last colonoscopy. No screening for prostate cancer at any age. (When a urologist gave me a PSA test even after I said I wasn't interested and called me with the results, I hung up before he could tell me. He ordered the test for himself, I told him, not for me.) After 75, if I develop cancer, I will refuse treatment. Similarly, no cardiac stress test. No pacemaker and certainly no implantable defibrillator. No heart-valve replacement or bypass surgery. If I develop emphysema or some similar disease that involves frequent exacerbations that would, normally, land me in the hospital, I will accept treatment to ameliorate the discomfort caused by the feeling of suffocation, but will refuse to be hauled off.

What about simple stuff? Flu shots are out. Certainly if there were to be a flu pandemic, a younger person who has yet to live a complete life ought to get the vaccine or any antiviral drugs. A big challenge is antibiotics for pneumonia or skin and urinary infections. Antibiotics are cheap and largely effective in curing infections. It is really hard for us to say no. Indeed, even people who are sure they don't want life-extending treatments find it hard to refuse antibiotics. But, as Osler reminds us, unlike the decays associated with chronic conditions, death from these infections is quick and relatively painless. So, no to antibiotics.

Obviously, a do-not-resuscitate order and a complete advance directive indicating no ventilators, dialysis, surgery, antibiotics, or any other medication—nothing except palliative care even if I am conscious but not mentally competent—have been written and recorded. In short, no life-sustaining interventions. I will die when whatever comes first takes me.

Paradigm clash

Emanuel's viewpoint can be seen as brave and selfless. It makes good sense within the paradigm through which he interprets the world:

- Medical costs continue to rise for elderly people, with society less able to meet these costs
- Previous hopes for progress in curing diseases such as dementia have proven unfounded
- Elderly people, when afflicted by drawn-out age-related diseases, experience a poor quality of life
- Society needs a rational, humane approach to dividing up its limited healthcare resources
- Elderly people have already lived the best years of their lives, including peak productivity and peak creativity.

Regarding the last point, Emanuel quotes Albert Einstein:

The fact is that by 75, creativity, originality, and productivity are pretty much gone for the vast, vast majority of us. Einstein famously said, "A person who has not made his great contribution to science before the age of 30 will never do so."

Notably, Emanuel is obliged to immediately contradict Einstein, before restating his own position in a less radical form:

[Einstein] was extreme in his assessment. And wrong. Dean Keith Simonton, at the University of California at Davis, a luminary among researchers on age and creativity, synthesized numerous studies to demonstrate a typical age-creativity curve: creativity rises rapidly as a career commences, peaks about 20 years into the career, at about age 40 or 45, and then enters a slow, age-related decline. There are some, but not huge, variations among disciplines. Currently, the average age at which Nobel Prize–winning physicists make their discovery—not get the prize—is 48. Theoretical chemists and physicists make their major contribution slightly earlier than empirical researchers do. Similarly, poets tend to peak earlier than novelists do. Simonton's own study of classical composers shows that the typical composer writes his first major work at age 26, peaks at about age 40 with both his best work and maximum output, and then declines, writing his last significant musical composition at 52.

However, Emanuel is further obliged to mention some counterexamples:

> About a decade ago, I began working with a prominent health economist who was about to turn 80. Our collaboration was incredibly productive. We published numerous papers that influenced the evolving debates around health-care reform. My colleague is brilliant and continues to be a major contributor, and he celebrated his 90th birthday this year. But he is an outlier—a very rare individual.

Such counterexamples are rare, Emanuel suggests, because of the complexity of the brain, and a resulting decline in its so-called "plasticity":

> The age-creativity curve—especially the decline—endures across cultures and throughout history, suggesting some deep underlying biological determinism probably related to brain plasticity.
>
> We can only speculate about the biology. The connections between neurons are subject to an intense process of natural selection. The neural connections that are most heavily used are reinforced and retained, while those that are rarely, if ever, used atrophy and disappear over time. Although brain plasticity persists throughout life, we do not get totally rewired. As we age, we forge a very extensive network of connections established through a lifetime of experiences, thoughts, feelings, actions, and memories. We are subject to who we have been. It is difficult, if not impossible, to generate new, creative thoughts, because we don't develop a new set of neural connections that can supersede the existing network. It is much more difficult for older people to learn new languages. All of those mental puzzles are an effort to slow the erosion of the neural connections we have. Once you squeeze the creativity out of the neural networks established over your initial career, they are not likely to develop strong new brain connections to generate innovative ideas—except maybe in those... like my outlier colleague, who happen to be in the minority endowed with superior plasticity.

In response to the question as to medicine cannot enable many more people to experience this same kind of extended creativity and productivity that he labels as "outlier", Emanuel can refer, again, to one of the planks of his paradigm:

- Previous hopes for progress in curing diseases such as dementia have proven unfounded.

The various planks of that paradigm, unsurprisingly, sit together well, and reinforce each other. That's where paradigms get their strength.

However, the same goal of reducing healthcare expenditure by elderly people can be met in a very different way – via the ideas of the anticipating-rejuveneering paradigm. If it turns out to be the case that smart, focused medical research can delay the onset and impact of aging (perhaps indefinitely), then society will benefit as follows. Increasing numbers of people will:

- Not become elderly and frail
- Not fall victim to diseases of aging (including diseases like cancer and heart diseases, whose likelihood and severity increases with aging)
- Not consume large amounts of health service costs, due to periods of extended ill-health
- Remain active, productive members of the workforce, full of vigour and zest.

As such, short-term investments will result in a sizeable financial and social dividend through increased health and delayed aging. This is known as the "longevity dividend".

The Longevity Dividend

The concept of the longevity dividend was introduced in a 2006 article in The Scientist, "In pursuit of the Longevity Dividend"[258]. The article was written by a quartet of deeply experienced researchers from various fields of aging:

- S. Jay Olshansky, professor of epidemiology and biostatistics at the University of Illinois, Chicago
- Daniel Perry, executive director for the Alliance for Aging Research in Washington, DC
- Richard A. Miller, professor of pathology at University of Michigan, Ann Arbor
- Robert N. Butler, president and CEO of the International Longevity Center in New York.

The article urged that

A concerted effort to slow aging [should] begin immediately – because it will save and extend lives, improve health, and create wealth.

The last of these reasons deserves highlighting: this effort to slow aging will *create wealth*.

The authors of the article are optimistic about the prospects for the science of aging:

> In recent decades biogerontologists have gained significant insight into the causes of aging. They've revolutionized our understanding of the biology of life and death. They've dispelled long-held misconceptions about aging and its effects, and offered for the first time a real scientific foundation for the feasibility of extending and improving life.
>
> The idea that age-related illnesses are independently influenced by genes and/or behavioural risk factors has been dispelled by evidence that genetic and dietary interventions can retard nearly all late-life diseases in parallel. Several lines of evidence in models ranging from simple eukaryotes to mammals suggest that our own bodies may well have "switches" that influence how quickly we age. These switches are not set in stone; they are potentially adjustable...
>
> The belief that aging is an immutable process, programmed by evolution, is now known to be wrong. In recent decades, our knowledge of how, why, and when aging processes take place has progressed so much that many scientists now believe that this line of research, if sufficiently promoted, could benefit people alive today. Indeed, the science of aging has the potential to do what no drug, surgical procedure, or behaviour modification can do—extend our years of youthful vigour and simultaneously postpone all the costly, disabling, and lethal conditions expressed at later ages.

As a result, they see many benefits ahead – including "enormous economic benefits":

> In addition to the obvious health benefits, enormous economic benefits would accrue from the extension of healthy life. By extending the time in the lifespan when higher levels of physical and mental capacity are expressed, people would remain in the labour force longer, personal income and savings would increase, age-entitlement programs would face less pressure from shifting demographics, and there is reason to believe that national economies would flourish. The science of aging has the potential to produce what we refer to as a "Longevity Dividend" in the form of social, economic, and health bonuses both for individuals and entire populations—a dividend that would begin with generations currently alive and continue for all that follow.

They go on to list a number of ways in which the extension of healthy life creates wealth for individuals and the nations in which they live:

- Healthy older individuals accumulate more savings and investments than those beset by illness.

- They tend to remain productively engaged in society.

- They spark economic booms in so-called mature markets, including financial services, travel, hospitality, and intergenerational transfers to younger generations.

- Improved health status also leads to less absenteeism from school and work and is associated with better education and higher income.

However, the authors also consider the alternative scenario, in which research on rejuvenation therapies is starved of resources, and makes slow progress. In this scenario, age-related diseases will exact an increasingly large cost on society.

Take, for instance, the impact of just one age-related disorder, Alzheimer disease (AD). For no other reason than the inevitable shifting demographics, the number of Americans stricken with AD will rise from 4 million today to as many as 16 million by mid-century. This means that more people in the United States will have AD by 2050 than the entire current population of the Netherlands.

Globally, AD prevalence is expected to rise to 45 million by 2050, with three of every four patients with AD living in a developing nation. The US economic toll is currently $80–$100 billion, but by 2050 more than $1 trillion will be spent annually on AD and related dementias. The impact of this single disease will be catastrophic, and this is just one example.

Cardiovascular disease, diabetes, cancer, and other age-related problems account for billions of dollars siphoned away for "sick care." Imagine the problems in many developing nations where there is little or no formal training in geriatric health care. For instance, in China and India the elderly will outnumber the total current US population by mid-century. The demographic wave is a global phenomenon that appears to be leading health care financing into an abyss.

In other words, these authors foresee the same financial crisis as discussed by Ezekiel Emanuel. But whereas Emanuel recommends a (voluntary) withdrawal of costly healthcare support once patients reach a certain age, such as seventy five, these four authors believe that anti-aging science can provide a different, better, solution – one without any cessation of medical support:

Nations may be tempted to continue attacking diseases and disabilities of old age separately, as if they were unrelated to one another. This is the way most medicine is practiced and medical research is conducted today. The National Institutes of Health in the United States are organized under the premise that specific diseases and disorders be attacked individually. More than half of the National Institute on Aging budget in the United States is devoted to AD. But the underlying biological changes that predispose everyone to fatal and disabling diseases and disorders are caused by the processes of aging. It therefore stands to reason that an intervention that delays aging should become one of our highest priorities.

Such interventions are, of course, the subject matter of this book. Indeed, I am arguing that treatments may be on hand, relatively soon, that would allow an indefinite extension of healthy lifespan. The proponents of the longevity dividend point out that, even if the extension falls far short of being indefinite – for example, even if it only results in an additional seven years of healthy life – it would still make a great deal of positive sense, from an economic as well as a humanitarian point of view:

We envision a goal that is realistically achievable: a modest deceleration in the rate of aging sufficient to delay all aging-related diseases and disorders by about seven years. This target was chosen because the risk of death and most other negative attributes of aging tends to rise exponentially throughout the adult lifespan with a doubling time of approximately seven years. Such a delay would yield health and longevity benefits greater than what would be achieved with the elimination of cancer or heart disease. And we believe it can be achieved for generations now alive.

If we succeed in slowing aging by seven years, the age-specific risk of death, frailty, and disability will be reduced by approximately half at every age. People who reach the age of 50 in the future would have the health profile and disease risk of today's 43-year-old; those aged 60 would resemble current 53-year-olds, and so on. Equally important, once achieved, this seven-year delay would yield equal health and longevity benefits for all subsequent generations, much the same way children born in most nations today benefit from the discovery and development of immunizations.

Quantifying the longevity dividend

Three arguments can be raised against the idea of the longevity dividend:

1. The first is the absolutist position that no amount of research is going to extend healthy human longevity by anything like the seven year period suggested; this position states that gains similar to what has happened in the past cannot be repeated in the present age, regardless of the investment made.

2. The second argument is the position that any such research will prove extremely expensive, so that the eventual economic benefits of longer healthspan will be outweighed by the huge costs to obtain these benefits.

3. Finally, the third argument is that the benefits of the longevity dividend are only temporary: significant healthcare expenditure on the elderly has not been cancelled, but only postponed.

Since you've made it to this late stage of my book, you'll realise that I reject the first of these arguments. I wholeheartedly reject the position of "no significant additional improvement, ever" for healthy longevity. Instead, the legitimate discussion is about "how much", "how quickly", and "what will it cost". That takes us to the second argument. That's an argument which deserves more attention. We should try to quantify the figures involved.

One approach to the figures is taken in a 2013 article by Dana Goldman, David Cutler, and collaborators, entitled "Substantial Health And Economic Returns From Delayed Aging May Warrant A New Focus For Medical Research"[259]. Goldman is professor of public policy and pharmaceutical economics and the director of the Schaeffer Center for Health Policy and Economics at the University of Southern California. Cutler is professor of economics at Harvard University.

These authors start by predicting that, *if healthcare systems continue on their present trajectory*, spending by Medicare (which provides health insurance for Americans aged 65 and older) is going to rise from 3.7% of the US national GDP (gross domestic product) in 2012 to a whopping 7.3% in 2050. This reflects findings about increased time spent in a state of disability by elderly people now than in the past:

> Although attacking diseases has extended life for younger and middle-aged people, evidence suggests it may not extend healthy life once people reach older ages. Increased disability rates are now accompanying increases in life expectancy, leaving the length of a healthy life span unchanged or even shorter than in the past…

As people age, they are now much less likely to fall victim to a single isolated disease than was previously the case. Instead, competing causes of death more directly associated with biological aging (for example, heart disease, cancer, stroke, and Alzheimer's disease) cluster within individuals as they reach older ages. These conditions elevate mortality risk and create the frailty and disabilities that can accompany old age.

The authors then looked at four different scenarios, each of which could arise from different sorts of medical progress in the time period between 2010 and 2050:

- The "status quo scenario", in which mortality rates for diseases remain unchanged over that period
- A "delayed cancer scenario", in which the incidence of cancer reduces by 25% from 2010 to 2030, and then remain constant
- A "delayed heart disease scenario", in which the incidence of heart disease reduces by 25% from 2010 to 2030, and then remain constant
- A "delayed aging scenario", in which "mortality from factors such as age, as opposed to exposure to external risks such as trauma or smoking... would decline by 20% by 2050".

The fourth of these scenarios fits the overall design that this book advocates. As the authors describe it,

Although this scenario altered the effects of getting disease, it was not the same as scenarios of disease prevention because it addressed the underlying biology of aging. The scenario reduced mortality and the probability of onset of both chronic conditions (heart disease, cancer, stroke or transient ischemic attack, diabetes, chronic bronchitis and emphysema, and hypertension) and disability by 1.25% for each year of life lived above age fifty (the period in life when most of these diseases emerge). This reduction was phased in over twenty years, starting with a 0% reduction in 2010 and increasing linearly until the full 1.25% reduction was achieved in 2030.

All three of the interventionist scenarios involved an increase in life expectancy. For example, someone aged 51 in 2030 would have a remaining life expectancy of 35.8 years (status quo scenario), 36.9 years (delayed cancer), 36.6 years (delayed heart disease), or 38.0 years (delayed aging). The delayed aging scenario fares best because the impact of a whole host of aging-related diseases is reduced, whereas in the other two cases, people remain vulnerable to diseases other than the one particularly targeted by the stated intervention.

The increases in life expectancy are modest – only about one year in the disease-specific scenarios, and 2.2 years in the delayed aging scenario. However, what is much more striking is the financial consequence of these delays, in the various models studied. Aggregating expected costs from public programmes such as Medicare, Medicaid, Disability Insurance, Supplementary Security Premium, and so on, and including estimates for the productivity benefits from increased quality of life, the authors estimate the economic value of the delayed aging scenario to be 7.1 trillion US dollars, over the period up to 2060. This benefit arises from two sources:

- A reduced number of disabled elderly people – up to five million fewer, in the USA, for each of the years 2030-2060
- An increased number of non-disabled elderly people – up to ten million more, in the USA, over the same time period – resulting in greater contributions (both production and consumption) to the economy.

Because the differences were much less in the other two scenarios – delayed cancer and delayed heart disease – the economic benefits in these cases are much smaller. That's yet another reason to raise the priority of rejuveneering, rather than continuing to just treat individual diseases.

Inevitably, there's a great deal of uncertainty in the numbers quoted. However, even if the headline figure of $7.1 trillion is wrong by an order of magnitude, the upside remains compelling. And what's particularly interesting is that these benefits arise from such a small increment in life expectancy – just 2.2 years. *Imagine how much larger the benefits could be from a more sizeable increment.*

Financial benefits from longer lives

Note that the savings described in the previous section depend upon significant changes to the rules governing entitlement for pay-outs from government welfare schemes. As Goldman, Cutler, and their colleagues state,

> Delayed aging would greatly increase entitlement outlays, especially for Social Security. However, these changes could be offset by increasing the Medicare eligibility age and the normal retirement age for Social Security.

Without changes to the onset and payment schedule of pension schemes, longer years of life will, indeed, store up additional financial problems. The extent of these problems was stated in a 2012 report by the International Monetary Fund, as summarised in a Reuters article by Stella Dawson entitled "Cost of aging rising faster than expected – IMF"[260]:

> People worldwide are living three years longer than expected on average, pushing up the costs of aging by 50%, and governments and pension funds are ill prepared, the International Monetary Fund said.
>
> Already the cost of caring for aging baby boomers is beginning to strain government budgets, particularly in advanced economies where by 2050 the elderly will match the numbers of workers almost one for one. The IMF study shows that the problem is global and that longevity is a bigger risk than thought.
>
> "If everyone in 2050 lived just three years longer than now expected, in line with the average underestimation of longevity in the past, society would need extra resources equal to 1 to 2 percent of GDP per year," it said...
>
> For private pension plans in the United States alone, an extra three years of life would add 9.0% to liabilities, the IMF said in urging governments and the private sector to prepare now for the risk of longer lifespans...

This adds up to some enormous figures:

> To give an idea of how costly this could prove, the IMF estimated that if advanced economies were to plug the shortfall in pension savings of an extra three years immediately, they would have to stash away the equivalent of 50% of 2010 GDP, and emerging economies would need 25%.
>
> These extra costs fall on top of the doubling in total expenses that countries can expect through 2050 from an aging population. The faster countries tackle the problem, the easier it will be to handle the risk of people living longer, the IMF said.

However, what this report sidesteps is:

- The potential for longer-lived people to contribute more to the economy (rather than just being a sink for its resources)
- The possibility of changing the age where pension payments start, in line with changes in average longevity.

A related point is made by Brookings economists Henry Aaron and Gary Burtless in their 2013 book "Closing the Deficit: How Much Can

Later Retirement Help?"[261]. Their conclusions are summarised by Walter Hamilton in the Los Angeles Times[262]:

> The book points out that people older than 60 have been steadily delaying retirement over the last 20 years. From 1991 to 2010, the employment rate increased by more than half among 68-year-old men and by about two-thirds among women the same age...
>
> As people... work longer in life, they'll generate additional tax revenue that could reduce federal budget deficits and spending on Social Security...
>
> The increase in work could boost government revenue by as much as $2.1 trillion over the next three decades...
>
> Expenditures on Social Security and Medicare could decrease by more than $600 billion as people delay tapping into those programs. The total effect, including savings on interest from smaller annual deficits, could narrow the gap between government revenue and spending by more than $4 trillion through 2040.

Yale economist William Nordhaus reached a broadly similar conclusion in his 2002 publication "The health of nations: the contribution of improved health to living standards"[263]. Nordhaus looked at the causes for the improvements in economic output throughout the twentieth century. His conclusion was that the increase in life expectancy was "about as large as the value of all the other consumption goods and services put together" in terms of increasing economic output. As they live longer, people work longer, produce more, and provide additional experience into the workforce and the community as a whole.

Nordhaus states the summary of his findings as follows, at the end of his paper:

> To a first approximation, the economic value of increases in longevity in the last hundred years is about as large as the value of measured growth in non-health goods and services... The medical revolution over the last century appears to qualify, at least from an economic point of view, for Samuel Johnson's accolade as "the greatest benefit to mankind."

University of Chicago economists Kevin Murphy and Robert Topel, in their 2005 review article "The Value of Health and Longevity"[264] perform another calculation of the historical gains from extended longevity. It's a lengthy calculation: the article extends to 60 pages of A4. Their conclusions can be read from the abstract:

> The historical gains from increased longevity have been enormous. Over the 20th century, cumulative gains in life expectancy were worth over $1.2 million per person for both men and women. Between 1970 and 2000 increased longevity added about $3.2 trillion per year to national wealth... Reduced mortality from heart disease alone has increased the value of life by about $1.5 trillion per year since 1970.

Murphy and Topel look forward to continuing gains from further healthcare improvements:

> The potential gains from future innovations in health care are also extremely large. Even a modest 1% reduction in cancer mortality would be worth nearly $500 billion.

But two questions remain:

- Might the costs to achieve this extension in healthy longevity exceed the potential economic benefit of (perhaps) trillions of dollars?
- Might the extra years of healthy longevity be followed, nevertheless, by particularly expensive years of healthcare (so that problems are being stored up for the future)?

Let's take these two questions in sequence.

The costs of developing rejuvenation therapies

It's not possible to reach any kind of certainty as to the costs required to develop rejuvenation therapies that would extend healthy lifespan by an average of, say seven years (as proposed in the abovementioned 2006 article "In pursuit of the Longevity Dividend" by Jay Olshansky and colleagues). There are too many unknowns involved, even to reach a plausible "order of magnitude" estimate. We don't know how hard it's going to be, to address whatever turns out to be the critical cellular and molecular drivers of age-related diseases.

However, we can draw some confidence from observing that projects to extend healthy lifespan have often easily covered their costs in the past. As an example, consider programmes to inoculate children against childhood diseases. The basic principle is "a stitch in time saves nine": prevention can work out much cheaper than cure. Indeed, according to Brian Kennedy[265], CEO of Buck Institute for Research on Aging, "The cost of prevention can be a twentieth of the cost of treatment".

Of course, at least some diagnostic scanning programmes have their critics. Some of these programmes, it is feared, have little proven utility, on account of false positives generated – people who the scan suggests may be carrying some cancerous cells, and who subsequent undergo expensive further tests and treatment, sometimes needlessly. For example, Archie Cochrane, the pioneer of evidence-based medicine discussed in the previous chapter, marshalled evidence[266] against the programme of screening for cervical cancer, stating such screening was ineffective. But that's no reason to shut down *all* efforts to develop diagnostic and preventive measures. It's reason to invest in research to *improve* these measures – to separate out the cost-effective ones from the cost-ineffective ones.

Here's the overall assessment of Kevin Murphy and Robert Topel, whose research was mentioned in the previous section:

> Between 1970 and 2000 increased longevity yielded a "gross" social value of $95 trillion, while the capitalized value of medical expenditures grew by $34 trillion, leaving a net gain of $61 trillion... Overall, rising medical expenditures absorb only 36% of the value of increased longevity.

They point out the implications of their analysis for setting the level of future investment in healthcare innovation:

> An analysis of the social value of improvements in health is a first step toward evaluating the social returns to medical research and health-augmenting innovations. Improvements in health and longevity are partially determined by society's stock of medical knowledge, for which basic medical research is a key input. The U.S. invests over $50 billion annually in medical research, of which about 40% is federally funded, accounting for 25% of government research and development outlays. The $27 billion federal expenditure for health related research in FY 2003, the vast majority of which is for the National Institutes of Health, represented a real dollar doubling over 1993 outlays. Are these expenditures warranted?

> Our analysis suggests that the returns to basic research may be quite large, so that substantially greater expenditures may be worthwhile. By way of example, take our estimate that a 1% reduction in cancer mortality would be worth about $500 billion. Then a "war on cancer" that would spend an additional $100 billion (over some period) on cancer research and treatment would be worthwhile if it has a 1-in-5 chance of reducing mortality by 1%, and a 4-in-5 chance of doing nothing at all.

Note the mention of probabilities. Investment can make sense, even if the probability of success is relatively low. This principle is already well understood by venture capitalists, who are prepared to accept low probabilities that a given company will succeed in its market goals, provided the extent of such a success (if it occurs) is large enough. A 5% chance of an eventual multi-billion dollar capitalisation of a company could support a significant investment – if, for example, the eventual valuation would exceed its present one by a factor of 100 or more.

This kind of consideration is familiar to anyone contemplating insurance policies. Disasters that have only a tiny probability of occurrence may nevertheless be well worth insuring against.

If only tiny probabilities deserve our attention, when the impact of occurrence is sufficiently huge, how much more attention should we give a possibility that has around a 50% probability of happening, with the financial consequences of that occurrence being in the trillions of dollars? That's the scenario if the rejuveneering programme would succeed in even a modest scale, compared to its overall ambitions.

Sources of additional funding

There are at least five potential sources for the funding that will accelerate rejuvenation therapies and therefore accelerate the realisation of the longevity dividend.

First, consider all the funding that, today, is targeted at individual diseases, in comparison to funding that targets the underlying mechanisms of aging. Of the 30 billion dollar annual budget for medical research[267] overseen by the US NIH (National Institute for Health), currently around 2.5 billion is targeted at aging, with the other 27.5 billion spread around numerous individual diseases. This present division of funding (which has echoes in other healthcare budgets worldwide) fits the mainstream "disease first" approach to improving healthcare. However, if aging is given a larger share of the overall budget – rising, perhaps, to 20% over the next ten years, rather than its present figure of around 8% – then many diseases could become less prevalent, and less severe, despite the reduction in research funding specifically linked to them. This assumes the validity of the alternative "aging first" approach to improving healthcare: biological aging exacerbates the body's tendency to being afflicted by diseases, and increases the likelihood of complications from these diseases.

A second way to achieve greater progress on rejuvenation is by an increase in the proportion of people's discretionary time that is spent on researching rejuvenation therapies. A small tweak in percentages is all that is required, on individual bases, to add up to a large increment across the entire population. For example, if just one person in a thousand devotes as little as four more hours per week to rejuvenation research – and four less hours to other leisure-time activities, such as watching light entertainment on TV – the total number of person hours spent on the subject in a country could rocket upwards. Of course, much of that effort could have little absolute significance, if it merely revisits what other people have already done, and if the people involved have limited access to experimental equipment. Nevertheless, if "collaborative rejuveneering" frameworks and processes are put in place, such as described in Chapter 6 of this book (including educational and mentoring activities), the overall benefit could, in due course, be substantial.

Third, rather than giving more of their time, individuals around the world can donate more of their personal funds to rejuvenation research initiatives. Rather than, say, donating on a regular basis to the college where they spent their formative years, or to their local church group, they can redirect at least some of these funds to philanthropic organisations in the anti-aging field. They can view these investments as a kind of parallel to contributions they make to pensions and health insurance schemes: the more people who pitch in with donations, the less the likelihood that family members, neighbours, and other acquaintances will suffer from aging-related diseases. With a dramatic change in public mood, along the lines discussed in this book, we could see a growing momentum of this kind of funding, similar to the way that other charitable campaigns have hit their own tipping points (for example, the ice bucket challenge in support of motor neuron disease).

Fourth, businesses (both large and small) may choose to invest in the field, seeing the potential to benefit financially from a share of the longevity dividend. After all, if these therapies really will generate more wealth for society – by increased positive economic activity, and by decreased drawn-out sick-care – there ought in principle to be some way for the companies providing these therapies to receive a portion of that additional wealth. If that kind of benefit-sharing can be engineered, it will allow more of the remarkable entrepreneurial power of the business world to assist the rejuveneering cause.

Fifth, we come to the subject of additional public funds (rather than the reallocation of existing public healthcare funds, as in the first paragraph above). Public funds can often bridge a gap that business funds cannot handle – a gap that requires greater patience, and where the benefits apply to society as a whole rather than being easily redirected to particular commercial suppliers. One example of this pattern is American's funding, to the tune of $13 billion dollars in 1940s value, of the Marshall Plan for the rebuilding of Western Europe after the devastation of the Second World War. Britain's public funding of the creation of the National Health Service also fits this pattern.

As one more example, consider Europe's investment in CERN, the European Organization for Nuclear Research, with its astonishing large hadron collider. This multi-billion euro investment, over many decades, was not undertaken with any simple thoughts of short-term economic benefit. Instead, politicians supported CERN out of a general view that it would contribute fundamental insight about nature – and, perhaps, create positive economic benefits in ways that could not be directly anticipated. The CERN project to detect the Higgs boson is, by itself, thought to have consumed[268] around $13.25 billion. As a long-time fan of fundamental physics, I have a warm space in my heart for the activities at CERN – and I admire the fact that the World Wide Web arose from work done at CERN by Tim Berners-Lee around 1989-1991. However, I believe there's a case for various public activities such as CERN (to give just one example) being relatively deprioritised, over the next few decades, in favour of more public research funding being applied instead to rejuvenation. We'll return to this suggestion in later chapters.

In summary, there are several sources of significant extra effort that can be applied to the rejuvenation project, with the expectation that at least some of that effort will result in very large economic benefits. It's an important decision for society to make how to prioritise these sources, and at what scale they should operate.

The final decision

One final question remains to be addressed in this chapter:

- Might extra years of healthy longevity be followed, nevertheless, by particularly expensive years of healthcare (so that problems are being stored up for the future)?

That's the question which worried the writers I quoted earlier in this chapter, including Ezekiel Emanuel and Francis Fukuyama. At this point, I'll concede that it remains an open question as to whether further progress with anti-aging medicine will result in large healthcare burdens once people have moved beyond the phase where the rejuvenation therapies are applicable.

One scenario is that rejuvenation therapies will lead to more people having the experience that characterises many centenarians: not only is their lifespan longer, but they tend to require less hospitalisation in their eventual period of decline. They live well and then they die well. Using terminology introduced[269] by Nir Barzilai of Albert Einstein College of Medicine of Yeshiva University, these centenarians are "super agers" with a notable tendency to "to avoid cardiovascular disease, insulin resistance and high blood pressure".

The same thought finds support from research reported for the BBC[270] by Nick Triggle in 2014:

Centenarians 'outliving diseases of old age'

Centenarians have found a way to beat the common diseases of old age, such as cancer and heart disease, research suggests.

The study by King's College London found they were more likely to die of infections such as pneumonia, unlike younger groups of elderly people.

Researchers said 28% of 100- to 115-year-olds died of "old age" and a fifth of pneumonia.

Cancer claimed the lives of fewer than 5% and heart disease fewer than 9%.

The study was based on an analysis of 36,000 death certificates.

By comparison, these diseases were the most common reasons for death among the 80- to 84-year-old age group, with cancer responsible for 25% of deaths and heart disease nearly a fifth...

Centenarians have outlived death from chronic illness... [and] may decline rapidly if they succumb to an infection or pneumonia.

On the other hand, it's possible that, as rejuvenation therapies push up the number of centenarians, these centenarians will still end up incurring large healthcare costs in the final stages of their life (especially at a time when rejuvenation therapies are still only partially effective – that is, while the project is still in an early phase). These new centenarians may not all become "super agers". If so, what is the point of investing in longevity when the eventual dividend is questionable?

To come to grips with this apparent conundrum it's worth emphasising that two questions are independent:

A. Should we decide to invest in favour of a longevity dividend, for the many benefits that is likely to bring (moral, social, and economic) over the extended period of time in which people will enjoy healthy lifespans?

B. What are our options for those who, for whatever reason, cannot be assisted by rejuvenation therapies, or who have gone beyond the time when rejuvenation therapies can keep them healthy?

I've already argued why the answer to A is 'yes'. Just because a separate question – Question B – arises doesn't mean the arguments in favour of Question A are worthless. Now let's look at possible answers to Question B. Three options that come easily to mind are:

1. We could take a leaf out of the recommendations by Ezekiel Emanuel, and hope (or even legislate) that people will voluntarily agree to abstain from expensive healthcare once they have reached a certain milestone age in their lives (75, 85, 95, or whenever bodily disintegration extends too far)

2. We could allow individuals to pay for these late-life healthcare costs, for themselves or family members, if they wish, but cut off their access to publicly funded schemes and general insurance support at a pre-agreed point

3. We could "grin and bear it", much the same as presently happens, without any formal rationing system.

The fact that we're unsure which option to select for Question B is no reason to cancel our efforts in favour of the longevity dividend. The costs of these options need be no higher than the costs presently incurred in the end of life phase. However, the longevity dividend will provide many advantages in the intermediate period.

There's also a fourth, more radical answer to Question B: cryonics. This is that increasing numbers of people may request the voluntary suspension of their bodily activities, via extreme low temperature storage, at the time when they have approached death.

Cryonics is one of the set of "radical alternatives" that I explore in Chapter 12. The motivation for cryonics is the possibility that, at some stage in the future, healthcare will have advanced to a state in which much more powerful rejuvenation therapies are available. Application of these future therapies would cure patients of whatever was on the point of killing them, before they were cryonically suspended. Application of these therapies would, in principle, restore patients to an excellent state of health. In the meantime, it is in principle a relatively low-cost matter to keep someone stored in a liquid nitrogen canister, more or less indefinitely.

There's a lot more to say about the possibility of cryonics, and about its economic consideration as well as its scientific plausibility (or, as critics would say, its implausibility). But before we resume that argument, it's time for one more digression. It's time to look beyond the economic arguments for or against rejuveneering, to the psychological ones.

10. Adverse psychology

I'll start this chapter by recapping. Technology is accelerating. As a consequence, rejuveneering is poised to jump ahead in leaps and bounds.

The waves of improvements to society that arose in the wake of the industrial revolution – the growth of the economy, better education, greater mobility, improved healthcare, richer opportunities – are set to continue, at an even more rapid pace than before. Ever larger numbers of people are both willing and capable to become involved in research and development activities, in multiple converging technology sectors, as part of a huge extended global network:

- More engineers, scientists, designers, analysts, entrepreneurs, and other change agents are being trained now, at universities and elsewhere, than ever before
- The available of high-quality online education material, often free-of-charge, means that these budding technologists are starting from a higher base point than most of their predecessors of just a few years ago
- People at later stages in their professional lives are able to jump into fertile new fields – perhaps initially "only browsing" – using some of their discretionary free time; this applies in particular to people who have retired from their previous work, or who have been made redundant but who still have many skills that they can deploy
- Connections between these different researchers, via a myriad of online communications channels, wikis, databases, AI linkages, and so on, mean that bright researchers can more quickly find out about promising lines of analysis happening elsewhere in the world
- The increasing prevalence of open source software, freely distributed, further helps to encourage wider participation.

It's this positive network effect – more people, better educated, better networked, building on top of each other's solutions – that leads me to the conclusion that, other things remaining equal, the overall pace of technology improvement is likely to rise and rise. The rapid breakthroughs of the last few decades in IT, smartphones, 3D printing, genetic engineering, brain scanning, and so on, are likely to be matched (if not surpassed) by similarly rapid breakthroughs in numerous other fields in the next few decades. Of critical importance, this pattern applies to innovation in medical treatments, and in particular, to innovation in rejuveneering.

As noted in Chapter 6, there exist many tough obstacles which impede progress in potential medical breakthroughs. This includes regulatory hurdles and other examples of system complexity and system inertia. Nevertheless, there are also an unprecedented number of well-educated, capable people who are already busy exploring possible solutions and workarounds for these hurdles. In a spirit of "divide and conquer", they're working on improved tools, libraries, test modules, methodologies, alternative regulatory pathways, AI analysis of big medical data, and much, much more. They can build creatively on each other's insights. And when they achieve good results, larger companies can join forces with them, to give their ideas any extra push needed.

As noted in Chapters 4 and 7, early signs of accomplishments by rejuveneering are all around us. The field can no longer be dismissed (as it used to be, by some critics) as quack medicine and snake oil. A host of interesting lines of inquiry await further research and development. Some of these lines of enquiry may turn out to be fruitless, but there's no reason to think that the field in its entirety will remain barren.

What's more, there are powerful economic reasons, reviewed in the previous chapter, for continuing this work. People who benefit from rejuveneering will, other things being equal, contribute more to the economy, and to the overall social capital. It makes strong financial sense for society to accelerate its investment in rejuveneering.

If there's a strong financial case for something happening, you'd think that society ought to be able to agree and say, "Let's do it". But that's far from being the case with rejuveneering. Instead, there are layers of opposition to it. It's time to dig more deeply into the roots of that opposition.

Varieties of objection

I've already reviewed, in Chapter 2, a whole set of objections to the rejuveneering project. As a reminder, I provided answers for questions such as:

- How does rejuveneering propose to address incurable diseases?
- Don't principles of physics, such as entropy, render rejuveneering impossible?
- Isn't the rejuveneering programme so inherently complicated it will require centuries of work?
- Aren't there natural limits to how long humans can live?
- Won't rejuveneering cause a dreadful population explosion?
- Won't long-lived people provide a brake on necessary societal change?
- In the absence of aging and death, what motivation will people have to get anything done?
- Won't the wealthy benefit disproportionately from rejuveneering?
- Isn't it egocentric to pursue rejuveneering?

The answers I gave in Chapter 2 were backed up with further exploration in later chapters. I believe that, in each case, rejuveneers have a strong case. Nevertheless, these good answers, by themselves, seem insufficient to change the minds of critics and sceptics. There's something deeper going on.

To understand what's happening, we need to distinguish *underlying motivation* from *supportive rationale*. In the vivid metaphor of the elephant and the rider, developed by social psychologist Jonathan Haidt in his book "The Happiness Hypothesis"[271], the conscious mind is akin to the human rider bestride a powerful elephant – the subconscious. Haidt develops this analogy in the first chapter[272] of his book:

> Why do people keep doing… stupid things? Why do they fail to control themselves and continue to do what they know is not good for them? I, for one, can easily muster the willpower to ignore all the desserts on the menu. But if dessert is placed on the table, I can't resist it. I can resolve to focus on a task and not get up until it is done, yet somehow I find myself walking into the kitchen, or procrastinating in other ways. I can resolve to wake up at 6:00 A.M. to write; yet after I have shut off the alarm, my repeated commands to myself to get out of bed have no effect…
>
> It was during some larger life decisions, about dating, that I really began to grasp the extent of my powerlessness. I would know exactly what I should do, yet, even as I was telling my friends that I would do it, a part of me was dimly aware that I was not going to. Feelings of guilt, lust, or fear were often stronger than reasoning…

> Modern theories about rational choice and information processing don't
> adequately explain weakness of the will. The older metaphors about
> controlling animals work beautifully. The image that I came up with for
> myself, as I marvelled at my weakness, was that I was a rider on the back
> of an elephant. I'm holding the reins in my hands, and by pulling one way
> or the other I can tell the elephant to turn, to stop, or to go. I can direct
> things, but only when the elephant doesn't have desires of his own. When
> the elephant really wants to do something, I'm no match for him.

The rider may think he or she is in control, but the elephant often has
its own firm ideas, particularly in matters of taste and morality. In such
cases, the conscious mind acts more like a lawyer than a driver. As Haidt
continues:

> Moral judgment is like aesthetic judgment. When you see a painting, you
> usually know instantly and automatically whether you like it. If someone
> asks you to explain your judgment, you confabulate. You don't really know
> why you think something is beautiful, but your interpreter module (the
> rider) is skilled at making up reasons... You search for a plausible reason
> for liking the painting, and you latch on to the first reason that makes
> sense (maybe something vague about colour, or light, or the reflection of
> the painter in the clown's shiny nose). Moral arguments are much the
> same: Two people feel strongly about an issue, their feelings come first,
> and their reasons are invented on the fly, to throw at each other. When
> you refute a person's argument, does she generally change her mind and
> agree with you? Of course not, because the argument you defeated was
> not the cause of her position; it was made up after the judgment was
> already made.
>
> If you listen closely to moral arguments, you can sometimes hear
> something surprising: that it is really the elephant holding the reins,
> guiding the rider. It is the elephant who decides what is good or bad,
> beautiful or ugly. Gut feelings, intuitions, and snap judgments happen
> constantly and automatically... but only the rider can string sentences
> together and create arguments to give to other people. In moral
> arguments, the rider goes beyond being just an advisor to the elephant; he
> becomes a lawyer, fighting in the court of public opinion to persuade
> others of the elephant's point of view.

In his follow-up book, "The Righteous Mind", Haidt builds upon that
metaphor to propose a cornerstone principle[273] of moral psychology:

Intuitions come first, strategic reasoning second.

Moral intuitions arise automatically and almost instantaneously, long before moral reasoning has a chance to get started, and those first intuitions tend to drive our later reasoning. If you think that moral reasoning is something we do to figure out the truth, you'll be constantly frustrated by how foolish, biased, and illogical people become when they disagree with you. But if you think about moral reasoning as a skill we humans evolved to further our social agendas—to justify our own actions and to defend the teams we belong to—then things will make a lot more sense. Keep your eye on the intuitions, and don't take people's moral arguments at face value. They're mostly post-hoc constructions made up on the fly, crafted to advance one or more strategic objectives.

The central metaphor… is that *the mind is divided, like a rider on an elephant, and the rider's job is to serve the elephant.* The rider is our conscious reasoning—the stream of words and images that hogs the stage of our awareness. The elephant is the other 99% of mental processes—the ones that occur outside of awareness but that actually govern most of our behaviour.

The biggest challenge facing the rejuveneering project isn't the set of supportive rationales that critics bring forward, as reasons for their opposition to the project. Instead, what urgently needs re-tuning is the underlying motivation that's guiding these critics, often without their conscious awareness. It's not the rider that we need to argue with. Instead, we have to find ways of directly engaging the elephant. That's my task in this chapter.

Managing terror

It's a fundamental fact of animals that they can experience terror. When facing a tangible threat of death, an animal's metabolism jumps into a different gear. Glands produce the hormones adrenaline and cortisol, which speed up heartbeat, dilate the pupils in the eye to take in more information about the impending danger, and increase blood flow to muscles and lungs in preparation for violent action. The animal is primed for either fight or flight. So that maximum energy is available for urgent self-preservation activities, other bodily processing is slowed down, including the digestion of food. Peripheral vision is reduced, so that the animal can concentrate more fully on the immediate threat at hand. Loss of hearing occurs too.

Terror is a state that serves a vital purpose when, indeed, the animal is under imminent mortal threat. In that state, the body is optimised to survive the immediate challenge. However, that state is far from optimised for longer-term existence. On the contrary, when in a state of panic, attention is restricted, thought patterns narrow, digestion suffers, and the body can be overtaken by convulsion and shaking. Uncontrollably releasing the contents of your bladder and sphincter may have the benefit of, perhaps, disgusting and repulsing would-be attackers, but it's not conducive to healthy social living at other times.

The human ability to vividly anticipate death ahead of time – that is, when not in any imminent danger – poses a problem for the management of the body's terror subsystem. If the thought of death becomes all-consuming, normal processing becomes impossible.

Worse, another aspect of animal psychology is that terror is contagious: if one animal in a group has spotted a predator nearby, the whole group can react quickly and decisively. Likewise, if one human becomes panic-stricken, their mood can swiftly spread, even in the absence of an objective cause for any panic.

The management of terror is, therefore, a key problem for human society. This has been the case right back into early prehistory, when humans started to acquire the capacities for self-awareness, planning, and introspective reflection. Observing the increasing frailty of group members who had, at younger times, been marvellously fit and healthy, early humans would be struck by the thought that a similar decline awaited them – and everyone else who they loved and cherished. In other words, mortal terror switched from being an occasional state, necessary for individual survival, to being something that could well up in someone's mind at any moment, unbidden by any external threat, leaving the person paralysed and panic-stricken.

What's more, the conscious anticipation of death from threats such as predators or competing bands of humans would tend, other things being equal, to cause strong risk-aversion. Behaviour that reduces short-term risk – such as remaining hidden in the depths of a cave – may well be far from the best for the long term progress of the group.

For these reasons, we can reasonably speculate that the groups of humans who successfully survived tended to be ones that developed social and psychological tools to manage the terror of the prospect of death – terror that would otherwise incapacitate the group. These tools in various ways denied the awfulness of the threat of death. These tools included mythology, tribalism, religion, ecstatic trances, and the *appearance* of contact with spirits. In later times, these tools also included cultural mores and thinking patterns which held out the promise of different kinds of transcendence of physical death, via the survival of our legacy, or the survival of a larger group of which we form an integral part. These thinking patterns are tied up with elements of our social philosophy – the way that we conceive of who we are, how we fit into our society, and how our society fits into the larger cosmos.

Our social philosophy, therefore, provides an important element of mental stability against the ever-lurking existential dread of mortality. But this means that anything which challenges our social philosophy – anything that suggests our philosophy has major flaws – is itself a danger to our mental well-being. Sensing this, our inner elephant can go wild, leading us to all sorts of irrational behaviour – behaviour which our inner lawyer/rider then hurries to rationalise.

What I've just described is a theory that was popularised by the philosopher Ernest Becker in his 1973 Pulitzer Prize-winning book "The Denial of Death"[274].

Beyond the denial of death

Becker wrote the following words at the start of "The Denial of Death":

> The prospect of death, Dr. Johnson said, wonderfully concentrates the mind. The main thesis of this book is that it does much more than that: the idea of death, the fear of it, haunts the human animal like nothing else; it is a mainspring of human activity—activity designed largely to avoid the fatality of death, to overcome it by denying in some way that it is the final destiny for man.

Sam Keen, contributing editor at Psychology Today, contributed a foreword to "The Denial of Death", in which he described Becker's philosophy as being "a braid woven from four strands":

> The first strand. The world is terrifying. To say the least, Becker's account of nature has little in common with Walt Disney. Mother Nature is a brutal bitch, red in tooth and claw, who destroys what she creates. We live, he says, in a creation in which the routine activity for organisms is "tearing

others apart with teeth of all types—biting, grinding flesh, plant stalks, bones between molars, pushing the pulp greedily down the gullet with delight, incorporating its essence into one's own organization, and then excreting with foul stench and gasses the residue."

The second strand. The basic motivation for human behaviour is our biological need to control our basic anxiety, to deny the terror of death. Human beings are naturally anxious because we are ultimately helpless and abandoned in a world where we are fated to die. "This is the terror: to have emerged from nothing, to have a name, consciousness of self, deep inner feelings, an excruciating inner yearning for life and self-expression—and with all this yet to die."

The third strand. Since the terror of death is so overwhelming we conspire to keep it unconscious. "The vital lie of character" is the first line of defence that protects us from the painful awareness of our helplessness. Every child borrows power from adults and creates a personality by introjecting the qualities of the godlike being. If I am like my all-powerful father I will not die. So long as we stay obediently within the defence mechanisms of our personality, what Wilhelm Reich called "character armour", we feel safe and are able to pretend that the world is manageable. But the price we pay is high...

The fourth strand. Our heroic projects that are aimed at destroying evil have the paradoxical effect of bringing more evil into the world. Human conflicts are life and death struggles—my gods against your gods, my immortality project against your immortality project. The root of humanly caused evil is not man's animal nature, not territorial aggression, or innate selfishness, but our need to gain self-esteem, deny our mortality, and achieve a heroic self-image. Our desire for the best is the cause of the worst. We want to clean up the world, make it perfect, keep it safe for democracy or communism, purify it of the enemies of god, eliminate evil, establish an alabaster city undimmed by human tears, or a thousand year Reich.

Becker's thesis is sweeping. It's one of a handful of ideas that attempt to show that human history has been shaped by forces that we often prefer not to acknowledge:

- Marx highlighted the role of class conflict and social alienation
- Freud highlighted repressed sexuality
- Becker highlighted our desire to deny the reality of death.

In common with all large theories of this form, Becker's thesis has critics who ask: *where is the evidence?* Sadly, Becker himself was unable to directly respond to such critics, as he had died even before the publication of "The Denial of Death", struck down by colon cancer. Sam Keen includes in his foreword a poignant account of him meeting Becker, for the first time, whilst Becker was at death's door:

> The first words Ernest Becker said to me when I walked into his hospital room were: "You are catching me in extremis. This is a test of everything I've written about death. And I've got a chance to show how one dies, the attitude one takes. Whether one does it in a dignified, manly way; what kinds of thoughts one surrounds it with; how one accepts his death…"
>
> Although we had never met, Ernest and I fell immediately into deep conversation. The nearness of his death and the severe limits of his energy stripped away the impulse to chatter. We talked about death in the face of death; about evil in the presence of cancer. At the end of the day Ernest had no more energy, so there was no more time. We lingered awkwardly for a few minutes, because saying "goodbye" for the last time is hard and we both knew he would not live to see our conversation in print. A paper cup of medicinal sherry on the night stand, mercifully, provided us a ritual for ending. We drank the wine together and I left.

Nevertheless, other researchers have stepped in, to provide a swathe of empirical evidence that fleshes out Becker's theory – evidence from a field sometimes called "experimental existential psychology". This new work was comprehensively summarised in the 2015 book "The Worm at the Core"[275] by social psychologists Jeff Greenberg, Tom Pyszczynski, and Sheldon Solomon.

The phrase used for the title of the book, "The worm at the core", comes from an extract from the 1902 publication "The varieties of religious experience: a study in human nature"[276] by philosopher William James. The authors quote that extract approvingly, and comment:

> There is now compelling evidence that, as William James suggested a century ago, death is indeed the worm at the core of the human condition. The awareness that we humans will die has a profound and pervasive effect on our thoughts, feelings, and behaviours in almost every domain of human life— whether we are conscious of it or not.
>
> Over the course of human history, the terror of death has guided the development of art, religion, language, economics, and science. It raised the pyramids in Egypt and razed the Twin Towers in Manhattan. It contributes to conflicts around the globe. At a more personal level, recognition of our mortality leads us to love fancy cars, tan ourselves to an

unhealthy crisp, max out our credit cards, drive like lunatics, itch for a fight with a perceived enemy, and crave fame, however ephemeral, even if we have to drink yak urine on *Survivor* to get it.

Terror Management Theory

Greenberg, Pyszczynski, and Solomon have coined the acronym TMT as shorthand for "Terror Management Theory" – which is their development of the ideas of Ernest Becker.

The Ernest Becker Foundation website carries a description[277] of TMT:

TMT posits that while humans share with all life-forms a biological predisposition toward self-preservation in the service of reproduction, we are unique in our capacity for symbolic thought, which fosters self-awareness and the ability to reflect on the past and ponder the future. This spawns the realization that death is inevitable and can occur at any time for reasons that cannot be anticipated or controlled.

The awareness of death engenders potentially debilitating terror that is "managed" by the development and maintenance of cultural worldviews: humanly constructed beliefs about reality shared by individuals that minimize existential dread by conferring meaning and value. All cultures provide a sense that life is meaningful by offering an account of the origin of the universe, prescriptions for appropriate behaviour, and assurance of immortality for those who behave in accordance with cultural dictates. Literal immortality is afforded by souls, heavens, afterlives, and reincarnations associated with all major religions. Symbolic immortality is obtained by being part of a great nation, amassing great fortunes, noteworthy accomplishments, and having children.

Psychological equanimity also requires that individuals perceive themselves as persons of value in a world of meaning. This is accomplished through social roles with associated standards. Self-esteem is the sense of personal significance that results from meeting or exceeding such standards.

The website also summarises three lines of the empirical evidence that support TMT:

1. The anxiety-buffering function of self-esteem is established by studies where **momentarily elevated self-esteem results in lower self-reported anxiety** and physiological arousal.

2. Making death salient by asking people to think about themselves dying (or viewing graphic depictions of death, being interviewed in front of a funeral parlour, or subliminal exposure to the word "dead"

or "death") **intensifies strivings to defend their cultural worldviews** by increasing positive reactions to similar others, and negative reactions toward those who are different.

3. Research verifies the existential function of cultural worldviews and self-esteem by demonstrating that **non-conscious death thoughts come more readily to mind when cherished cultural beliefs or self-esteem is threatened**.

TMT has generated empirical research (currently more than 500 studies) examining a host of other forms of human social behaviour, including aggression, stereotyping, needs for structure and meaning, depression and psychopathology, political preferences, creativity, sexuality, romantic and interpersonal attachment, self-awareness, unconscious cognition, martyrdom, religion, group identification, disgust, human-nature relations, physical health, risk taking, and legal judgments.

I had the opportunity to watch one of these authors, Tom Pyszczynski, present the ideas of TMT at the SENS6 conference in Cambridge in September 2013. I was struck by the relevance of his ideas to the question as to why so many people produce a string of ill-thought-out objections to the possibility of rejuveneering. I blogged about it[278] at the time:

My impression from the attendees at SENS6 that I met, over the four days I spent at the conference, is that the vast majority of them would give a resounding 'No' as the answer to the question, "Is it good that we grow old, weak, disease-prone, and eventually succumb, dead, to the ravages of aging?"

What's more, they shared a commitment that action should be taken to change this state of affairs. In various ways, they described themselves as *fighters against aging, healthy longevity activists,* and as *campaigners for negligible senescence.* They share an interest in the declaration[279] made on the page on the SENS Research Foundation website describing the conference:

"The purpose of the SENS conference series, like all the SENS initiatives, is **to expedite the development of truly effective therapies to postpone and treat human aging** by tackling it as an engineering problem: not seeking elusive and probably illusory magic bullets, but instead enumerating the accumulating molecular and cellular changes that eventually kill us and identifying ways to repair – to reverse – those changes, rather than merely to slow down their further accumulation."

But not everyone sees things like this. SENS6 attendees agreed on that point too. Over informal discussions throughout the event, people time and again shared anecdotes about their personal acquaintances being opposed to the goals of SENS. You can easily see the same kind of negative reactions, in the online comments pages of newspapers, whenever a newspaper reports some promising news about potential techniques to overcome aging.

For example, the Daily Mail in the UK recently published a well-researched article, "Do lobsters hold the key to eternal life? Forget gastronomic indulgence, the crustacean can defy the aging process"[280]. For healthy longevity activists, there was lots of good news in the article. This information, however, was too much for some readers to contemplate. Some of the online comments make for fascinating (but depressing) reading. Here are four examples, quoted directly from the comments:

1. How would humankind cope with tens of millions of extremely old and incredibly crabby people?

2. People have to die and they're not dying quickly enough. Soon the earth will run out of water and food for the ever increasing masses.

3. These "researchers" should watch [the film] Death Becomes Her

4. The only guarantee of eternal life is to read your Bibles. Though even if you don't, eternal life of another kind exists, though it's not particularly appealing: "And the smoke of their torment ascendeth up for ever and ever" (Rev 14:11).

In my blogpost, I provided some answers to the questions posed by these readers, but then went on to remark:

I believe that there are deeper roots to the opposition that many people have to the idea of extending healthy lifespans. People may offer intellectual rationalisations for their opposition (e.g. "How would humankind cope with tens of millions of extremely old and incredibly crabby people?") but these rationalisations are not the drivers for the position they hold.

Instead, their opposition to extending healthy lifespans comes from what we can call faith.

This thought crystallised in my mind as I reflected on the very last presentation from SENS6. The speaker was Thomas Pyszczynski of the University of Colorado, and his topic was "Understanding the paradox of opposition to long-term extension of the human lifespan: fear of death, cultural worldviews, and the illusion of objectivity"[281].

The paradox of opposition to extended healthspan

Here's the "paradox" to which Pyszczynski referred in the title of his talk: Nobody wants to die, but many people object to long-term extension of the human lifespan by reversing the aging process. Pyszczynski's explanation is that it's the operation of an entrenched "anxiety buffering system" – a mix of culture and philosophy – which leads people to oppose the idea that we could have longer healthy lives. This anxiety buffering system was originally an adaptive response to the disturbing underlying fact that something we deeply desire – indefinitely long healthy lives – is unachievable.

For all of history up until the present age, the aspiration to have an indefinitely long healthy life was at stark variance to everything else that we saw around ourselves. Death seemed inevitable. To reduce the risk of collapsing into terror at this realisation, we needed to develop rationalisations and techniques that prevented us from thinking counterproductively about our own finitude and mortality. That's where key aspects of our culture arose, creating and sustaining our elaborate anxiety buffering system. Meeting an important social need, these aspects of our culture became deeply rooted.

Our culture often operates below the level of conscious awareness. We find ourselves being driven by various underlying beliefs, without being aware of the set of causes and effects. However, we find comfort in these beliefs, especially when "other people like us" also espouse these beliefs, providing a measure of social validation. This faith (belief in the absence of sufficient reason) helps to keep us mentally sane, and keeps society functional, even as it prepares us, as individuals, to grow infirm and die.

To be clear, the "faith" described here, as intrinsic to the continuation of the accepting-aging paradigm, may *or may not* involve (for any specific individual) a belief in a supernatural "life beyond death", such as many religions describe. But the faith does, in all cases, involve the view that good members of society should accept death when their time comes, that society could not function properly if individuals ignored that principle, and that the fundamental meaning of an individual's life is tied up in the longer-term flourishing of the society or tradition of which they are part.

In case any new ideas challenge this faith, adherents often find themselves compelled to lash out against these ideas, even without taking the time to analyse them. Their motivation is to preserve their core culture and faith, since that's what provides the foundation of meaning in their lives. They fight the new ideas, even if these new ideas would be a better solution to their underlying desire to live an indefinitely long, healthy life. Paradoxically, it's their fear of death that makes them upset about the contrary ideas. These ideas generate feelings of alienation, even though they don't see the actual mental connections between the ideas. In summary, their faith causes us to lose their rationality.

Another useful metaphor here, Pyszczynski suggests, is to see our anxiety buffering system as a psychological immune system that seeks to destroy incoming ideas which would cause us mental distress. Like our physical immune system, our psychological immune system sometimes malfunctions, and attacks something that would actually bring us greater health.

Aubrey de Grey, the chief science officer of SENS, has also written on this topic. In chapter two of his 2007 book "Ending Aging"[282], he notes the following:

There is a very simple reason why so many people defend aging so strongly – a reason that is now invalid, but until quite recently was entirely reasonable. Until recently, no one has had any coherent idea how to defeat aging, so it has been effectively inevitable. And when one is faced with a fate that is as ghastly as aging and about which one can do absolutely nothing, either for oneself or even for others, it makes perfect psychological sense to put it out of one's mind – to make one's peace with it, you might say – rather than to spend one's miserably short life preoccupied by it. The fact that, in order to sustain this state of mind, one has to abandon all semblance of rationality on the subject – and, inevitably, to engage in embarrassingly unreasonable conversational tactics to shore up that irrationality – is a small price to pay....

De Grey continues this theme at the start of chapter three of his book:

We've recently reached the point where we can engage in the rational design of therapies to defeat aging: most of the rest of this book is an account of my favoured approach to that design. But in order to ensure that you can read that account with an open mind, I need to dispose beforehand of a particularly insidious aspect of the pro-aging trance: the fact that most people already know, in their heart of hearts, that there is a possibility that aging will eventually be defeated.

Why is this a problem? Indeed, at first sight you might think that it would make my job easier, since surely it means that the pro-aging trance is not particularly deep. Unfortunately, however, self-sustained delusions don't work like that. Just as it's rational to be irrational about the desirability of aging in order to make your peace with it, it's also rational to be irrational about the feasibility of defeating aging while the chance of defeating it any time soon remains low. If you think there's even a one percent chance of defeating aging within your lifetime (or within the lifetime of someone you love), that sliver of hope will prey on your mind and keep your pro-aging trance uncomfortably fragile, however hard you've worked to convince yourself that aging is actually not such a bad thing after all. If you're completely convinced that aging is immutable, by contrast, you can sleep more soundly.

In this extract, de Grey refers to "the pro-aging trance", on account of what he describes[283] as "the depth of irrationality that is exhibited by so many people". Other writers refer to the concept of "deathism"; for example, the website "Fight Aging!" has published what it called "An Anti-Deathist FAQ"[284]. I personally prefer the term "Accepting-aging paradigm", since it is less pejorative and may lower the temperature of what can already be a heated discussion.

Engaging the elephant

Let's return to excellent advice offered by Jonathan Haidt, regarding changing the direction of the "elephant" which represents our subconscious tendencies. If we recognise that these tendencies are flawed, as in the case of the accepting-aging paradigm, what can we do to change them?

The following is from the third chapter, "Elephants Rule", of his book "The Righteous Mind"[285]:

The elephant is far more powerful than the rider, but it is not an absolute dictator. When does the elephant listen to reason? The main way that we change our minds on moral issues is by interacting with other people. We are terrible at seeking evidence that challenges our own beliefs, but other people do us this favour, just as we are quite good at finding errors in other people's beliefs. When discussions are hostile, the odds of change are slight. The elephant leans away from the opponent, and the rider works frantically to rebut the opponent's charges. But if there is affection, admiration, or a desire to please the other person, then the elephant leans toward that person and the rider tries to find the truth in the other person's arguments. The elephant may not often change its direction in response to objections from its own rider, but it is easily steered by the mere presence of friendly elephants or by good arguments given to it by the riders of those friendly elephants…

Under normal circumstances the rider takes its cue from the elephant, just as a lawyer takes instructions from a client. But if you force the two to sit around and chat for a few minutes, the elephant actually opens up to advice from the rider and arguments from outside sources. Intuitions come first, and under normal circumstances they cause us to engage in socially strategic reasoning, but there are ways to make the relationship more of a two-way street…

The elephant (automatic processes) is where most of the action is in moral psychology. Reasoning matters, of course, particularly between people, and particularly when reasons trigger new intuitions. Elephants rule, but they are neither dumb nor despotic. Intuitions can be shaped by reasoning, especially when reasons are embedded in a friendly conversation or an emotionally compelling novel, movie, or news story.

This provides us with three ways to change the elephant's opinion, on a matter as controversial as whether healthy life extension is ultimately a desirable or an undesirable outcome. People are more likely to accept advice, on potentially difficult topics, if that advice:

1. Comes from someone perceived as being "one of us" – that is, a friend, from a similar demographic, rather than being a strange outsider

2. Is supported by "an emotionally compelling novel, movie, or news story"

3. Exists in a context where the elephant feels that its own needs are well understood and well supported.

The first of these conditions matches a well-known principle of technology marketing – that of companies needing to change their marketing approach while "crossing the chasm" from the set of early adopters of a new technology, to the larger market of "early majority". Geoffrey Moore brought attention to this idea in his 1991 book "Crossing the Chasm"[286], which in turn drew on rich observations by Everett Walker's 1962 work "The Diffusion of Innovation"[287]. The key insight is as follows: whereas early adopters of a new idea are prepared to act as visionaries, access to the mainstream market is controlled by pragmatists whose strong instinct is to "stick with the herd". In general, such people will only adopt a solution (or an idea) if they see others from their own herd who have already adopted it and endorse it.

There's an important implication here. Advocates and slogans that were successful in attracting an initial community of supporters to a new cause – such as the anticipating-rejuvenation paradigm – often need to be changed, before potential mainstream supporters will be prepared to listen. Talk of, for example, immortality, or mind uploading, which appealed to early supporters of rejuveneering, can be counterproductive as the movement seeks to gain a wider circle of supporters. People who might endorse the longevity dividend might be repelled by talk of the defeat of death.

The second and third of the above three conditions were addressed in a presentation by another speaker at the same SENS6 event where I first heard Tom Pyszczynski speak. This speaker was Mair Underwood of the University of Queensland. Her presentation was entitled "What reassurances do the community need regarding life extension? Evidence from studies of community attitudes and an analysis of film portrayals"[288].

Underwood's presentation pointed out the many ways in which would-be rejuveneers are depicted in a bad light in popular films including "The Fountain", "Death Becomes Her" (as mentioned by the Daily Mail commentator quoted above), "Highlander", "Interview with the Vampire", "Vanilla Sky", "Dorian Gray", and so on. Rejuveneers, these films imply, are emotionally immature, selfish, reckless, obstructive, narrow-minded, and generally dislikeable. The heroes in these films – the characters who are portrayed as calm, rational, praiseworthy, and mentally healthy – are the characters that voluntarily choose *not* to extend their lives.

Films with a contrary, affirmative impression of life extension are much less common; "Cocoon", directed by Ron Howard, is perhaps the best known example.

One reason negative stereotypes prevail in popular films is, no doubt, because dystopia tends to sell better than utopia. However, Hollywood stereotypes draw their strength from pre-existing cultural norms. As such, these films reflect and magnify viewpoints about life extension that are already widely distributed among the general population:

- Life extension would be boring and repetitive
- Long term relationships would suffer
- Life extension would mean the extension of chronic illness
- Life extension would be unfairly distributed.

To counteract these negative viewpoints, and to help free society from its accepting-aging paradigm, Underwood gave the following advice to the rejuveneering community:

1. Avoid berating the general public for having "breath-taking stupidity" on the subject of life extension
2. Provide assurances that life extension science, and the distribution of life extension technologies, are ethical and regulated, and seen to be so
3. Assuage community concerns about life extension as "unnatural" or "playing god"
4. Provide assurances that life extension would involve an extension of healthy lifespan
5. Provide assurances that life extension does not mean a loss of sexuality or fertility
6. Provide assurances that life extension will not exacerbate social divides, and that those with extended lives will not be a burden on society
7. Create a new cultural framework for understanding life extension.

I've been aiming to follow that advice throughout this book. In the next chapter, I'll spend some time painting a positive picture of the kind of society that can develop in the wake of rejuveneering – the "new cultural framework for understanding life extension".

11. Towards Humanity+

It's time for me to offer some friendly words of advice to a number of passionate advocates of rejuveneering. The advice is this: it's not sufficient to play "the freedom card".

This card typically comes into play in response to critics of rejuveneering who state that they would not want, themselves, to take advantage of rejuvenation therapies.

Consider this 2001 interview by Michael Rose, the longevity researcher and evolutionary biologist from the University of California at Irvine who we already met in previous chapters. Rose was answering the question, "How do people respond to your ideas about extending human life?" He gave the following answer[289]:

> There are all kinds of people who are opposed to us doing anything. The Federal Government has this need for us to die on our due date, so you don't bankrupt Social Security or Medicare. And I have on a number of occasions heard people give very moving addresses as to why we should die as soon as possible. I think the phrase that most stuck in my mind was "So that we can know God's love sooner." And let me just say for the record, I am all for those people dying. They can go ahead.
>
> I just know other people who *don't* want to die, and least of all by the horrible and unattractive process of aging, and I don't see any reason why they shouldn't be allowed to go on living.

What Rose is asking for (and he's by no means alone) is a spirit of toleration. Some critics of rejuveneering may well choose to reject the options *for themselves* to take any advantage of life-extending health-enhancing rejuvenation therapies. They may decide that these options lie outside their personal preferences. They may elect to grow old and die. If that's their choice for themselves, Rose can respect their decision. But he objects – strongly – when these critics want to prevent other people from developing and accessing such therapies. That would seem to be an intolerable imposition on personal liberty.

Beyond the freedom card

However, society sometimes decides that personal liberties need to be constrained.

For example, we constrain each other against drinking and driving, against making loud noises in quiet neighbourhoods, against making misleading advertising claims, and against emitting toxic pollutants. We carefully monitor and limit the spread of powerful armaments. We insist that high standards of hygiene are followed during food preparation. We demand that everyone vaccinates their children against dangerous infectious diseases – to prevent these diseases from regaining a foothold in the population, from which they might morph into new, incurable variants. We have rules to prevent over-fishing of shared fishing stocks – and other rules to protect various so-called "commons" which would otherwise be depleted by individuals taking more than their fair share. People have no absolute freedoms in such cases.

Could the same apply to the freedom to pursue rejuveneering?

Critics and sceptics of rejuveneering fear that lots of people with longer lives would have adverse economic or social consequences. I addressed the economic consequences in Chapter 9, "Money Matters", but even after reviewing these arguments, critics may still be apprehensive about the social consequences. They are driven by something like the following line of thought:

- If individuals live longer, that may be good for them, as individuals (assuming they retain good health), but it could cause large problems for society as a whole
- It could be similar to the way that, if individuals are prescribed antibiotics by their doctors, too freely, just on the outside chance that they could do some good to the individual, it can result in the growth of bacteria that are resistant to antibiotics (something that's bad for everyone)
- As another analogy, consider the way in which well-intentioned but naïve human interventions in a complex natural ecosystem, such as culling carnivore predators, can have unforeseen disastrous effects – such as a boom in the population of an animal species that was formerly kept in check by the predators, resulting in widespread destruction of vegetation and consequent ecosystem collapse
- Examples of foreseeable potential undesired consequences from rejuveneering are the elimination of time-proven social mechanisms for leadership to pass to younger individuals,

upheavals to family dynamics, the devastation of the natural environment due to unchecked growth of human population, and the fragmentation of the human species into "near immortals" and "definitely mortals" – the haves and have-nots of the future

- As well as considering foreseeable changes, we should also consider follow-on changes that are less foreseeable; the larger the original change, the greater the likelihood of larger unforeseen consequences.

I gave some answers to this kind of question in Chapter 2, "Rejuveneering 101". The biggest concern in the mix may be the one about large unforeseen consequences arising from the magnitude of the change if, indeed, aging is abolished. In this chapter, it's time to further explore the possibility of these larger consequences.

Embracing radical transformation

Rejuveneers have, in broad terms, a choice of three responses to the possibility of there being large unforeseen consequences from advances in rejuvenation biotech.

The first potential response is a simple, optimistic, upbeat one. It says that humanity is a clever, innovative species, with a track record of responding well to changes that weren't anticipated in advance. So we don't need to be unduly worried by such changes. We don't need any long list of what these changes might be. We can be confident that we'll take things in our stride.

The second potential response is more cautious and minimalist. It downplays the magnitude of any future changes, and claims that any future disruptions will be a small price to pay for the huge advantage of the abolition of aging. For example, the pension age would be raised, but that's OK, since we'll all be healthier. Again, therefore, we don't need to be unduly worried by such changes. Anything we have to take in our stride will be relatively small.

I'm sympathetic to both these responses, but I see them both as being inadequate. I prefer, instead, a third response. Rather than *simple optimism* or *cautious minimalism*, this response is one of *embracing radical transformation*. In order to describe that response, we have to be clearer about the scope of changes which technological progress is likely to bring.

The short summary is that we cannot simply say "we'll all be living longer and healthier, but everything else will be basically the same as before". The same engines of technological progress that will enable the abolition of aging will, in parallel, enable other profound changes in human nature. These changes will result in humans who not only live longer but are much smarter, much stronger, and much more capable. New sensory experiences will become possible – such as seeing ultraviolet or sensing magnetic fields. New depths of emotional experience and heightened consciousness beckon, as do abilities to temporarily alter aspects of our body. Simple examples of morphological experimentation include the acquisition of gills that would enable us to swim underwater, fish-like, and wings that would enable us to fly through the air, bird-like. We might switch our genders. Going further, we humans could become cyborgs, enmeshing our original physical bodies in mechanical prosthetics, silicon add-ons for enhanced memory and calculation, and numerous other "wearable" and "embedded" computers.

These radical changes won't just impact individuals. The human species as a whole stands poised to undergo a new, accelerated phase of evolution, in which intelligent life remoulds itself by conscious, thoughtful re-design. That re-design can fix the worst bugs that we have inherited from our biological evolution and from our history – bugs such as cognitive blind spots, systematic biases and prejudices, flawed rationality, and perverse incentive schemes. In short, we're contemplating, not only the abolition of aging but also the abolition of stupidity and the abolition of avarice. Rather than looking forward to "humans with longer healthspans", what we're really talking about is the advent of "Humanity+", namely a step-up from present-day humanity that could be every bit as significant as the prehistoric step-up from ape to human.

(Disclosure: I have been a Director of the international Humanity+ organisation[290] since 2013.)

In that Humanity+ future, our greater intelligence is likely to bring whole new fields of thought into our experience. However, from our present baseline vantage point of Humanity v1.0 (so to speak), we will inevitably struggle to anticipate the content and format of these new fields of thought. It would be like pre-human primates trying to conceive of the theorem of Pythagoras, the elliptical motion of planets around the sun, the mechanics of nuclear fusion, the pros and cons of the offside rule in football and the LBW rule in cricket, the beauty of sacrificing your queen in chess to force a checkmate five moves later, or the Darwinian principle of evolution through natural selection. Such concepts are simply beyond comprehension for our evolutionary antecedents. Nor could these primates appreciate the moral dilemmas addressed by *Hamlet* or *Breaking Bad*. All these features of human culture would have been inconceivable to pre-humans. Many elements of Humanity+ culture are likewise inconceivable to us today.

This "impossible to foresee" conundrum – which is part of what is meant by the oft-used phrase "technological singularity", meaning a time beyond which our present predictive abilities fail – is bound to cause some psychological distress. If we cannot know what kinds of thoughts future humans will think, or what kinds of actions they will undertake, how can we know whether things will turn out favourably? Given that unknowability, shouldn't we apply a sharp brake against the acceleration of technology? Shouldn't we take steps to ensure that the essential positive features of human existence are going to be preserved? And given that rejuveneering is an essential part of the journey to that unknowable future, shouldn't we be campaigning against rejuveneering, despite the benefits individuals may well gain from that project?

That line of thought is, in my view, what underpins a lot of the hostility against rejuveneering. It's what gives more strength to the accepting-aging paradigm. It's a line of thought that adds *apprehension of change* to *dislike of the alien (the different)*. The prospect of the world being populated and governed by something significantly different from present-day humans brings its own terror, which mingles with our underlying age-old terror regarding death. No wonder it's such a potent force.

From precautionary to proactionary

Neither the "simple optimism" response nor the "cautious minimalism" response, both of which I described earlier, will be strong enough to overcome this entrenched terror-driven hostility. Nor will it suffice to appeal to the principle of personal liberty. Instead, we need to be able to help people see the radical change ahead as being full of positive potential, for humanity as well as for individuals, rather than being a treacherous step into an unknowable abyss. People will be much more inclined to campaign to enable these radical changes if they see the future as attractive rather than as terrifying.

In other words, we need to be able to move away from a *precautionary* stance to one that is *proactionary*:

- The precautionary stance urges *avoidance of action* in areas where there are potential dangers and where there is uncertainty about the circumstances in which the dangers might occur. If a new technology (such as genetically modified food) operates in an environment where the cause-and-effect mechanisms are poorly understood, and if there is a risk that some of these mechanisms could have a major deleterious effect (such as interfering with the wider natural ecosystem in unexpected ways), the precautionary stance is opposed to the deployment of that new technology

- The proactionary stance, instead, urges *avoidance of inaction* in areas where there are potential dangers, even if there is uncertainty about the circumstances in which the dangers might occur. Doing nothing is, in itself, risky: a region may suffer from a shortage of food. And millions are dying needlessly, every year, due to aging-related diseases which sustained action could eradicate.

The proactionary stance does not *ignore* risks; far from it, it aims to identify risks and then *manage* these risks. The acceleration of technological progress brings, indeed, a multitude of new risks, and magnifies some previous risks into a more serious form. These risks need to be monitored, understood more fully, and addressed by whatever means is judged most suitable. But where the precautionary stance would throttle back any technology which is connected to a potential existential risk, the proactionary stance points out that these technologies may well be become incorporated as part of the solution, rather than as part of the problem. For example, genetic modification can create humans who are stronger, wiser, kinder, and less prone to foolish or egotistical action. And artificial intelligence can build better models of complicated system interactions (such as for the climate) which can then clarify the best actions to de-risk the system.

Your choice between precautionary and proactionary depends, in turn, on your assessment of the likely capabilities of the people who will be monitoring developments: are they going to spot real dangers in good time, and will they be able to devise *and implement* appropriate solutions to these dangers? Or will they prove themselves to be blind and/or weak?

It turns out, in other words, that your assessment of the likely *future* of humanity – whether you believe the radical transformation that technology brings will be for good or for ill – depends on your assessment of the *present* state of humanity. Do you see humanity's existing governing processes and decision-making systems as being competent or incompetent? If you assess them as essentially competent, you'll be inclined to accept the proactionary stance for technological advances. If you assess them as essentially incompetent, you'll be fearful of the consequences of ever-faster technological change, and you'll adopt a precautionary stance.

The ultimate decision, between these two different evaluations of the competence of present-day humanity, is one of the great unknowns of rejuveneering to which I'll return in the final chapter of this book. In the meantime, I'll try to take some heat out of the issue by filling in some of the gaps about how a future Humanity+ society might operate. The following suggestions will hopefully provide some balance to the dystopian visions of the future that Hollywood helps to keep in the public mind.

A better future for humanity

The positive future I foresee isn't one of stasis (lacking change). It's one in which plenty of challenges continue to arise, prompting ongoing social growth and development. However, in that positive future, society is able to reflect, on a regular basis, about the kinds of changes it would like to make, well in advance of any time deadline that would force the decision one way or the other.

That's a principle which should already be adopted, in the present day. The goal is to consciously remould the future, as we collectively judge best, rather than to sleepwalk into a scenario which we ought to have recognised in advance as being highly undesirable.

For example, consider the potential remoulding of the great human institution of marriage. In a world in which death may be indefinitely postponed, what happens to the idea, enshrined in the marriage vows of Christian denominations worldwide, of "until death do us part"?

In her role as agony aunt in the Guardian newspaper, social commentator Mariella Frostrup proposed one possible change. Responding to the enquiry from a reader, "I'm unhappy with my wife of 30 years. Should I leave?"[291] Frostrup offered the following reflections:

> I blame [your dilemma] less on your partner and more on medical science and healthier lifestyles. The reason a golden wedding anniversary attracts so much attention is that it's meant to be rare. "Till death us do part" is a noble aspiration, but it dates back to the days when you weren't committing to much more than a couple of decades. Nowadays, if you're young and a fool for love, you could tie the knot at 18, leaving yourself with 70 years or more to "enjoy" the company of your "one and only". For many that is more of a life sentence than a romantic idyll, and though such staying power represents an admirable ambition, it's nigh on impossible to live up to.
>
> If we're increasingly headed towards life expectancies of up to a century, an awful lot of what we take for granted when it comes to jobs, children and mating needs to be examined. For a start, when attempting such Olympian heights of relationship longevity, regular reassessment periods – making departure a less complicated, messy and emotionally wearing process than divorce – would be an improvement on the current contract. How about creating a nuptial contract renewable on a 10-year basis and marking each passing decade that you stay together with a party for all those who have helped you stay the course, from in-laws and friends, to children and exes? Rather than token gifts for longevity of tenure, how about a "get out of jail free" card that you can choose to use or lose every decade? That way you offer incentives to each other and to those around you to keep the marriage boat afloat. One wedding, one reception and then a lifetime together with no punctuation, rolling along like waves on a beach, seems an altogether measly ratio of enjoyment to commitment.

I'm not going to say that Frostrup's recommendation of renewable 10-year marriage contracts is the right one to adopt more widely. I'm mentioning it as an example of the kind of suggestion we can expect to be raised more often. Marriage can evolve without society necessarily suffering a crisis as a result.

Indeed, rejuvenation therapies can help our minds to be renewed, as well as keeping our bodies youthful. These therapies may well help our personalities to transcend the limitations of sameness which might otherwise push a long-term relationship into a state of weariness. We might be pleasantly surprised by new depths that become visible in our spouses.

What about the ancient human trait of giving birth to children? That, too, is something which technology can change – not only by making caesarean deliveries much more common, but by altogether doing away with the requirement for the baby to develop in a womb inside a mother's body. The technology of ectogenesis would allow a fertilised zygote to develop for nine months in an external, synthetic womb, where it would receive all the nutrients and nourishment required for proper growth. This technology will extend and unify two capabilities that already exist outside of the womb: in-vitro fertilisation at the very beginning of life, and the protection of babies in hospital incubators when they are born premature. The technique will provide opportunities for aspiring parents who, for whatever reason, find themselves unable (or unwilling) to have children by the "natural" route.

The thought of ectogenesis – originally described by JBS Haldane[292] in 1924 – brings its own share of apprehension, fuelled by its depiction in Aldous Huxley's 1932 novel "Brave New World". In that novel, the concept of motherhood is held up to ridicule, as is that of live birth, as being fit only for savages. In that dystopia, children belong only to the state, not to families – and "everyone belongs to everyone else". This is a future free from love. However, there's no inherent reason why ectogenesis would have to evolve in such a direction.

"Brave New World" forecast wide future use, not only of ectogenesis, but also of eugenics – the careful control of the attributes which would be present in any given child in the next generation. In the novel, this included the deliberate creation of "lower castes" (such as "epsilons") with reduced mental capacities, consisting of people suited to menial tasks. It's no surprise that eugenics has a dreadful reputation – particularly due to its association with ideas of racial superiority and inferiority, and with the zeal of the Nazis to prevent various types of people from having children. Nevertheless, the core concept of eugenics can in principle be used in ways that everyone benefits:

- Rather than children being designed as "dumbed down" (like the epsilons in Brave New World), genetic precursors for positive features can be selectively accentuated, including creativity, sociability, generosity, open-mindedness, musicality, and persistence

- It's not just new generations that can be enhanced in this way, but existing people from earlier generations (including you and me), who can have our genetic makeup incrementally upgraded, helping us to overcome some of our innate negative dispositions.

For a good discussion of the possibilities here, see the book "Babies by design: the ethics of genetic choice" [293] by Ronald Green.

These options for creating children – genetic selection followed by ectogenesis – are part of the reason why I part company with those forecasters who seem sure that longer lifespans will inevitably lead to smaller families. Historically, the two factors have indeed been correlated: as life expectancy has increased, the average size of families has declined. Because parents had a greater confidence that their offspring would still be alive when the parents decline in health, the parents felt less pressure to have additional children as a kind of "extended insurance policy". An extrapolation of this trend would be one reason to discount any fear that greater lifespans will, by itself, pose a strong risk of overpopulation. That line of reasoning is expressed in, for example, the article "Dying doesn't really affect overpopulation" [294] by Martin Borch Jensen. Jensen writes:

> I think it's reasonable to assume that any country that had the capacity to eliminate aging and disease would have very low birth rates... The global average birth rate is 2.5. The EU average is 1.6, the US 2. Japan, Hong Kong, Taiwan and South Korea are all below 1.4. The majority of African countries lie between 4 and 7, which brings up the average. Empirically, birth rates have a very strong negative correlation with child mortality and overall level of education. An example of this effect can be seen in South Korea, which in 1970 had a birth rate of 4.53. Concurrent with its explosive economic growth, this rate dropped to its present value of 1.2.
>
> It thus seems reasonable to assume that any society advanced enough to eliminate aging and disease would already have low birth rates, quite possibly well below 2 children per woman... Other societal changes, both planned and unplanned, are likely to affect the population dynamics of a society where death is voluntary. One possibility is that when we gain the right to live indefinitely, we lose the right to reproduce without limits...

Talk of "losing the right to reproduce" is likely to provoke opposition. But I see it as unnecessary. As I explained in Chapter 2, I believe the current global population remains far short of the overall carrying capacity of the earth – a figure that could be as high as 100 billion. In that case, there's no special need, any time soon, to reduce the number of children per parent.

Accordingly, the following scenario would be possible. At least some of the adults who remain indefinitely youthful might decide to become parents again, and again, once every 10-20 years, say – perhaps with different genetic partners each time. Such a trend would be in line with what researcher Mikko Myrskylä and colleagues have already suggested is happening. These authors suggested the following in a 2009 article in Nature, "Advances in development reverse fertility declines"[295]:

> During the twentieth century, the global population has gone through unprecedented increases in economic and social development that coincided with substantial declines in human fertility and population growth rates. The negative association of fertility with economic and social development has therefore become one of the most solidly established and generally accepted empirical regularities in the social sciences...
>
> [However] we show, using new cross-sectional and longitudinal analyses of the total fertility rate and the human development index (HDI), a fundamental change in the well-established negative relationship between fertility and development as the global population entered the twenty-first century. Although development continues to promote fertility decline at low and medium HDI levels, our analyses show that at advanced HDI levels, further development can reverse the declining trend in fertility. The previously negative development–fertility relationship has become J-shaped, with the HDI being positively associated with fertility among highly developed countries.

The same authors provided further explanation in a follow-up paper two years later, "High Development and Fertility: Fertility at Older Reproductive Ages and Gender Equality Explain the Positive Link"[296]:

> A fundamental switch in the fertility-development relationship has occurred so that among highly developed countries, further socioeconomic development may reverse the declining fertility trend. Here we shed light on the mechanisms underlying this reversal by analyzing the links between development and age and cohort patterns of fertility, as well as the role of gender equality. Using data from 1975 to 2008 for over 100 countries, we show that the reversal exists... and is mainly driven by increasing older reproductive-age fertility. We also show that the positive impact of development on fertility in high-development countries is conditional on gender equality: countries ranking high in development as

measured by health, income, and education but low in gender equality continue to experience declining fertility.

One concern that some people have about a growing population is a shortage of food or energy. However, as I've argued, the earth receives more than enough energy from the sun to be able to meet the needs of a much larger population than already exists. Improvements in agriculture and synthetic biology (including the cultivation of plants that thrive in salt water) should address that concern. The greater amount of waste that ever larger global populations create, as a by-product of living, needn't pose any problems either. New technology should enhance our ability to recycle that waste – similar, in fact, to the way that rejuvenation therapies will be repairing damage and waste that occurs inside our bodies.

Nor is any problem posed by the need to *eventually* find more living space than exists on the earth. Humanity can evolve in due course from being earth-bound to being sun-bound, that is, to living in extensive collections of fabricated space satellites, complete with their own versions of gravity, food, safety shields, and so on. These space cities would initially be close to the earth, but would later travel more widely in the solar system. Over a longer period of time, humanity would transition one more time, from being sun-bound to being galaxy-bound.

In parallel with our future journeys through outer space, we may also spend increasing amounts of time exploring inner space, including immense new virtual worlds. The detailed characteristics of these new virtual worlds lie beyond our present comprehension, similar to how people who lack awareness of the rules of a board game such as chess or go cannot appreciate the exquisite sophistication of the moves played by experts in these games – and similar to how people untutored in mathematics cannot initially appreciate the beauties of higher algebra and multi-dimensional geometries. But that's no reason for us to fear these new worlds. On the contrary, we can see these new worlds as being full of choice and experience.

The future of faith

One more great institution of humanity deserves consideration: the institution of faith. Religion is so pervasive in human culture that it seems likely that it must serve important needs.

I am sympathetic to the viewpoint expressed by David Sloan Wilson in his 2002 book "Darwin's Cathedral: Evolution, Religion, and the Nature of Society"[297], namely, that religion has in general survived inasmuch as it helped groups of people to achieve greater cohesion and thereby acquire greater fitness compared to other groups of people. This kind of religion has practical effect, independent of whether or not its belief system corresponds to factual reality. (It can hardly be denied that, in most cases, the belief system does *not* correspond to factual reality.) As pioneering sociologist Emile Durkheim put it[298], religions can have great "secular utility".

Wilson's book has some great examples – from the religions in hunter-gatherer societies, which contain a powerful emphasis on sharing out scarce resources completely equitably, through examples of religions in more complex societies. His chapter on protestant John Calvin was eye-opening, describing how Calvin's belief system brought stability and prosperity to Geneva. Even more fascinating was a section on the water-irrigation religion of Indonesian island Bali, which makes it clear that the religion has vital pragmatic side-effects.

If aging is abolished, what will happen to religion? With humans dying much less often – perhaps having an average lifespan of thousands of years (if the likelihood of death in any one year is as low as, say, 1 in 10,000[299], in the absence of aging-related diseases) – will religion lose its force over people's lives? And in that case, what will happen to the cohesion religion supplied to society for centuries?

Of course, religion has led to horrendous division as well as to cohesion. The analysis in Wilson's book makes it crystal clear why many religious groups have treated outsiders so badly (despite treating insiders so well): the cohesion they promote is centred on a particular in-group, not on humanity as a whole.

What's more, religion is declining for reasons other than the extension of lifespan: worldviews populated with angels and demons and ghosts and spirits sit dreadfully uneasily with what science teaches us about ourselves. Overbearing theories about human sinfulness and wrathful deities are being superseded by powerful modern insights about human psychology. Thankfully, morality is increasingly seen as having its roots in the requirements of social living, rather than being dependent on commandments supposedly carved onto ancient tablets of stone or breathed into primeval scripture. As the Internet makes us aware of the bizarre, untenable aspects of the religious beliefs of our neighbours from different historical cultures, we are shocked to realise, in moments of honest reflection, that the religious beliefs we may have inherited from our own forefathers are just as bizarre and untenable. No, any force that is capable of providing modern society with much-needed cohesion will need, first and foremost, to be grounded in science and rationality, rather than age-old mythology.

Along these lines, David Sloan Wilson offers the following thoughts, in an essay entitled "The future of religion"[300]:

> It is often said that all cultures throughout history have had some sort of religion. Testing this proposition requires a rigorous definition of religion, which is notoriously difficult, but another proposition is easier to defend: all cultures throughout history have had some sort of meaning system, defined as a system of beliefs and practices that receive environmental information as input and result in action as output. There are no exceptions to this rule. We are such a cultural species that every individual requires an elaborate meaning system to make it through every single day... Durkheim was on the mark when he said, "In all its aspects and at every moment in history, social life is only possible thanks to a vast symbolism."
>
> Once we focus on the universality of meaning systems, we can begin to make sensible statements about the meaning systems worth wanting in the future. They need to solve problems of coordination and cooperation at a planetary scale. To do this, they must be highly respectful of scientific knowledge. Anything less will result not only in a lack of knowledge about how to behave, but the evolution of social entities that are well-designed for their own survival but are cancerous with respect to the long term welfare of the planet.
>
> Is the human race capable of creating a single meaning system or federation of meaning systems that works together for the common good? Will such a meaning system or federation be religious or secular according to conventional definitions? Nobody knows the answers to those questions, but scientific knowledge about the cultural evolution of meaning systems will be required to find out.

To my mind, the Humanity+ vision can provide at least the core of what Wilson calls a "meaning system" that can enable people to "work together for the common good".

If faith means a commitment to a belief that is consistent with the known evidence and the best current theories, but which may go beyond that evidence and these theories, then I am ready to say that I have a faith in Humanity+. The Humanity+ vision is something which should be able to provide coherence and direction for increasing numbers of people, around the world. The Humanity+ initiative provides a larger sense of meaning and purpose for the rejuveneering project and the abolition of aging.

The Humanity+ vision

The term "Humanity+" was devised and adopted[301] by members of the global transhumanist community in 2008.

The word "transhumanism" itself indicates "going beyond" ("transcending") the existing condition and capabilities of humanity. I like this definition from the Transhumanist FAQ[302]:

What is transhumanism?

Transhumanism is a way of thinking about the future that is based on the premise that the human species in its current form does not represent the end of our development but rather a comparatively early phase.

Transhumanism is a loosely defined movement that has developed gradually over the past two decades. "Transhumanism is a class of philosophies of life that seek the continuation and acceleration of the evolution of intelligent life beyond its currently human form and human limitations by means of science and technology, guided by life-promoting principles and values." (Max More 1990) ...

Transhumanism can be viewed as an extension of humanism, from which it is partially derived. Humanists believe that humans matter, that individuals matter. We might not be perfect, but we can make things better by promoting rational thinking, freedom, tolerance, democracy, and concern for our fellow human beings. Transhumanists agree with this but also emphasize what we have the potential to become. Just as we use rational means to improve the human condition and the external world, we can also use such means to improve ourselves, the human organism. In doing so, we are not limited to traditional humanistic methods, such as education and cultural development. We can also use technological means that will eventually enable us to move beyond what some would think of as "human".

The Humanity+ mindset rejects some widespread opinions which often influence decisions in today's world. These "Humanity v1.0" opinions include:

- Evolution has done the best possible job in designing humans; what it has produced cannot be surpassed
- Except for relatively peripheral matters, "natural methods" are generally the best ones
- Any significant improvements in human condition are likely to take centuries
- Attempts to redesign human nature – or otherwise to "play God" – will inevitably cause disaster.

It's true that attempts to redesign human nature are fraught with danger. It's also true that more powerful technology brings new menaces. More powerful technology augments our capability to wreak havoc, as well as our ability to heal, educate, and flourish. The same YouTube that distributes wonderful Khan Academy educational videos also distributes contemptible footage of Islamic State atrocities, inducing widespread outrage and hatred. The same synthetic biology that can repair damaged human organs, improving them in the process, can also produce deadly pathogens with virulence beyond the worst existing diseases. The same computer guidance systems that navigate us to holiday destinations can also navigate lethal cruise missiles to explode in the midst of large human populations.

Technology has always been a two-edged sword, but it's now sharper and more potent than ever before. We are therefore in the midst of an urgent race between, on the one hand, technological improvement and, on the other, a growing risk of crisis. It's as expressed by futurist Ramez Naam in his excellent book "The infinite resource: the power of ideas on a finite planet"[303]:

> A long time ago Dickens wrote these words in the opening of *A Tale of Two Cities*: "It was the best of times, it was the worst of times". This pretty much captures the current discussion of what's happening on this planet. In a lot of ways we're living in the greatest age humanity has ever seen, but in a lot of ways we're facing some of the worst risks also. So you see sort of highest levels of optimism in some parts of society, and the highest levels of pessimism in other parts.

I fully support the solution advocated by Naam in his book:

- Human ingenuity has the capability to solve the problems that humanity is facing
- Even though these problems are becoming harder, human ingenuity can grow to match them
- Nevertheless there is nothing predetermined about the outcome; history has shown many previous examples of civilisations collapsing, after a prior period of extended consumption
- Whereas in the past, collapses of civilisation only affected parts of the earth, future collapses could terminate humanity altogether; we therefore face what has been called a set of "existential risks"
- The wise, considerate use of new technology should play a fundamental role in avoiding our existential risks, augmenting our human ingenuity.

Note this is *not* a "technology first" approach. Technology is the prime enabler, but the goal is the enhancement of humanity, rather than technological progress for its own sake.

A manifesto for Humanity+

To summarise the core message of this chapter, I'll include the text for a "Humanity+ manifesto" from a 2013 blogpost of mine[304]. As befits a manifesto, the language is deliberately provocative.

Humanity is on the brink of a momentous leap forwards in evolution. If we are wise and strong, we can – and should – make that leap.

This evolutionary transformation takes advantage of rapidly improving technology – technology that arises from positive virtuous cycles and unprecedented interdisciplinary convergence. This technology will grant us awesome powers: the power to capture ample energy from the Sun, the atom, and beyond; the power to synthesise new materials to rejuvenate our environment and fuel our societies; the power to realise an unparalleled abundance of health, security, vigour, vitality, creativity, knowledge, and experience; the power to consciously, thoughtfully, proactively remake Humanity.

Through imminently available technology, our lives can be radically enhanced, expanded, and extended. We can be the generation that banishes disease, destitution, decay, and death. Our societies can become marvels of autonomy and inclusion, featuring splendid variety and harmony. We can move far beyond the earth, spreading ever higher consciousness in both inner and outer space. We can transcend our original biological nature, and become as if divine; we'll be as far ahead of current human capabilities as current humans exceed the prowess of our ape forebears.

But technology is a two-edged sword. Alongside the potential for transcendent improvement lies the potential for existential destruction. We face fearsome perils of environmental catastrophe, unstoppable new plagues and pathogens, rampant unemployment and alienation, the collapse of world financial markets, pervasive systems of unresponsive computers and moronically intelligent robots that act in frustration to human desires, horrific new weaponry that could easily fall into the wrong hands and precipitate Armageddon, and intensive mechanisms for draconian surveillance and thought control.

Continuing the status quo is not an option. Any quest for sustainability of current lifestyles is a delusion. We cannot stay still, and we cannot retreat. The only way to survive is radical enhancement – moving from Humanity to Humanity+.

We'll need great wisdom and strength to successfully steer the acceleration of converging technology for a positive rather than a negative outcome. We'll need to take full advantage of the best of current Humanity, to successfully make the leap to Humanity+.

Grand battles of ideas lie ahead. In all these grand battles, smart technology can be our powerful ally – technology that can unlock and enhance our human capacities for insight, innovation, compassion, kindness, and solidarity.

We'll need to transcend worldviews that insist on viewing humans as inherently diminished, incapable, flawed, and mortal. We'll need to help individuals and societies rise above cognitive biases and ingrained mistakes in reasoning. And we'll need to accelerate a reformation of the political and economic environment, so that the outcomes that are rationally best are pursued, instead of those which are expedient and profitable for the people who currently possess the most power and influence.

As more and more people come to appreciate the tremendous attractiveness and the credibility of the Humanity+ future, they'll collectively commit more of their energy, skills, and resources in support of realising that future. But the outcome is still far from clear.

Time is short, risks are high, and there is much to do. We need to open minds, raise awareness, transform the public mood, overturn prejudices, establish rights, build alliances, resist over-simplification, avoid the temptations of snake oil purveyors, dispel distractions, weigh up the best advice available, take hard decisions, and accelerate specific research and development. If we can navigate these slippery paths, with wisdom and strength, we will indeed witness the profound, glorious emergence of Humanity+.

The future of death

As I said, a manifesto uses provocative language. The 576 words that I've just quoted, originally written in early 2013, are well sprinkled with exhortation and urgency. I make no apology – except, in part, for one word.

The strongest claim in that manifesto comes in the final word of this clause, "We can be the generation that banishes disease, destitution, decay, and death." The abolition of *death* would, of course, be a huge step up from the abolition of aging. As I've been at pains to point out throughout this book, whilst rejuvenation therapies have the potential to eradicate aging-related diseases, including most of the biggest killers of contemporary society, these therapies cannot, by themselves, eradicate many of the other causes of death. Nor does the potential that such therapies might be developed over the next few decades provide comfort for someone who is already afflicted with a mortal disease with a much shorter life expectancy. What can Humanity+ say in response to such questions?

It's time to look at some radical alternatives – ideas that are complementary to the main rejuveneering project which has been the main focus of my book so far.

12. Radical alternatives

For most people who have ever lived, rejuveneering is coming too late. It's coming too late for them, either because they've already grown old and died, in the present century or in one of the many preceding ones, or because, although they're still alive, they're likely to die before effective rejuvenation therapies become widely available. Either way, they belong to the BR era – the Before-Rejuvenation era.

However, within the broad rejuveneering community, some researchers dare to suggest there might be hopes for the regeneration of people from the BR era. Collectively, these ideas form a set of radical alternatives and complements to the methods I've covered in previous chapters in this book. In this chapter, I'll take a look at these ideas.

An ambulance to the future

One of the most important innovations in medical history can be said to be the creation of the ambulance. If someone is injured, or suffers a medical emergency, the timely arrival of an ambulance can make all the difference between life and death. Such a person was the victim of "being in the wrong *place*"; they needed medical help, but they weren't in a location where medical help was immediately available. However, an ambulance meant they could be transported to a facility with the resources to treat them: equipment, medicines, and trained healthcare professionals.

There may be scope for observers to quibble about the costs of any given ambulance service. Some critics might say that an ambulance service could be provided at less cost, whilst still being able to meet the majority of the demands placed upon it. However, it's rare to find someone who complains about the very idea of an ambulance service. You don't hear people saying that if someone experiences a medical emergency away from a hospital, that's simply too bad – they should stoically accept their fate. Nor is it said that any family members who request an ambulance for their injured parent, child, or sibling are being selfish or immature. Instead, society embraces the idea that it is natural to demand speedy, safe transport away from the initial danger zone into a place where the medical emergency can be properly dealt with. That way, the injured person has a chance to be treated, and to live on, potentially for many decades to come.

But consider our attitude towards someone who suffers a medical emergency at "the wrong *time*". They happen to have a disease which is about to kill them, but which medical science is likely to be able to cure in, say, thirty years' time. What should we think about the provision of a possible "ambulance to the future" for such a person? Suppose, for the sake of argument, there was a chance of at least 5% that such an "ambulance" might work. To be precise, the mechanism under consideration is the low-temperature cryonic preservation of the person, in such a way that they enter something akin to deep coma in which all their normally physiological processing is suspended. Should we embrace the possibility of such a rescue vehicle? Or should we instead urge the victim of this medical crisis to avoid thinking about any such possibility? Should we tell them, in other words, to stoically accept their fate (their impending death)? And if any of their family members, wishing to be able to converse and interact with the dying person in the future, request the provision of this kind of ambulance service, should we rebuke them for being selfish or immature?

Of course, the analogy is far from perfect. With an ambulance that transports a patient through space, to a hospital, there are plenty of previous examples of the journey succeeding. But with cryonics, the journey of a human patient through decades of low-temperature bodily suspension has never yet completed. We can read about people *starting* that journey, when they are cryopreserved by organisations such as Alcor Life Extension Foundation[305], Cryonics Institute[306], or KrioRus[307]. (These companies are headquartered in, respectively: Scottsdale Arizona, USA; Clinton Township Michigan, USA; and Moscow, Russia). We can also see photographs of the storage cylinders inside which cryonics patients are preserved – sometime their entire bodies, and sometimes just their heads (under the expectation that the science of the future will be able to regrow a new body around the person's brain). But there is no guarantee that medical science will ever progress to the point where these patients can be successfully reanimated.

The arguments against the idea of cryonics mirror the arguments against rejuveneering that I mentioned right at the start of this book. Some critics say cryonics *cannot* succeed: the technical challenges of wakening someone from such a low temperature state are unfathomably difficult. The process of lowering the body to ultra-low temperatures may have irreparably damaged it, despite the careful use of antifreeze, cryoprotectants, and other sophisticated chemicals. After all, these chemicals are toxins in their own right, and the process of cooling large organs may introduce fractures. Other critics say that cryonics *should not even be considered*, because it is morally wrong. They allege that it's a misuse of valuable resources, a wicked delusion, a financial scam, or worse.

My response to these criticisms is – like my response to the corresponding criticisms of rejuveneering – to profoundly disagree. In both cases, I view the majority of the criticisms to be ill-informed, or to be motivated by faulty reasoning and other (often repressed) ulterior drives.

In both cases – rejuveneering and cryonics – I accept that the engineering task will be hard. But I see no reason in either case why the task will be impossible. In time, high quality solutions can be created. In both cases, I see a series of precursors already in place, which point the way towards an eventual comprehensive engineering solution.

One precursor for cryonics is the field known as therapeutic hypothermia. In 1999, trainee doctor Anna Bågenholm was skiing off-piste in a steep descent in a remote region of northern Norway, when she fell into a frozen mountain stream. By the time a rescue helicopter arrived, she had been in freezing water for 80 minutes, and her blood circulation had been stopped for 40 minutes, as reported in a subsequent article in the Lancet, "Resuscitation from accidental hypothermia of 13·7°C with circulatory arrest"[308]. Writing in the Guardian, in an article entitle "Between life and death – the power of therapeutic hypothermia"[309], David Cox provides further details:

> By the time Bågenholm was brought to the University Hospital of North Norway in Tromso, her heart had stopped for well over two hours. Her core temperature had plunged to 13.7C. She was in every sense clinically dead.
>
> However, in Norway, there has been an old saying for the past three decades that you're never dead until you're warm and dead. Mads Gilbert is the head of emergency medicine at the hospital and, from experience, he knew that there was a slim chance the extreme cold had actually kept her alive.
>
> "Over the last 28 years, there have been 34 victims of accidental hypothermia with cardiac arrest who were rewarmed on cardiopulmonary bypass and 30% survived," he said. "The key question is: are you cooled

before you have the cardiac arrest or are you first having a circulatory arrest and then getting cooled?"

Cox goes on to explain some of the key biology involved:

While lowering the body temperature will stop the heart, it also reduces the oxygen demand of the body and, in particular, the brain cells. If the vital organs have been sufficiently cooled before the cardiac arrest occurs, then the inevitable cell death from the lack of circulation will be postponed, buying emergency services an extra time window to try and save the person's life.

"Hypothermia is so fascinating because it's a double-edged sword," Gilbert said. "On the one side it can protect you but, on the other side, it will kill you. But it's all a question of how controlled the hypothermia is. Anna was probably cooled quite slowly but efficiently so that, when her heart stopped, her brain was already so cold that the oxygen need in the brain cells was down to zero. Good CPR can provide up to 30-40% of the blood circulation to the brain and in these cases that is often sufficient to keep the person alive for sometimes seven hours while we try to restart the heart."

Thankfully, Bågenholm made almost a complete recovery. Ten years later, she was working as a radiologist in the hospital where her life had been saved.

Bågenholm had experienced *accidental* hypothermia. Increasingly, doctors are deliberately *inducing* hypothermia, to obtain time to carry out complicated medical procedures. In his book "Extreme Medicine"[310], Kevin Fong tells the story of the treatment in 2010[311] of Esmail Dezhbod:

Esmail Dezhbod's symptoms had begun to worry him. He felt pressure in his chest, at times great pain. A body scan revealed that Esmail was in trouble. He had an aneurysm of his thoracic aorta, a swelling of the main arterial tributary leading from his heart. This vessel had doubled in size, to the width of a can of Coke.

Esmail had a bomb in his chest that might go off at any moment. Aneurysms elsewhere can usually be repaired with relative ease. But in this location, so close to the heart, there are no easy options. The thoracic aorta carries blood from the heart and into the upper body, supplying oxygen to the brain, among other organs. To repair the aneurysm, flow would have to be interrupted by stopping the heart. At normal body temperatures, this and the accompanying oxygen starvation would damage the brain, leading to permanent disability or death within three or four minutes.

Esmail's surgeon, cardiac specialist John Elefteriades, MD, decided to carry out the procedure under the conditions of deep hypothermic arrest. He used a heart-lung bypass machine to cool Esmail's body to a mere 64.4°F before stopping his heart completely. Then, while the heart and circulation were at a standstill, Dr. Elefteriades performed the complicated repair, racing the clock while his patient lay dying on the operating table...

It's a delicate operation:

Though Dr. Elefteriades is an old hand with hypothermic arrest, he says that every time feels like a leap of faith. Once circulation has come to a standstill, he has no more than about 45 minutes before irreversible damage to the patient's brain occurs. Without the induced hypothermia, he would have just four.

The doctor lays the stitches down elegantly and efficiently, making every movement count. He has to cut out the diseased section of the aorta, a length of around six inches, then replace it with an artificial graft. The electrical activity in Esmail's brain is, at this point, undetectable. He is not breathing and has no pulse. Physically and biochemically, he is indistinguishable from someone who is dead.

That phrase is worth emphasising: "Physically and biochemically, he is indistinguishable from someone who is dead". However, he is still capable of revival. Fong continues:

After 32 minutes, the repair is complete. The team warms Esmail's freezing body, and very quickly his heart explodes back to life, pumping beautifully, delivering a fresh supply of oxygen to his brain for the first time in over half an hour.

Fong reports that he visited the patient in the intensive care unit the following day:

He is awake and well. His wife stands by his bed, overjoyed to have him back.

Who would deny the patient's wife the chance to have that joyous reuniting with her husband? Nevertheless, the critics of cryonics would deny many other people the chance to anticipate a similarly joyous reuniting with their loved friends and families at the culmination of a cryonics suspension. They would say that the extrapolation from therapeutic hypothermia to cryonics is too big a chasm. The temperature involved in cryonics is much lower – the temperature of liquid nitrogen – and the timescale of the suspension is much longer. In response, I maintain there are promising grounds to believe this chasm can, indeed, be bridged.

Not freezing

A second precursor that points the way to successful cryonics technology is the fact that some organisms can already survive various kinds of sub-zero hibernation. For example, the Artic ground squirrel hibernates for up to eight months each year, during which time its core temperature drops from 36°C to -3°C, whilst external temperatures can reach as low as -30°C. The New Scientist reports[312] that

> To prevent their blood from freezing, the squirrels cleanse it of any particles that water molecules could form ice crystals around. This allows the blood to remain liquid below zero, a phenomenon known as supercooling.

Various fish in polar regions can survive in salt water that is below the freezing point of fresh water. They seem to manage this, without their blood freezing, with the help of so-called antifreeze proteins (AFPs). AFPs suppress the growth of ice crystals. Species of insects, bacteria, and plants also take advantage[313] of AFPs. Remarkably, larvae of the Alaskan beetle have been reported[314] as surviving temperatures as low as -150°C, by means of adopting a glass-like vitrified state.

The champion species for surviving ultra-low temperatures is the tardigrade, which is sometimes known as the "water bear". It's actually tiny: it grows to less than 2mm. The species is also evolutionarily ancient, having been in existence some 500 million years ago, in the Cambrian era. An article on BBC Earth[315] describes their tolerance of temperatures actually below that of liquid nitrogen as used in cryonics (-196°C). It refers to experiments carried out in the 1920s by Gilbert Franz Rahm, a Benedictine monk:

> Rahm... immersed [tardigrades] in liquid air at -200°C for 21 months, in liquid nitrogen at -253°C for 26 hours, and in liquid helium at -272°C for 8 hours. Afterwards the tardigrades sprang back to life as soon as they came into contact with water.
>
> We now know that some tardigrades can tolerate being frozen to -272.8°C, just above absolute zero... The tardigrades coped with a

profound chill that does not occur naturally and must be created in the lab, at which atoms come to a virtual standstill.

The biggest hazard tardigrades face in the cold is ice. If ice crystals form inside their cells, they can tear apart crucial molecules like DNA.

Some animals, including some fish, make antifreeze proteins that lower the freezing point of their cells, ensuring that ice doesn't form. But these proteins haven't been found in tardigrades.

Instead it seems tardigrades can actually tolerate ice forming within their cells. Either they can protect themselves from the damage caused by ice crystals, or they can repair it.

Tardigrades may produce chemicals called ice nucleating agents. These encourage ice crystals to form outside their cells rather than inside, protecting the vital molecules. Trehalose sugar may also protect those that produce it, as it prevents the formation of large ice crystals that would perforate the cell membranes.

The *C. elegans* nematode worm, whose variable longevity has featured in many of the experiments covered in previous chapters in this book, makes an important appearance in this chapter too. On this occasion, what's noteworthy is the preservation of memories over the process of *C. elegans* individuals being cryonically suspended (to the temperature of liquid nitrogen) and then reanimated. The experiment was carried out by Natasha Vita-More of the University of Advancing Technology, Tempe, Arizona, and Daniel Barranco of Universidad de Sevilla, Spain. Here's the description of the experiment from the abstract of their October 2015 article[316] in Rejuvenation Research:

Persistence of Long-Term Memory in Vitrified and Revived *Caenorhabditis elegans*

Can memory be retained after cryopreservation? Our research has attempted to answer this long-standing question by using the nematode worm *Caenorhabditis elegans*, a well-known model organism for biological research that has generated revolutionary findings but has not been tested for memory retention after cryopreservation. Our study's goal was to test *C. elegans'* memory recall after vitrification and reviving. Using a method of sensory imprinting in the young *C. elegans*, we establish that learning acquired through olfactory cues shapes the animal's behaviour and the learning is retained at the adult stage after vitrification. Our research method included olfactory imprinting with the chemical benzaldehyde for phase-sense olfactory imprinting at the L1 stage, the fast-cooling

SafeSpeed method for vitrification at the L2 stage, reviving, and a chemotaxis assay for testing memory retention of learning at the adult stage. Our results in testing memory retention after cryopreservation show that the mechanisms that regulate the odorant imprinting (a form of long-term memory) in *C. elegans* have not been modified by the process of vitrification or by slow freezing.

In an article co-authored by Vita-More in MIT Technology Review, "The Science Surrounding Cryonics"[317], the significance of this *C. elegans* result is put in context. The question under discussion is whether there is any possibility that human memory and consciousness could survive cryonic suspension. Vita-More and colleagues write as follows:

The exact molecular and electrochemical features of the brain that underlie the conscious mind remain far from completely explored. However, available evidence lends support to the possibility that brain features that encode memories and determine behaviour can be preserved during and after cryopreservation.

Cryopreservation is already used in laboratories all over the world to maintain animal cells, human embryos, and some organized tissues for periods as long as three decades. When a biological sample is cryopreserved, cryoprotective chemicals such as DMSO or propylene glycol are added and the temperature of the tissue is lowered to below the glass transition temperature (typically about -120°C). At these temperatures, molecular activities are slowed by more than 13 orders of magnitude, effectively stopping biological time.

Although no one understands every detail of the physiology of any cell, cells of virtually every conceivable kind are successfully cryopreserved. Similarly, while the neurological basis for memory, behaviour, and other features of a person's identity may be staggeringly complex, understanding this complexity is a problem largely independent of being able to preserve it.

Vita-More and colleagues then highlight the evidence from *C. elegans* that memories can survive cryopreservation:

For decades *C. elegans* have commonly been cryopreserved at liquid nitrogen temperatures and later revived. This year, using an assay for memories of long-term odorant imprinting associations, one of us published findings that *C. elegans* retain learned behaviours acquired before cryopreservation. Similarly, it has been shown that long-term potentiation of neurons, a mechanism of memory, remains intact in rabbit brain tissue following cryopreservation.

Reversibly cryopreserving large human organs, such as hearts or kidneys, is more difficult than preserving cells but is an active area of research with important public health benefits, since it would greatly increase the supply of organs for transplant. Researchers have made progress in this area, successfully cryopreserving and later transplanting sheep ovaries and rat limbs, and routinely recovering rabbit kidneys after cooling to -45°C. Efforts to improve these technologies provide indirect support for the idea that the brain, like any other organ, may be adequately cryopreserved by current methods or methods under development.

Note that the cryonicists are very clear that the preservation methods they use should be described as "vitrification" rather than "freezing". The difference is explained straightforwardly, with easily understood graphics, on the website of Alcor[318], one of the leading providers of cryonics services. Here's the key conclusion:

Because no ice is formed, vitrification can solidify tissue without structural damage.

Given that point, it's (almost) remarkable that various high-profile critics of cryonics seek to discredit the whole concept by theatrically demonstrating the structural damage done to fruit and vegetables – such as strawberries and carrots – when they are frozen and then thawed. The critics almost sneer: *how could the cryonicists be so stupid?* I'm tempted to sneer in return: *how could these critics get their basic facts so badly wrong?* Are these critics really unaware of the successful cryopreservation of human embryos (pivotal in IVF treatments)? Have they not heard about the 2002 vitrification[319] by Greg Fahy and colleagues at 21st-Century Medicine of a rabbit kidney, which was lowered to -122°C before being thawed and successfully transplanted, as an operational organ, into another rabbit?

To answer my own question: there's more going on here than rational debate. It's another example of a gulf of two paradigms, with pressures of adverse psychology making it hard for some observers to take seriously the possibility of cryonics. The possibility that cryonics might work poses a strong threat to the framework of ideas with which many people have surrounded themselves – the framework (as discussed in Chapter 10) that says that "good people accept the inevitability of aging and death, and shouldn't fight that conclusion". People who have grown comfortable with that conclusion are therefore motivated to find fault with the cryonics worldview. That can explain why they blithely parrot technical objections, economic objections, or sociological objections which, frankly, don't hold up to serious scrutiny.

The forthcoming surge in cryonics

There's a great deal more than can be said about cryonics, from multiple viewpoints. It takes considerable time to sort through all the objections and misunderstandings that have grown up around cryonics. For an engaging introduction to the subject, I recommend the comprehensive March 2016 Wait But Why article "Why Cryonics Makes Sense"[320] by Tim Urban. In turn, that article includes pointers to lots of additional material. Readers may also value the wealth of perspectives contained in the volume "Preserving Minds, Saving Lives"[321] that is available from the Alcor website.

Here, I'll restrict myself to a small number of final comments on cryonics:

- The economic costs for cryonic preservation, long-term storage, and (assuming all goes well) an eventual reanimation, can presently be met from a life insurance policy
- The economic costs for an individual cryonic patient could decline by orders of magnitude if the number of patients grows significantly; this is the familiar principle of benefiting from "the economics of scale"
- As long as the "accepting aging" paradigm remains so pervasive within society, most people will feel strong social and psychological pressure against investigating cryonics and, subsequently, signing the relevant contracts. However, as this paradigm wilts (as I believe will happen) under greater publicity being given to rejuveneering breakthroughs, greater numbers of people will become open to the possibility of cryonics
- The increased interest in the subject will also result in more people carrying out research into improvements in cryonics – including improvements in the technology, engineering, support networks, business models, organisational frameworks, and methods to communicate about the subject to wider audiences. In turn, the innovations that result will accelerate the attractiveness of the cryonics option

- As high profile figures from fields such as entertainment, business, academia, and the arts increasingly endorse the idea, it will open the way for wider members of the general public to feel comfortable about identifying themselves as cryonicists.

But cryonics is far from being the only idea whereby people might be transported (so to speak) from the present BR (Before Rejuvenation) era into AR (After Rejuvenation).

Head transplants

If someone's body is badly damaged, but their brain is still in good shape, one approach that can be considered, at least in principle, is to transplant the healthy head onto a new body.

But before I write another word on this subject, I probably need to address the strong feelings of revulsion that usually arise whenever any possibility of a head transplant is mentioned. Recall that the idea of a heart transplant used to evoke similar shudders. How... *distasteful* that one person might have someone else's heart placed inside them! How... *Frankensteinian*!

In time, as the positive examples were publicised of people returning to good health after receiving a heart transplant, in the late 1960s and early 1970s, these initial powerful feelings of disgust became tempered. Rather than being seen as revolting, the process became re-evaluated as deeply humane.

In time, a similar transformation of mood may take place regarding head transplants. The surgeon who gained notoriety for transplanting the head of one rhesus monkey onto the decapitated body of another, in 1970, Dr Robert White, was motivated[322] to find a solution for quadriplegics or for sufferers of amyotrophic lateral sclerosis whose bodies had totally stopped functioning. Over his long career, White carried out more than 10,000 surgeries. A 2010 obituary for him[323] by Grant Segall contained fulsome praise:

> Bishop Anthony Pilla, former head of the Cleveland Catholic diocese, called White "a brilliant mind, a world-respected surgeon and researcher, a person with a much-needed, keen sense of moral values and their impact on science and medicine." He said White helped shift devout people of many faiths from opposing extraordinary medicine to supporting it as pro-life...

White pioneered what became widespread methods of draining fluids and chilling injured parts of the brain for surgery…

His many awards included papal knighthoods, honorary doctorates, visiting professorships and the 1997 Humanitarian Award of the American Association of Neurological Surgeons. He was one of 85 doctors portrayed in the book "Modern Neurosurgical Giants".

White gained some of his important insights about chilling injured parts of brains from his controversial experiments on animal brains. The rhesus monkey mentioned earlier, when it awoke after its head had been transplanted onto a new body, was able[324] to see, hear, taste, and smell. It even – typical for a rhesus monkey, apparently – tried to bite the finger[325] of one of the medical team. However, the new body was paralysed, due to lack of nerve reconnection. It needed mechanical assistance to breathe. The monkey died several days afterwards, when the body's immune system rejected the head.

During the 1990s, a severely disabled former diver, Craig Vetovitz, would frequently give interviews alongside Dr White, supporting his work. A Clevescene article by Laura Putre with the ghoulish title "The Frankenstein Factor"[326] gives the details:

For the past five or six years, White has regularly done interviews on head transplant surgery with a partner – Craig Vetovitz, a biker and polymer engineer who broke his neck 25 years ago in a diving accident, when he was 19…

Vetovitz is technically not a quadriplegic, because he has some movement in his hands, and he can even stand up, with help. "My feet are very ticklish," he says. But like most quads, he expects his internal organs to start failing in middle age, his life cut short. So if head transplants become available, he'll be the first in line.

"Everybody always thinks, 'Oh, what a gross, horrible, mean thing to do to a person,' he says of the surgery. "Well, pretend you're a total quad. Let's say you're real thirsty – ask somebody to get you a glass of water, or ask somebody to help you transfer to the toilet when you have to go. When you become disabled, you lose all privacy. Your life is a schedule."

Vetovitz was full of praise for Dr White:

Vetovitz calls White, who has advised him on medical matters, "a very noble character."

"He's not the type of person that's just gonna switch a head, unless there's a very high chance of full recovery. He knows what it's like being behind the eyes – because he sees it all the time, he sees the misery."

Any risks involved don't matter, says Vetovitz. When your life is changed forever because you landed in the pool the wrong way, risks are all relative.

Despite his enthusiasm at the prospect, no such operation was to take place for Vetovitz. The costs would have been enormous. The challenges of overcoming tissue rejection seemed insurmountable. And the ethical climate was strongly opposed. In the meantime, more conventional methods of care for quadriplegic have improved – witness the remarkable life of Professor Stephen Hawking, despite his debilitating amyotrophic lateral sclerosis. White died at the age of 84 without coming close to carrying out the kind of experiment which, in his middle age, he had expected would eventually become almost as common as heart transplants.

As it happens, White sometimes regretted that media fascination with his idea of a head transplant took interest away from what he saw as another great accomplishment of his – an accomplishment with considerable relevance for the topic of cryonics. As Laura Putre reports:

White's first medical breakthrough was not head transplantation, but a technique of cooling the spinal cord that slowed down the damage enough so that doctors could operate on it. Then came his advances in extracorporeal perfusion, the isolation and cooling of the brain -- a technique now used in the Mayo Clinic and most other top hospitals. Sometimes he wonders why all the reporters don't ask him about those achievements, since they've actually been put in practice.

"We discovered that you can keep a human brain going without any circulation," he says. "It's dead for all practical purpose – for over an hour – then bring it back to life. If you want something that's a little bit science fiction, that is it, man, *that is it!*"

But as often happens with new technology, an idea which is premature at one point can return to significance after a suitable passage of time. In 2013, Dr Sergio Canavero of the Advanced Neuromodulation Group at Turin, Italy, announced that he believed such an operation would be feasible by around 2017. The New Scientist[327] reported his ambitions:

He wants to use the surgery to extend the lives of people whose muscles and nerves have degenerated or whose organs are riddled with cancer. Now he claims the major hurdles, such as fusing the spinal cord and preventing the body's immune system from rejecting the head, are surmountable, and the surgery could be ready as early as 2017.

As evidence of progress towards the possibility of reconnecting a broken spinal cord, consider a video produced in early 2016 by a colleague of Canavero, C-Yoon Kim of the School of Medicine at Konkuk University in South Korea. As the New Scientist[328] comments:

The video… [appears to show] mice sniffing and moving their legs, apparently weeks after having the spinal cord in their necks severed and then re-fused. C-Yoon Kim, at Konkuk University School of Medicine in South Korea, who carried out the procedure, says his team have demonstrated the recovery of motor function in the forelimbs and hindlimbs of the animals. "Therefore I guess it is possible to reconnect the [spinal] cord after complete severance," he says.

Key to the successful refusing, according to Canavero and Kim, is the use of a chemical called polyethylene glycol (PEG) when the cut is made: this allows the preservation of the nerve membranes.

As news of Canavero's work spread, it particularly caught the attention of Valery Spiridinov, a 31-year old software engineer who suffers from the muscle wasting Werdnig Hoffman disease, also known as spinal muscular atrophy.

Just as, two decades earlier, Craig Vetovitz was ready to be the pioneering patient for any head transplant carried out by Dr Robert White, Spiridinov is ready to be the first participant in an experiment overseen by Canavero. Guardian writer Sam Thielman reports[329] that Spiridinov sees his current body as "just mechanics that I want to have removed". Spiridinov told Luke Heighton of the Daily Telegraph[330] that he looked forward to no longer being constrained by the limits of his present, failing, physical body:

"If I have a chance of full body replacement I will get rid of the limits and be more independent."

Heighton's article proceeds to explain the three stages of the envisaged surgery — surgery that is likely to last for two days, and involve a medical team of around 150 people:

Stage one involves cooling the patient and donor's bodies in order to prevent the brain cells from dying during the operation. Next, the neck is partially severed and the blood vessels from one body linked to the other with tubes…

Stage two sees the spinal cord cut with an extremely fine blade to minimise damage. The donor head is then removed, placed on the recipient's body, and the spinal cord fused back together again using polyethylene glycol, a compound used both in medicine and industrial manufacturing...

Stage three involves knitting together the survivor's blood vessels and nerves... The body is then kept in a coma for several weeks to prevent movement and allow time for the spinal cord to glue itself back together.

Heighton quotes Matthew Crocker, a consultant neurosurgeon at St George's Hospital, London, confirming that key parts of the proposed operation already have grounding in established medical practice:

"Excluding blood vessels that supply blood to the brain then restoring them with tubes is very well recognised... Lowering the temperature of the whole body head and brain to between 10 and 20 degrees, usually around 15 to 17 degrees, is a very well recognised technique used for complex neurosurgery or cardiovascular surgery in which there is an expectation that the brain will be starved of its blood and oxygen supply for a substantial period...

"The idea of cutting the spinal cord sharply rather than bluntly has a little medical support. The only well recognised success with spinal cord injury surgery came from a man who had a stab injury rather than a blunt injury."

At time of writing, Canavero remains set on preparations to carry out the procedure at some stage during 2017 – probably in Russia. As a striking example of how breakthrough new medical procedures may find their strongest support in what were formerly third world countries, Professor Trinh Hong Son, director of the National Co-ordination Centre in Vietnam, has suggested[331] that his Centre in Hanoi could be used for subsequent cases.

For a small number of people whose bodies are on the point of total failure, this kind of head transplant may represent a viable route to continued mobility. Learnings from any such experiments may also provide important insight about how to repair broken spinal cords. But my reason for including this possibility in this chapter is as a prelude to a more radical idea. Rather than someone having their head transplanted onto a new body (donated, in effect, by someone whose own brain had died), their head could be placed inside a totally new kind of body, sometimes called a "robot body" or "full body prosthetic".

Full body prosthetics

The last few years have seen remarkable improvements in replacement limbs. Hugh Herr, a professor in MIT Media Lab, leads the MIT Biomechatronics group which creates so-called "smart prosthetics". This includes a replacement knee which contains a small computer chip that constantly monitors the position of the joint and the stresses it is experiencing. This new knee supplies the following functionality (according to a commercial website[332] advertising the product):

- Advanced actuator and resistance control ensure best possible resistance, e.g. more support in stair descent and minimum effort needed in level ground gait

- Effortless swing initiation enables a smoother gait, even in crowds and confined spaces

- Smart gait detection, including kinematic sensor technology, ensures stability and dynamic response in every situation

- Magnetorheologic technology enables an instant response so that users never have to wait for the knee to catch up with them.

A separate "ankle-foot" prosthetic, with a built-in battery, enables amputees[333] "to walk with normal levels of speed and metabolism as if their legs were biological".

The positive impact of these smart prosthetics can be appreciated from a remarkable TED talk given by Herr in 2014. From the TED website, here's the description[334] of that talk:

Hugh Herr is building the next generation of bionic limbs, robotic prosthetics inspired by nature's own designs. Herr lost both legs in a climbing accident 30 years ago; now, as the head of the MIT Media Lab's Biomechatronics group, he shows his incredible technology in a talk that's both technical and deeply personal — with the help of ballroom dancer Adrianne Haslet-Davis, who lost her left leg in the 2013 Boston Marathon bombing, and performs again for the first time on the TED stage.

These prosthetics combine elements of a replacement skeleton (exoskeleton), electromechanics, biomimicry, new materials, computer control, and adaptive learning. When I saw Herr speaking at an event in Shoreditch, London, he remarked, half-joking, half-serious, that some non-amputees were almost jealous of the replacement limbs that he was using.

Let's consider where this could be leading. A full set of smart prosthetic limbs, combined with replacement synthetic organs (heart, lungs, and so on), could provide an entire replacement body that could host someone's brain. This vision is spelt out in the document "Extracorporeal artificial life support system for a full body prosthetic"[335] authored by John LaRocco, Head of Engineering at the company Humai which was publicly launched in January 2016. Humai's website[336], under the tagline "Transcending human biology through robotics", state the company's aims as follows:

> We want to transplant your brain into an elegantly designed bionic body called Humai. It will use a brain-computer interface to communicate with the sensory organs and limbs of your new bionic body.
>
> Artificial intelligence will be integrated into synthetic organs, so they can operate independently. Sensor technology will allow you to feel the essence of human experience.

LaRocco's document gives more details:

> The implementation of a full body prosthetic requires the development of a full extracorporeal artificial life support system. The cornerstone of the proposed approach is an artificial circulatory system that moves blood plasma between different artificial organs. The proposed system relies upon a cell-free environment to sustain a transplanted head or decanted brain. The specific implementation is a closed-loop circuit beginning and terminating at the blood vessels of the transplanted head. The system would send nutrients and oxygenated blood in to the common carotid artery, after dealing with deoxygenated blood and metabolic waste. The system comprises a cerebral module, a cardiopulmonary module, a renal module, a filtration module, and a nutritional module. Additional modules can be added or subtracted based upon individual cases. In addition to assisting the development of a full-body prosthetic, the system could improve conditions for patients suffering from organ failure or in need of long-term life support for surgical procedures.

Humai recognise that any such system is unlikely to be available any time soon. Their website highlights the use of cryonics to preserve brains, from the point of legal death, until such time as a full-body prosthetic may become available:

> We believe by leveraging cryonics to preserve the brain to potentially restore it later will be the core breakthrough for human resurrection.
>
> Cryonics is a method used to freeze the brain. We will preserve the brain immediately after death as there is only a certain time frame after death

that we can safely remove the brain and cryonically preserve it for possible later restoration. We endorse cryonics technology but we are not a cryonics company.

The best case scenario however, would actually be to successfully transplant a live person's brain to the Humai body. The ultimate goal is to achieve a point where no one has to die at all.

One member of the Humai team, Ira Pastor, is working on various associated technologies through his own company Bioquark[337] – tagline "next generation therapeutics for human regeneration and repair" – and the spin-out project ReAnima[338]. ReAnima states its focus as:

Biomedical interventions for brain death utilizing the most cutting edge neuro-regeneration and neuro-reanimation technologies available

The ReAnima website further declares that:

Comprehensive neuro-regeneration and neuro-reanimation is a possibility.

In an article[339] he wrote for Singularity Weblog, Pastor gave more details of the envisioned regeneration mechanism, and how it would alter current conceptions of when brains can be declared as irretrievably dead. First, Pastor stated the usual definitions of "death":

Death is defined as the termination of all biological functions that sustain a living organism.

Brain death, the complete and irreversible loss of brain function (including involuntary activity necessary to sustain life) as defined in the 1968 report of the Ad Hoc Committee of the Harvard Medical School, is the legal definition of human death in most countries around the world.

Either directly through trauma, or indirectly through secondary disease indications, brain death is the final pathological state that over 60 million people globally transfer through each year.

We are repeatedly told through the medical establishment (as well as through popular culture, in recent public cases such as those surrounding Jahi McMath and Bobbi Kristina Brown) that brain death is "irreversible" and should be considered the end of the line.

Then he points out that various animals have the ability to regenerate parts of their CNS (central nervous system):

While it is true that human beings lack substantial regenerative capabilities in the CNS, many non-human species, such as amphibians, planarians, and certain fish, can repair, regenerate and remodel substantial portions of their brain and brain stem even after critical life-threatening trauma.

These… capabilities have been leveraged experimentally in past decades to perform complex brain transplantation in organisms such as salamanders, as well as to study the dynamics of memory storage.

Extensive study over the last century has shed a substantial amount of knowledge on the processes of… regeneration and the unique and multi-mechanistic dynamics that are involved in re-starting a defined generative developmental pattern to specifically fill in missing or damaged tissues and organs in a living organism.

He suggests there is some evidence of similar abilities being latent in humans too:

Despite the label of irreversibility associated with the 1968 Harvard Ad Hoc Committee definition, there are several documented cases in the literature of potential brain death reversal, primarily associated with younger subjects whose CNS maintained some degree of underlying neuroplasticity.

Bioquark's website explains[340] that the proposed regenerative mechanism, named BQ-A, is being targeted in the first instance at the regeneration of kidney:

The first organ that the company is focusing on, based on a combination of unmet medical need and minimal competitive landscape, is the human kidney.

While humans can live normally with just one kidney, when the amount of functioning kidney tissue is greatly diminished by disease or damage, chronic kidney disease will develop leading towards a progressive loss in function. This loss of kidney function leads to a downward spiral throughout the body including negative effects on the cardiovascular system, nervous systems, and endocrine function.

Dialysis or kidney transplant can prolong life, but quality of life is severely affected, supplies are limited, and costs of long term maintenance are exorbitant. Additionally, as the kidney is one of the more anatomically complex organs, it has proven refractory to stem cell-based regenerative techniques to date.

Work on the regeneration of the brain will follow. The page on the website ends with a flourish:

> We are at a very unique moment in history where the convergence of the tools of regenerative biology, resuscitation / reanimation research, and clinical neuroscience have placed us on the verge of major scientific breakthroughs.

Accordingly, the Humai website is able to foresee "extensive tissue repair and regeneration, including the repair of individual brain cells" for the brains of people placed into the Humai full body prosthetic. In other words, after an incident when disease or accident would normally have killed them, people can live on, with their brains being repaired and improved, and transferred inside a brand new body which is stronger and more resilient than their original one.

A roadmap of avatars

Humai isn't alone in offering a vision of a future life inside a robot body. The idea came to public attention through the "2045" project[341] of Russian multi-millionaire Dmitry Itskov. Itskov organised conferences in Moscow (2012) and New York (2013) around the theme of a four-fold progression of different kinds of robot interfaces. The New York event attracted an audience of around 900 (I was one of the 900) and featured 34 speakers. Some speakers highlighted technology that already exists:

- Nigel Ackland, a former metal worker whose arm was amputated below the elbow following a horrific factory accident, demonstrated the bionic lower arm which has been attached to his upper arm stub and which is controlled by muscle impulses; his new arm allows him to tie shoelaces and play cards

- Japanese professor Hiroshi Ishiguro demonstrated his "geminoid" robot avatars, which at first glance are hard to distinguish from the people upon which they are modelled (including Ishiguro himself)

- Professor Theodore Berger of the University of Southern California described replacing part of the hippocampus, inside the brains of rats, with a small electronic chip that provides equivalent functionality (the hippocampus has a key role in the transfer of memory from short-term to long-term storage)

- Jose Carmena and Michel Maharbiz of the University of California, Berkeley, reviewed the power of deep brain stimulation to provide relief to the terrible shudders of sufferers of Parkinson's Disease, and also described some rudimentary examples of patients controlling their wheelchairs via brain-machine interfaces

- Russian professor Alexander Kaplan described work in the "Walk Again Project" to prepare for someone wearing an exoskeleton to kick a football during the opening of the 2014 World Cup tournament.

Other speakers looked ahead at credible projections of improvements in related technology:

- Prosthetic arms that provide users with tactile feedback
- Connections into the brain that are much less intrusive but which will allow additional degrees of freedom of control
- Brain computer interfaces that take advantage of machine learning and neuroplasticity to improve their performance
- A support system for a living brain, including a brain incubator, sensors, and a perfusion system
- Methods to slice a brain into very thin slices whose contents can then be scanned into a massive data storage system.

Itskov's 2045 initiative slots expected outcomes from present and forthcoming technology projects into a four-stage series of more sophisticated avatars:

- Avatar A is a robotic copy of a human body (similar to the ones created by Professor Ishiguro) that can be remotely controlled by a brain-computer interface from a human "pilot"
- Avatar B is a robot into which someone's brain can be transplanted at the end of their life
- Avatar C is a robot with its own artificial brain, into which a human personality can be transferred (via copying the data from the human brain) at the end of their life
- Avatar D is described as a "hologram-like avatar" and would have an even higher level of indestructibility.

The initiative suggests[342] that Avatar A might be ready by 2020, Avatar B by 2025, Avatar C by 2035, and Avatar D by 2045. One reason to be sceptical about these dates is that, since the public flourish in New York in 2013, the project has communicated little further about tangible plans. A BBC Horizon programme in March 2016, "The Immortalist"[343], included interviews with Itskov and his colleagues from the 2045 project, but gave no tangible updates on what was already discussed at the event in New York. On the other hand, aspects of the project are being adopted by other companies – such as Humai (as noted above).

To gain a fuller appreciation of both the strengths and weakness of the "Avatar C" style of solution – in which there's a transfer, not of a brain, but of a mind – we need to take a step back, and resume our consideration of cryonics.

Brain duplication

As noted earlier in this chapter, one of the big unknowns of cryonics is the extent to which human memory and consciousness might survive the long journey through initial vitrification, storage over multiple decades (perhaps even centuries), and the envisaged eventual re-animation of the body. One risk is that, despite all precautions, the brain structure will have deteriorated too badly in the process. Something might go wrong during the storage period. The vitrified brain may be badly disturbed as a result of earthquakes, political upheavals, terrorist attacks, commercial failures, social collapse, regulatory interference, or technical incompetence.

As an example, consider the sad case of Dr Raymond Martinot and his wife Monique. A Guardian article by Angelique Chrisafis[344] provides the background:

> Raymond Martinot, a doctor who once taught medicine in Paris, spent decades preparing for his demise in the belief that if he was frozen and preserved scientists would be able to bring him back to life by 2050. In the 1970s he bought a chateau near Samur in the Loire valley and began preparing a freezer unit for himself. But his wife, Monique Leroy, died first, of ovarian cancer, in 1984, and was the first to enter the intricate stainless steel freezer unit in the chateau's vaulted cellars.
>
> She remained in the freezer for almost 20 years while Dr Martinot met his high refrigeration bills by allowing paying visitors to visit the cellar... In 2002 Dr Martinot died of a stroke, aged 84, and his son followed his orders to inject him with the same anti-coagulants and store him alongside.

The Martinot's son, Rémy, then commenced a lengthy legal argument with the French authorities, who demanded that both bodies be removed from storage and buried. He was preparing to take his case to the European Court of Human Rights in Strasbourg. Unfortunately, Remy shortly afterwards discovered that the freezer unit had suffered a fault, whose seriousness was compounded by the failure of a monitoring alarm system to detect that the temperature was rising. Chrisafis explains the outcome:

> The French couple's journey into the future ended prematurely when, 22 years after his mother's body was put into cold storage, their son discovered the freezer unit had broken down and they had started to thaw.
>
> The couple's bodies were removed from their faulty freezer and cremated this week…
>
> Rémy Martinot said he had no choice but to cremate his parents' bodies after the technical fault had seen their temperatures rise above the constant level required of -65C (-85F).

It seems that the temperature had risen to -20C for several days. The son commented,

> "I don't feel any more bereaved today than I did when my parents died; I had already done my grieving. But I feel bitter that I could not respect my father's last wishes. Maybe the future would have shown that my father was right and that he was a pioneer."

This incident shows two of the threats to cryonics success: government interference, and technical fault. Other episodes in the history of cryonics had equally sad outcomes, including the so-called "Chatsworth Scandal"[345] of 1978. Modern cryonics companies are making every effort to guard against future mishaps. But it is in this context that a different idea may come to seem attractive: rather than seeking to store the brain intact, as a potentially fragile organ vulnerable to destruction if it heats up too much, why not create a *digital copy* of the brain? Digital copies could be stored in several different places, as extra precaution in case of any accidents affecting individual copies.

This approach can be named as "digital cryonics", as compared to the original "organic cryonics". Both variants of cryonics envisage three problems to be solved:

1. The initial "data collection" phase, which in the organic case involves securing the brain in a stable state, and in the digital case involves copying all of its contents
2. The "long-term storage" phase

3. The "reanimation phase", in which the brain is either reconstituted from its data (in the digital case) or is sufficiently repaired and warmed up so that consciousness restarts (in the organic case).

Both approaches see the reanimation phase to be considerably harder than the data collection phase. Both approaches are relying on far-future technology to enable the reanimation. The data collection phase, whilst still hard, is seen as being more tractable – as something that present-day technology can already solve (in the organic case) or may solve within the next few decades (in the digital case). In both approaches, the long-term storage phase is seen as the easiest of the three.

What I've called digital cryonics would be commenced by a process of *chemopreservation*: the brain has its contents "fixed" by the application of various chemicals. Sometimes this is called "plastination", as the technique adopts ideas from the process developed in the late 1970s[346] by Gunther von Hagens to preserve parts of bodies for display or teaching purposes. In turn, the process has its roots in the way that ancient creatures have sometimes been preserved, to a remarkable amount of detail, by amber (fossilised tree resin). This includes[347] ants from 99 million years ago, lizards and scorpions from 20 million years ago, and even dinosaur feathers from 80 million years ago. Morticians use embalming fluids such as aldehyde for a similar purpose. This kind of embalming won't prevent the internal microstructure of the body from deteriorating. But modern chemopreservation methods are believed to achieve that goal. In a 2012 article in io9, "How to Live Forever By Turning Your Brain Into Plastic"[348], George Dvorsky reports a description of modern brain plastination by John Smart, the Vice President of the Brain Preservation Foundation:

> Moments after your death, a response team will start the process of emergency glutaraldehyde perfusion (EGP) for protein fixation (a kind of advanced embalming process). This has to happen within 15 minutes of your death, otherwise the first phase of neural degradation will start to set in; brain cells start to die on account of oxygen deprivation.
>
> The infusion of this molecule by the response team basically freezes your brain into place, creating a snapshot of your identity and your long term memories – though you might lose some short-term memories when you resume life after reanimation, just as sometimes happens after brain trauma today. "Glutaraldehyde is a very small chemical that gets into all your cells, and locks down your proteins and cytoskeleton, creating a kind

of molecular cage," said Smart, "all protein-related interactions grind to a halt because of this crosslinking."

After this, your body will be moved to a centralized facility where, over the course of several months, your brain will be carefully removed and placed into a bath. Unlike cryonics, this stage is not time sensitive (whereas the standard saying at cryonics facilities is "time is trauma"). It's at this point that a chemical called osmium tetroxide fixes all the fats and fluid membranes in the brain cells. Then, a series of acetone-like solvents are used to convert the brain into plastic where it can be stored at room temperature. "All the water gets leached, out, but all the protein (and presumably, the other critical features) is still there," says Smart, "and so are all the neural connections, as are all the neural weightings – including the three dimensional structure."

The next line in the io9 article makes the all-important claim:

Indeed, because the exact 3D structure of the brain is preserved, it can be reconstructed.

Note this looks forward to a *reconstruction* of the brain, rather than a *removal* of the plastination that was applied to the original brain. This is a key difference between cryopreservation (at low temperature) and chemopreservation (at room temperature): the former is believed to be reversible, whereas the latter is not. The route forward for someone whose brain has been chemopreserved is for their memories and their consciousness to be reinstantiated in a futuristic new brain – perhaps one that is composed of silicon-based semiconductors, rather than biological neurons. The idea is similar to how a single piece of software can run on multiple different computers – indeed, on multiple different *kinds* of computer.

The concept underlying digital cryonics is that a human mind doesn't depend on any specific feature of the biological brain in which it was originally located. Instead, the mind is a *pattern* of interactions. If these interactions are replicated on a different brain – biological, silicon, or whatever – and if the memories have been transferred too, then (in this viewpoint) the mind is the same. It will experience an awakening similar to coming out of general anaesthetic; it will recognise (sooner or later) that it is now housed in a different body from before, but outsiders would recognise that mind as being the same person as prior to the brain plastination exercise began. The mind, which was previously "downloaded" from the plastinated brain into a massive computer storage file, has now been said (in the jargon) to be "uploaded" into the new brain, and restarted.

Chemopreservation vs. cryopreservation

The cryonics community has mixed views on whether cryopreservation or chemopreservation is the best option to pursue. For example, in an evaluation entitled "Plastination versus cryonics"[349], the blogger Gwern finds six factors in favour of chemopreservation (two being particularly significant, in his view), and only two in favour of cryopreservation (one being significant). Gwern states his conclusion as follows:

> The fundamental question is, does the rapid advance of scanning and the robustness against organizational failure of plastination outweigh the risk that cryonics uniquely preserves key information?

The point about a potential rapid advance of scanning is this: progress in improving cryopreservation techniques can be evaluated as slow, since the cryopreservation community is small. In contrast, there are now huge projects (outside of the world of cryonics) benefiting from government funding, in both the US and the EU, that involve improvements in the kinds of scanning techniques that are needed to extract information from plastinated brains.

Gwern states the point about organisational failure as follows:

> One rough year and your brain is a pile of rotting maggots with cryonics. One rough year with plastination, and your brain is a bit dusty. A plastinated brain doesn't even need an organization: it may be preserved as a time capsule, a family heirloom, a curiosity, or perhaps just buried somewhere; but a cryogenically stored brain must have a sophisticated support system which will supply it regularly with liquid nitrogen, and that rules out pretty much everyone but a cryonics organization.

Taking a different view, Aschwin de Wolf of Alcor has written an article entitled "Chemical Brain Preservation and Human Suspended Animation"[350], with the following executive summary:

> Scientific and practical considerations strongly support cryopreservation rather than chemopreservation for the stabilization of critically ill patients. Technology for achieving solid state chemopreservation of brains larger than a mouse brain does not yet exist. Chemical fixation is irreversible without very advanced technologies. Chemical fixation permits no functional feedback or development pathway toward reversible suspended

animation. By contrast, cryopreservation seeks to maintain viability of the brain as far downstream as our capabilities and resources permit — an approach that reflects our view of cryonics as an extension of contemporary medicine. Cryopreservation preserves more options in that a cryopreserved brain could be scanned in future, or later chemically fixed, but the process of chemical fixation cannot be reversed and replaced by just low temperature storage. The cost benefits of chemopreservation over cryopreservation are exaggerated, largely because the standby and treatment procedures for effective chemopreservation would be just as extensive as for cryopreservation, if not more so, even assuming that highly toxic chemicals could be worked with safely in the field. Chemopreservation is being inherently tied to mind uploading, an association that is likely to limit its acceptance as a form of experimental critical care medicine by apparently requiring acceptance of the idea of substrate independent minds.

The Brain Preservation Foundation was created in 2010 to encourage and evaluate improvements in techniques to preserve brain structure – whether by cryopreservation or by chemopreservation. The Foundation set out its intentions in what it called an "Open Letter to the Medical, Scientific, and Government Communities Regarding Brain Preservation"[351]. This contained the following conclusion:

Over the last half century medical practice has seen some startling additions – routine organ transplants, minimally invasive laparoscopic surgery, robot- assisted surgery, profound hyperthermia and circulatory arrest, cochlear implants, Lasik eye surgery, deep brain stimulation, frozen embryos used for in- vitro fertilization, and sex reassignment surgery. We are moving quickly into an era where the scanning of whole animal brains at the nanometer level will be commonplace, and there is already serious contemplation of producing an entire connection- level atlas of a human brain.

With these recent advances in mind, it is no longer appropriate to simply dismiss the possibility of brain preservation as a medical procedure. Preservation should instead be evaluated with an open mind as a means for putting a person in suspended animation in order that they reach future medical technology able to cure them.

The Foundation also announced a Technology Prize[352] in support of its aims:

> **Technology Prize – Prize purse as of June 12, 2010: $100,000 US**
>
> The nonprofit Brain Preservation Foundation (BPF) hereby officially announces a cash prize for the first individual or team to rigorously demonstrate a surgical technique capable of inexpensively and completely preserving an entire human brain for long-term (>100 years) storage with such fidelity that the structure of every neuronal process and every synaptic connection remains intact and traceable using today's electron microscopic (EM) imaging techniques.
>
> This prize competition is structured into two stages:
>
> - Stage#1 - Preservation of an entire mouse brain (or similar small mammalian brain) using a technique that is applicable to a laboratory environment.
>
> - Stage#2 - Preservation of a large mammalian brain (a pig for example) using a surgical technique meeting all the medical standards necessary for it to be applied (as an elective procedure) to a human patient in a hospital setting, and using a procedure that, with minor modifications, might potentially be offered for less than US$20,000 by appropriately trained medical professionals.
>
> The first group to complete stage#1's requirements will win 1/4 of the total prize purse accumulated up to that date. The first group to complete stage#2's requirements will win the remaining prize purse, or the entire prize purse if no one has previously met stage#1's requirements.

In February 2016 came news that the Stage#1 prize had been won by researchers at the company 21st Century Medicine[353]. Interestingly, the winning approach used a combination of techniques of cryopreservation and chemopreservation. The press release[354] gives the details:

> The Small Mammal Brain Preservation Prize has officially been won by researchers at 21st Century Medicine. Using a combination of ultrafast chemical fixation and cryogenic storage, it is the first demonstration that near-perfect, long-term structural preservation of an intact mammalian brain is achievable, thus directly answering what has been a main scientific criticism against cryonics…
>
> A team from 21st Century Medicine (21CM), spearheaded by recent MIT graduate Robert McIntyre, has discovered a way to preserve the delicate neural circuits of an intact rabbit brain for extremely long-term storage using a combination of chemical fixation, cryoprotectants, and cryogenic cooling. Proof of this accomplishment, and the full "Aldehyde-Stabilized

Cryopreservation" protocol, was recently published in the journal Cryobiology and has been independently verified by the BPF through extensive electron microscopic examination. This answers a challenge issued to the scientific and cryonics communities five years ago by the BPF, and carries an award of $26,735. Kenneth Hayworth, a PhD neuroscientist who is president of the BPF and one of the prize's judges said: "Every neuron and synapse looks beautifully preserved across the entire brain. Simply amazing given that I held in my hand this very same brain when it was a vitrified glassy solid ... This is not your father's cryonics."

Equally significant was the fact that another team, using different techniques, also came very close to winning this prize. The press release explains:

Throughout the contest, the 21CM team was in a tight race with Max Planck researcher Shawn Mikula to be the first to meet the prize's strict requirements. Although the prize will be awarded to 21CM, a BPF spokesman emphasized that a mouse brain entry submitted by Dr. Mikula also came extremely close to meeting the prize requirements. Dr. Mikula's laboratory is attempting to perfect not only brain preservation (using a different method based on chemical fixation and plastic embedding) but whole brain electron microscopic imaging as well.

Writing in the Scientific American, renowned sceptic Michael Shermer offered his thoughts, in an article entitled "Can Our Minds Live Forever? Can a brain's connectome be preserved forever?"[355]

The soul is the pattern of information that represents you—your thoughts, memories and personality—your self. There is no scientific evidence that something like soul stuff exists beyond the brain's own hardwiring, so I was curious to visit the laboratories of 21st Century Medicine in Fontana, Calif., to see for myself an attempt to preserve a brain's connectome – the comprehensive diagram of all neural synaptic connections...

I witnessed the infusion of a rabbit brain through its carotid arteries with a fixative agent called glutaraldehyde, which binds proteins together into a solid gel. The brain was then removed and saturated in ethylene glycol, a cryoprotective agent eliminating ice formation and allowing safe storage at −130 degrees C as a glasslike, inert solid. At that temperature, chemical reactions are so attenuated that it could be stored for millennia. If successful, would it be proof of concept?

Think of a book in epoxy resin hardened into a solid block of plastic, McIntyre told me. "You're never going to open the book again, but if you

> can prove that the epoxy doesn't dissolve the ink the book is written with, you can demonstrate that all the words in the book must still be there ... and you might be able to carefully slice it apart, scan in all the pages, and print/bind a new book with the same words."

The fact that no one is ever "going to open the book again" – that is, to reanimate this brain – provokes worries among some cyronicists. One set of worries is whether enough information is captured by this preservative mechanism. This worry is put into words by Shermer:

> I have my doubts. Is a connectome precisely analogous to a program that can be uploaded in machine-readable format into a computer? Would a connectome so preserved and uploaded into a computer be the same as awakening after sleep or unconsciousness? Plus, there are around 86 billion neurons in a human brain with often 1,000 or more synaptic connections for each one, for a total of 100 trillion connections to be accurately preserved and replicated. Staggering complexity. And this doesn't include the rest of the nervous system outside the brain, which is also part of your self that you might want resurrected.

A second worry is whether the original self is killed by this process, and the new brain is a different consciousness. Even if the new consciousness, in the new brain, remembers the same memories as the original person, and expresses the same personality as the original, it can still be queried whether this is a mere copy, rather than the original consciousness somehow reincarnated.

Killed by bad philosophy?

Kenneth Hayward is someone who sees this second worry as "bad philosophy". He wrote a powerful essay[356] in 2010 that addresses this topic. It's worth reading all the way through. Here's how it starts:

> ### A tragic miscalculation
>
> You wake up with a splitting headache and weakness on one side of your body. Your wife rushes you to the hospital where a CT scan reveals what is wrong. You have a massive aneurysm that is about to burst in your brain and will surely kill you when it does. Furthermore, the position of the aneurysm is deep within the brain making a traditional surgical approach impossible. You are given some drugs to ease the pain and the doctor explains your options to you and your wife.
>
> The doctor suggests the use of an untested surgical procedure that may give the surgeons enough time to clip the aneurysm and save your life. The

procedure will involve lowering your body and brain temperature down to 10° Celsius and then stopping your heart and blood flow for a full hour. This stopping of blood flow will allow the surgeons to complete the complicated surgery without the risk of catastrophic blood loss, and the low temperature will protect your brain from metabolic damage during the hour it will be without oxygenated blood flow.

Perplexed, you ask your doctor "Will my brain still be active during the surgery?" "No", your doctor says, "At 10° Celsius all communications between neurons is halted. In fact this will be one of the tests we will use to make sure we have your brain's temperature low enough to begin the procedure." Incredulous you ask, "Then you are saying I will be dead for a full hour, and then you will attempt to bring me back to life?!?" The doctor attempts to reassure you, "Well technically you will meet most of the legal requirements of death during that hour, but our research on animals suggests that once we rewarm your brain and restart your heart you will simply 'reboot'. You should wake up just like you would from anaesthesia following a normal surgery."

The doctor leaves the room to let you and your wife discuss. She is religious and says she believes that your soul will be called up to heaven as soon as your brain stops functioning. Being an agnostic with a scientific educational background, you are offended by such an obviously illogical juxtaposition between the metaphysical and biological. At a different time you would have sarcastically responded to your wife by asking her "Exactly which passage in the bible makes this connection between an immaterial soul and patterned neural firing in the brain?" But at this moment, with your life at stake, you are only deeply saddened that you cannot rely on your wife's counsel. However, your own scientific background can do little better. You recall a spate of popular science articles you have read about the functioning of the brain, all ending with vague statements about the remaining mystery of human consciousness. You also recall several philosophical articles suggesting that our conscious self is an emergent phenomenon of the complex neural activity within the brain, possibly having something to do with its quantum state or some such thing. These all suggest to you that being brain dead for a full hour is not reversible. You start to imagine your doctor happily presenting you as a drooling Frankenstein- like zombie to your wife after the surgery and egotistically declaring that the surgery was a complete success. In the end you decide not to undergo the surgery, reasoning that it has essentially zero chance of success but would cost your grieving family several thousand dollars even after insurance. You comfort yourself that perhaps the aneurysm will not burst and in time may disappear. A week later the aneurysm does burst and you die of a massive cerebral haemorrhage. Your wife and young son mourn the loss of the father he will never know.

But as in many tales in which a death occurs, there's a "whodunit" angle that provides the real interest in the story:

A few years later your wife reads a newspaper article about how a new surgical procedure is proving phenomenally successful at treating previously intractable aneurysms and how a dozen patients are now living normal lives after undergoing the procedure. With a sick feeling she realizes that the doctor described in the article is the same one that had suggested the surgical procedure for her husband. She is sad and disturbed but rationalizes by thinking "it was God's decision". However many years later when relating the story to her, now adult, son, he has a different interpretation of this chain of events: "So what you're telling me mom is that dad was not killed by a burst aneurysm. He was actually killed by bad philosophy!"

Profound Hypothermia and Circulatory Arrest

How realistic is the above scenario? Very. The procedure describe above is called Profound Hypothermia and Circulatory Arrest (PHCA) and it is a real surgical technique used for treating, amongst other things, hard to reach brain aneurysms. It has been in limited use since the late 1950's and it does indeed lower the temperature of the brain to such a degree that all communication and patterned activity between neurons is halted for up to an hour. The only part of this scenario that is unrealistic is the doctor letting his patient commit suicide over such a flimsy philosophical argument. A doctor today would simply point to the hundreds of reports of patients leading high- functioning lives after undergoing the procedure. I do not know if the first patients to undergo a PHCA procedure had such philosophical misgivings.

The next section of the essay draws out the implications for brain preservation:

I hope you agree with me that it would be particularly pathetic for a son to realize that his father died because of his misplaced faith in "bad philosophy". In retrospect i.e. now that we know that people do survive the PHCA procedure, we can see how foolish it would be for the man in the story above to simply assume that stopping brain activity would result in his irreversible death. If the man had consulted a neuroscientist the sarcastic response obtained might have been "Exactly which passage in your [philosophical] bible makes this connection between an immaterial soul and patterned neural firing in the brain?"

I am belabouring this point because I am virtually certain that our grandchildren will be saying the same thing about us. They will say that we died not because of heart disease, cancer, or stroke, but instead that we died pathetically out of ignorance and superstition. They will say we were killed by our "bad philosophy". In one hundred years they will ask in disbelief, "Our grandparents had the technology to preserve the precise neural circuitry of their brains for long- term storage. The best science of our grandparent's era stated unequivocally that this unique patterning of neural circuitry was the seat of the self; in it was written all memories, skills, and personality. Our grandparents seemed to grasp the quickening pace of technology, and understood that full brain scanning and simulation was around the corner. Why then did grandpa and the rest of his generation reject brain preservation and mind uploading as a means of overcoming death?" …

Much as I admire Hayworth's essay (of which I have quoted around the first 15%), I hesitate to endorse any conclusion in favour of "brain preservation and mind-uploading" being the uniquely best approach to ensure indefinite life extension. I share the assessment of Michael Shermer, quoted earlier, that this digital cryonics project involves a "staggering complexity", which may exceed by some margin the scale of the other hard tasks discussed in this book:

- The task of comprehensive biological rejuvenation, addressed in all chapters in this book apart from this one
- The task of cryopreservation (organic cryonics), addressed at the start of this chapter.

To dig further into this question, it's useful to consider an incomplete version of digital cryonics, in which only *part* of the essential structure of someone's brain is successfully captured and recreated. This brings us to the topic of "Mindfiles".

Mindfiles

In April 2016, news broke that a piece of AI software had created a new portrait in the style of the celebrated Dutch artist Rembrandt. The software studied an extensive database consisting of 346 paintings by Rembrandt, to identify key underlying patterns and methods. These principles were then applied in the creation of an original portrait.

Bas Korsten, head of the team that created this new portrait, explained his thinking in an NPR article "A 'New' Rembrandt: From The Frontiers Of AI"[357]:

"I thought, well, if you can basically take historical data and then create something new out of it, why can't we distil the artistic DNA of a painter out of his body of work and create a new artwork out of that?"

The article gives more details about the project:

Everything about the painting — from the subject matter (a Caucasian man between the age of 30 and 40) to his clothes (black, wide-brimmed hat, black shirt and white collar), facial hair (small moustache and goatee) and even the way his face is positioned (facing right) — was distilled from Rembrandt's body of work.

"A computer learned, with artificial intelligence, how to re-create a new Rembrandt right eye," Korsten explains. "And we did that for all facial features, and after that, we assembled those facial features using the geometrical dimensions that Rembrandt used to use in his own work."

It's a remarkable accomplishment. Applications of the technology include improvements in the process of restoring paintings which have been partially damaged.

But to what extent could this software be said to bring Rembrandt himself back to life, almost 450 years after his death? To what extent is a word such as "ghost" justified, as in the title of an RT article covering the same story, "Ghost of Rembrandt: AI taught to paint like master Dutch artist"[358]?

Before answering these questions, let's consider some potential extensions of similar software that may be realised in the next 5-10 years:

- Software that studies all the known musical compositions of Beethoven could output potential new 10th and 11th symphonies, in the style of the master composer
- Other software could study the cannon of the Beatles – both as individual artists and in combination – and create an album "as if" all four Beatles were alive and cooperating musically in 2020 (one track on that album could be "When I'm 84")
- Software could also study records of great scientists, such as Albert Einstein and Richard Feynman, and produce avatars of these

personalities giving their reactions to scientific experiments that took place after their death.

It's not just world-renowned people whose personality and ideas could be reincarnated in such a way. The Terasem Movement[359], headquartered in Florida, is one of several organisations which seek to help collect and store sufficient data about its members to allow the recreation of their personalities in the future. These records are known as "mindfiles" and aim to include someone's mannerisms, recollections, attitudes, beliefs, values, and other aspects of their personality. One of Terasem's project has the name "Lifenaut" – chosen for its similarity to the word "astronaut" – and it has created a robot known as Bina48. The Lifenaut website[360] describes Bina48 as follows:

Bina48 is one of the worlds most advanced social robots based on a composite of information from several people including, Bina Aspen, co-founder of the Terasem Movement. She was created using video interview transcripts, laser scanning life mask technology, face recognition, artificial intelligence and voice recognition technologies. As an "ambassador" for the LifeNaut project, Bina48 is designed to be a social robot that can interact based on information, memories, values, and beliefs collected about an actual person.

As such, Bina48 is an early demonstration of the Terasem Hypothesis, which states:

- A conscious analog of a person may be created by combining sufficiently detailed data about the person (a mindfile) using future consciousness software (mindware).

Terasem say it is willing to revise its opinions in the light of new experimental findings. One of its ongoing projects, to help it tune its understanding of what may (or may not) be possible, is CyBeRev[361]:

CyBeRev means cybernetic beingness revival. The CyBeRev project is part of a multi-decade experiment to test the comparability of single person human consciousness with a digital representation of the same person created by personality software that draws upon a database comprised of the original person's digitized interactions, as assessed by expert psychological review. The purpose of the CyBeRev project is to preserve sufficient digital information about a person so that, should the experiment validate the comparability of such consciousnesses, recovery of the digitized personality will remain possible. The Terasem Movement believes that future technology will enable full recovery of functionality for CyBeRev participants in this manner...

The first step toward achieving that goal, and the purpose of this website, is for participants to store digital reflections of their mannerisms, personality, recollections, feelings, beliefs, attitudes and values with as great a fidelity as is possible...

In an interview with Anthony Cuthbertson of IB Times, "Virtual reality heaven: How technology is redefining death and the afterlife"[362], Gabriel Rothblatt of Terasem provides a big picture vision for how these records may in due course even enable a kind of immortality:

"The end goal of Terasem is similar to other religions, these ideas of joyful immortality in the afterlife. But for us it's not simply a spiritual concept, it's a mechanical challenge. Technology could one day make this a reality through digital backups – the idea of transferring a person's consciousness on to a hardrive, which could then be placed into quasi-utopian conditions. Heaven could be a virtual reality world hosted on a computer server somewhere."

I see it as reasonably likely that, in due course, AI representations of people will be created that demonstrate more and more details of the personality and memories of given individual humans. These emulations will improve, as AI improves, and as fuller mindfile records can be created. The Portuguese company Eter9[363], for example, could succeed at least partially in its goal to create virtual beings that can continue to contribute postings to social networks on our behalf, even when we are no longer alive. BBC Newsbeat summarised the possibility in its headline "Eter9 social network learns your personality so it can post as you when you're dead"[364].

However, there's a gulf between software that emulates part of someone's personality, and that software actually *being* the continuation of that person's consciousness. After all, people can be quite good at mimicking one another, without actually *becoming* each other. And although children often demonstrate the mannerisms of their parents surprisingly accurately, that doesn't mean that the consciousness of the parent has been moved inside the brains of their offspring.

I can concede that, in the future, such software actually will become conscious. I have no trouble in accepting that consciousness can exist on a silicon substrate, as well as in carbon-based biological brains. That consciousness might do a great job of persuading onlookers that it is, *in some sense*, a continuation of the original person: it has the memories and personality to match. But the fact that *multiple* copies might exist at the same time causes me unease with any simple identity claim.

It's possible that, at some time in the decades ahead, I will find myself face to face with a robotic copy of myself. That copy might be a better version of me, with a stronger body, and a faster brain. I might see that copy functioning in the world in a continuation of all the projects that I care about, making strong progress in ways for which I had hoped. But if doctors then suggest that I be terminated, since my consciousness is now also present in a new copy, I suspect I will strongly hesitate.

On the other hand, I imagine that more and more people will put effort into collecting mindfiles of themselves, for the purposes of assisting future successful reanimation of themselves out of a long-term cryopreservation. In case parts of their brain have been damaged by the processes of vitrification or subsequent storage, the information in these mindfiles could serve an invaluable function of augmenting the memories and personality that remain intact.

Copying the dead to the future?

One radical alternative idea suggests that even those people who died, without a careful copy of their brain structure being preserved, may be brought back to life at some stage in the future. This is the ultimate jump from BR (Before Rejuvenation) to AR (After Rejuvenation).

This idea has, of course, been held throughout history by many people of a religious disposition. It's a statement of the Christian idea of future resurrection. In that conception, it is a cosmic being – God – who is able to recreate humans, on account of divine access to all information from previous times in history.

Some thinkers in modern times suggest that future descendants of humans will attain similar powers. These thinkers often trace their ideas to Nikolai Fedorov, a Russian who lived from 1828 to 1903. Fedorov spoke at length about a "common task" which future generations would master Nature, colonize the stars, and resurrect the dead. A 2013 article by Eric Naiman[365] in the Times Literary Supplement provides some details:

According to Tolstoy, Nikolai Fyodorov was a saint, whose programme for the universal resurrection of the dead was "not devoid of sense"...

Fyodorov was an outstanding librarian, who pioneered the practice of inter-library (and international) borrowing and served as an invaluable resource for scholars conducting research in a wide variety of fields. What he is remembered for, however, is the project he outlined in unpublished articles and letters, as well as in discussions with visitors and disciples and which, after his death in 1903, two lifelong acolytes published as The Philosophy of the Common Task.

"The common task" was the physical resurrection of the dead. All mankind, Fyodorov wrote, was under a moral obligation to identify and collect the dust of its ancestors; this was a duty every son owed to his forefathers, a duty constantly under threat from the blind forces of nature, by which Fyodorov meant the elemental forces outside and within man: not only the climate but also human sexuality. The hunt for these lost particles was to be an act of gigantic filial labour and "positive chastity". Motivated by piety, sons and daughters were to devote themselves fully to scientific discoveries that would make the task of resurrection possible. These discoveries would entail not only bringing the dead back to life, but finding space for them to dwell. The deserts would have to be made fertile; other planets would need to be made habitable, and modes of transport to other worlds developed. In effect, Fyodorov was providing a scientific basis for religious myth, the way other nineteenth-century scholars traced the historical existence of Jesus Christ.

In his 2007 review article "Nikolai Fedorov and the Dawn of the Posthuman"[366], Nader Elhefnawy highlighted what Fyodorov had in mind:

Overcoming death was the only doctrine "which demands not separation but reunification ... the doctrine of kinship" among not living human beings, but their predecessors, "the fathers". A fully developed sense of kinship meant defeating death on their behalf as well, shifting from the "mythical petrification" of ancestor worship to "actual resuscitation", which he termed "the supreme good, the supreme task"...

Taking a purely materialistic view of the mind-body problem, which he somewhat facetiously describes as consciousness relating to the body "like bile to the liver", meant that if you "reassemble the machine ... consciousness will return to it". Though he was careful not to exclude other hypotheses, he believed that the means of such "reassembly" would be the "gathering of the scattered dust and its reconstitution into bodies, using radiation or outlines left by the waves caused by the vibration of molecules". Since those vibrations travel into space, the extension of human control into space was again critical to recovering all the scattered particles.

Transhumanists Ben Goertzel and Giulio Prisco have published "Ten Cosmist convictions"[367] that, in effect bring the ideas of Fyodorov up-to-date. Here are the first six of these convictions:

1) Humans will merge with technology, to a rapidly increasing extent. This is a new phase of the evolution of our species, just picking up speed about now. The divide between natural and artificial will blur, then disappear. Some of us will continue to be humans, but with a radically expanded and always growing range of available options, and radically increased diversity and complexity. Others will grow into new forms of intelligence far beyond the human domain.

2) We will develop sentient AI and mind uploading technology. Mind uploading technology will permit an indefinite lifespan to those who choose to leave biology behind and upload. Some uploaded humans will choose to merge with each other and with AIs. This will require reformulations of current notions of self, but we will be able to cope.

3) We will spread to the stars and roam the universe. We will meet and merge with other species out there. We may roam to other dimensions of existence as well, beyond the ones of which we're currently aware.

4) We will develop interoperable synthetic realities (virtual worlds) able to support sentience. Some uploads will choose to live in virtual worlds. The divide between physical and synthetic realities will blur, then disappear.

5) We will develop spacetime engineering and scientific "future magic" much beyond our current understanding and imagination.

6) Spacetime engineering and future magic will permit achieving, by scientific means, most of the promises of religions — and many amazing things that no human religion ever dreamed. Eventually we will be able to resurrect the dead by "copying them to the future".

Prisco offers a number of suggestions on how this "copying to the future" might work, and how, therefore, the bold ideas of Fyodorov might in due course be fulfilled. These are included in his recent article "Technological resurrection concepts from Fyodorov to quantum archaeology"[368]:

In "The Light of Other Days," a science fiction novel written in 2000 by Stephen Baxter based on a synopsis by Arthur C. Clarke, near-future scientists discover that the fabric of space-time is full of micro wormholes, and develop technology to establish wormhole data links to anywhere and anytime. By combining past viewing and neural sensing technologies, the scientists will find ways to copy the dead from the past and upload them to the present, achieving Fyodorov's vision.

Time scanning technologies similar to those described by Clarke and Baxter are often called "Quantum Archaeology" (QA), which reflects the assumption that time-magic tech would use weird quantum effects. Quantum reality could be weird enough to permit connecting every space-time pixel to every other space-time pixels by information conduits that, perhaps, future engineers will be able to exploit to bring the dead back. Current speculations are centred on the mysterious instant correlations of quantum entanglement and proposals for extending the current quantum physics framework in ways that could permit instant data channels between different places, different times, and different universes.

Prisco reflects on some comparisons between these more recent ideas and the earlier thoughts of Fyodorov:

These contemporary technological resurrection ideas dressed in warped space-time and weird quantum fields seem very different from Fyodorov's "naive" ideas of technological resurrection by finding and reassembling the molecular dust left behind by the deceased. But Fyodorov formulated his ideas using the science and language of his time – just like contemporary scientists formulate modern ideas using the science and language of our times. I guess contemporary ideas will seem naive to future scientists, just like Fyodorov's ideas seem naive to us.

Perhaps – and why not? – the universe spontaneously provides immortality and resurrection, embedded in the fabric of reality. Perhaps we and all persons (and animals, and ETs) who ever lived are stored in "Akashic records" in some still hidden dimension of reality. If Akashic records exist, I am sure future science will find them and learn how to read them. Perhaps our reality is a "simulation" computed in a higher-level reality by extra-dimensional scientists, and someday we will find ways to break free. Time, as always, will tell.

I don't know future science, but I think Shakespeare's "There are more things in heaven and earth, Horatio, than are dreamt of in your philosophy" could remain true forever. Our scientific understanding of the universe could grow without bonds, but always find new fractal depths of unexplained phenomena, in a big infinite fractal onion universe to be explored by future scientists.

Assessment

I cannot deny the possibility that unexpected future breakthroughs in scientific understanding will in due course enable something akin to the universal technological resurrection discussed by Giulio Prisco and others. As it happens, I'm sceptical about exploiting quantum entanglement to achieve "instant data channels between different places, different times, and different universes". My opinion in this case reflects the four years of postgraduate research[369] I carried out, in the 1980s, into the philosophy of quantum mechanics. But Prisco is right that remarkable new surprises could lie ahead. For example, our entire universe might actually be a simulation, as he describes in an article "Christianity and Transhumanism are much closer than you think"[370]:

> ### A 'sysop' God in a higher reality
>
> Another mental model for God inspired by Transhumanist eschatology is the reality-as-a-simulation model, which treats our reality as a simulation computed by intelligent entities in a higher level of reality. You, and I, and everything around us, are but information bits that live and move in a supercomputer beyond space and time, operated by a God-like creator.
>
> "Science-fiction authors… have even suggested (and I cannot think how to disprove it) that we live in a computer simulation, set up by some vastly superior civilization," said Dawkins in "The God Delusion." Dawkins is open to the reality-as-a-simulation concept, but doesn't think of the simulators as God. "But the simulators themselves would have to come from somewhere," he adds. "They probably owe their existence to a (perhaps unfamiliar) version of Darwinian evolution."
>
> However, the sysop God has all the properties of the Christian God, and the reality-as-a-simulation concept is totally indistinguishable from religion. God is omniscient, omnipresent, and omnipotent, wrote the laws of our physics, and can choose to violate them in case of need. Or, in the formulation of Augustine and [Wolfhart] Pannenberg, God can subtly influence our reality without needing to violate its laws. In particular, God can copy people from our world before death and run the copies again in a better new world.

However, I offer the following personal assessment of the relative probabilities of the various scenarios discussed in this chapter:

- The most plausible scenario is that of organic cryonics: cryopreservation followed by awakening from cryonic suspension

- The scenario of transplanting a brain into a new robotic body sits in parallel with that of organic cryonics: the two scenarios complement each other, especially in the case when cryonics only preserves the head of a patient, rather than their entire body

- Less plausible is that of digital cryonics: chemopreservation followed by the digital reinstantiation of consciousness in a new brain

- Least plausible of the three is any notion of quantum archaeology (or similar).

It makes sense for parts of the broad rejuveneering community to invest effort into all of these projects. Different people will find themselves drawn in different directions. But inasmuch as the first two may be closest to completion, I believe they deserve the greatest portion of attention.

The Russian researcher Alexey Turchin has developed a four-level "Roadmap to immortality"[371] (by which he says he means[372] "potentially indefinite life extension") which examines many of the same themes as I've explored in this chapter, reaching similar conclusions. Turchin describes the four levels of his plan[373] as follows:

> The Roadmap to Personal Immortality is list of actions that one should do to live forever. The most obvious way to reach immortality is to defeat aging, to grow and replace the diseased organs with new bioengineered ones, and in the end to be scanned into a computer. This is Plan A. It is the best possible course of events. It depends on two things – your personal actions (like regular medical checkups) and collective actions like civil activism and scientific research funding. The map is showing both paths in Plan A.
>
> However, if Plan A fails, meaning if you die before the victory over aging, there is Plan B, which is cryonics. Some simple steps can be taken now, like calling your nearest cryocompany about a contract.
>
> Unfortunately, cryonics could also fail, and then you can move to Plan C. Of course it is much worse – less reliable and less proven. Plan C is the so called digital immortality, that means one could be returned to life based on the existing recorded information about that person. It is a not the best plan, because we are not sure how to solve the identity problem, which will arise, and also we don't know if collected amount of information would be enough. But it is still better than nothing.

Lastly, if Plan C fails, we have Plan D. It is not a plan in fact – it is just hope or a bet that immortality already exists somehow, maybe there is quantum immortality, or maybe the future AI will bring us back to life.

All Plans demand particular actions now – we need to prepare to all of them simultaneously.

As for which actions are the most pressing: that is the topic of my final chapter.

13. Future uncertain

The rejuveneering project has made a great deal of progress over the last three decades. Aging is understood much better today than in any previous era. What's more, as previous chapters have shown, there are many grounds for anticipating an acceleration of progress over the next two or three decades. This progress should see the creation of practical bioengineering therapies that will take increasing advantage of our expanding theoretical knowledge. There are credible scenarios ahead, for the establishment by around 2040 of a Humanity+ society in which the terrible diseases of aging have become as rare as, say, polio and smallpox are today.

Nevertheless, many uncertainties lie ahead. These aren't just uncertainties in detail – over, for example, which drug will prove to have the biggest short-term impact on healthy lifespan, or which AI algorithm will deliver the most important insights into modifications in gene pathways. Instead, these are uncertainties over fundamentals – problems that could jeopardise the entire rejuveneering project.

It's time to look more closely at what could be the biggest obstacles on the pathway to the abolition of aging. Out of all the questions that audiences ask me when I talk to them about the potential for rejuveneering, these are the hardest to answer.

Exceptional engineering complications?

Sometimes, problems prove much harder to solve than people expected. Consider nuclear fusion. It's commonly said that nuclear fusion is always thirty years in the future. A recent article by Nathaniel Scharping in Discover, "Why Nuclear Fusion Is Always 30 Years Away"[374], summarises the experiences of the nuclear fusion industry:

> Nuclear fusion has long been considered the "holy grail" of energy research. It represents a nearly limitless source of energy that is clean, safe and self-sustaining. Ever since its existence was first theorized in the 1920s by English physicist Arthur Eddington, nuclear fusion has captured the imaginations of scientists and science-fiction writers alike.
>
> Fusion, at its core, is a simple concept. Take two hydrogen isotopes and smash them together with overwhelming force. The two atoms overcome

their natural repulsion and fuse, yielding a reaction that produces an enormous amount of energy.

But a big payoff requires an equally large investment, and for decades we have wrestled with the problem of energizing and holding on to the hydrogen fuel as it reaches temperatures in excess of 150 million degrees Fahrenheit...

The most recent advancements have come from Germany, where the Wendelstein 7-X reactor recently came online with a successful test run reaching almost 180 million degrees, and China, where the EAST reactor sustained a fusion plasma for 102 seconds, although at lower temperatures.

Still, even with these steps forward, researchers have said for decades that we're still 30 years away from a working fusion reactor. Even as scientists take steps toward their holy grail, it becomes ever more clear that we don't even yet know what we don't know.

The problem, apparently, is that each step forwards seems to throw up new issues which are just as hard to solve as the previous ones:

For every answer, more questions

The Wendelstein 7-X and EAST reactor experiments were dubbed "breakthroughs," which is an adjective commonly applied to fusion experiments. Exciting as these examples may be, when considered within the scale of the problem, they are only baby steps. It is clear that it will take more than one, or a dozen, such "breakthroughs" to achieve fusion.

"I don't think we're at that place where we know what we need to do in order to get over the threshold," says Mark Herrmann, director of the National Ignition Facility in California. "We're still learning what the science is. We may have eliminated some perturbations, but if we eliminate those, is there another thing hiding behind them? And there almost certainly is, and we don't know how hard that will be to tackle."

Might a similar set of ever harder problems lie ahead of the rejuveneering project? Perhaps each new tweak to the human biology, that enhances some aspect of healthy longevity, will have its own drawbacks. For example, we might strengthen the immune system, but this enhancement might cause the immune system to attack cells which the body needs for its normal healthy functioning – similar to the way that type 1 diabetes can result from an over-aggressive immune system destroying the islet cells in the pancreas which would otherwise produce insulin. And a second engineering intervention to fend off that unintended side-effect might, in turn, generate yet further complications. Similarly, lengthened telomeres might cause an increase in the incidence of cancer, as discussed in Chapter 7.

One reason to be doubtful that any such fundamental engineering impasse lies ahead is because we can already see other animals – including some that experience negligible senescence – that can have much longer lifespans than humans. Nevertheless, it's possible in principle that our unique human attributes might somehow get in the way of engineering modifications that would provide negligible senescence for us. In ways that we don't yet understand, it could be the case that rejuveneering will suffer the same fate as nuclear fusion, with its advent being repeatedly delayed.

After all, sometimes a problem that is comparatively easy to state can require enormous processing to solve. The mathematical problem known as Fermat's Last Theorem is one example. The theorem was stated in the margin of a copy of a textbook by Pierre de Fermat in 1637. It's very short: "the equation $a^n + b^n = c^n$ has no solutions in positive integers, if n is an integer greater than 2". Nevertheless, the theorem took the entire mathematical community a total of 358 years to prove. The proof, by Andrew Wiles, with support from my former Cambridge mathematics colleague Richard Taylor, occupied over 120 pages when it was published in two articles in the Annals of Mathematics[375] in 1995, including nearly 10 pages of references to previous mathematical papers. This centuries-long saga of development would surely have shocked Fermat, if he could have foreseen it; in fact Fermat had convinced himself that he already had worked out a proof of the theorem, that was, however, too long for him to write into that same margin.

Despite the possible comparisons to nuclear fusion and to Fermat's Last Theorem, I personally think it's unlikely that insoluble engineering hurdles lie ahead on the rejuveneering footpath. It's not as if there is only one engineering technique that can be investigated. On the contrary, numerous different types of rejuveneering intervention can be considered.

Moreover, the slow progress with nuclear fusion can be attributed to factors other than sheer technical difficulty. In his Discovery article, Scharping states that the fusion project has lacked sufficient funding, and is being held up by the political difficulties of international cooperation:

More Than a Scientific Problem

Ultimately, the question may be one of funding. Multiple sources said they were confident that their research could progress faster if they received more support. Funding challenges certainly aren't new in scientific research, but nuclear fusion is particularly difficult due to its near-generational timescale. Although the potential benefits are apparent, and would indeed address issues of energy scarcity and environmental change that are relevant today, the day when we see a payoff from fusion research is still far in the future.

Our desire for an immediate return on our investments dampens our enthusiasm for fusion research, says Laban Coblentz, the head of Communication at ITER.

"We want our football coaches to perform in two years or they're out, our politicians have two or four or six years and they're out — there's very little time to return on investment," he said. "So when somebody says we'll have this ready for you in 10 years, that's a tough narrative to tell."

In the U.S., fusion research receives less than $600 million in funding a year, including our contributions to ITER. This is a relatively small sum when compared to the $3 billion the Department of Energy requested for energy research in 2013. Overall, energy research represented 8% of the total funding the U.S. gave out for research that year.

"If you look at it in terms of energy budgets, or what's spent on military development, it's not really a lot of money that's going to this," says Thomas Pedersen, division head at the Max-Planck Institut für Plasmaphysik. "If you compare us to other research projects, it seems very expensive, but if you compare it to what goes into oil production or windmills or subsidies for renewables, its much, much less than that."

Sharping concludes that the progress of nuclear fusion will come down to a question of political will:

Fusion power is always 30 years away.

However, the finish line has been visible for some time now, a mountaintop that seems to recede with every step forward. It is the path that is obscured, blocked by obstacles that are not only technological, but also political and economic in nature. Coblentz, [Hutch] Neilson and [Duarte] Borba expressed no doubts that fusion is an achievable goal. When we reach it however, may be largely dependent on how much we want it.

Soviet physicist, Lev Artsimovich, the "Father of the Tokamak" may have summed it up best:

"Fusion will be ready when society needs it."

In this aspect, the comparison between fusion and rejuveneering is actually an apt one:

- The engineering challenges are deeply hard, in both cases, but are by no means insoluble
- Progress in solving these challenges will depend upon large international collaboration, backed by political support of the sort I'll cover later in this chapter
- The speed at which this large international collaboration can be created and supported depends, in turn, on the level of public demand for a solution.

As an aside, I suspect that, if the survival of the human race had been manifestly dependent upon someone finding a proof of Fermat's Last Theorem, such a proof could have been found a lot more quickly than actually happened. A wartime siege mentality mindset can work wonders – *so long as there still exists an infrastructure adequate to support the collaboration of brilliant minds.*

Social turmoil ahead?

The possibility just mentioned, of a failure of social infrastructure, needs to be listed as another major risk for the attainment of the goals of rejuveneering. My argument in earlier chapters has been that an extended, powerful coalition is in the process of being formed, consisting of academics, entrepreneurs, designers, engineers, educators, story-tellers, humanitarians, and professionals from numerous fields – a coalition that has the collective ability to solve whatever challenges still exist before rejuvenation therapies become widely available. But such a coalition is dependent on the possibility for collaborative research and development to continue to take place. If society changes in ways that prevent this from happening, all bets are off. If the engines for innovation are destroyed, we may reach a new dark age rather than the Humanity+ vision I have indicated.

History has seen such setbacks before, on local or temporary scales. Geographer Jared Diamond raised awareness of many examples in his book "Collapse: How societies choose to fail or succeed"[376]. These examples show that there is no simple rule that, just because a society has done well in the past, it is bound to do well in the future. On the contrary, many cultures seemed in their day to be all-powerful, before the changes in circumstances which led to their downfalls.

Our present era therefore needs to keep in mind two contrasting visions of possible futures. One vision is the Humanity+ future I have outlined in previous chapters. In that scenario, human society is able to harness for very beneficial ends the tremendous power of new technologies, including green technology, synthetic biology, artificial intelligence, and robotics. But the other vision sees the potential of a global social collapse – akin, but on a grander scale, to the sorts of disasters described by Diamond.

In combination, these two conflicting visions might seem to be an unlikely pair of extreme possibilities. Most readers may imagine that some kind of middle-of-the-road scenario, far from either extreme, is much more credible – a scenario in which society is changed in only small ways from its present situation. But as a futurist who has spent a lot of time looking at the pace and likely impact of forthcoming technological disruptions, I believe we should open our minds to the potential of larger changes. Not only are we seeing fast improvements in the diverse fields of technology already mentioned. We're also seeing:

- Deepening impacts of these technologies in many new areas of life and society
- Stresses and strains of rapidly increasing resource usage
- The perception (and, often, the reality) of increasing social inequality
- New ideas and fads, often with little substance, spreading like wildfire around the world, undermining previous consensus
- Swiftly changing lifestyles, with unforeseeable consequences
- Gridlock in the mechanisms for international collaboration, being challenged by intense pent-up pressures.

The same technologies which can, collectively, enable a new Humanity+ era of sustainable abundance and personal rejuvenation can also, in different configurations, seriously threaten social and environmental health. Examples include the risks of:

- New pathogens and fast-spreading disease pandemics
- The proliferation of nuclear weapons among both state and non-state actors

- Genetically modified organisms having unexpected adverse effect on the environment
- New nano-particles causing pollution akin (but much worse) to that from asbestos dust
- Artificial intelligence systems, such as those monitoring financial trading or supervising vital energy infrastructure, suffering major faults in their software (faults in implementation and/or faults in specification)
- Increasingly extreme weather, triggered by runaway increases in atmospheric greenhouse gases
- Experimental geo-engineering projects, designed as an emergency measure to combat global warming, but which accidentally cause even worse changes in the environment
- Social chaos caused by an increasing sense of alienation, displacement, and rampant inequality
- The destruction of our data infrastructure by an escalation of cybercrime
- Terrorists or other malcontents gaining access to various sorts of horrific "weapons of mass destruction"
- Governments feeling snowballing pressure and adopting extreme measures, including pre-emptive strikes against perceived enemies, with the result of stirring up even worse reprisals.

It's hard to estimate the probabilities of any one of these risks. But I believe they add up in combination to probably the largest factor standing in the way of the successful abolition of aging.

It's for this reason that I believe that the rejuveneering project needs to run hand-in-hand with a parallel project to identify, assess, and champion the best responses to what have been called "existential risks"[377]. Without such a project, the danger is too high that we'll end up in a dramatically worse situation in the future than at present – as opposed to the dramatically better one which I believe we *ought* to be able to reach.

Naïve politics?

There are four possible responses to the threat that I have just described, of technological change posing existential risks to human society in the coming decades. I call these responses[378], respectively, the *technosceptical, technoconservative, technolibertarian*, and *technoprogressive* responses.

The technosceptical viewpoint denies that technology will have anything like the magnitude of impact that I have just described. This technosceptical response accepts that there has been rapid change over the last 10-20 years, but also asserts the following:

- There have been other times of rapid change in the past – as when electrification was introduced, or when new railways quickly criss-crossed the world; there is nothing fundamentally different about the present age; society coped with massive disruptive change in the past and will take new disruptive change in its stride in the future

- Past inventions such as the washing machine arguably transformed lives (especially women's lives) at least as much as modern inventions such as smartphones

- Although there have been many changes in ICT (information and communications technology) in the last 10-20 years, other areas of technology have slowed down in their progress; for example, commercial jet airliners don't fly any faster than in the past (indeed they fly a lot slower than Concorde)

- Past expectations of remarkable progress in fields such as flying cars, and manned colonies on Mars, have failed to be fulfilled

- Although some people are living longer, other demographic groups are experiencing greater health issues and declining life expectancies

- It may well be that the majority of the "low hanging fruit" of technological development has been picked, leaving much slower progress ahead.

My counter to this view will be evident to anyone who has reached this late point in this book. I point to positive feedback cycles, which accelerate technological innovation, as well as to escalating crossovers of ideas between different overlapping fields of enquiry (such as nanotech, infotech, biotech, and cognotech):

- Technology magnifies people's knowledge and intelligence, which in turn allows more technology to be created

- Technology improves everyone's ability to access cutting-edge information, via free online encyclopaedias, massive open online courses, and open source software
- Critically, this information is available to vast numbers of bright students, entrepreneurs, hackers, and activists, throughout the emerging world as well as in countries with longer-established modern economies
- Technology improves the ability for smart networking of prospective partners – people in one corner of cyberspace can easily improve and extend ideas that arose elsewhere
- The set of pre-existing component solutions keeps accumulating through its own positive feedback cycles, serving as the basis for yet another round of technological breakthrough
- Insight, tools, and techniques from one technology area can quickly transfer (often in innovative ways) into new technology areas.

It's very unlikely that technological progress will run out of steam of its own accord. But since every technology is a two-edged sword, capable of destructive usage just as much as constructive use, this means that the potential for existential risk is likely to grow in the forthcoming decades, rather than shrinking. I therefore assess technosceptics as being ill-informed – *dangerously* ill-informed.

That takes me to the technoconservative approach. Whereas technosceptics say, in effect, "there's no need to get worked up about the impact of technological change, since that change is going to slow down of its own accord", technoconservatives say "we *need* to slow that change down, since otherwise bad things are going to happen – *very* bad things".

Technoconservatives take seriously the linkage between ongoing technological change and the threats to society and humanity that I listed earlier. Unless that engine of change is brought under serious control, they say, technology is going to inflict terrible damage on the planet.

Technoconservatives want to cry out, "Enough!" They want to find ways to apply the brake on our technological steamroller – or (to change the metaphor) to rip out the power cable that keeps the engine of technological progress humming. Where technologists keep putting more opportunities into people's hands – opportunities to remake what it means to be human – technoconservatives argue for a period of prolonged reflection. "Let's not play God", some of them might say. "Let's be very careful not to let the genie out of the bottle."

They'll argue that technology risks leading people astray. Instead of us applying straightforward, ordinary, common-sense solutions to social problems, we're being beguiled by faux techno-solutions. Instead of authentic, person-to-person relations, we're spending too much time in front of computer screens, talking to virtual others, neglecting our real-world neighbours. Instead of discovering joy in what's natural, we're losing our true nature in quests for technotopia. These quests, argue the technoconservatives, aren't just misguided. They're deeply dangerous. We might gain a whole universe of electronic and chemical satiation, but we'll lose our souls in the process. And not only our souls, but also our lives, if some of the existential risks come to fruition.

But whenever a technoconservative says that technology has already developed enough, and there's no need for it to continue any further, I'll point out the vicious impediments that still blight people's lives the world over – disease, squalor, poverty, ignorance, oppression, aging.

Think of the terrible pain still inflicted by numerous diseases, both in young people and in the elderly. Think of the heartache caused by neurodegeneration and dementia. Rejuvenation biotechnology has the latent ability to make all these miseries as much a thing of the past as deaths from tuberculosis, smallpox, typhoid, or the bubonic plague. Anyone who wants to block this progress by proclaiming "Enough" has a great deal of explaining to do.

In any case, I don't believe the technoconservative programme to be feasible. Could the rate of pace of technological change really be significantly slowed down? I doubt it. Any such action is going to require large-scale globally coordinated agreements. It's not sufficient for any one company to agree to avoid particular lines of product development. It's not sufficient for any one country to ban particular fields of technological research. Everyone would need to be brought to the same conclusion, the world over. And everyone would need to be confident that everyone else is going to honour agreements to abstain from various developments.

Since the global technology engine is delivering huge numbers of good outputs, in parallel with its potential for bad outputs, I don't believe any technoconservative blanket ban is feasible. The technoconservative approach is too blunt, and is bound to fail. But while we cannot imagine voluntarily dismantling that great engine of progress, what we can – and should – imagine is to *guide* that engine more powerfully. Instead of seeking to stop it, we can seek to shape it. That's the approach favoured by technoprogressives. I'll come to that shortly.

First, though, some words about the technolibertarian approach. The technolibertarian view is a near direct opposite of the technoconservative one. Whereas the technoconservatives say "stop – this is going too fast", technolibertarians say "go faster".

It's not that technolibertarians are blind to the threats which cause so much concern to the technoconservatives. On the whole, they're aware of these threats. However, they believe that technology, given a free hand, will solve these problems.

For example, excess greenhouse gases may well be sucked out of the atmosphere by clever carbon capture systems, perhaps involving specially engineered bio-organisms. In any case, green energy sources – potentially including solar, geothermal, biofuels, and nuclear – will soon become cheaper than (and therefore fully preferable to) carbon-based fuels. As for problems with weaponry falling into the wrong hands, suitable defence technology could be created. Declines in biodiversity could be countered by Jurassic Park style technology for species resurrection. Ample fresh water can be generated by desalination processes from sea water, with the energy to achieve this transformation being obtained from the sun. And so on.

Broadly speaking, I'm sympathetic to this view. Where I differ from technolibertarians, however, is in my attitude towards the roles of government and economic markets.

The main request of technolibertarians to politicians is "hands off". They want government to provide a free rein to smart scientists, hard-working technologists, and innovative entrepreneurs – a free rein to pursue their ideas for new products. It is these forces, they say, which will produce the solutions to society's current problems and any impending existential risks.

Technolibertarians echo the sentiment of Ronald Reagan[379] that the nine most terrifying words in the English language are, "I'm from the government and I'm here to help." Governments suffer, in this view, from a number of deep-rooted problems:

- Politicians seek to build ever larger empires
- Politicians have little understanding of the latest technologies
- Politicians generally impose outdated regulations – which are concerned with yesterday's problems rather than with tomorrow's opportunities
- Regulators are liable to "capture" – an over-influence from vested interests, resulting in so-called "crony capitalism"
- Politicians have no inherent ability to pick winners
- Political spending builds a momentum of its own, behind "white elephant" projects.

The technolibertarian recipe to avoid potential existential risks, accordingly, is technology plus innovation plus free markets, minus intrusive regulations, and minus government interference. The role of government should be minimised – perhaps even privatised.

Now I certainly understand the impulse to minimise the power of politicians. Political and legislative intervention in technological development is often cumbersome, self-serving, and misguided. It can unnecessarily hinder the speedy development of innovative products.

But I cannot accept the conclusion that, therefore, *all that needs to be done* is to direct as much effort as possible into developing and deploying new technologies, such as rejuvenation therapies. Such a conclusion is politically naïve. New technologies can have awful side-effects, as listed earlier, such as accidental nuclear war, the destruction of the natural ecosystem by powerful pesticides, and runaway climate change. In the field of medicine, apparent new "wonder drugs" can, likewise, have awful unintended consequences: consider thalidomide and Vioxx[380]. So what rejuveneers need to advocate, rather than "no regulations", is "smart regulations". And rather than "less government", we need to advocate "better government".

Market failures?

The need for smart regulations and, more generally, for informed state guidance over technological development, is underscored by a number of other observations. What these observations have in common is that an economic free market, if left to itself, often produces outcomes that are far from optimal – and, indeed, can be disastrous.

One example is the way that pharmaceutical companies routinely deprioritise the development of drugs for diseases that only impact populations that have low incomes. The organisation "Drugs for Neglected Diseases initiative" (DNDi) was set up in 2003 to address that issue. The DNDi website[381] gives sobering details of some of these "neglected diseases":

- Malaria – kills one child every minute in sub-Saharan Africa (about 1,300 children every day)
- Paediatric HIV: 2.6 million children below 15 years of age are living with HIV globally, mainly in sub-Saharan Africa, and 410 of them die every day
- Filarial Diseases – 120 million people are infected with Elephantiasis and 25 million with River Blindness
- Sleeping sickness – endemic in 36 African countries with 21 million people at risk
- Leishmaniasis – occurs in 98 countries with 350 million people at risk worldwide
- Chagas disease – endemic in 21 countries across Latin America; kills more people in the region than malaria.

In summary:

Neglected diseases continue to cause significant morbidity and mortality in the developing world. Yet, of the 850 new therapeutic products approved between 2000 and 2011, only 4% (and only 1% of all approved NCEs [New Chemical Entities]) were indicated for neglected diseases, even though these diseases account for 11% of the global disease burden.

This situation shouldn't come as a surprise, given the shareholder constraints under which pharmaceutical companies operate. For example, the stated policy of pharmaceutical giant Bayer was described in an article by Glyn Moody in early 2014. The article carried the headline "Bayer's CEO: We Develop Drugs For Rich Westerners, Not Poor Indians"[382]. It quoted Bayer Chief Executive Officer Marijn Dekkers stating this principle:

"We did not develop this medicine for Indians. We developed it for western patients who can afford it."

That policy aligns with the for-profit motivation that the company pursues, in service of the needs of its shareholders to maximise returns. It's for that reason that DNDi advocate an "alternative model", stating their organisational vision as follows:

> To improve the quality of life and the health of people suffering from neglected diseases by using an alternative model to develop drugs for these diseases and by ensuring equitable access to new and field-relevant health tools.
>
> In this not-for-profit model, driven by the public sector, a variety of players collaborate to raise awareness of the need to research and develop drugs for those neglected diseases that fall outside the scope of market-driven R&D. They also build public responsibility and leadership in addressing the needs of these patients.

Glyn Moody, after noting the stark comments by Bayer CEO Dekkers mentioned above, points out how pharmaceutical companies have, in the past, shown broader motivation. He refers to this quote from 1950 from George Merck[383] (emphasis added):

> "We try never to forget that medicine is for the people. It is not for the profits. The profits follow, and if we have remembered that, they have never failed to appear. The better we have remembered it, the larger they have been…
>
> "We cannot step aside and say that we have achieved our goal by inventing a new drug or a new way by which to treat presently incurable diseases, a new way to help those who suffer from malnutrition, or the creation of ideal balanced diets on a worldwide scale. *We cannot rest till the way has been found, with our help, to bring our finest achievement to everyone.*"

What determines whether the narrow financial incentives of the market govern behaviours of companies with the technology (possibly unique technology) that enables significant human enhancement? Other factors need to come into play – not just financial motivation.

Even within their own parameters – the promotion of optimal trade and the accumulation of wealth – free markets often fail. The argument for smart oversight and regulation of markets is well made in the 2009 book "How markets fail: the logic of economic calamities"[384] by the New Yorker journalist John Cassidy[385].

The book contains a sweeping but compelling survey of a notion Cassidy dubs "Utopian economics", before providing layer after layer of decisive critique of that notion. As such, the book provides a useful guide to the history of economic thinking, covering Adam Smith, Friedrich

Hayek, Milton Friedman, John Maynard Keynes, Arthur Pigou, Hyman Minsky, among others.

The key theme in that book is that markets do fail from time to time, potentially in disastrous ways, and that some element of government oversight and intervention is both critical and necessary, to avoid calamity. This theme is hardly new, but many people resist it, and Cassidy's book has the merit of marshalling the arguments more comprehensively than I have seen elsewhere.

As Cassidy describes it, "utopian economics" is the widespread view that the self-interest of individuals and agencies, allowed to express itself via a free market economy, will inevitably produce results that are good for the whole economy. The book starts with eight chapters that sympathetically outline the history of thinking about utopian economics. Along the way, he regularly points out instances when free market champions nevertheless described cases when government intervention and control was required.

Next, Cassidy devotes another eight chapters to reviewing the history of criticisms of utopian economics. This part of the book is entitled "Reality-based economics", and covers topics such as:

- Game theory ("the prisoners dilemma")
- Behavioural economics (pioneered by Daniel Kahneman and Amos Tversky) – including disaster myopia
- Problems of spillovers and externalities (such as pollution) – which can only be fully addressed by centralised collective action
- Drawbacks of hidden information and the failure of "price signalling"
- Loss of competiveness when monopoly conditions are approached
- Flaws in banking risk management policies (which drastically under-estimated the consequences of larger deviations from "business as usual")
- Problems with asymmetric bonus structure
- The perverse psychology of investment bubbles.

These factors all obstruct markets from discovering the optimal solutions.

In summary, Cassidy lists four "illusions" of utopian economics:

1. The illusion of harmony: that free markets always generate good outcomes
2. The illusion of stability: that free market economy is sturdy
3. The illusion of predictability: that distribution of returns can be foreseen
4. The illusion of Homo Economicus: that individuals are rational and act on perfect information.

These illusions remain pervasive in many parts of economic thought. These illusions also lie behind technolibertarian optimism that technology, without government intervention, will be able to solve social and climatic problems such as terrorism, surveillance, environmental devastation, extreme fluctuations in weather, threats from new pathogens, and the growing costs of diseases of old age.

Indeed, free markets and innovative technology have, together, been a tremendous force for progress in recent history. However, they need smart oversight and regulation if they are going to reach their fullest potential. Indeed, without such oversight and regulation, they may lead society into a new Dark Age, rather than a Humanity+ age of sustainable abundance and healthy longevity for all. These convictions lie at the core of the technoprogressive stance.

It's for these reasons that, in November 2014 in a meeting in Paris, I joined with a number of colleagues from the international transhumanist community in helping to draft, and then sign, the Technoprogressive Declaration[386]. That Declaration starts as follows:

> The world is unacceptably unequal and dangerous. Emerging technologies could make things dramatically better or worse. Unfortunately too few people yet understand the dimensions of both the threats and rewards that humanity faces. It is time for technoprogressives, transhumanists and futurists to step up our political engagement and attempt to influence the course of events.
>
> Our core commitment is that both technological progress and democracy are required for the ongoing emancipation of humanity from its constraints…
>
> We must intervene to insist that technologies are well-regulated and made universally accessible in strong and just societies. Technology could exacerbate inequality and catastrophic risks in the coming decades, or especially if democratized and well-regulated, ensure longer, healthy and

more enabled lives for growing numbers of people, and a stronger and more secure civilization…

As artificial intelligence, robotics and other technologies increasingly destroy more jobs than they create, and senior citizens live longer, we must join in calling for a radical reform of the economic system. All persons should be liberated from the necessity of the toil of work. Every human being should be guaranteed an income, healthcare, and life-long access to education.

Evidently, this Declaration aims at liberation – similar to the technolibertarian stance. But the methods in the Declaration listed include

- Thoughtful reform of the economic system
- Smart regulation of new technologies
- The democratisation of access to new technologies
- Stepping up political engagement.

Here's the key significance for the rejuveneering project. Without these technoprogressive actions in the political sphere, we might see one or more of the following unfold:

- Rejuvenation therapies fail to be developed, because there is no business model whereby pharmaceutical companies can make adequate short-term profits from these products; in effect, aging would become a "neglected disease"
- Practical rejuvenation therapies do get developed, but are only available to the very wealthy in society, exacerbating an "us versus them" distinction which then prompts something like a class war, urban terrorism, and worse
- As a result of growing social alienation, political extremists come to power worldwide; pandering to religious sensibilities, these extremists implement draconian technoconservative policies, setting back the development of rejuvenation therapies by decades, centuries, or even millennia.

Destructive inequality?

A counterargument can be raised, against the position I have just outlined. It's important to take the time to hear this counterargument, before observing its shortcomings. This counterargument states that the benefits of rejuvenation therapies will be so clear and compelling that any remotely

361

rational system of government and economics will soon yield to popular pressure and ensure that these therapies quickly become widely available. Any additional central expenditure needed to assist this wide deployment will be more than repaid, numerous times over, by the economic and financial benefits of better health – benefits that I described in Chapter 9, "Money matters". Any government that is slow to provide such measures will be swept away in the next round of democratic elections.

In this analysis, rejuvenation therapies may start off by being expensive, but they'll quickly reach lower prices, either by the normal engines of business innovation, or by subsidies put in place by governments. It will be like smartphones, which were initially only available to the wealthy, but subsequently could be bought by virtually everyone on the planet, regardless of income bracket. It will be like many other consumer products too, that likewise quickly became more affordable after prohibitively expensive debut prices.

Mary Meeker's annual KPCB reviews of Internet trends contain some eye-popping statistics of declining costs. Here are some call-outs from her 2014 presentation[387]:

- Computational costs have declined 33% annually from 1990 to 2013: a million transistors cost $527 in 1990 but only 5 cents in 2013
- Storage costs declined 38% annually from 1992 to 2013: a Gigabyte of storage came down in price over that time from $569 to 2 cents
- Bandwidth costs declined 27% annually from 1999 to 2013: connectivity of 1 Gbps came down in price over that time from $1,245 to $16
- Even smartphones, despite their ever-greater functionality, have seen their costs decline 5% annually from 2008 to 2013.

Yuri Van Geest of the Singularity University picks up the analysis, in an attractive slideset introduction[388] to his 2014 book "Exponential Organizations"[389]. These slides illustrate remarkable price reductions for (broadly) like-for-like functionality in a range of fast-improving technological fields:

- Industrial robots: 23-fold reduction in 5 years
- Neurotech devices for brain-computer interface (BCI): 44-fold reduction in 5 years

- Autonomous flying drones: 142-fold reduction in 6 years
- 3D-printing: 400-fold reduction in 7 years
- Full DNA sequencing: 10,000-fold reduction (from $10M to $1,000) in 7 years.

Similar price reductions, it can be argued, will take all the heat out of present-day unequal access to goods. In the meantime, technolibertarians urge two sets of action:

- Let's press forwards quickly with further technological advances
- Let's avoid obsessing about present-day inequalities (and, especially, the *appearance* of present-day inequalities), since the more they're spoken about, the greater the likelihood of people becoming upset about them and taking drastic action.

However, here's my counter to the counterargument. At the same time as technology can reduce prices of products that have already been invented, it can also result in the creation of fabulous new products. Some of these new products will inevitably start off as extremely expensive – especially in fields such as advanced healthcare. Sectors such as rejuvenation biotech and neuro-enhancement may well see the following *accelerating "winner take all" outcomes*:

- Initial therapies are scarce and expensive, but deliver a decisive advantage to the people who can afford to pay for them
- With their brains enhanced – and with their bodies made more youthful and vigorous – the super-wealthy will be in a pole position to become even wealthier
- People who are unable to pay for these treatments will therefore fall even further behind
- Social alienation and angst will grow, with potentially explosive outcomes.

Unequal access to healthcare, in the United States, is already at near scandalous levels. That's despite wider access to healthcare being a "clear and compelling" target from a rational point of view. Alas, for the reasons covered in "How markets fail" by John Cassidy – and also in "Animal spirits: how human psychology drives the economy"[390] by Nobel laureates George Akerlof and Robert Schiller – there are no guarantees that the free market economy will deliver rational outcomes. And, similarly, there are no guarantees that democracies will collectively adopt and champion the policies that make the best rational sense. Politics, like economics, is too often governed by its own "animal spirits".

The factors behind the growing inequalities of "winner takes all" outcomes are described in, for example, the book "The Second Machine Age"[391] by Erik Brynjolfsson and Andrew McAfee, of MIT:

- The digitization of more and more information, goods, and services, allowing the owners of powerful data analysis platforms to gain even more insight into improvement possibilities
- The vast improvements in telecommunications and transport – the best products can, therefore, be used in every market worldwide
- The increased importance of networks and standards – new capabilities and new ideas can be combined and recombined more quickly, by those who are well-positioned.

As a result, winning companies take a much larger share of rewards than in previous times. That's great news for the winners, but potentially bad news for everyone else.

This effect is also known as "the economics of superstars", using a term coined in 1981[392] by Sherwin Rosen:

> The phenomenon of Superstars, wherein relatively small numbers of people earn enormous amounts of money and dominate the activities in which they engage, seems to be increasingly important in the modern world.

This analysis explains why the photo sharing company Instagram, with only 13 employees at the time (but with 100 million registered users) was valued at $1B when acquired by Facebook in April 2012. In contrast, another company in the field of photography, Kodak, had its peak valuation of $30B in 1997, when it had 86,000 employees. This seems to imply that Instagram employees had, on average, 2,000 times the productivity of Kodak employees. This productivity advantage was due to how Instagram took special advantage of pre-existing technology, and created their own online network which users found addictive. As winners in their space, Instagram reaped huge benefit.

The analysis is continued in a landmark MIT Technology Review article by David Rotman, "Technology and inequality"[393]:

The signs of the gap—really, a chasm—between the poor and the super-rich are hard to miss in Silicon Valley. On a bustling morning in downtown Palo Alto, the centre of today's technology boom, apparently homeless people and their meagre belongings occupy almost every available public bench. Twenty minutes away in San Jose, the largest city in the Valley, a camp of homeless people known as the Jungle—reputed to be the largest in the country—has taken root along a creek within walking distance of Adobe's headquarters and the gleaming, ultramodern city hall.

The homeless are the most visible signs of poverty in the region. But the numbers back up first impressions. Median income in Silicon Valley reached $94,000 in 2013, far above the national median of around $53,000. Yet an estimated 31% of jobs pay $16 per hour or less, below what is needed to support a family in an area with notoriously expensive housing. The poverty rate in Santa Clara County, the heart of Silicon Valley, is around 19%, according to calculations that factor in the high cost of living.

Even some of the area's biggest technology boosters are appalled. "You have people begging in the street on University Avenue [Palo Alto's main street]," says Vivek Wadhwa, a fellow at Stanford University's Rock Center for Corporate Governance and at Singularity University, an education corporation in Moffett Field with ties to the elites in Silicon Valley. "It's like what you see in India," adds Wadhwa, who was born in Delhi. "Silicon Valley is a look at the future we're creating, and it's really disturbing."

Rotman goes on to quote legendary venture capitalist Steve Jurvetson, Managing Director at Draper Fisher Jurvetson. Jurvetson was an early investor in Hotmail and sits on the boards of SpaceX, Synthetic Genomics, and Tesla Motors:

> "It just seems so obvious to me [that] technology is accelerating the rich-poor gap," says Steve Jurvetson... In many discussions with his peers in the high-tech community, he says, it has been "the elephant in the room, stomping around, banging off the walls."

Just because there is strong market logic to the way in which technological superstars are able to command ever larger incomes, this does not mean, of course, that we should acquiesce in this fact. An "is" does not imply an "ought". An enlightened self-interest should cause a rethink within "the 1%" (and their supporters on lower incomes – who often aspire to being to reach these stellar salary levels themselves). A plea for such a rethink was issued in 2014 by one of the wealthiest members of that 1%,

Nick Hanauer. In an article in Politico[394], Hanauer introduced himself as follows:

> You probably don't know me, but like you I am one of those .01%ers, a proud and unapologetic capitalist. I have founded, co-founded and funded more than 30 companies across a range of industries—from itsy-bitsy ones like the night club I started in my 20s to giant ones like Amazon.com, for which I was the first nonfamily investor. Then I founded aQuantive, an Internet advertising company that was sold to Microsoft in 2007 for $6.4 billion. In cash. My friends and I own a bank. I tell you all this to demonstrate that in many ways I'm no different from you. Like you, I have a broad perspective on business and capitalism. And also like you, I have been rewarded obscenely for my success, with a life that the other 99.99% of Americans can't even imagine. Multiple homes, my own plane, etc., etc.

But Hanauer was not writing to boast. He was writing to warn. The title of his article made that clear: "The Pitchforks Are Coming... For Us Plutocrats". This extract conveys the flavour:

> The problem isn't that we have inequality. Some inequality is intrinsic to any high-functioning capitalist economy. The problem is that inequality is at historically high levels and getting worse every day. Our country is rapidly becoming less a capitalist society and more a feudal society. Unless our policies change dramatically, the middle class will disappear, and we will be back to late 18th-century France. Before the revolution.
>
> And so I have a message for my fellow filthy rich, for all of us who live in our gated bubble worlds: Wake up, people. It won't last.
>
> If we don't do something to fix the glaring inequities in this economy, the pitchforks are going to come for us. No society can sustain this kind of rising inequality. In fact, there is no example in human history where wealth accumulated like this and the pitchforks didn't eventually come out. You show me a highly unequal society, and I will show you a police state. Or an uprising.

In short: technolibertarians inhabit a blinkered paradigm, which gives various core ideas far too much priority: the dangers of government, the drawbacks of regulation, and the apparent super-competence of free markets. To the extent that they place whole-hearted trust in free markets, technolibertarians are accepting a very dangerous risk. They could end up triggering a social and economic collapse that would destroy the mechanisms necessary for future technological advance. As such, they could kill the rejuveneering project, stone dead.

A broken dialogue?

Despite what I have just said, I have no desire to see the technolibertarian viewpoint being completely crushed. After all, that viewpoint puts its finger on a set of valid concerns, which need to be integrated into our collective response to technological possibilities. Governments and regulatory schemes suffer, as mentioned earlier, from tendencies towards deep problems: empire-building, poor understanding of new tech, regulations that become outdated and ossified, regulatory capture, and white elephant projects.

Rather than technoprogressives somehow vanquishing technolibertarians, in debate over the next 2-3 years, I instead look forwards to the best insights of both positions being integrated into an improved transhumanist political platform.

Indeed, there is much more that unifies technolibertarians and technoprogressives than what divides them. They can both be seen as part of what pioneering futurist FM Esfandiary[395]used to call "up wing" as opposed to either "right wing" or "left wing". In this light, these two positions are opposed to the "down wing" technoconservative position, as well as to the "no wing" technosceptical position. (Esfandiary also endorsed the term "transhuman", via his 1989 book "Are You a Transhuman? Monitoring and Stimulating Your Personal Rate of Growth in a Rapidly Changing World"[396].)

Accordingly, I look forward to the following features of the political dialogue of the next 10-20 years:

1. The evolution and maturation of *an integrated transhumanist political position*, that respects and enhances the best insights of both technolibertarians and technoprogressives
2. The growing recognition of *the fundamental inadequacies of both the technoconservative and technosceptical viewpoints*.

Given the inertia present in current political systems and prevailing mindsets, the second of these tasks may prove harder than the first. Old habits die hard, and old beliefs hang on, long past their "sell by" date. But the first task may turn out to be the enabler for the second.

Without progress in constructing a compelling unified political vision, and the demonstration of a series of positive incremental outcomes arising from it, one or more of the following outcomes may happen.

First, technolibertarians may gain too much power, and will dismantle the wise "visible hand" of government. That will increase the risk of market failures. Indeed, prices of medical treatment for diseases such as cancer are already rising, steeply, rather than falling – as noted in the May 2016 National Daily Press article "Cancer becomes one of the most expensive and riskiest diseases to treat"[397]:

> A new study shows that cancer drugs have become significantly more expensive compared to the drugs used 15 years ago.
>
> It's no secret that treating cancer is no walk in the park and it could leave someone's bank account in the red. Treating cancer today with drugs has been found to be costlier than treating the disease with drugs several years ago.
>
> Researchers have showed that the cost for a month of treatment with the latest cancer drugs from 2014 cost six times more than cancer drugs from 2000. That is even after adjusting the prices for inflation.
>
> To put that into more understandable figures, the researchers said that the cancer drugs from 2000 had an average cost of $1,869 per month. The cancer drugs from 2014 cost $11,325 which is nearly $10000 more.

A similar stark escalation of costs applies for insulin, pushing access beyond the means of large numbers of patients. This is described by Gary Stoller writing in the Connecticut Health-Team[398]:

> The high cost of insulin, which has risen by triple-digit percentages in the last five years, is endangering the lives of many diabetics who can't afford the price tag, say Connecticut physicians who treat diabetics.
>
> The doctors say that the out-of-pocket costs for insulin, ranging from $25 to upwards of $600 a month, depending on insurance coverage, are forcing many of their low-income patients to choose between treatment and paying their bills...
>
> A study by Philip Clarke, a professor of health economics at the University of Melbourne in Australia, reported that the price of insulin has tripled from 2002-2013...

These extra costs fly in opposition to the cosy assumption that prices are bound to fall over time, by the sheer magic of the invisible hand of free market economics. They're indications of more severe examples that could jeopardise social well-being if technolibertarian principles are more widely applied.

The second bad outcome that may occur is that technoconservatives gain too much power, and implement an overbearing precautionary principle, which is opposed to the kinds of breakthrough changes in technology and society that are needed for rejuveneering to flourish. Note that something that will embolden technoconservatives, making them want to assert their policies more forcibly, is them seeing the risk of technolibertarians gaining unbridled power. In contrast, what will calm technoconservatives down is if they see technoprogressives who clearly understand the same apprehensions, and who are setting out a credible plan to steer around the risks arising.

In summary, rather than being dismantled, the governmental and regulatory systems of the near future need to become significantly enhanced, slicker, more effective versions of today's incumbent systems. We need government 2.0 and regulations 2.0.

For more on the need to balance the invisible hand of the free market with the visible hand of smarter government, I recommend the recent excellent book "American Amnesia: How the War on Government Led Us to Forget What Made America Prosper"[399] by political scientists Jacob Hacker and Paul Pierson. These authors give a damning assessment of the argument for downsizing government, which echoes the discussion of bloodletting from Chapter 8 of my own book:

> There is no recipe for prosperity that doesn't involve extensive reliance on effective political authority. The... vision of shrinking government to a size that will make it 'safe' from cronyism is the economic equivalent of bloodletting.

In other words, that 'cure' is worse than the disease. Much worse!

Poor ways of doing good?

For readers for whom the discussion of politics in the last few sections extended far beyond their comfort zone, I have some good news. In this section, the narrative transitions away from politics, into an area that might be best described as "philosophy".

One of the biggest threats to the rejuveneering project is that muddled thinking will prevail, in the public mind, about what kind of actions are admirable. People who wish to behave in an admirable way may, nevertheless, be guided by ideas that end up doing harm rather than good. As victims of social and psychological pressure, they'll be stuck, consciously or unconsciously, in the accepting aging paradigm. Their personal philosophies will lead them to take actions that actually cause damage, to themselves and to their fellow citizens.

Specifically, if people are convinced that it's praiseworthy to accept ongoing aging and impending death, as some kind of "natural order of things", they'll be inclined to oppose measures that would enable radically extended healthspans. Consciously or unconsciously, they'll (wrongly) see such measures as somehow unfair, or unbalanced, or disproportionate, or grasping, or egotistical, or juvenile.

People locked into that mindset will prefer that society invests its discretionary time and effort into projects that accept aging as a given. For example, they may support projects that seek to help the elderly by providing them with neighbourly contact, lower cost transport, or improved "assisted living" facilities. Other projects they may be comfortable to support would be that more people can live long enough to become elderly, instead of being stricken by accidents or diseases in their youth or middle age. Or they'll support an expansion of education for people at all ages. They'll see all these projects as admirable, acceptable ways of doing good. But they'll be blinded to the possibility that there could be a *better way for them to do good*.

The phrase "Doing good better"[400] forms the title of a book written in 2015 by William MacAskill, who at the age of 28 was one of the youngest professors at Oxford University. The book's subtitle is "Effective Altruism and how you can make a difference". On his website, MacAskill introduces the book as follows:

> Do you care about making the world a better place? Perhaps you buy ethical products, donate to charity or volunteer your time in the name of *doing good*. But how often do you know what impact you really have?
>
> In my book, I argue that many ways of making a difference achieve little, but that, by targeting our efforts on the most effective causes, we each have an enormous power to make the world a better place.

A couple of representative examples from MacAskill's book feature in a Guardian book review[401] by David Shariatmadari:

A popular US charity called Books for Africa distributes donated educational material to schools across the continent. According to its website, it has sent 33m books to 49 countries since 1988, and last year it raised $2.3m (£1.5m) to cover the costs of shipping. It is highly rated by the evaluation body Charity Navigator and has been praised by Kofi Annan.

Surely it stands to reason that a greater abundance of books will result in better educated children, and all the benefits that flow from that? Except that the impact of increasing the number of books in schools has been tested, and, in the absence of teacher training, "providing textbooks has either no discernible effect on children's school performance, or only a limited effect on the most able students".

Do you know what does improve educational outcomes, and in dramatic fashion? Deworming. Parasitic infections make children unwell, more likely to miss school and fall behind. Supplying cheap and effective medicine to treat them reduced absenteeism in Kenya by 25%. Ten years later, it was found that the children who had been de-wormed earned 20% more than those who hadn't. Give to a deworming charity and you'll stand a real chance of improving hundreds of lives.

LinkedIn founder Reid Hoffman provided a glowing review[402] too, starting as follows:

Compassionate Utilitarianism: Balancing the head and the heart in the pursuit of philanthropy

No one donates money to try really hard to cure cancer, or deeply empathize with Siberian tigers. The goal is to eradicate cancer. The goal is to save Siberian tigers from extinction.

And yet while philanthropy is oriented around specific outcomes, it's often driven by emotion more than measurements and analysis. Instead of trying to identify the most leverageable causes through rational evaluation, people gravitate toward the most dramatic and evocative ones.

That's a flawed approach. In his recently published book, *Doing Good Better*, Oxford philosophy professor William MacAskill evangelizes, dispassionately but engagingly, on behalf of calculated and reflective charitable giving.

The Effective Altruism[403] community which MacAskill co-founded, based around the ideas given voice in "Doing good better", has quickly become one of the most exciting and impressive movements for positive social change. Hoffman suggests that Effective Altruism can be described as quantified selflessness. That seems right to me. I welcome the rigour that it brings to choices between different uses of time and money.

I had the pleasure to attend a two-day Effective Altruism Summit in Oxford in August 2015. I observed a community that was open-minded, ready to be self-critical, yet full of people who wanted to find the best ways to make a positive difference in the world. I was particularly struck by a presentation at that Summit by another Oxford University philosopher, Toby Ord. Ord's analysis is available online in a PDF, "The moral imperative towards cost-effectiveness"[404].

One of the examples explored by Ord is the relative cost-effectiveness of a number of treatments for HIV and AIDs:

> Let us consider four intervention types: surgical treatment for Kaposi's sarcoma (an AIDS defining illness), antiretroviral therapy to fight the virus in infected people, prevention of transmission of HIV from mother to child during pregnancy, condom distribution to prevent transmission more generally, and education for high risk groups such as sex workers. It is initially very unclear which of these interventions would be best to fund, and one might assume that they are roughly equal in importance. However, the most comprehensive compendium on cost-effectiveness in global health, Disease Control Priorities in Developing Countries 2nd edition, lists their estimated cost-effectiveness…
>
> Note the wide discrepancies between the effectiveness of each intervention type…
>
> Treating Kaposi's sarcoma is considered cost-effective in a rich country setting. Antiretroviral therapy is estimated to be 50 times as effective as treatment of Kaposi's sarcoma; prevention of transmission during pregnancy is 5 times as effective as this; condom distribution is about twice as effective as that; and education for high risk groups is about twice as effective again. In total, the best of these interventions is estimated to be 1,400 times as cost-effectiveness as the least good.

The comparison is carried out using the metric of DALYs gained per $1,000 spent – where DALY stands for Disability Adjusted Life Year. The DALY is a standard measure in global health. As the WHO website[405] explains,

> One DALY can be thought of as one lost year of "healthy" life. The sum of these DALYs across the population, or the burden of disease, can be thought of as a measurement of the gap between current health status and

an ideal health situation where the entire population lives to an advanced age, free of disease and disability.

In his analysis, Ord goes on to note that the variance in cost-effectiveness becomes even more striking when considering interventions targeting different illnesses:

Consider the progress that has been made on saving lives lost to immunization preventable illness, diarrhoea, malaria, and smallpox... In all cases, our interventions have led to at least 2.5 million fewer deaths per year... In each of the four of these disease areas, our health interventions save more lives than would be saved by a lasting world peace.

Moreover, these gains have been achieved very cheaply. For instance in the case of smallpox, the total cost of eradication was about $400 million. Since more than 100 million lives have been saved so far, this has come to less than $4 per life saved... Moreover, the eradication also saved significant amounts of money. Approximately $70 million was being spent across developing countries per year in routine vaccination and treatment for smallpox, and more than $1,000 million was lost per year in reduced productivity. Even just in the United States, smallpox vaccination and vigilance cost $150 million per year before eradication. The eradication programme thus saved more lives per year than are lost due to war, while *saving* money for both donors and recipients, paying back its entire costs every few months. It serves as an excellent proof of just how cost-effective global health can be.

Ord then underlines what he sees as the moral conclusion:

In these examples, we have seen how incredibly variable cost-effectiveness can be within global health. The least effective intervention in the HIV/AIDS case produces less than 0.1% of the value of the most effective, and if we are willing to look at different kinds of disease, this fraction drops to less than 0.01%. Ignoring cost effectiveness thus does not mean losing 10% or 20% of the potential value that a health budget could have achieved, but can easily mean losing 99% or more...

In practical terms, this can mean hundreds, thousands, or millions of additional deaths due to failure to prioritize. In non-life-saving contexts it means thousands or millions of people with untreated disabling conditions...

Learning how to correctly factor these other ethical issues into our decision making is an important and challenging problem, but we are currently failing at a much more basic, more obvious, and more important problem: choosing to help more people instead of fewer people, to produce a larger health benefit instead of a smaller one.

Some people find this kind of cold calculation to be unsettling. It can seem somewhat dehumanised. But the Effective Altruism advocates make a strong case that, by failing to think through these kinds of considerations, we would be falling short of our own potential for improving the human condition. If our aim is truly to improve the human condition – rather than just to *feel good* about *gestures* we make with the implied aim at improving the human condition – then we need to be able to rethink our priorities.

Any such rethink should weigh up the possibility that extending healthy lifespans, by the abolition of aging, might turn out to be *an even more cost-effective intervention*, when we recognise that the increase in DALYs from successful rejuvenation therapies would be very considerable indeed.

The Chief Science Officer of the SENS Research Foundation, Aubrey de Grey, made a similar argument in a presentation at Oxford in 2012, "The cost-effectiveness of anti-aging research"[406]:

- If we truly care about preventing deaths, we should pay close attention to the factor which is responsible for around two thirds of all deaths worldwide, namely aging (note that the figure includes all deaths from aging-related diseases – deaths that would not occur in the absence of aging)

- That high fraction (which rises to over 90% in the industrialised world) makes aging "unequivocally the world's most serious problem"

- The importance of abolishing aging increases even further, when we additionally consider the many years of declining functionality and increasing disability that precede deaths from aging

- Treatments that retard aging will have the benefit of delaying frailty and the onset of diseases of aging; treatments that, additionally, *repair* the bodily and cellular damage caused by aging have the potential to indefinitely prevent frailty and the diseases of aging – thereby *further increasing* the expected DALYs metric

- The costs required to make significant progress with rejuvenation therapies don't need to be particularly huge; a budget of around $50 million per year, over 5-10 years, could well be enough to advance the rejuveneering therapies proposed by SENS to the point where they can be applied to middle-aged mice with dramatic effect

- Once middle-aged mice, who had previously not received any special treatment, have their remaining healthy lifespan increased by upwards of 50% following the administration of rejuvenation therapies, lots of other funding would quickly follow: governments, businesses, and philanthropists would by that time all understand and acknowledge the great potential of these therapies for humans too.

The task that is urgent, de Grey argues, is to carry out intelligent advocacy for the needed research budgets in the shorter-term – up to the point when a manifest demonstration of robust mouse rejuvenation causes a wholesale change in public mindset. This shorter term intelligent advocacy can build momentum, once more people take the time to think things through dispassionately, and perhaps employ the conceptual methods of Effective Altruism. But it's still going to take a lot of effort – and a lot of smart marketing – to overcome the public's deep-rooted "accepting aging" apathy.

Public apathy?

Broadly speaking, there are two approaches to overcome apathy and to change the world. Either you change the world directly, or you change people's minds about the importance of changing the world (so that one of them changes the world instead). In other words, either you get involved in *actually doing things*, or you *talk* about how good it would be if people did various things.

The first approach involves action. The second involves ideas. The first approach can be adopted by engineers, entrepreneurs, designers, and so forth. The second approach is, in principle, available to everyone – everyone who can speak up about the importance of an idea.

I'm a fan of both approaches, but I recognise the second has come under a lot of criticism.

In an age of instant messaging, with legions of people who can click an online "Like" button whilst still in pyjamas or lounging on their sofas, it has become fashionable to decry so-called "slacktivism" (also known, less pithily, as "armchair activism"). Critic Evgeny Morozov, in his NPR article

"Brave New World Of Slacktivism"[407], was withering in his scorn of the practice:

> "Slacktivism" is an apt term to describe feel-good online activism that has zero political or social impact. It gives those who participate in "slacktivist" campaigns an illusion of having a meaningful impact on the world without demanding anything more than joining a Facebook group. Remember that online petition that you signed and forwarded to your entire contacts list? That was probably an act of slacktivism.

> "Slacktivism" is the ideal type of activism for a lazy generation: why bother with sit-ins and the risk of arrest, police brutality, or torture if one can be as loud campaigning in the virtual space? Given the media's fixation on all things digital — from blogging to social networking to Twitter — every click of your mouse is almost guaranteed to receive immediate media attention, as long as it's geared towards the noble causes. That media attention doesn't always translate into campaign effectiveness is only of secondary importance…

> The real issue here is whether the mere availability of the "slacktivist" option is likely to push those who in the past might have confronted the regime in person with demonstrations, leaflets, and labour organizing to embrace the Facebook option and join a gazillion online issue groups instead. If this is the case, then the much-touted tools of digital liberation are only driving us further away from the goal of democratization and building global civil society.

In contrast to this negative assessment, I see a very important role for online advocacy, in the battle to raise public awareness of the profound opportunities of rejuveneering and the profound risks from the potential misuse of the same underlying technologies.

For an upbeat example of the positive power of online advocacy, that contrasts with the scepticism of Morozov, consider this 2012 Financial Times report[408] by Matthew Green into the dramatic effect of a short video, "Invisible children", about the previously neglected scandal of the so-called "Lord's Resistance Army" of the theocratic guerrilla leader Joseph Kony in Uganda:

Invisible Children has sparked a global discussion of a forgotten evil

What would Joseph Kony make of it all? Running the Lord's Resistance Army rebel group has never been easy. That the Ugandan warlord has survived for a quarter of a century is testimony to his acumen and canny ability to forecast – and not merely with the help of his spirit guides. But even he will not have foreseen that his nemesis might not be in the form of the Ugandan army, but a generation of "slactivists" – hipsters intent on using Facebook, YouTube and Twitter, plus some wristbands, to bring him to justice.

What has happened in the past week has been momentous. A tiny group of people have forced one of the world's monsters into the spotlight by making a film that has gone viral about him and his crimes. They did not aspire to journalistic objectivity, but to create a clamour to bring Kony to justice. They have achieved more with their 30-minute video than battalions of diplomats, NGO workers and journalists have since the conflict began 26 years ago.

The "Invisible children" video[409] has been viewed more than 100 million times on YouTube. So far, no rejuveneering video has come close to that kind of viewing figure. The video by Peter Brietbart, Marco Vega and colleagues, "PostHuman: An introduction to transhumanism"[410], which features the concept of super longevity (along with super intelligence and super wellbeing), is perhaps one of the best made that I have seen; it has notched up over 150,000 views. Also worth mentioning is the 2005 short story by philosopher Nick Bostrom, "The Fable of the Dragon-Tyrant"[411]. This fable analogises the accepting aging paradigm to a centuries-long acquiescence by the citizens of a fictional country to the demands of a giant dragon:

> It demanded from humankind a blood-curdling tribute: to satisfy its enormous appetite, ten thousand men and women had to be delivered every evening at the onset of dark to the foot of the mountain where the dragon-tyrant lived. Sometimes the dragon would devour these unfortunate souls upon arrival; sometimes again it would lock them up in the mountain where they would wither away for months or years before eventually being consumed…

Max More is another philosopher with an imaginative touch. I remember being struck by the thoughtfulness of his 1999 "Letter to Mother Nature"[412], which starts as follows:

> Dear Mother Nature:
>
> Sorry to disturb you, but we humans—your offspring—come to you with some things to say. (Perhaps you could pass this on to Father, since we never seem to see him around.) We want to thank you for the many wonderful qualities you have bestowed on us with your slow but massive,

distributed intelligence. You have raised us from simple self-replicating chemicals to trillion-celled mammals. You have given us free rein of the planet. You have given us a life span longer than that of almost any other animal. You have endowed us with a complex brain giving us the capacity for language, reason, foresight, curiosity, and creativity. You have given us the capacity for self-understanding as well as empathy for others.

Mother Nature, truly we are grateful for what you have made us. No doubt you did the best you could. However, with all due respect, we must say that you have in many ways done a poor job with the human constitution. You have made us vulnerable to disease and damage. You compel us to age and die—just as we're beginning to attain wisdom. You were miserly in the extent to which you gave us awareness of our somatic, cognitive, and emotional processes. You held out on us by giving the sharpest senses to other animals. You made us functional only under narrow environmental conditions. You gave us limited memory, poor impulse control, and tribalistic, xenophobic urges. And, you forgot to give us the operating manual for ourselves!

What you have made us is glorious, yet deeply flawed. You seem to have lost interest in our further evolution some 100,000 years ago. Or perhaps you have been biding your time, waiting for us to take the next step ourselves. Either way, we have reached our childhood's end.

We have decided that it is time to amend the human constitution.

We do not do this lightly, carelessly, or disrespectfully, but cautiously, intelligently, and in pursuit of excellence. We intend to make you proud of us. Over the coming decades we will pursue a series of changes to our own constitution, initiated with the tools of biotechnology guided by critical and creative thinking. In particular, we declare the following seven amendments to the human constitution:

Amendment No.1: We will no longer tolerate the tyranny of aging and death. Through genetic alterations, cellular manipulations, synthetic organs, and any necessary means, we will endow ourselves with enduring vitality and remove our expiration date. We will each decide for ourselves how long we shall live…

When done well, all the following can contribute to a seismic change in public mindset from being stuck in "accepting aging" to being receptive, and then fully supportive, of "anticipating rejuvenation": short videos, powerful online blogposts, soulful poems, eye-catching animations, witty limericks, clever jokes, dramatic performances, concept art, novellas, soaring anthems, chants, slogans, and evocative "memes" consisting of a picture and an associated memorable quote. All can help to dismantle public apathy. And if slacktivists identify and highlight the best contributions from the many that are created, so that these contributions receive more attention, and hasten the weakening of the bastions of the accepting aging paradigm, that's something I heartily applaud. Once minds have been changed, actions can follow. When the groundwork is laid, new ideas can spread quickly.

In 1861, the French writer Gustave Aimard expressed the following thought in his novel "The freebooters"[413]:

> There is something more powerful than the brute force of bayonets: it is the idea whose time has come and hour struck.

That thought has itself evolved over the years, commonly being attributed to Aimard's more famous contemporary, Victor Hugo[414], who said something similar:

> One withstands the invasion of armies; one does not withstand the invasion of ideas.

Or, in the paraphrased form in which it is frequently quoted:

> Nothing is stronger than an idea whose time has come.

What's hard, of course, is to know what time is the right time for a particular idea. If someone repeatedly cries wolf too early, they lose their credibility – and their audience. But I see plenty of reason why the present time is ripe for the idea that we can, and should, abolish aging. That idea can be backed up by a host of observations:

- Examples of animals that experience negligible senescence
- Genetic manipulations that can significantly extend lifespan (and healthspan)
- Fascinating possibilities from stem cell therapies
- The game-changing possibilities of CRISPR genetic editing
- The increasing viability of nano-interventions, such as nano-surgery and nano-bots
- Early indications that synthetic organs can be created
- Research projects targeting each of seven identified underlying causes of aging
- Encouraging progress in new ideas for treating cancer, as well as other diseases of aging

- Promising results from big data analysis by increasingly powerful artificial intelligence
- Financial models that show the tremendous economic benefits of the longevity dividend
- Examples from other technological fields of unexpectedly rapid progress
- Examples from other activist projects of rapid changes in social mindset.

These observations provide the environment in which the idea of the abolition of aging can thrive, but the task still remains to actually champion that idea:

- Finding better, more effective ways to express the idea, for different audiences
- Analysing the objections that people raise to the idea, and finding good responses to these objections
- Appreciating the *underlying circumstances* which make people want to object to the idea (or even just to ignore it), and taking steps, where possible, to transform these circumstances.

If these tasks get left undone, the idea may languish, being of interest only to a small minority. In that case, the accepting aging paradigm will remain dominant. Investment – both public and private – will go into fields other than rejuveneering. Regulatory hurdles will persist, that frustrate efforts by innovators to develop and deploy rejuvenation therapies. And upwards of 100,000 people will continue to die, every day, of diseases of aging that are actually avoidable. That would be the terrible cost of ongoing public apathy about the potential to abolish aging.

A lack of conviction?

I chose the phrase "The abolition of aging" as the title of this book, by analogy with the phrase "The abolition of slavery". The abolition of slavery has a strong case to be one of the high points of human history. Drawing on the material in the magisterial book "Inhuman Bondage: The Rise and Fall of Slavery in the New World"[415] by veteran Yale historian David Brion Davis, Donald Yerxa of Boston University offers this assessment[416]:

> After receiving hundreds of antislavery petitions and debating the issue for years, the British Parliament passed the Abolition of the Slave Trade Act

in March 1807. Starting May 1, 1807, no slaver could legally sail from a British port. Following the Napoleonic Wars, British abolitionist sentiment increased, and substantial public pressure was brought to bear on Parliament to gradually emancipate all British slaves. In August 1833, Parliament passed the Great Emancipation Act, which made provision for the gradual emancipation of slaves throughout the British Empire. Abolitionists on both sides of the Atlantic hailed it as one of the great humanitarian achievements in history. Indeed, the prominent Irish historian W.E.H. Lecky famously concluded in 1869 that "the unwearied, unostentatious, and inglorious crusade of England against slavery very may probably be regarded as among the three or four perfectly virtuous acts recorded in the history of nations."

As the distinguished historian David Brion Davis observes, however, in his brilliant synthesis of slavery in the New World, British abolitionism is "controversial, complex, and even baffling." It has occasioned a significant historiographical debate lasting over sixty years. The key issue has been how to account for abolitionists' motives and the groundswell of public support for the antislavery cause. Davis suggests that historians find it difficult to accept that something as economically significant as the slave trade could be abolished on essentially religious and humanitarian grounds. After all, by 1805 "the colonial plantation economy," he informs us, "accounted for about one-fifth of Britain's total trade." Prominent abolitionists like William Wilberforce, Thomas Clarkson, and Thomas Fowell Buxton used Christian arguments to combat "inhuman bondage," but surely other, material factors were in play. A great deal of ink has been spilled assessing the relationship of antislavery to capitalism and free market ideology. And the upshot of this research is that the antislavery impulse went against British economic interests, both real and perceived.

So how do we explain the successes of a humanitarian movement advocating reforms that could have precipitated economic disaster? Davis concludes that while it is important to appreciate the complex interplay of economic, political, and ideological factors, we must recognize the significance of a moral vision that "could transcend narrow self-interest and achieve genuine reform."

The analysis by Davis makes it clear that:

- The abolition of slavery was by no means inevitable or predetermined
- There were strong arguments against the abolition of slavery – arguments raised by clever, devout people in both the United States

and the United Kingdom – arguments concerning economic well-being, among many other factors

- The arguments of the abolitionists were rooted in a conception of a better way of being a human – a way that avoided the harsh bondage and subjugation of the slave trade, and which would in due course enable many millions of people to fulfil a much greater potential

- The cause of the abolition of slavery was significantly advanced by public activism – including pamphlets, lectures, petitions, and municipal meetings.

With its roots in the eighteenth century, and growing in momentum as the nineteenth century proceeded, the abolition of slavery eventually became an idea whose time had come – thanks to brave, smart, persistent activism by men and women with profound conviction.

With a different set of roots in the late twentieth century, and growing in momentum as the twenty-first century proceeds, the abolition of aging can, likewise, become an idea whose time has come. It's an idea about an overwhelmingly better future for humanity – a future that will allow *billions* of people to fulfil a much greater potential. But as well as excellent engineering – the creation of reliable, accessible rejuvenation therapies – this project will also require brave, smart, persistent activism, to change the public landscape from one hostile (or apathetic) to rejuveneering into one that deeply supports it.

Noise swamping the signal?

In my applause for activism in favour of rejuveneering, I don't mean to endorse *all* the rhetoric that can be found, online or in books, in favour of this project. Far from it. Indeed, much that is said in support of rejuveneering is probably counterproductive:

- Rash, unwarranted claims about the effectiveness of individual tonics or therapies

- Distortions of the research findings from particular experiments, with an eye to bolstering the market perception of products under commercial development

- Tiresome repetitions of misleading over-simplifications of more sophisticated principles

- Hurtful allegations about the competence or motivation of critical researchers who are actually carefully following established scientific processes
- Claims that are well understood to be false but which nevertheless keep being repeated, out of naivety and/or carelessness, by people who are well-intentioned but misinformed
- People being urged to undergo treatments which are actually dangerous.

The dangers of this kind of misrepresentation include various sorts of backlash:

- To protect patients from being misled and harmed, legislators may impose stricter regulation, that clamps down on good innovation as well as on purveyors of perceived "snake oil"
- Capable academics may want to dissociate themselves from the entire field, in order to avoid reputational damage
- Researchers may waste lots of time duplicating work that has already been done, and whose results ought to have been known in advance (but that knowledge was drowned out in the noise of low quality communications)
- The public may tire of hearing of forthcoming rejuveneering therapies, and decide that the field is suspect and hype-laden
- Potential funding may be removed from the field, being routed instead to completely different kinds of project.

For these reasons, the rejuveneering community needs to work hard on improving its own knowledge management. Enthusiastic new members should be welcomed, but then be quickly brought up to speed in terms of the actual best state of current knowledge. They should be able to access online knowledge about:

- The community's best thoughts as to credible **roadmaps** for progress that can be made in the rejuveneering project in the years ahead
- The strengths and weaknesses of various **theories of aging**
- The **treatments and therapies** that are being developed or which are proposed

- The **lifestyle changes** which have the best chance, upon adoption, to keep individuals alive and healthy until such time as "Bridge 2" therapies become available
- The **history** of the overall field (to avoid needless repetition of previous mistakes)
- The broader **political**, **social**, **psychological**, and **philosophical** dimensions of rejuveneering
- The **projects** which are actively looking for assistance, and which the community judges to be worthy of support
- The **memes** of various sorts, at any given time, which are the most effective at winning new supporters and in responding to criticism
- The **skills** which are in short supply within the community, and the best ways in which various skills can be deployed in support of the rejuveneering goals
- The areas where **genuine differences of opinion** exist, and the proposed methods for how the community may be able to resolve these differences
- The **risks** which the community is tracking, and the proposed **mitigations** for these risks.

Evidently, the present book aims to cover many of the topics listed above. However, rejuveneering is a fast-changing field. Much of what I've written on these pages will be out-of-date, or otherwise incomplete, by the time you read it. For pointers to information that is more up-to-date and more comprehensive, please see the community page[417] on the website that accompanies this book.

To be clear, I'm *not* saying that any new supporter of rejuveneering should be obliged to digest huge amounts of information before he or she is allowed to open their mouths in any public forum. The community's best knowledge about rejuveneering needs to be layered, easily searchable, and engaging. That way, when someone feels inspired to publicly address a particular topic, they should be able to quickly discover the community's best advice on what to say about it. They should also be able to find supportive, knowledgeable friendly people with whom they can discuss any issues arising. Whatever new insight arises from these conversations should be captured online, so that the knowledge base improves. As a result, the rejuveneering project can continue to move forwards. As it must.

Making a real difference?

In this chapter, I've reviewed some of the biggest risks facing the rejuveneering project. The project might become bogged down in enormous technical challenges that are harder than rejuveneers anticipate. It may alienate potential important supporters because of ill-chosen words and/or deeds, thereby cutting itself off from much-needed advice and finance. Other latent support may fail to materialise, due to prevailing public apathy, with the accepting-aging paradigm remaining dominant. Yet other supporters could prove to be net hindrances to the project, magnifying confusion rather than actually helping. Technoconservative politicians may put huge barriers in place of the research needed to create and deploy rejuvenation treatments. Technolibertarians might unwittingly precipitate an economic meltdown due to misguidedly dismantling public policies. Existential risks such as runaway climate change, highly virulent pathogens, or terrorist access to horrific weapons of mass destruction, could herald a terrible new dark age.

Also in this chapter, I've indicated actions that can be taken by supporters of rejuveneering, to handle these risks, and to heighten the positive forces that sit alongside these negative risks. I ask each reader to consider which actions are the ones that best play to their own personal strengths.

Answers will vary from person to person. But I expect the following six types of action will feature prominently.

First, we need to strengthen our ties to **communities** that are working on at least parts of the rejuveneering project. We should find out which communities can nurture and inspire us, and where we can help, in turn, to nurture and inspire others. The resulting network ties will give us all greater strength to face the difficulties ahead.

Second, we need to improve our personal **understanding** of aspects of rejuveneering – the science, roadmaps, history, philosophy, theories, personalities, platforms, open questions, and so on. With a better understanding, we can see more clearly what contributions we can make – and we can help others to make similar decisions for themselves. In some cases, we can help to document a better understanding of specific topics, by creating or editing knowledgebases or wikis.

Third, many of us can become involved with **marketing** of one sort or another. We might work on the creation and distribution of various marketing messages, presentations, videos, websites, articles, books, and so on. We might identify particular audiences – sets of people – and deepen the community's understanding of the issues high in the minds of these audiences. We might take the time to build better relationships with key influencers (potential new supporters of rejuveneering). We might even develop our political skillsets, improving our ability to influence others, forge alliances, broker coalitions, and create draft legislation in politician-friendly manner.

Fourth, some of us can undertake original **research** – into any of the unknowns of rejuveneering. This could be part of formal educational courses, or it could be a commercial R&D undertaking. It could also be part of a decentralised activity, in the style of "citizen science". See the book's website, https://theabolitionofaging.com/, for some suggestions for next steps.

Fifth, many of us can provide **funding** to projects that we judge to be particularly worthwhile. We can take part in specific fundraising initiatives, or we can donate some of our personal wealth. We can also decide to change our jobs, in order to earn more money, so we can make larger donations to the projects about which we care the most.

Last, but not least, we can work on our **personal effectiveness** – our ability to get things done. Having become aware of the historical importance of this present time period – a time period in which human society could make either a remarkable turn for the better or a remarkable turn for the worse – we should find ways to rise above the distractions and inertia of day-to-day "life as normal". Instead of just being interested observers standing on the side lines of the culminating acts of humanity's oldest quest, occasionally offering cheers of encouragement, we can transform ourselves to become active participants in that quest. If we put our lives in order, each one of us can make a very real difference.

Acknowledgements

The contents of the book were greatly improved due to feedback from Alan Boulton, Alexander Karran, Aubrey de Grey, Bruce Lloyd, Catarina Lamm, Dalton Murray, Hyesoon Wood, James Littlejohn, Jenina Bas, Rob Lawrence, Ted Howard, and Terry Raby. Shortcomings that remain are my own responsibility.

The book cover incorporates CC0 public domain graphics from Pixabay – from users ArtsyBee[418] and PublicDomainPictures[419]. The cover design was improved due to feedback from Alexander Karran, Alper Erel, Catarina Lamm, Hyesoon Wood, and Martin Kleman. The inclusion of enhanced DNA should be no surprise. For the reason why the cover features a high-flying bird, see Chapter 3, "From flight to rejuvenation".

Writing this book kept me away from other projects for many months. I deeply appreciate everyone's patience at my slow responsiveness during this time. May the sacrifices prove to be worthwhile!

Endnotes

Note: for the convenience of readers, the online page https://theabolitionofaging.com/contents/endnotes/ provides an easily clickable version of the contents of the following list of endnotes.

---

1 https://theabolitionofaging.com/author/
2 http://www.grg.org/SC/SCmain.html
3 https://www.youtube.com/watch?v=jZLfVk_pXRg
4 https://en.wikipedia.org/wiki/Wilfred_Owen#Death
5 http://www.warpoetry.co.uk/owen1.html
6 https://en.wikipedia.org/wiki/Serenity_Prayer
7 https://en.wikibooks.org/wiki/Introduction_to_Philosophy/What_is_Buddhist_Philosophy%3F
8 https://archive.org/stream/epictetus02epicuoft#page/140/mode/2up/search/freedom
9 https://en.wikipedia.org/wiki/Meditations
10 https://web.archive.org/web/19990819170545/http://salon.com/news/1999/02/cov_02news.html
11 http://99u.com/articles/24401/a-makers-guidebook-9-stoic-principles-to-nurture-your-life-and-work
12 http://www.mindfulpurpose.com/personal-change/acceptance-is-the-first-step-toward-change
13 http://99u.com/articles/24401/a-makers-guidebook-9-stoic-principles-to-nurture-your-life-and-work
14 https://www.poets.org/poetsorg/poem/do-not-go-gentle-good-night
15 http://www.bbc.co.uk/arts/0/24748894
16 http://www.theguardian.com/books/2013/jun/15/iain-banks-the-final-interview
17 https://www.littlebrown.co.uk/a-personal-statment-iain-banks.page
18 http://www.presidency.ucsb.edu/ws/?pid=3275
19 http://er.jsc.nasa.gov/seh/ricetalk.htm
20 http://news.nationalpost.com/2013/03/15/war-on-cancer/
21 http://data.worldbank.org/indicator/SP.DYN.LE00.FE.IN
22 http://www.econ.ku.dk/okocg/VV/VV-Economic%20Growth/articles/artikler-2006/Broken-limits-to-life-expectancy.pdf

23

http://science.sciencemag.org/content/suppl/2002/05/09/296.5570.1029.DC1

[24] http://www.ncbi.nlm.nih.gov/pmc/articles/PMC2625386/

[25] http://www.ncbi.nlm.nih.gov/pmc/articles/PMC2587384/

[26] http://www.inspiredinsider.com/michael-rose-55theses-interview/

[27] https://www.youtube.com/watch?v=slXmh7igkZA

[28] http://www.ncbi.nlm.nih.gov/pubmed/8608934/

[29] http://www.ncbi.nlm.nih.gov/pmc/articles/PMC3001308/

[30] http://www.ncbi.nlm.nih.gov/pubmed/8247153/

[31] https://www.ncbi.nlm.nih.gov/pmc/articles/PMC2885961/

[32] http://www.nature.com/news/destroying-worn-out-cells-makes-mice-live-longer-1.19287

33

https://en.wikipedia.org/wiki/List_of_world_records_in_masters_athletics

[34] http://youtu.be/xI38YRz1bbQ

[35] http://sens.org/research/introduction-to-sens-research

[36] http://www.ncbi.nlm.nih.gov/pmc/articles/PMC3836174/

[37] https://cogforlife.org/Hayflick.NatureNotImmortal.pdf

[38] http://www.nature.com/news/quantum-gas-goes-below-absolute-zero-1.12146

[39] http://www.amazon.com/Pleasure-Finding-Things-Out-Richard/dp/0465023959

40

http://content.time.com/time/specials/packages/article/0,28804,1884779_1884782_1884758,00.html

[41] http://www.amazon.com/Ageless-Generation-Advances-Biomedicine-Transform/dp/0230342205/

[42] https://londonfuturists.com/2013/09/01/biomedical-discoveries-and-the-ageless-generation/

[43] https://www.woodlibrarymuseum.org/library/pdf/S_ADVA.pdf

[44] http://www.general-anaesthesia.com/images/queen-victoria.html

[45] http://metrocosm.com/world-population-split-in-half-map/

[46] http://shrinkthatfootprint.com/how-big-is-a-house

[47] http://www.techinsider.io/this-is-the-potential-of-solar-power-2015-9

[48] http://www.nytimes.com/2015/05/30/world/middleeast/water-revolution-in-israel-overcomes-any-threat-of-drought.html?_r=2

[49] https://en.wikiquote.org/wiki/Max_Planck

50

https://web.archive.org/web/20060107100252/http://www.sagecrossroads.net/Portals/0/transcript13.pdf

[51] http://www.thenewatlantis.com/publications/ageless-bodies-happy-souls

[52] https://www.washingtonpost.com/archive/opinions/2003/07/13/think-baby-louise-and-dont-be-afraid/dffccc74-237a-4d1c-8a5a-12a986368cc8/

[53] http://www.theguardian.com/commentisfree/2014/jul/07/life-extension-dictators-ultra-rich-longevity-science

[54] http://aeon.co/magazine/health/will-new-drugs-mean-the-rich-live-to-120-and-the-poor-die-at-60/

[55] http://www.theatlantic.com/health/archive/2013/07/the-vitamin-myth-why-we-think-we-need-supplements/277947/

[56] https://books.google.com/books?id=xconQZv0rBAC&pg=PA485

[57] https://books.google.co.uk/books?id=crLx9_3RulUC&pg=PT766

[58] https://www.reddit.com/r/IAmA/comments/2tzjp7/hi_reddit_im_bill_gates_and_im_back_for_my_third/co3q1lf

[59] http://www.bartleby.com/157/6.html

[60] http://www.jstor.org/stable/25105260

[61] http://zapatopi.net/kelvin/papers/letters.html#baden-powell

[62] http://www.wright-brothers.org/History_Wing/Wright_Story/Inventing_the_Airplane/Not_Within_A_Thousand_Years/Not_Within_A_Thousand_Years.htm

[63] http://www.flyingmachines.org/langaer.html

[64] https://en.wikipedia.org/wiki/Simon_Newcomb#Other_work

[65] http://www.amazon.com/When-Hull-Freezes-Over-Massachusetts/dp/1596290994/

[66] https://www.foresight.org/news/negativeComments.html

[67] http://www.skygod.com/quotes/times1903.pdf

[68] http://www.amazon.com/Rudyard-Kipling-Something-Myself-original/dp/052140584X

[69] http://aerostories.free.fr/precurseurs/lilien/page2.html

[70] http://zapatopi.net/kelvin/papers/interview_aeronautics_and_wireless.html

[71] https://airandspace.si.edu/exhibitions/wright-brothers/online/age/1908/index.cfm

[72] http://www.amazon.com/Side-Lights-Astronomy-Kindred-Popular-Science-ebook/dp/B018PLI4EY/

[73] http://oecdinsights.org/2011/04/12/the-future-is-not-what-it-used-to-be/

[74] http://www.amazon.com/No-Longer-Island-Brothers-1902-1909/dp/0804712654/

75
http://www.smithsonianeducation.org/educators/lesson_plans/wright/flights_future.html

76 https://www.newspapers.com/newspage/71188203/

77 http://blog.modernmechanix.com/sun-is-energy-source/

78 https://en.wikipedia.org/wiki/Ernest_Rutherford#Nuclear_physics

79 http://www.post-gazette.com/ae/book-reviews/2007/04/20/Einstein-His-Life-and-Universe-by-Walter-Isaacson/stories/200704200408

80
https://archive.org/stream/einsteinhislifea011653mbp/einsteinhislifea011653mbp_djvu.txt

81 http://www.dannen.com/lostlove/

82 https://edge.org/response-detail/26157

83 http://www.humanity.org/voices/commencements/lewis-lapham-st.johns-college-speech-2003

84 http://www.nytimes.com/2012/12/02/magazine/can-a-jellyfish-unlock-the-secret-of-immortality.html

85 https://www.ucl.ac.uk/news/news-articles/0614/200614-salamander-limb-regeneration

86 http://www.heraldsun.com.au/news/worldfirst-australian-stem-cell-marvel-that-regrows-damaged-cartilage-could-make-joint-surgery-unnecessary/news-story/5ce4837e91fe06a8e0ba7ae5dc655c62

87 http://www.theaustralian.com.au/higher-education/new-program-takes-stem-out-of-stem-cells/news-story/522ff43c30f22efcafd5e2a74d70df9b

88 http://www.karger.com/Article/Pdf/215589

89 http://www.nature.com/news/2007/070619/full/news070618-6.html

90 http://sciencenordic.com/new-record-world%E2%80%99s-oldest-animal-507-years-old

91 http://www.slideshare.net/redescma/biologa-y-ecologa-del-alimoche, slide 9

92 https://whyevolutionistrue.wordpress.com/2014/11/09/moar-bears/panda-001/

93 http://www.birdcare.com/bin/shownews/69

94 http://green.blogs.nytimes.com/2011/03/08/albatross-is-a-mother-at-60/?_r=2

95 http://longevityletter.com/10-animal-species-that-made-cancer-a-thing-of-the-past/

96 http://www.fs.fed.us/database/feis/plants/tree/pinlon/all.htm

97 http://www.nytimes.com/2010/09/14/science/14williams.html

98 http://www.jstor.org/stable/2406060

99 http://www.amazon.com/Youth-Pill-Scientists-Anti-Aging-Revolution/dp/1617230081

100 http://www.ncbi.nlm.nih.gov/pubmed/147113

101 http://longevity-science.org/Evolution.htm

102 http://www.normandoidge.com/?page_id=1639

103 http://www.mpg.de/7470432/planarian-regeneration

104 http://www.scientificamerican.com/article/new-limb-regeneration-ins/

105 http://optn.transplant.hrsa.gov/converge/latestData/rptData.asp

106 http://www.nature.com/news/tissue-engineering-how-to-build-a-heart-1.13327

107

http://poptech.org/blog/poptech_interview_gabor_forgacs_on_the_realit
y_of_3d_organ_printing

108 http://www.wsj.com/articles/can-3-d-printing-of-living-tissue-speed-up-drug-development-1424145654

109 http://www.cbsnews.com/news/elephants-from-mice/

110 http://news.harvard.edu/gazette/story/2014/07/new-way-to-regrow-human-corneas/

111 http://www.nytimes.com/2014/05/05/science/young-blood-may-hold-key-to-reversing-aging.html?_r=0:

112 http://www.nature.com/nm/journal/v20/n6/pdf/nm.3569.pdf

113 http://www.cbsnews.com/news/promising-duke-university-polio-brain-cancer-trial-given-breakthrough-status-60-minutes/

114 https://news.osu.edu/news/2016/02/23/dnatrojan/

115 http://www.tum.de/en/about-tum/news/press-releases/short/article/32983/

116 http://sabinehauert.com/

117 https://www.youtube.com/watch?v=sn1gmcs-HXU

118 http://www.pnas.org/content/105/37/13987.full

119 http://embomolmed.embopress.org/content/4/8/691

120 http://drdaveunleashed.com/2012/05/a-giant-step-for-mankind-that-started-with-a-mouse/

121 http://www.amazon.com/Autobiography-Values-Charles-A-Lindbergh/dp/0156094029

122 http://news.bbc.co.uk/1/hi/7420026.stm

123 http://www.amazon.com/Immortalists-Charles-Lindbergh-Alexis-Forever/dp/0060528168/

124 http://www.buzzfeed.com/hunterschwarz/how-many-photos-have-been-taken-ever-6zgv#

125 http://www.slideshare.net/kleinerperkins/internet-trends-2014-05-28-14-pdf

126 http://www.arraycomm.com/technology/coopers-law/

127

https://web.archive.org/web/20150602193727/http://www.idc.com/getdoc.jsp?containerId=244709
128 http://www.amazon.com/The-Mythical-Man-Month-Engineering-Anniversary/dp/0201835959
129 http://www.stevemcconnell.com/ieeesoftware/eic08.htm
130 http://firstmonday.org/article/view/578/499
131 http://en.wikipedia.org/wiki/Netscape_6
132 http://www.joelonsoftware.com/articles/fog0000000069.html
133 http://www.joelonsoftware.com/news/20030601.html
134 http://smartphonesandbeyond.com/
135

https://web.archive.org/web/20160203233154/http://www.bloomberg.com/bw/stories/2005-08-16/google-buys-android-for-its-mobile-arsenal
136 http://www.amazon.com/Next-Fifty-Years-Science-Twenty-first/dp/0375713425
137 http://arep.med.harvard.edu/gmc/nexgen.html
138 http://www.nanalyze.com/2016/03/does-full-genome-sequencing-really-cost-1000-now/
139 http://www.nature.com/nrd/journal/v11/n3/full/nrd3681.html
140

http://blogs.sciencemag.org/pipeline/archives/2012/03/08/erooms_law
141 http://techonomy.com/2012/09/why-drug-development-is-failing-and-how-to-fix-it/
142 http://www.amazon.com/Bad-Pharma-Companies-Mislead-Patients/dp/0865478007
143 https://www.youtube.com/watch?v=2BjKYvkHQeM
144 http://www.forbes.com/sites/matthewherper/2012/02/10/the-truly-staggering-cost-of-inventing-new-drugs/
145 http://www.amazon.com/Cure-Code-Century-Undermining-Medicine/dp/0465050689/
146 http://www.manhattan-institute.org/html/unlocking-code-health-6016.html
147 http://casmi.org.uk/
148

http://www.ema.europa.eu/docs/en_GB/document_library/Press_release/2014/03/WC500163410.pdf
149 http://casmi.org.uk/2014/08/fda-uses-adaptive-approach-championed-by-casmi-for-experimental-ebola-treatment/
150 http://med.stanford.edu/news/all-news/2013/03/clinical-trials-in-a-dish-may-be-more-reliable-than-standard-way-of-measuring-drug-effects-on-heart-researchers-say.html

151 http://www.drugwatch.com/vioxx/recall/

152 http://londonfuturists.com/2015/02/01/blue-skies-the-future-of-regenerative-medicine-with-stephen-minger/

153 https://www.youtube.com/watch?v=2LPboySOSvo

154 http://advances.sciencemag.org/content/1/4/e1400142.full

155 https://cosmosmagazine.com/life-sciences/how-i-discovered-viagra

156 http://www.enterprisetech.com/2015/12/09/gpu-accelerated-deep-neural-nets-look-for-cures-that-already-exist/

157 http://www.nytimes.com/2005/06/18/business/fda-restricts-access-to-cancer-drug-citing-ineffectiveness.html?_r=0

158 https://www.manhattan-institute.org/html/testimony-peter-huber-senate-subcommittee-space-science-and-competitiveness-6368.html

159 https://www.quora.com/What-questions-were-asked-in-the-Jeopardy-episode-involving-Watson

160 http://www.slate.com/articles/arts/culturebox/2011/02/my_puny_human_brain.single.html

161 http://www.pcworld.com/article/2600360/paging-dr-watson-ibms-medical-adviser-for-the-future.html

162 http://uk.businessinsider.com/r-ibms-watson-to-guide-cancer-therapies-at-14-centers-2015-5?_ga=1.211924119.2051919762.1445418669

163 http://dl.acm.org/citation.cfm?id=1073017

164 https://www.youtube.com/watch?v=yvDCzhbjYWs

165 http://googleresearch.blogspot.co.uk/2015/03/large-scale-machine-learning-for-drug.html

166 http://www.amazon.com/Master-Algorithm-Ultimate-Learning-Machine/dp/0465065708/

167 http://www.kdnuggets.com/2015/02/facebook-open-source-deep-learning-torch.html

168 http://arstechnica.co.uk/information-technology/2015/12/facebooks-open-sourcing-of-ai-hardware-is-the-start-of-the-deep-learning-revolution/

169 https://code.facebook.com/posts/1687861518126048/facebook-to-open-source-ai-hardware-design/

170 https://www.tensorflow.org/

171 http://www.kdnuggets.com/2015/12/update-google-tensorflow-deep-learning-is-improving.html

172 http://uk.businessinsider.com/google-on-machine-learning-2015-10

173 https://medium.com/backchannel/were-hoping-to-build-the-tricorder-12e1822e5e6a#

174 http://www.amazon.com/Innovators-Prescription-Disruptive-Solution-Health/dp/0071592083/

[175] http://www.sciencemag.org/news/2015/12/and-science-s-breakthrough-year

[176] http://spectrum.ieee.org/biomedical/diagnostics/software-helps-gene-editing-tool-crispr-live-up-to-its-hype

[177] http://www.fantastic-voyage.net/

[178] http://www.fantastic-voyage.net/Chapter1.htm

[179] http://www.fantastic-voyage.net/ShortGuidehtml.htm

[180] http://www.healio.com/hematology-oncology/news/print/hemonc-today/%7B241d62a7-fe6e-4c5b-9fed-a33cc6e4bd7c%7D/cigarettes-were-once-physician-tested-approved

[181] http://www.amazon.com/Science-Yoga-Risks-Rewards/dp/1451641427/

[182] http://lpi.oregonstate.edu/new-recommendations-dietary-antioxidants-response-and-position-statement-linus-pauling-institute

[183] http://www.theatlantic.com/health/archive/2013/07/the-vitamin-myth-why-we-think-we-need-supplements/277947/

[184] http://onlinelibrary.wiley.com/doi/10.1111/j.1749-6632.2002.tb02115.x/abstract

[185] http://sens.org/research/introduction-to-sens-research/extracellular-crosslinks

[186] http://sens.org/research/introduction-to-sens-research/intracellular-junk

[187] http://sens.org/research/introduction-to-sens-research/deathresistant-cells

[188] http://sens.org/research/introduction-to-sens-research/cell-loss-and-atrophy

[189] http://sens.org/research/introduction-to-sens-research/mitochondrial-mutations

[190] http://sens.org/research/introduction-to-sens-research/cancerous-cells

[191] http://sens.org/research/introduction-to-sens-research/extracellular-junk

[192]

http://www.sens.org/sites/srf.org/files/reports/SENS%20Research%20Foundation%20Annual%20Report%202015.pdf

[193] http://www.sens.org/donate

[194] http://www.michaelfossel.com/book

[195] http://www.michaelfossel.com/blog/?p=148

[196] http://www.amazon.com/Reversing-Human-Aging-Michael-Fossel/dp/0688153844

[197] https://www.singularityweblog.com/the-search-for-immortality/

[198] http://onlinelibrary.wiley.com/doi/10.1111/j.1474-9726.2011.00700.x/full

199 http://www.nature.com/news/2010/101128/full/news.2010.635.html

200 http://jama.jamanetwork.com/article.aspx?articleid=186171

201 http://blogs.scientificamerican.com/guest-blog/aging-too-much-telomerase-can-be-as-bad-as-too-little/

202 http://bioviva-science.com/telomere-theory-of-aging/

203 http://www.popsci.com/science/article/2011-07/man-who-would-stop-time

204
http://www.sierrasci.com/documents/bill_andrews_on_telomere_basics_c uring_aging.pdf

205 http://www.imdb.com/title/tt3267194/

206 http://www.michaelfossel.com/blog/?p=88

207 http://www.michaelfossel.com/blog/?p=139

208 http://www.eurekalert.org/pub_releases/2016-04/brf-fgt042116.php

209 https://www.technologyreview.com/s/542371/a-tale-of-do-it-yourself-gene-therapy/

210 https://www.youtube.com/watch?v=z1TQ1KV1Q2I

211 http://www.prnewswire.com/news-releases/gero-physics-meets-biology-to-help-defeat-aging-523209361.html

212 https://www.ncbi.nlm.nih.gov/pmc/articles/PMC2885961/

213 http://www.nature.com/articles/srep13589

214 http://ieet.org/index.php/IEET/more/konovalenko20150901

215 http://www.ncbi.nlm.nih.gov/pmc/articles/PMC1691385/

216 http://senescence.info/telomeres_telomerase.html

217 http://www.ncbi.nlm.nih.gov/pmc/articles/PMC3357623/

218 http://www.nytimes.com/2011/02/17/science/17longevity.html

219 http://genomics.senescence.info/genes/

220
http://www.press.uchicago.edu/ucp/books/book/chicago/L/bo13920974 .html

221 http://www.xconomy.com/boston/2013/03/12/glaxosmithkline-shuts-down-sirtris-five-years-after-720m-buyout/

222 http://www.humanlongevity.com/milken-institute-global-health-conference-video/

223 http://www.humanlongevity.com/human-longevity-inc-hli-launched-to-promote-healthy-aging-using-advances-in-genomics-and-stem-cell-therapies/

224 http://www.wired.co.uk/news/archive/2015-04/24/brad-perkins-human-longevity-wired-health-2015

225 https://translate.google.com/about/intl/en_ALL/

226 http://www.faculty.uci.edu/profile.cfm?faculty_id=5261

227 http://www.worldsciencefestival.com/participants/michael_rose/

[228] https://55theses.org/

[229] https://michaelroses55.files.wordpress.com/2011/05/55-theses-explained-final.pdf

[230] http://mathworld.wolfram.com/Rabbit-DuckIllusion.html

[231] http://www.moillusions.com/vase-face-optical-illusion/

[232] http://well.blogs.nytimes.com/2008/04/28/the-truth-about-the-spinning-dancer/?_r=0

[233] http://www.amazon.com/Alfred-Wegener-Creator-Continental-Science/dp/0816061742/

[234] http://www.smithsonianmag.com/science-nature/when-continental-drift-was-considered-pseudoscience-90353214/

[235] https://www.e-education.psu.edu/earth520/content/l2_p12.html

[236] http://folk.ntnu.no/krill/krilldrift.pdf

[237] http://www.mantleplumes.org/WebDocuments/Oreskes2002.pdf

[238] http://www.macleans.ca/society/science/the-meaning-of-alphago-the-ai-program-that-beat-a-go-champ/

[239] http://geologylearn.blogspot.co.uk/2016/02/paleomagnetism-and-proof-of-continental.html

[240] http://semmelweis.org/about/dr-semmelweis-biography/

[241] https://en.wikipedia.org/wiki/Carl_Braun_(obstetrician)#Views_on_puerperal_fever

[242] http://jama.jamanetwork.com/article.aspx?articleid=400956

[243] http://www.amazon.com/Effectiveness-Efficiency-Random-Reflections-Services/dp/185315394X/

[244] http://www.nuffieldtrust.org.uk/sites/files/nuffield/publication/Effectiveness_and_Efficiency.pdf

[245] http://www.amazon.com/Taking-Medicine-Medicines-Difficulty-Swallowing/dp/1845951506/

[246] http://www.cochrane.org/about-us

[247] http://community-archive.cochrane.org/cochrane-reviews

[248] http://www.cochrane.org/evidence

[249] https://www.rcpe.ac.uk/sites/default/files/thomas_0.pdf

[250] http://www.bcmj.org/premise/history-bloodletting

[251] http://www.theguardian.com/world/2008/nov/27/japan

[252] http://www.theguardian.com/world/2013/jan/22/elderly-hurry-up-die-japanese

[253] http://www.nytimes.com/1984/03/29/us/gov-lamm-asserts-elderly-if-very-ill-have-duty-to-die.html

[254] http://www.theatlantic.com/magazine/archive/2014/10/why-i-hope-to-die-at-75/379329/

255 http://www.amazon.com/Reinventing-American-Health-Care-Outrageously/dp/1610393457

256 https://web.archive.org/web/20110110154034/http://www.sagecrossroads.net/files/transcript01.pdf

257 http://www.ncbi.nlm.nih.gov/pmc/articles/PMC1361028/

258 http://sjayolshansky.com/sjo/Background_files/TheScientist.pdf

259 http://scholar.harvard.edu/cutler/publications/substantial-health-and-economic-returns-delayed-aging-may-warrant-new-focus

260 http://www.reuters.com/article/us-imf-aging-idUSBRE83A1C020120412

261 http://www.brookings.edu/research/books/2013/closing-the-deficit

262 http://articles.latimes.com/2014/jan/08/business/la-fi-mo-sure-you-have-to-work-in-retirement-but-look-on-the-bright-side-20140108

263 http://www.nber.org/papers/w8818

264 https://web.archive.org/web/20061018172529/http://www.econ.yale.edu/seminars/labor/lap04-05/topel032505.pdf

265 http://www.northbaybusinessjournal.com/northbay/marincounty/4138872-181/quest-to-redefine-aging#page=0

266 http://www.spiked-online.com/newsite/article/9669#

267 https://report.nih.gov/categorical_spending.aspx

268 http://www.forbes.com/sites/alexknapp/2012/07/05/how-much-does-it-cost-to-find-a-higgs-boson/

269 http://www.einstein.yu.edu/news/releases.asp?ID=582

270 http://www.bbc.co.uk/news/health-27682376

271 http://www.happinesshypothesis.com/

272 http://www.happinesshypothesis.com/happiness-hypothesis-ch1.pdf

273 http://righteousmind.com/about-the-book/introductory-chapter/

274 http://www.amazon.com/Denial-Death-Ernest-Becker/dp/0684832402/

275 http://www.amazon.com/Worm-Core-Role-Death-Life/dp/1400067472/

276 http://www.amazon.com/Varieties-Religious-Experience-William-James/dp/1482738295/

277 http://ernestbecker.org/?page_id=60

278 http://dw2blog.com/2013/09/17/when-faith-gets-in-the-way-of-progress/

279 http://www.sens.org/outreach/conferences/sens6

280 http://www.dailymail.co.uk/sciencetech/article-2418252/Do-lobsters-hold-key-eternal-life-Forget-gastronomic-indulgence-crustacean-defy-ageing-process.html

281 https://www.youtube.com/watch?v=biNF_a5QbwE

282 http://www.amazon.com/Ending-Aging-Rejuvenation-Breakthroughs-Lifetime/dp/0312367074/

283 https://www.youtube.com/watch?v=RITCdrOEO9Y

284 https://www.fightaging.org/archives/2014/07/an-anti-deathist-faq.php

285 http://www.amazon.com/Righteous-Mind-Divided-Politics-Religion/dp/0307455777/

286 http://www.amazon.com/gp/product/0062292986/

287 http://www.amazon.com/Diffusion-Innovations-5th-Everett-Rogers/dp/0743222091/

288 https://www.youtube.com/watch?v=vg4lTZvfIz8

289 http://discovermagazine.com/2001/may/breakdialogue

290 http://humanityplus.org/about/board/

291 http://www.theguardian.com/lifeandstyle/2016/jan/31/im-unhappy-with-my-wife-of-30-years-should-i-leave-mariella-frostrup

292 http://www.thenewatlantis.com/docLib/TNA03-Rosen.pdf

293 http://www.amazon.com/Babies-Design-Ethics-Genetic-Choice/dp/0300143087

294 http://www.martinborchjensen.com/hypotheses/overpopulation/

295 http://www.nature.com/nature/journal/v460/n7256/full/nature08230.html

296 http://repository.upenn.edu/cgi/viewcontent.cgi?article=1029&context=psc_working_papers

297 http://www.amazon.com/o/ASIN/0226901351/189-6785645-1607002

298 https://evolution-institute.org/article/is-religion-useful-a-test-involving-common-pool-resource-groups/

299 http://webarchive.nationalarchives.gov.uk/20160105160709/http:/www.ons.gov.uk/ons/rel/vsob1/death-reg-sum-tables/2013/sty-mortality-rates-by-age.html

300 http://www.slate.com/bigideas/what-is-the-future-of-religion/essays-and-opinions/david-sloan-wilson-opinion

301 http://metamagician3000.blogspot.co.uk/2008/07/wta-changes-its-image.html

302 http://humanityplus.org/philosophy/transhumanist-faq/

303 http://rameznaam.com/the-infinite-resource/

304 http://dw2blog.com/2013/02/04/responding-to-the-call-for-a-new-humanity-manifesto/

305 https://www.alcor.org/

306 http://www.cryonics.org/

307 http://kriorus.ru/en

308 http://www.thelancet.com/journals/lancet/article/PIIS0140-6736(00)01021-7/

309 https://www.theguardian.com/science/blog/2013/dec/10/life-death-therapeutic-hypothermia-anna-bagenholm

310 http://www.amazon.com/Extreme-Medicine-Exploration-Transformed-Twentieth/dp/1594204705

311 http://www.rd.com/true-stories/survival/hypothermia-cheat-death/

312 https://www.newscientist.com/article/dn23107-zoologger-supercool-squirrels-go-into-the-deep-freeze/

313 https://www.sciencedaily.com/releases/2011/04/110411152533.htm

314 http://jeb.biologists.org/content/213/3/502.full

315 http://www.bbc.co.uk/earth/story/20150313-the-toughest-animals-on-earth

316 http://www.ncbi.nlm.nih.gov/pmc/articles/PMC4620520/

317 https://www.technologyreview.com/s/542601/the-science-surrounding-cryonics/

318 http://www.alcor.org/Library/html/vitrification.html

319 http://www.bbc.com/future/story/20140224-can-we-ever-freeze-our-organs

320 http://waitbutwhy.com/2016/03/cryonics.html

321 http://www.alcor.org/book/index.html

322 http://www.dichotomistic.com/mind_readings_head_transplant.html

323 http://www.cleveland.com/obituaries/index.ssf/2010/09/dr_robert_j_white_was_a_world-.html

324 http://news.bbc.co.uk/1/hi/health/1263758.stm

325 http://homepage.ntlworld.com/david.bennun/interviews/drwhite.html

326 http://www.clevescene.com/cleveland/the-frankenstein-factor/Content?oid=1473264

327 https://www.newscientist.com/article/mg22530103.700-first-human-head-transplant-could-happen-in-two-years/

328 https://www.newscientist.com/article/2073923-head-transplant-carried-out-on-monkey-claims-maverick-surgeon/

329 https://www.theguardian.com/science/2015/jun/13/neurosurgeon-first-head-transplant-america-sergio-canavero

330 http://www.telegraph.co.uk/news/2016/03/22/russian-man-to-undergo-worlds-first-full-head-transplant/

331 http://vietnamnews.vn/society/281124/vn-prepares-for-first-head-transplant-in-2017.html

332 http://www.ossur.co.uk/prosthetic-solutions/products/knees-and-legs/bionic-knees/rheo-knee-3

333 https://www.ted.com/speakers/hugh_herr

334 https://www.ted.com/talks/hugh_herr_the_new_bionics_that_let_us_run_climb_and_dance

335 http://humaitech.com/HumaiArtificialLifeSupportSystem.pdf

336 http://humaitech.com/

337 http://www.bioquark.com/

338 http://reanima.tech/

339 https://www.singularityweblog.com/is-death-reversible/

340 http://www.bioquark.com/therapeutic-programs/bq-a-clinical-plans/

341 http://2045.com/

342 http://2045.com/project/

343 http://www.bbc.co.uk/programmes/b0747199

344 https://www.theguardian.com/science/2006/mar/17/france.internationalnews

345 http://www.cryocare.org/index.cgi?subdir=&url=history.txt

346 http://www.bodyworlds.com/en/plastination/idea_plastination.html

347 http://www.forbes.com/sites/shaenamontanari/2015/08/13/the-six-most-incredible-fossils-preserved-in-amber/

348 http://io9.gizmodo.com/5943304/how-to-preserve-your-brain-by-turning-it-into-plastic

349 https://www.gwern.net/plastination

350 http://www.alcor.org/Library/html/chemopreservation2.html

351 http://www.brainpreservation.org/wp-content/uploads/2015/08/Open-Letter-On-Brain-Preservation.pdf

352 https://web.archive.org/web/20100628175250/http://www.brainpreservation.org/index.php?path=prize

353 http://www.21cm.com/

354 http://www.prweb.com/releases/2016/02/prweb13191956.htm

355 http://www.scientificamerican.com/article/can-our-minds-live-forever/

356 http://www.brainpreservation.org/content-2/killed-bad-philosophy/

357 http://www.npr.org/sections/alltechconsidered/2016/04/06/473265273/a-new-rembrandt-from-the-frontiers-of-ai-and-not-the-artists-atelier

358 https://www.rt.com/news/338681-3d-printed-rembrandt-painting/

359 http://www.terasemcentral.org/

360 https://www.lifenaut.com/bina48/

361 https://cyberev.org/

362 http://www.ibtimes.co.uk/virtual-reality-heaven-how-technology-redefining-afterlife-1532429

363 https://www.eter9.com

364 http://www.bbc.co.uk/newsbeat/article/34015307/eter9-social-network-learns-your-personality-so-it-can-post-as-you-when-youre-dead

365 http://www.the-tls.co.uk/tls/public/article1342505.ece

366 http://futurefire.net/2007.09/nonfiction/fedorov.html

367 http://turingchurch.com/2012/01/02/ten-cosmist-convictions/

368 http://turingchurch.com/2015/09/28/technological-resurrection-concepts-from-fedorov-to-quantum-archaeology/

369 https://dw2blog.com/2008/11/16/schrodingers-rabbits/

370 http://ieet.org/index.php/IEET/more/Prisco20160410

371 http://hpluspedia.org/wiki/Immortality_Roadmap

372 https://www.youtube.com/watch?v=We3CTL3WLZE

373 http://immortality-roadmap.com/2015/06/26/immortality-roadmap/

374 http://blogs.discovermagazine.com/crux/2016/03/23/nuclear-fusion-reactor-research/

375 http://www.jstor.org/stable/2118559

376 http://www.jareddiamond.org/Jared_Diamond/Collapse.html

377 http://hpluspedia.org/wiki/Existential_risks

378 https://transpolitica.org/2015/07/24/four-political-futures-which-will-you-choose/

379 http://www.reaganfoundation.org/reagan-quotes-detail.aspx?tx=2079

380 http://bigpictureeducation.com/tale-two-drugs

381 http://www.dndi.org/about-dndi/

382 https://www.techdirt.com/articles/20140124/09481025978/big-pharma-ceo-we-develop-drugs-rich-westerners-not-poor.shtml

383 http://todayinsci.com/M/Merck_George/MerckGeorge-Quotations.htm

384 http://www.amazon.com/How-Markets-Fail-Economic-Calamities/dp/0374173206/

385 http://www.newyorker.com/magazine/bios/john_cassidy/search?contributorName=john%20cassidy

386 http://ieet.org/index.php/IEET/more/tpdec2014

387 http://www.businessinsider.com.au/mary-meekers-2014-internet-presentation-2014-5

388 http://www.slideshare.net/vangeest/exponential-organizations-h

389 http://www.exponentialorgs.com/

390 http://press.princeton.edu/titles/8967.html

391 http://www.secondmachineage.com/

392 http://users.polisci.wisc.edu/schatzberg/ps616/Rosen1981.pdf

393 http://www.technologyreview.com/featuredstory/531726/technology-and-inequality/

394 http://www.politico.com/magazine/story/2014/06/the-pitchforks-are-coming-for-us-plutocrats-108014.html

395 http://fm2030.us/about/

396 http://fm2030.us/are-you-a-transhuman/

397 http://www.nationaldailypress.com/2016/05/01/now-cancer-become-one-of-the-most-expensive-and-riskiest-diseases-to-treat/

398 http://c-hit.org/2016/04/10/low-income-diabetics-paying-high-price-for-insulin/

399 http://books.simonandschuster.co.uk/American-Amnesia/Jacob-S-Hacker/9781451667820

400 http://www.williammacaskill.com/#book

401 http://www.theguardian.com/books/2015/aug/20/doing-good-better-william-macaskill-review

402 https://www.linkedin.com/pulse/compassionate-utilitarianism-balancing-head-heart-pursuit-hoffman

403 http://www.effectivealtruism.com/

404

https://www.givingwhatwecan.org/sites/givingwhatwecan.org/files/attachments/moral_imperative.pdf

405

http://www.who.int/healthinfo/global_burden_disease/metrics_daly/en/

406 https://www.youtube.com/watch?v=jDJ_IjMwT20

407 http://www.npr.org/templates/story/story.php?storyId=104302141

408 http://www.ft.com/cms/s/0/882c6c6a-6c34-11e1-8c9d-00144feab49a.html

409 https://www.youtube.com/watch?v=Y4MnpzG5Sqc

410 https://www.youtube.com/watch?v=bTMS9y8OVuY

411 http://www.nickbostrom.com/fable/dragon.html

412 http://strategicphilosophy.blogspot.co.uk/2009/05/its-about-ten-years-since-i-wrote.html

413 https://babel.hathitrust.org/cgi/pt?id=chi.087603619;view=1up;seq=67

414 https://en.wikiquote.org/wiki/Victor_Hugo

415 http://www.amazon.com/Inhuman-Bondage-Rise-Slavery-World/dp/0195339444

416 http://www.bu.edu/historic/london/conf.html

417 https://theabolitionofaging.com/community/

418 https://pixabay.com/en/eagle-bird-silhouette-animal-1181513/

419 https://pixabay.com/en/dna-biology-science-helix-protein-163710/

Index

100 billion people 53, 290

2040 .... 31, 119, 134

2045 project 320

21st Century Medicine 309, 328

3D bio-printing 102

50% probability 31

55 Theses 212

A stitch in time saves nine 254

Aaron, Henry 252

Accelerating "winner take all" outcomes 363

Accelerating the acceleration 164

Acceleration of history 116

Ackland, Nigel 320

Additional public funds 258

Advanced glycation end-products (AGEs) 181

After Rejuvenation (AR) era 311, 337

age-1 gene 36

Aging as a "neglected disease" 361

Aimard, Gustave 379

Akerlof, George 364

Alaskan beetle 306

Alcock, John 76

Alcor 302, 310

Aldrin, Buzz 76

Alemayehu, Berhanu 240

Ambulance to the future 302

American Amnesia (book) 369

Ames Dwarf Mouse 108

Amortality 46

Amyloid 182

An Introduction to Transhumanism (video) 377

Andrews, Bill 196

Android OS 128, 131

Animal Spirits (book) 363

Annual budget for medical research .. 256

Antifreeze proteins (AFPs) 306

Antioxidants 179

Anton, Ted 206

Anxiety buffering system 275

ApoptoSENS 186

Architecture 128

Are You a Transhuman? (book) 367

Armchair activism 376

Armstrong, Neil 76

Arnst, Catherine 137

Artic ground squirrel 306

Aso, Taro 235

Aurelius, Marcus 20

Avatar roadmap 321

Babies by Design (book) 290

Bacon, Francis 62, 63

Bad Pharma (book) 139

Bad philosophy? 330

Baden-Powell, Baden 71

Bågenholm, Anna 303

Banko, Michele 159

Banks of human cells 147

Banks, Iain 24

Bannister, Roger 45

Barranco, Daniel 307

Barzilai, Nir 259

Becker, Ernest 269, 271

Before Rejuvenation (BR) era 301, 337

Bell, Eric 159

Benign dictator 123

Berger, Theodore 320

Berlin, Irving 61

Berners-Lee, Tim 258

Big Data 159

Big Sur hardware 164

Biggest risks facing rejuveneering 385

Bina48 335

Biomechatronics 316

Bioquark 318

BioViva Sciences 197

Birth rate 52

Blasco, Maria 108, 191

Bleriot, Louis 76

Bloodletting 232, 369

Bodily regeneration 85

Book of Genesis 45, 48

Bostrom, Nick 377
Bountra, Chas 140
Bowhead whale 89
Brain plasticity 244
Brain Preservation Foundation .. 324, 327
Braun, Carl 226
Brave New World 289
Bridge One journey 177
Bridges 2A and 2B 210
Brietbart, Peter 377
Bristlecone pine tree 91, 110
Broad, William 176
Brooks, Fred 120
Brooks' Law 120
Brown, Arthur 76
Brown, Louise 57
Brown-Séquard, Charles-Édouard . 61, 63
Brynjolfsson, Erik 364
Buddha, Gautama 20
Buddhism 20
Burch, Druin 230
Burtless, Gary 252
Bush, George W. 56
Business As Usual lifespan extension .. 34
Butler, Robert N. 245
Byrd, John 106
C. elegans 36, 307
Calico 167
Callaway, Ewen 191
Calment, Jeanne Louise 13, 45
Calvin, John 293
Canavero, Sergio 313
Carmena, Jose 320
Carrel, Alexis 113
CASMI 144
Cassidy, John 358
Castro, Carlos 106
CERN (funding) 258
Chamberlin, Rollin 221
Change in mindset 215
Charpentier, Emmanuelle 171
Chatsworth Scandal 323
Chemopreservation 324
Childbirth 49, 83, 225, 289
Chloroform 49
Chrisafis, Angelique 322

Christensen, Clayton 167
Christianity 341
Church, George 134
Citizen science 386
Citizen scientist rejuveneers 119
Civilisational collapse 297
Clayton, Paul 33
Clinton, Bill 20
Closing the Deficit (book) 252
Cochrane Collaboration 231
Cochrane, Archie 228, 231, 255
Collaboration frameworks 129
Collaboration platforms 130
Collapse (book) 350
Commercial investments 257
Comorbidities 241
Complexity multiplication factor (N) .. 81, 110
Connor, Kristina 91
Conrad, Andrew 167
Constraints on personal freedoms 282
Context of discovery 65
Context of justification 65
Continental drift 220
Coolidge, Calvin 111
Cooper, Martin 117
Cooper's Law 117
Copernican revolution 39
Copying to the future 339
Cosmetics industry 119
Costliness of drug development 140
Counterproductive rhetoric 383
CRISPR 170
Critser, John 103
Crocker, Matthew 315
Crony capitalism 356
Crossing the Chasm (book) 278
Crowdsourced medicine 141
Cryonics 260, 302
Cryonics Institute 302
Curing Aging (book) 196
Cutler, David 249
CyBeRev project 335
Daedalus 50
daf-2 gene 36
Daley, George 100

Darwin's Cathedral (book) 293
Davis, David Brion 381
Dawkins, Richard 92, 133
Dawson, Stella.................................... 252
de Grey, Aubrey.... 40, 182, 196, 276, 374
de Magalhaes, Joao Pedro 206
de Wolf, Aschwin 326
Deathism 277
Declining prices 362
Deep learning 163
Dekkers, Marijn 357
Delayed aging scenario 250
Demographic crisis.............................. 241
Dendrocoelum lacteum 99
DePinho, Ronald 191
Desalination..53
Detuning.. 213
Dezhbod, Esmail 304
Diagnostic scanning programmes 255
Diamandis, Peter 207
Diamond, Jared 349
Diet.. 175
Dietary supplements 178
Dietz, Hendrik 106
Digital copy of the brain 323
Digital vs. organic cryonics................. 323
Disability Adjusted Life Year (DALY)
.... 372
Discretionary time 257
Dislike of the alien............................. 285
Divine curse..48
DNA origami 105
DNA sequencing................................. 133
Do not go gentle into the good night 23
Does Aging Stop (book) 211
Doidge, Norman..................................98
Doing Good Better (book)................... 370
Domingos, Pedro 163
Don't play God....................................51, 354
Donations..........................187, 257, 386
Doumergue, Gaston 111
Drugs for Neglected Diseases initiative
(DNDi) 357
du Toit, Alex...................................... 220
Dublin, Louis.......................................32
Dulce et decorum est 16

Dunnet, George 90
Durkheim, Emile 293
Dvorsky, George.................................. 324
Ebola 145
Economic benefits............................... 246
Economics of superstars 364
Ectogenesis 289
Effective Altruism 370, 372
Effectiveness and Efficiency (book) .. 228
Einstein, Albert 78, 79, 243
Elephant and rider (metaphor)... 265, 277
Elhefnawy, Nader 338
Elixir of life 43
Emanuel, Ezekiel 237, 241, 247, 259, 260
Embracing radical transformation...... 283
Ending Aging (book) 276
Enforced bed rest 230
Engaged community 124
Entropy.. 44
Epictetus... 20
ERK pathway 86
Eroom's Law 136
Esfandiary, FM.................................... 367
Eter9 336
Eugenics 289
Euthanasia.. 241
Evidence-based medicine........... 228, 231
Evolutionary Biology of Aging (book)
.... 211
Evolutionary biology vs. molecular
biology.. 213
Exceptional responders 155
Existential risks 351
Exoskeleton 321
Experimental existential psychology.. 271
Exponential Organizations (book)..... 362
Extreme Medicine (book) 304
Facebook 164
Factoring complexity.......................... 167
Fahy, Greg.. 309
Fantastic Voyage (book)...................... 174
Fedorov, Nikolai................................. 337
Fermat's Last Theorem 347
Feynman, Richard............................... 45
Fight or flight..................................... 267
Finch, Caleb 88

Firefox project 125
Fong, Kevin 304
Forgacs, Gabor 102
Fossel, Michael 188, 192, 194, 196
Four minute mile 45
Four Noble Truths 20
FOXO3 gene 108
Frankenstein 311
Free radicals 178
Freezer failure 323
Friedman, David 113
Frostrup, Mariella 287
Fruit fly lifespan 36
Fukuyama, Francis 240
Full body prosthetic 315
Fulmar 57 90
Fundamentalist approaches to aging.. 182
Funding for rejuveneering 256
Future shock 12
Galen of Pergamum 232
Galileo 219
Galka, Max 52
Gates, Bill 65
Gavrilova, Leonid and Natalia 96
Geminoid robot avatars 320
GenAge Database 206
Genomic stability theory of aging 202
Germ theory of disease 226
Geron Corporation 190, 196
Global social collapse 350
Goertzel, Ben 339
Goldacre, Ben 139
Goldman, Dana 249
Gompertz Law 88, 201
Gompertz, Benjamin 89
Good Samaritan 23
Google 129, 155, 161, 165
Google Translate 209
Grandparents 15
Green, Ronald 290
Greenberg, Jeff 271
Greenhouse gases 53
Greenstone, Gerry 233
Gromeier, Matthias 105
Grossman, Jerome 167
Grossman, Terry 174

Guevara-Aguirre, Jaime 204
Gwern (blogger) 326
Hacker, Jacob 369
Hadoop 152
Haidt, Jonathan 265, 277
Haldane, JBS 289
Haldane, Lord Richard 75
Hallmarks of Aging 41
Hanauer, Nick 366
Hand-washing 225
Harley, Calvin 190
Harrison, David 194
Harvey, William 232
Hauert, Sabine 107
Hayflick limit 44, 189
Hayflick, Leonard 44
Hayward, Kenneth 330
Head transplant 311, 314
Heart transplant 101, 311
Heart-lung machine 114
Heighton, Luke 314
Herr, Hugh 316
Hinton, Geoffrey 223
Hippocampus 320
Hippocrates of Kos 232
Hippocratic Oath 227
Hoffman, Reid 371
Hollywood stereotypes 279, 287
Horace (Roman poet) 16
How Markets Fail (book) 358, 363
Howard, Ron 279
Huber, Peter 143, 154
Hughes Bennett, John 233
Hugo, Victor 379
Humai 317
Human ingenuity 297
Human Longevity Inc (HLI) 207
Humanity v1.0 .... 284, 296
Humanity+ 284, 287, 294, 350
Huxley, Aldous 289
Hwang, Jason 167
I'm from the government and I'm here
    to help 356
IBM 156
Icarus 50
Ice bucket challenge 257

Immortal jellyfish..................................84
Immortality 46
Impact of technological disruptions .. 350
Infectious diseases 38
Inhuman Bondage (book)................... 381
Insilico Medicine............................... 151
In-silico testing.................................. 150
Instagram... 364
Integrated transhumanist political
    position 367
International Monetary Fund............. 252
Invisible Children (video) 376
In-vitro fertilisation (IVF)....................57
iOS... 131
Iressa 153
Ishiguro, Hiroshi................................ 320
Itskov, Dmitry................................... 320
James, William 271
Jeffreys, Harold 221
Jensen, Martin Borch 290
Jeopardy quiz show 156
Joel on Software................................. 126
Johnson & Johnson............................. 158
Johnson, Tom 36
Jun, Paul 20
Jurvetson, Steve 365
Kahneman, Daniel............................... 359
Kaplan, Alexander 321
Karma 47
Kass, Leon 56
Keen, Sam 269
Kelvin, Lord 71, 74
Kennedy, Brian 207, 254
Kennedy, John F...................................27
Kenyon, Cynthia 36
Kerridge, IH 234
Khan Academy.................................... 296
Kim, C-Yoon 314
Kipling, Rudyard..................................73
Knowledgebase for rejuveneering...... 383
Kodak "Brownie" camera................... 116
Konovalenko, Maria 202
Kony, Joseph 376
Kope, Mike 187
Korsten, Bas 334
KrioRus 302

Kubota, Shin 85
Kurzweil, Ray 174
Lamm, Richard.................................... 236
Langley, Samuel.................................... 72
Lanner, Ronald 91
LaRocco, John 317
Laron syndrome 204
Letter to Mother Nature...................... 377
Levy, Stephen 167
Lifenaut 335
Lilienthal, Otto 71, 74
Lin28a gene 100
Lindbergh, Charles 111, 112
Linus' Law 123
Linux, growth of 123
Live long enough to live forever........ 173
London Futurists 47, 148, 183
Longevity dividend..............245, 248, 260
Longevity gap 59
Longwell, Chester 221, 222
López-Otín, Carlos............................... 41
Lord's Resistance Army....................... 376
Losing the right to reproduce............. 290
Louis, Pierre Charles Alexandre.......... 233
Lovelace, Ada 118
Lowe, Derek 136
Lowe, M... 234
LysoSENS 186
Lysosomes 181
MacAskill, William............................. 370
Maharbiz, Michel 320
Manifesto 297
Manly, Charles 72
Mao (as dictator) 55
Market failures 359
Marketing of rejuveneering................. 386
Marriage 287
Marsa, Linda 59
Marshall Plan 258
Martin, George M. 95
Martinot, Raymond 322
Mayer, Catherine 46
McAfee, Andrew................................. 364
McConnell, Steve 121
Medical costs...................................... 237
Medicare 249

Meeker, Mary 117, 362
Melville, George W. 70
Memories surviving cryopreservation 308
Mencken, H.L. 111
Merck, George 358
Metabolic stability theory of aging 181
Metabolome 208
Metchnikoff, Ilya 61, 63
Metformin 37
Microbiome 208
Miller, Richard A. 245
Millikan, Robert. 77
Mind as a pattern of interactions 325
Mind uploading 326
Mindfiles 333
Minger, Stephen 148
Misery in old age 239
Mitochondrial theory of aging 181
Monbiot, George 57
Montgolfier brothers 80
Moody, Glyn 357
Moore, Geoffrey 278
Moore's Law 118, 133
Moral psychology 266
More, Max 377
Morozov, Evgeny 376
Morphological experimentation 284
Morrow, Elisabeth 112, 114
Mozilla project 126
Multiple copies vs. simple identity 337
Murphy, Kevin 253, 255
Myrskylä, Mikko 291
Naam, Ramez 296
Naiman, Eric. 337
Naked mole-rats 90
Nano-engineering 105
Nano-surgery 106
Natural remedies 177
Neel, Benjamin 27
Neglected diseases 357
Negligible senescence 88, 201
Netscape project 125
New cultural framework 280
New Dark Age 349, 360
New sensory experiences 284
Newcomb, Simon 72, 75

Niebuhr, Reinhold 20
Niépce, Nicéphore 116
Nissen, Steven. 180
Nixon, Richard 26
Non-communicable diseases (NCDs) . 38
Nordhaus, William 253
Norvig, Peter. 160
Nuclear fusion 345
Ocean trenches 224
Och, Franz. 209
Oeppen, Jim 32
Offit, Paul 61, 179
Okada, Jun-ichi 150
Olshansky, S. Jay 245, 254
Oncology 158
Opinion vs. experiment 229
Ord, Toby 372
Oreskes, Naomi 222
Organovo. 103
Ott, Harald 102
Owen, Wilfred 16
Paleomagnetism 224
Parabiosis 104
Paradigm 2, 219, 227, 243, 309
Paradox of opposition to extended
    healthspan 275
Parrish, Elizabeth 197
Partitionable tasks 129
Pasteur, Louis 226
Pastor, Ira 318
Pauling, Linus 61, 178
Perkins, Brad 209
Perry, Daniel 245
Personal effectiveness 386
PI3K-null gene 36
Pichai, Sundar 166
Pierson, Paul 369
Planck, Max 55
Plasticity of lifespan 36
Plastination vs. cryonics 326
Pleiotropy 92
Pluralist approaches to aging 182
Political will 348
Pollack, Andrew 153
Population explosion 51
Positive feedback cycles 352

PostHuman (video) 377
Precautionary stance 286
Preference for "modest" theories 224
Preserving Minds, Saving Lives (book)
.... 310
Prisco, Giulio 339, 341
Proactionary stance 286
Pro-aging trance 277
Probabilities 256
Procrastination 56
Profound conviction 382
Protecting the commons 282
Psychological immune system 276
Putre, Laura 312
Pyszczynski, Tom 271, 273
Qin Shi Huang (emperor) 62
Quadriplegics 311
Quahog clam 89
Quantified selflessness......................... 372
Quantum archaeology.......................... 339
Rahm, Gilbert Franz 306
Ramsundar, Bharath............................ 161
Randomised control trials 229
Rapamycin...36
Rapid Software Development (book) 121
Raymond, Eric 122
Reagan, Ronald 356
Reality-based economics 359
ReAnima... 318
Reconnecting broken spinal cord....... 314
Regeneration of the brain 319
Regulatory capture.............................. 356
Regulatory reform 142
Rehman, Jalees 193
Reinventing American Health Care
    (book).. 238
Reis, Robert Shmookler 199
Rejuvenation of minds 288
Rejuveneering community 383
Religion...47, 293
Rembrandt 333
Replacement cornea 104
Replacement kidney 102
Resistance to antibiotics 282
Reversing Human Aging (book)......... 190
Riley, Patrick 161

Rink, Jochen...................................... 99
Risk management................................ 286
Riskiness of drug development.......... 140
Ritalin 151
Robust mouse rejuvenation 375
Rose, Michael.........................35, 211, 281
Rosen, Sherwin.................................. 364
Rothblatt, Gabriel 336
Rotman, David 365
Rowbotham, Judith 33
Rubin, Andy...................................... 128
Rush, Benjamin 232
Rutherford, Ernest 77
Salamander.. 85
Sanocrysin 230
Scharping, Nathaniel 345
Schiller, Robert.................................. 364
Scurvy.. 43
Second Law of Thermodynamics........ 44
Semmelweis, Ignaz 225, 227
Senescent cells 182
Senolytics.. 36
SENS.................. 40, 42, 140, 182, 273
Serenity prayer 20
Shariatmadari, David.......................... 371
Shaw, George Bernard 69
Shermer, Michael 329
Sierra, Felipe 40
Simpson, James Young......................... 49
Sirtris Pharmaceutical......................... 207
Six actions in support of rejuveneering
.... 385
Slacktivism... 376
Slavery 3, 381
Slowness of drug development........... 140
Smart prosthetics 316
Smart regulations 356
Smart, John 324
Smartphone industry.................. 131, 362
Smartphones and Beyond (book)....... 128
Solar panels 53
Solomon, Sheldon.............................. 271
Space stations 54
Spiridinov, Valery 314
Spiritual immortality........................... 48
Spolsky, Joel...................................... 126

Stalin (as dicator) 55
Stem cells 182
Stipp, David 95
Stoic philosophy 20
Sub-zero hibernation 306
Super agers 259
Symbian 128, 131
Szilard, Leo 78
Takagi, Sunada 21
Taking the Medicine (book) 230
Talking serpent 50
Tardigrade 306
Taylor, Doris 101
Taylor, Richard 347
Technoconservative approach 353
Technolibertarian approach 355, 367
Technological resurrection 339
Technological singularity 285
Technology and inequality 365
Technology marketing 278
Technology Prize 327
Technoprogressive approach 361, 367
Technoprogressive Declaration 360
Technosceptical approach 352
Telomerase 108
Telomeres 188, 195
Ten Cosmist convictions 339
TensorFlow 165
Terasem 335
Terror 267
Terror Management Theory (TMT) ... 272
Texas 52
The Ageless Generation (book) 46
The Brain That Changes Itself (book) . 98
The Cathedral and the Bazaar (book) 122
The cost-effectiveness of anti-aging
    research 374
The Cure in the Code (book) 143
The Denial of Death (book) 269
The Diffusion of Innovation (book) . 278
The Fable of the Dragon-Tyrant 377
The freedom card 281
The Happiness Hypothesis (book) 265
The Immortalists (book) 113
The Infinite Resource (book) 296
The Innovator's Prescription (book) . 167

The Longevity Seekers (book) 206
The Master Algorithm (book) 163
The moral imperative towards cost-
    effectiveness 372
The Mythical Man-Month (book) 120
The Pitchforks Are Coming 366
The right time for an idea 379
The Righteous Mind (book) 266, 277
The Science of Yoga (book) 176
The Second Machine Age (book) 364
The son of Moore's Law 133
The Telomerase Revolution (book) ... 188
The Unreasonable Effectiveness of Data
    160
The Worm at the Core (book) 271
The Youth Pill (book) 95
Theories of aging 178
Theory of "bad air" (miasma) 226
Therapeutic hypothermia 303
Thomas, DP 232
Thomas, Dylan 23
Three "Bridges" 174
Tobacco industry 176
Tonsillectomy 229
Topel, Robert 253, 255
Torch deep learning system 164
Torvalds, Linus 123
Transdifferentiation 85
Transhumanism 295, 341
Trinh Hong Son 315
Turchin, Alexey 342
Tversky, Amos 359
Two-edged sword 296
Underlying motivation 267
Underwood, Mair 279
Unequal access to healthcare 363
Unforeseeable consequences 283
Until death do us part 287
Up wing vs. right or left wing 367
Urban, Tim 310
UT-Heart 150
Utopian economics 358
Van Geest, Yuri 362
Vaupel, James 32
Vega, Marco 377
Venter, Craig 207

Verily 167
Veritas Genetics 134
Vetovitz, Craig 312
Viagra 151
Victoria, Queen 49
Victorian London 33
View from the Window at Le Gras 116
Villeda, Saul 105
Vioxx 148
Visible hand of government 368
Visual illusions 219
Vitamin C 178
Vita-More, Natasha 307
Vitrification vs. freezing 309
von Hagens, Gunther 324
Voronoff, Serge 61
Wade, Nicholas 205
Walk Again project 321
Walker, Everett 278
War on cancer 26
Warner, Kenneth E 240
Waste recycling 53
Watson supercomputer 156

Webster, Dale 161
Wegener, Alfred 220, 225
Wellcome Trust 141
Wells, HG 78
What do we want to want? 11
When I'm 84 334
White, Robert 311
Why Cryonics Makes Sense 310
Why I Hope to Die at 75 237
Wiles, Andrew 347
Willcox, Bradley 108
Willeit, Peter 193
Williams, George C. 91, 107
Wilson, David Sloan 293, 294
Winner Takes All outcomes 364
Woynarowski, Dave 109
Wright brothers 69, 71, 80
Wu, Joseph 147
Yerxa, Donald 381
Yoga 176
Yun, Max 86
Zhavoronkov, Alex 46, 151

About the author

David W. Wood, D.Sc., was one of the pioneers of the smartphone industry. He is now a futurist consultant, speaker and writer.

Wood spent 25 years envisioning, architecting, designing, implementing, and avidly using smart mobile devices. This includes ten years with PDA manufacturer Psion PLC, and ten more with smartphone operating system specialist Symbian Ltd, which he co-founded in 1998. At different times, his executive responsibilities included software development, technical consulting, developer evangelism, partnering and ecosystem management, and research and innovation. His software for UI and application frameworks was included on 500 million smartphones from companies such as Nokia, Samsung, LG, Motorola, Sony Ericsson, Fujitsu, Sharp, Siemens, and Panasonic.

From 2010 to 2013, Wood was Technology Planning Lead (CTO) of Accenture Mobility. During this time, he also co-led Accenture's "Mobility Health" business initiative. Wood is now CEO of the independent futurist consultancy and publisher Delta Wisdom.

As chair of London Futurists, Wood has organised regular meetings in London since March 2008 on futurist and technoprogressive topics. Membership of London Futurists reached 5,000 in June 2016.

Wood was the lead editor of the volume "Anticipating 2025: A guide to the radical changes that may lie ahead, whether or not we're ready", published in June 2014. His own book "Smartphones and beyond: lessons from the remarkable rise and fall of Symbian" was published in September 2014 and has been described as "One of the most candid and revealing books a technology executive has ever written".

Wood has a triple first class mathematics degree from Cambridge and undertook doctoral research in the Philosophy of Science. He has an honorary Doctorate in Science from Westminster University. In 2009 he was included in T3's list of "100 most influential people in technology". He has been a Fellow of the Royal Society of Arts (FRSA) in London since 2005, a Director of Humanity+ since November 2013, and a Fellow of the IEET (Institute for Ethics and Emerging Technologies) since January 2015.

He blogs at dw2blog.com and tweets as @dw2.

About Delta Wisdom

Delta Wisdom is an independent futurist consultancy and publisher.

Delta Wisdom helps clients to anticipate:

- The dramatic impact of rapidly changing technology on human individuals and communities
- Opportunities to apply technology in new solutions to deep-rooted problems.

Clients of Delta Wisdom include individuals, businesses, organisations, and governments around the world.

Please contact Delta Wisdom regarding the availability of David Wood to facilitate workshops, present keynotes, catalyse change initiatives, tailor research reports, or to deliver TED-style talks, on any of the following topics:

- Anticipating the future: the key methods and scenarios
- Twenty technologies that could cause major disruptions by 2025
- Scenarios for the future of healthy human life extension
- Anticipating the better politics of tomorrow
- Transforming the future of education, employment, and security
- The future of artificial intelligence – how worried should we be?
- Assessing radical futurism: learning from the history of futurism
- Anticipating 2040: existential risks and existential opportunities
- Options for handling disruptive technology: innovation vs. inertia
- The creative transformation of medicine and healthcare
- What's next for smartphones? Wearables, the IoT, and next gen UI
- Learning from the smartphone industry: platforms and agility
- Thriving in times of profound change: vision and execution

For more details, see deltawisdom.com.

Made in the USA
Lexington, KY
04 April 2018